Scripturalizing Jewishness through Blackness

SCRIPTURALIZATION
DISCOURSE, FORMATION, POWER

Series Editor

Vincent L. Wimbush

This series aims to advance creative and provocative transdisciplinary thinking and conversation about, original research projects into, and wide dissemination of, the patho-, social-cultural-, and economic-political-logics and reverberations of mimetic practices, social relations, orientations that have been conceptualized by the independent scholarly research group called The Institute for Signifying Scriptures (ISS) (www.signifyingscriptures.org) and shorthanded by the term "scripturalization."

Titles in the Series

Scripturalizing Jewishness through Blackness: Black Jews in France, by Aurélien Mokoko Gampiot

Wild Races: Scripturalizing Empire in British India, by Lalruatkima

Masquerade: Scripturalizing Modernities Through Black Flesh, edited by Vincent L. Wimbush

Scripturalizing Jewishness through Blackness

Black Jews in France

Aurélien Mokoko Gampiot

LEXINGTON BOOKS/FORTRESS ACADEMIC
Lanham • Boulder • New York • London

Published by Lexington Books/Fortress Academic
Lexington Books is an imprint of The Rowman & Littlefield Publishing Group, Inc.
4501 Forbes Boulevard, Suite 200, Lanham, Maryland 20706
www.rowman.com

86-90 Paul Street, London EC2A 4NE, United Kingdom

Copyright © 2024 by The Rowman & Littlefield Publishing Group, Inc.

All rights reserved. No part of this book may be reproduced in any form or by any electronic or mechanical means, including information storage and retrieval systems, without written permission from the publisher, except by a reviewer who may quote passages in a review.

British Library Cataloguing in Publication Information Available

Library of Congress Cataloging-in-Publication Data

Names: Mokoko Gampiot, Aurélien, author.
Title: Scripturalizing Jewishness through Blackness : Black Jews in France / Aurélien Mokoko Gampiot.
Description: Lanham, Maryland : Lexington Books, an imprint of The Rowman & Littlefield Publishing Group, Inc., [2024] | Series: Scripturalization: discourse, formation, power | "Published by Lexington Books/Fortress Academic"—Title page verso. | Includes bibliographical references and index. | Summary: "This book describes the multiple ways in which Black Jews in France practice and claim their Judaism, relate to their fellow Jews, and reconstruct their identities. After fifteen years of fieldwork, Dr. Aurélien Mokoko Gampiot offers an original analysis of their individual and collective itineraries"—Provided by publisher.
Identifiers: LCCN 2024019077 (print) | LCCN 2024019078 (ebook) | ISBN 9781978716568 (cloth) | ISBN 9781978716575 (epub)
Subjects: LCSH: Black Hebrews—France. | Black people—France—Social conditions. | Black people—Religion. | Black race. | France—Race relations. | France—Ethnic relations.
Classification: LCC BP605.B64 M65 2024 (print) | LCC BP605.B64 (ebook) | DDC 305.6/9608996044—dc23/eng/20240509
LC record available at https://lccn.loc.gov/2024019077
LC ebook record available at https://lccn.loc.gov/2024019078

To my wife Cécile and our two sons Antoine and Vincent

Contents

Acknowledgments	ix
Introduction	1
Chapter 1: History of the Presence of Jews and Blacks in France	11
Chapter 2: Self-Identification or Quest of Jewishness	53
Chapter 3: Patterns of Conversion of Africans and West Indians to Judaism: From Christian to Jew	81
Chapter 4: Black Jews' Insertion in the French Jewry	121
Chapter 5: Black Jewish Organizations in France	149
Chapter 6: Interracial Marriages	167
Chapter 7: Being Black and Jewish in France Today	205
Conclusion	237
Glossary	243
Bibliography	247
Index	263
About the Author	269

Acknowledgments

At the moment of putting the finishing touches to this work, my first thanks are for my partner Cécile Coquet-Mokoko, professor of American studies at the University of Paris Saclay, for her considerable input during the making of this book. Not only did she have a part in setting out the research project with me, but she also accompanied me several times during the fieldwork and was greatly helpful in our enlightening discussions on the topic, not to mention her translating the entire manuscript from French into English.

I am also indebted to Professor Vincent Wimbush, director of the Institute for Signifying Scriptures, who has always been supportive of my work and given it invaluable exposure. I am highly appreciative of his suggestions for this manuscript, as well as those of the anonymous reviewer. Professor Pierre-Jean Simon has my gratitude for transmitting me his knowledge in the sociology of race and ethnicity as well as a solid methodology of research, while his wife, ethnology professor Ida Simon-Barouh, was kind enough to read the first draft of the manuscript and make the first suggestions for improvement.

I wish to thank my fellow scholars, members of the Groupe Sociétés Religions et Laïcité (GSRL-CNRS) hosted by the Sorbonne, and especially the members of the axe Judaïsme, for their interest in my research and their consideration. My discussions with the members of the International Society for the Study of African Judaism (ISSAJ) have also been precious in deepening my understanding of the complexity of Jewish cultures and practices.

Of course, I extend my heartfelt thanks to those without whom this study of Black Jews in France would never have materialized: namely, Guershon Nduwa, the president of the Fédération internationale des Juifs noirs; Hortense Tsiporah Bilé, president of Am-Israël-Farafina; Rabbi Marah Pinhas Eliyahou Saday; Albert Messan; Yvon Aloula; and all the respondents who put their trust in me by accepting to candidly answer my questions.

Finally, to all of you who expressed interest in this study, encouraged me, and waited impatiently for the book to come out, I want to say thank you.

Introduction

It is three decades since the phenomenon of Jewish identity claims among Blacks first emerged in France. It is observable in the transnational dynamics of believers hailing from sub-Saharan Africa and the Caribbean, who have recently emerged within the French Jewry. For outsiders, it is surprising to evoke the presence of Black persons within the French Jewish community, for Jews in France as well as in the rest of Europe and "the West" are not usually identified as Blacks. The new visibility of Black Jews in France, which began with the twenty-first century, first poses the question of inter-ethnic relations, as defined by Pierre-Jean Simon's pioneering work in the 1980s, in which he explored "the process of ethnic Othering and its connection with race as a social and ideological construct."[1] Some French Africanists, among whom Jean-Loup Amselle and Elikia M'Bokolo,[2] recommend using the concept of "Otherness" (*altérité*) rather than "ethnicity," which, they contend, remains inseparable from the reification of human groups and the dominant posture of White mainstream groups, and ultimately reinforces the social exclusion of migrants. However, ethnicity is also observable among groups that have integrated the White mainstream, as the case of French Jews will exemplify in the following pages.

As a matter of fact, the other question raised by a focus on Black Jews is the relation between two minority groups in France, one of which now positions itself as a mainstream group when dealing with racialized believers in its midst. Albert Bastenier considers that ethnic consciousness develops both among majority and minority groups, and supports using the concept of ethnicity "in its attempt to account for the social organization of difference." He stresses that it can take the form of accommodation, competition for resources, conflict, as well as mobilization and innovation. The notion of "ethnic consciousness" is central to demonstrating that "from a sociological standpoint, ethnicity has no existence per se" but only "within the frame of a consciousness belonging to the historically-established, as opposed to the newcomers."[3] Thinking in terms of ethnic consciousness is useful to account for the situation of Black Jews within Jewish milieus in France, for religion is by definition a field that lends itself to the study of ethnicity. Indeed, the ethnic dimension behind the assertion of religious identities is made all the more visible as the assertion of Jewish identity increasingly entails explicit or implicit constructions of Otherness, particularly when diversity is at stake in the Jewish world. As Western communities of the Jewish diaspora become more diverse, the evolution of believers has modified group interactions in such a way that majority-group members are players of ethnicity as much as minority-group members are. The articulation between minority and majority is tied to the connections between universal and particular, as well as to processes of differentiation and hierarchization.[4] In this case, what is considered universal is the Ashkenazi/Sephardic binary, which assigns all other Jews (among whom Black Jews) to minority particularism or periphery. The purpose of this work is to explore the majority/minority relations in the case of Jews from Africa and the Caribbean, who are doubly in a minority situation in their interactions with fellow Jews who, while being part of a minority religious group, behave as a majority group when faced with the prospect of a racially diverse Jewry.

African and Caribbean Jews find justifications in the Torah to vindicate their Jewishness and/or Judaism in the eyes of a French Jewry that sometimes welcomes them and sometimes struggles to integrate them among its estimated 650,000 members.[5] Indeed, in spite of the diversity of origins among Jews around the world, the Jewish landscape in France is shaped by the binary between Ashkenazim and Sephardim, the former originating from Central Europe and the latter from France's former colonies in North Africa, who emigrated to France in the early 1960s. The two groups differ in their practices of Jewishness, with distinct customs and rituals, languages, geographical roots, cultural heritage, culinary and musical traditions; and their coexistence implies dynamics of both inclusion and exclusion of one another, as a result of their respective feelings of superiority. The Sephardic community is numerically larger than the Ashkenazi; but in spite of its linguistic and cultural proximity with the North African minority, it identifies and is perceived as White, just like the Ashkenazi group, and both groups assume that no Jewish person can also be Black, save Ethiopian Jews.

However, the increasing number of Black people identifying as Jewish on the African continent has drawn the attention of several researchers from various academic disciplines. Among the earliest is the French ethnologist Maurice Dorès, who in 1992 wrote a first historical account of relations between Blacks and Jews in his classic book *La beauté de Cham*.[6] His documentary entitled *Black Israël*, released in 2003, showed several testimonies of Black converts to Judaism hailing from a variety of countries. Tudor Parfitt,[7] a pioneer in the field of Black African Jewish Studies, first identified several mechanisms shared by the African tribal groups that came to identify as the descendants of Biblical Israelites. Then, the collective work he co-edited with Emanuela Trevisan-Semi[8] showed the role of colonialism in the development of Judaising movements around the world, including the African continent. Édith Bruder[9] wrote on the Jews of Africa, as well as Magdel Le Roux,[10] who studied the identity claims of the Lembas of South Africa. Daniel Lis[11] and William Miles[12] discussed those of the Jews of Nigeria, while Lisa Anteby-Yemini[13] and Don Seeman[14] did fieldwork on the Ethiopian Jews of Israel. In his ethnographic study of the African Hebrew Israelites, John L. Jackson Jr. showed how a group of African Americans identifying with ancient Israel chose to leave the United States for Israel and build a Promised Land there.[15] Other noteworthy scholarly work was published by Jaap Van Slageren,[16] Nicole Lapierre,[17] Harold Brackman and Ephraim Isaac,[18] Maurice Dorès,[19] and Édith Bruder,[20] analyzing the relations between Jews and Blacks through history and around the globe.

Yet, Jewish believers are not found solely in Africa or Israel; they travel the world and some have settled in France, where, alongside the Ashkenazi/Sephardic binary, they add their own experiences of Judaism and Jewishness to those of African and Caribbean converts who discovered their calling in France. The US anthropologist Katya Gibel Azoulay, building partly on her personal experience as the daughter of an interracial couple, showed in her book[21] how the biracial offspring of Black/Jewish couples position themselves vis-à-vis the two communities. On the same topic, in France, autobiographical essays have been published by biracial sons and daughters of Jewish mothers, among which Raphaël Ben Gad's *Je Suis Juif, Je Suis Noir Et J'en Suis Fier!*[22] ("I'm Jewish, I'm Black and I'm Proud") or Rachel Kahn's *Racée*[23]("full-blooded"). Two Congolese converts also penned autobiographical essays in French: Marah Saday,[24] *Tu seras juif mon fils* ("you'll be a Jew, my son") and Guershon Nduwa,[25] *Manifeste des Juifs Noirs: Essai pour la tolérance* ("Black Jews' manifesto: a plea for tolerance").

So far, there have been very few studies of Black Jews within the French Jewry. The present work seeks to fill this gap by exploring their life stories and the converts' spiritual itineraries from Christianity to Judaism. As a consequence of processes of acculturation—which, the French sociologist Pierre-Jean Simon explains, may be forced, desired, or sought after—as well as processes of assimilation, which are usually imposed but may sometimes be desired, "individual social players are not doomed to remain forever true to their initial selves in terms of ethnicity, and may, if they choose to, become new selves. This is particularly true in modern societies where they generally enjoy greater spatial mobility."[26] Conversion offers non-Jewish individuals the possibility of becoming new selves that identify, and seek to be recognized, as Jews. Pierre-Jean Simon's emphasis on the connection between greater mobility and greater acculturation and assimilation in modern societies is echoed by the French sociologist of religion Danièle Hervieu-Léger,[27] when she depicts the convert as the exemplum of the modern believer, to the extent that they testify to the mobility and individual or collective circulation between the established religions, both in spatial and sociological terms.

In such a context, several parameters factor in to diversify the present landscape of Judaism, running counter to common assumptions. Asking herself, "Who are 'the Jews'? What does it mean to be a Jew?" the French ethnologist Ida Simon-Barouh answered eloquently:

> [o]ften perceived as a homogeneous group, they actually exhibit a dizzying diversity—of ethnic origins, and therefore, of familial and national histories; of individual and collective self-definitions; of assigned identities; of ways in which they make Jewishness real. "The Jew" does not exist. Jews do, in the plural, distinct forms in which their social lives unfurl from day to day.[28]

In the nineteenth century, the French historian Ernest Renan was more insightful than most of his contemporaries in this respect, when he concluded a famous conference as follows:

> Originally, Judaism was a national religion. Nowadays, it is a closed religion again. But in the interval, over a span of many centuries, Judaism was open, and considerable masses of peoples who were not Israelites by blood embraced Judaism; so that the meaning of the word, from an ethnographic perspective, has become very unstable.[29]

Within this diverse Jewry, Black believers from Africa and the African diaspora, whether native Jews or converts, are currently demanding a new phase of openness.[30]

I approached this subject after investigating the articulation between religion and Blackness in an African Initiated Church known as Kimbanguism, which develops a unique appropriation of the Scriptures, where Adam and Eve are Blacks and the Garden of Eden is located in the church's Holy City of Nkamba-Jerusalem, in the present-day Democratic Republic of Congo.[31] The syncretism observed in that church transforms all the parameters of Jewishness mentioned in the Bible in order to offer what the French Africana scholar Roger Bastide called "a reinterpretation of the Christian message through the African intellect and sensitivity."[32] It made sense for me to pursue the reflection by exploring other cases of African(-descended) believers seeking to articulate their experiences of racialization with their religious beliefs, specifically in association with Biblical Scriptures. As a native of Brazzaville in the Republic of Congo, where I was raised until I moved to France for my studies, I have an insider's grasp of African worldviews which has allowed me to understand how Africans may relate to Jewish customs. I began working on Black Jews in France in 2009, soon after they first became visible in the country's media. Listening to a radio talk where Guershon Nduwa was invited as France's "first Black rabbi,"[33] I became aware of the presence in France of Black Jews who were not necessarily Ethiopian, and most of whom are converts. Fifteen years later, the present work aims to analyze their conceptualization of Blackness and Jewishness by means of a qualitative sociological approach.

In effect, conversions to Judaism, contrary to conversions to Islam, are not visible yet in France, because most people assume that it is impossible to convert to Judaism. However, conversions do take place, even if they receive no publicity. Black Jews in France, whether native or converts, are drawing more attention, even if they are among the least documented minorities, as they are not yet integrated as a subgroup within the French Jewry and the broader French society. It is worth mentioning a documentary film entitled *Être juif et noir en France* (Being Jewish and Black in France), made in 2014 by Annick N'Guessan,[34] which premiered at the Centre Alliance Edmond J. Safra in Paris and featured various public figures, including Joël Mergui, the then president of the Consistory; Roger Cukierman, the then President of the CRIF; Gilles Bernheim, then France's Chief Rabbi, and academics of international renown. Black Jews' quest for visibility makes them less invisible. As distinct from African Jews based in African countries (such as the Lembas or the Ethiopian Jews), who have been Jewish for a very long time, the presence of Black Jews in France only became perceptible in the 2000s, when community organizations (the Fraternité Judéo-Noire and Am-Israël-Farafina) gained media exposure, although I interviewed a person who converted as early as 1970.

While on the African continent, conversion to Judaism or identification to the Jewish people are rather collective phenomena, in France, these are individual decisions. Indeed, in France, conversion to Judaism results from a person's deliberate choice. While, in Africa, Black Jews live outside of a rabbinical authority that controls a person's Jewishness, in France, candidates are submitted to examination by such an authority, and often see their admission into the community postponed by means of various disincentives. Consequently, two reactions may be observed. On the one hand, African and Caribbean Jews manifest a strong will of integration into the French Jewry; on the other hand, they express a tendency to keep to themselves when this aspiration is hindered by the color line they encounter in some synagogues. The resulting negotiations between Black Jews and the religious authorities vary, following the tenets of their particular stream of Judaism.

This study offers an insight into the modes of religious expression observable in the negotiation strategies implemented by African and Caribbean believers with each of the religious traditions and denominations making up modern-day Judaism in France. Who are these believers? How did they become Jewish? How do they articulate their Black experience with their experience of Judaism? How do the converts among them vindicate their Jewish faith considering both the Scripturalization of Jewishness and the cultural legacy of Christianity in the African and Caribbean cultures they grew up in? How do they carve a place for themselves in the French Jewry? What meaning do they give to the idea of Jewishness?

Scripturalization proves appropriate to account for Black believers' relation to Judaism as a modern social-cultural dynamic and phenomenon, in a more textured modern-world and contemporary psycho-social-cultural and political analysis. Scripturalization, Vincent Wimbush reminds us,

> broadly refers to the ideology and power dynamics and social and cultural practices built around texts. It refers to the use of texts, textuality and literacy as a means of constructing and maintaining society, as a legitimation of authority and power. It becomes shorthand for a type of structure and arrangement of power relations and communications of society, the ultimate politics of language. It is nothing less than magic, a powerful and compelling construction, make-believe.[35]

In this book, I seek to elaborate a framework to describe, understand, and analyze Jewishness in order to shed a new light on the articulation between Judaism, ethnicity, and race in interracial contexts—in other words, Black Jews' expression of Jewishness and Judaism through the prism of the Torah. My interest in Black Jews is dictated not by my belonging to that community, but by my interest in scientifically analyzing the interplay between religion and racialization and more particularly, the Scripturalization of Black identities. To go about this project, I conducted a qualitative sociological fieldwork from 2009 to 2023 among self-identified Black Jews living in the greater Paris area. I applied the methods of participant observation, field survey in community centers and synagogues, and semi-structured interviews combined with analyses of the media discourses, documentaries, and scientific literature in order to reconstruct the respondents' individual itineraries. In parallel, over the same span of time, I observed the evolution of the Black community organizations born within the French Jewry. I collected a total of forty-seven semi-structured interviews with Black Jews aged from seventeen to sixty-five. Among them, twenty (including twelve men and eight women; no respondent identified as non-binary) identified as Jewish-born, because either their mothers were Jewish or their parents had converted before their births. The twenty-seven other respondents (including eighteen men and nine women) identify as converts. I also interviewed one rabbi from the

Masorti[36] movement; my efforts to reach out to rabbis of the other denominations of Judaism proved unsuccessful, as I received no answers. To preserve the anonymity of the respondents, all of their names, save those of the leaders of Jewish institutions and Black Jewish organizations, have been modified.

The findings of the study are detailed in seven chapters. Chapter 1 describes the historical backdrop of the presence of Jews and people of African descent in metropolitan France, with a comparative perspective on antisemitism and anti-Black racism. Chapter 2 offers analyses of Black Jews' quest for Jewishness and self-definitions. Chapter 3 follows the spiritual itineraries of converts who formerly identified as Christians. Chapter 4 explores the modes of insertion of Black Jews into the French Jewry. Chapter 5 discusses Black Jewish organizations, namely, the Fédération internationale des Juifs noirs (FJN) and Am-Israël-Farafina (AM-I-FA), which were founded in reaction to the frustrations experienced in Jewish milieus and in interactions with the Consistory, which officially acts as a gatekeeper of Jewishness in France. Chapter 6 addresses interracial marriages between White Jews and Black Jews or non-Jews. Finally, chapter 7 shows how Black Jews struggle for integration and visibility in the broader French society.

NOTES

1. See Pierre-Jean Simon, "Propositions d'un schéma pour l'analyse des attitudes et des politiques dans le domaine des relations interethniques," *Bastidiana*, no. 23–24 (1986): 167–81. Translation by Cécile Coquet-Mokoko. Unless indicated otherwise, all translations from the French are by Cécile Coquet-Mokoko.

2. Jean-Loup Amselle and Elikia M'Bokolo, eds., *Au cœur de l'ethnie. Ethnies, tribalisme et État en Afrique* (Paris: La Découverte, collection Poche, 1999).

3. Albert Bastenier, *Qu'est-ce qu'une société ethnique? Ethnicité et racisme dans les sociétés européennes d'immigration* (Paris: Presses Universitaires de France, collection "Sociologie d'aujourd'hui," 2004), 190.

4. Pierre-Jean Simon, *Pour une sociologie des relations interethniques et des minorités* (Rennes: Presses Universitaires de Rennes, 2006).

5. See Sergio dellaPergola, "World Jewish Population 2020 [archive]," *Berman Jewish Data Bank*, accessed 3 March 2024, jewishdatabank.org/api/download/?studyId=1149&mediaId=bjdb\2020_World_Jewish_Population_(AJYB_DellaPergola)_FinalDataBank.pdf

6. Maurice Dorès, *La beauté de Cham: Mondes juifs, Mondes noirs* (Paris: Ballard, 1992); Maurice Dorès, *Black Israël* (Production / Diffusion, Les Films Esdés, 2003).

7. Tudor Parfitt, *Black Jews in Africa and the Americas* (Cambridge, MA: Harvard University Press, 2013).

8. Tudor Parfitt and Emanuela Semi, eds., *Judaising Movements: Studies in the Margins of Judaism in Modern Times* (London and New York: Routledge Jewish Studies series, 2002).

9. Édith Bruder, *Black Jews: Les juifs noirs d'Afrique et le mythe des tribus perdues* (Paris: Albin Michel, 2020).

10. Magdel Le Roux, *The Lemba, a Lost Tribe of Israel in Southern Africa?* 2nd edition (Pretoria: Unisa, University of South Africa, 2015).

11. Daniel Lis, *Jewish Identity Among the Igbo of Nigeria, Israel's "Lost Tribe" and the Question of Belonging in the Jewish State* (Trenton, NJ: Africa World Press, 2015).

12. William F. S. Miles, *Jews of Nigeria: An Afro-Judaic Odyssey* (Princeton, NJ: Markus Wiener Publishers, 2012).

13. Lisa Anteby-Yemini, *Les Juifs éthiopiens en Israël: les paradoxes du paradis* (Paris: CNRS Éditions, 2004); *Les Juifs d'Éthiopie de Gondar à la Terre promise* (Paris: Albin Michel, 2018).

14. Don Seeman, *One People, One Blood: Ethiopian-Israelis and the Return to Judaism* (New Brunswick, NJ: Rutgers University Press, 2010).

15. John L. Jackson Jr., *Thin Description: Ethnography and the African Hebrew Israelites of Jerusalem* (Cambridge, MA: Harvard University Press, 2013).

16. Jaap Van Slageren, *Influences juives en Afrique. Repères historiques et discours idéologiques* (Paris: Éditions Karthala, 2009).

17. Nicole Lapierre, *Causes communes. Des Juifs et des Noirs* (Paris: Stock, series "Un ordre d'idées," 2011).

18. Harold Brackman and Ephraim Isaac, *From Abraham to Obama: A History of Jews, Africans and African Americans* (Trenton, NJ: Africa World Press, Inc., 2015).

19. Maurice Dorès, *Négritude et Judéité: Balades en noir et blanc* (Paris: Édition Indes savantes, Collection 5 points, 2021).

20. Édith Bruder, *Les Relations entre Juifs et Noirs. De la Bible à Black Lives Matter* (Paris: Albin Michel, 2023).

21. Katya Gibel Azoulay, *Black, Jewish, and Interracial: It's Not the Color of Your Skin, but the Race of Your Kin, and Other Myths of Identity* (Durham, NC: Duke University Press, 1997).

22. Raphaël Ben Gad, *Je suis juif, je suis noir et j'en suis fier!* (Saint Maur-des-Fossés: Éditions Jets d'Encre, 2022).

23. Rachel Kahn, *Racée* (Paris: Éditions de l'Observatoire, 2021).

24. Marah Saday, *Tu seras juif mon fils* (Paris: Biblieurope, 2013).

25. Guershon Nduwa, *Manifeste des Juifs Noirs: Essai pour la tolérance* (Orthez: Publishroom, 2016). This work was self-published.

26. Pierre-Jean Simon, *Pour une sociologie,* 68–69.

27. Danièle Hervieu-Léger, *La religion en miettes ou la question des sectes* (Paris: Calmann-Lévy, 2001) and *Le pèlerin et le converti. La religion en mouvement* (Paris: Flammarion, 1999), 121–24.

28. Ida Simon-Barouh, *Juifs à Rennes. Étude ethnosociologique* (Paris: L'Harmattan, 2009), 9.

29. Ernest Renan, "Le Judaïsme comme race et comme religion," conference given at the Cercle Saint-Simon on January 27, 1883 (Paris: Editions Calmann Lévy, formerly Michel Lévy Frères, 1883), accessed October 28, 2019, https://fr.wikisource.org/wiki/Le_Judaisme_comme_race_et_comme_religion.

30. See Édith Bruder, *The Black Jews of Africa: History, Religion, Identity* (London and New York: Oxford University Press 2008); *Black Jews, Les Juifs noirs d'Afrique et le mythe des Tribus perdues* (Paris: Albin Michel, 2014).

31. Aurélien Mokoko Gampiot, *Kimbanguism: An African Understanding of the Bible* (Signifying (on) Scriptures series, University Park, PA: Pennsylvania State University Press, 2017). Available in Open Access at http://www.oapen.org/search?identifier=627658; *Kimbanguisme et Identité noire* (Paris: L'Harmattan, 2004); *Les Kimbanguistes en France, Expression messianique d'une Eglise afro chrétienne en contexte migratoire* (Paris: L'Harmattan, 2010).

32. Roger Bastide, *Les Christs noirs,* preface to Martial Sinda, *Le messianisme congolais et ses incidences politiques* (Paris: Payot, 1972), 11.

33. In many earlier publications, and on the basis of his self-presentation, I referred to Nduwa as being in the process of becoming a rabbi; yet after many interviews, I realized that this is actually a project he had.

34. Annick N'Guessan, *Être juif et noir en France,* documentary film, production TV Mondiapress, 2014.

35. Vincent L. Wimbush, *White Men's Magic: Scripturalization as Slavery* (Oxford and New York: Oxford University Press, 2012), 87. Italics in the text.

36. "Masorti Judaism celebrates the diversity of our contemporary Jewish community while making its own, distinctive contribution. We have a steadfast commitment to integrating traditional Judaism with modern values, and maintain traditional observance while being fully inclusive and intellectually open-minded." Definition retrieved from the website https://masorti.org.uk/articles/what-is-masorti/ accessed September 28, 2023.

Chapter 1

History of the Presence of Jews and Blacks in France

JEWS IN FRANCE

The Diaspora of Jews around the world was due to the war between Jews and Romans in 70 C.E., which ended with the fall of Jerusalem and the destruction of the second temple. Exile began then for most Jews. Settling down in countries where they had to obey non-Jewish rulers, they were nevertheless under the spiritual authority of religious leaders who made observance of the Kashrut and marriage alliances more stringent, as unions with natives of these countries were banned. As a consequence of this as well as minority status, Jews did not assimilate with native populations, since their religious practice demanded that they follow a separate calendar, consume distinct food, and keep Shabbat and festivals unique to their faith.

In Europe and especially in France, the early Jewish communities were unwelcome minorities, considered as having lost the favors of God, as the French philosopher Alexis Rosenbaum explains:

> The Christians thus inherit the election the Jews are dispossessed of, because they have proven unworthy of it. The Bible is interpreted as a prophetic indictment of the former elect, whose role is regularly denigrated. The fall of the temple of Jerusalem and the Diaspora are considered as divine punishments. The [Catholic] church therefore developed and facilitated the rise of an anti-Jewish rhetoric that no longer accuses them of misanthropy or self-segregation, but of impiety and sinfulness against God. The most dreadful and unforgivable of these sins is obviously the death of Christ, the infamous deicide, which they were rapidly blamed for as a people.[1]

As a result, in France the anti-Judaic sentiment translated into the social marginalization of and discrimination against Jews, whose presence dates back at least to the fifth century C.E. and in all likelihood, to the first century C.E., in the immediate aftermath of the fall of Jerusalem.[2] As in other countries, French Jews adjusted to the situation and elaborated collective survival strategies in response to changing political contexts. Their community organization, throughout history, has been based on shared religious values and a common understanding of their history and destiny as a people. From the eleventh to the late thirteenth centuries, Jewish communities became more numerous in Europe, both within and in the outskirts of urban centers, partly because Jews were forbidden to own land in Christian countries. Medieval societies across Europe were divided into three social castes: the aristocracy, the clergy, and the taxpaying laypeople (merchants, craftspeople, and peasants). Jews, being a religious minority, were only partly accepted in the third group, and the thriving of some in occupations such as banking or medical science often caused the entire group to be targeted by the church or the kings (who repeatedly seized their possessions, banned those who refused conversion, and allowed them back into the country against the payment of a ransom, in 1182, 1254, 1306, 1394 C.E.).

The protection of the Catholic church was ambiguous, as it oscillated between a policy of forced conversions and a theological discourse presenting the Jewish people as an accursed "witness" whose presence was necessary to testify to the superiority of Christianity and the divine election of Christians as the "New Israel." To ensure that Jews would be visibly distinguished from Christians at first sight, the Fourth Council (1215) forced them to wear a roundel, that is, a round, yellow patch sewn on their garments, which helped local authorities to police them, restrict their liberties, and implement other discriminatory policies. As mentioned above, several occupations became forbidden to Jews, who, being excluded from the "guilds" in which skilled craftsmen had organized and being denied the right to gain revenue from land ownership, were confined to the peddling of textile and used clothes, the trading of cattle, horses, grain and wine, hospitality, butchery, and usury, which was their only—but risky—option for investing their savings. As money lending at high interest rates was forbidden by the Catholic church, this activity, which was nonetheless necessary to the wealthiest members of medieval French society, helped build the persistent anti-Semitic stereotype embodied by the Shakespearean character of Shylock, even though the vast majority of European Jews were as needy as their Christian neighbors.

The legal separation from the Christian majority was materialized and reinforced by the confinement of Jewish inhabitants to ghettos (known as "juiveries") within French cities, which usually implied insecurity on a daily basis and exposure to violent raids, discriminatory policing, and an easier rounding up for the deportations regularly ordered by kings. As the famous sociologist Edgar Morin pointed out,

> The separation between Jews and Gentiles became near-total in the West from the eleventh century, save for Spain and Portugal [then under Muslim rule]. In the Middle Ages, a dual logic created and reinforced the self-isolation of both Christians and Jews. This self-isolation, on the one hand, hampered any communication on an equal footing, any intermarriage and, with some exceptions, any intellectual exchange; on the other hand, the Mosaic religion's own tendency towards self-isolation, rooted in the privilege of divine election, casts the Gentiles as impure and bans outmarriages. The extraordinary survival of Jewishness [in Europe] should be understood on the basis of this loop, where the closure of Judaism both fuels and is fueled by anti-Judaism. The uniqueness of Jewishness is perpetuated by the dynamics of self-assertion of both systems of beliefs, which leads each of them to the denial of the other.[3]

Yet, in spite of this (self-)segregation, Jewish institutions have known evolutions in various times and places, with their own styles and models of self-government. As the US historian Elisheva Carlebach notes,

> In some respects, internal governance was the same in most communities: Jews were entitled to choose their representatives, legislate, settle disputes, share out taxes, punish civil offenses and organize themselves for purposes of charity, education, and religious life. The emergence of community organizations was much more unplanned, their mutual relations were more decentralized and their structures much more diverse as had been assumed. Yet, their existence as well as the services they performed remain undeniable.[4]

This form of community organization, prompted both by the specificity of Jewish legislation and religious practices and by the structural inequality maintained by French society, made Jews appear "as a form of anomaly, or even led to accusing them of trying to form a State within the State."[5] The period between the sixteenth and eighteenth centuries is marked by a double realization, as explained by Elisheva Carlebach: "the States, which were involved in a process of centralization, became aware of the functioning of secondary societies in their midst, while Jewish communities became aware of their place in a world made wider."[6] The networks of the Jewish diaspora allowed a sizable development of trading and banking activities. The status of Jews also became more complex, with the emergence of the figure of the "court Jew," who played a role in European monarchies to facilitate financial transactions and help manage public finances or levy taxes. However, this status was viewed unfavorably by the rising middle class and the guilds, which feared competition. Additionally, the Inquisition was a major turning point in the construction of France as a modern nation, as in previous centuries, French Jews' refusal of assimilation through forced conversions to Christianity caused them to be massacred or cast out of the country. As the political science scholar Pierre-André Taguieff notes,

> the century of progress was also that of the emancipation of Jews in a context where the nationalist principle prevailed, imposing the norm of homogeneity to the various groups making up the people and therefore eradicating all "distinctive identities." This placed Jews in a tragic dilemma: either they must stop being Jewish, by putting down roots unreservedly in the host nation (and thus following a principle of total assimilation or radical loss of distinctiveness), or they must leave the homeland (by forced emigration), unless they were willing to accept discrimination, stigmatization and social exclusion.[7]

In the late eighteenth century, Jews were eventually "emancipated," that is, freed from legal restrictions in France and other European countries, but as individuals rather than as a distinct group of citizens. During the French Revolution of 1789, the cleric Abbé Henri Grégoire played a considerable part in theorizing the advantages of such a policy:

> [i]nstead of closing the gap separating Jews from us, we have worked to deepen it; and far from giving them incentives to inform and improve themselves, we have shut in their faces all the gates of the temple of virtue and honor. What hope was left to the Jew, oppressed as he was by despotism, branded as an outcast by our laws, covered with indignity, and tortured by hatred? No sooner had he stepped out of his cabin that he was faced with enemies and suffered humiliation. The sun shone on his pains only. A martyr to public opinion, he had nothing to lose or gain before the tribunal of public esteem, even if he converted, as no one would believe in his sincerity or virtue. He was scorned, and thus became despicable. Had we been in his place, we may have been even worse.[8]

Undeniably, Abbé Grégoire's essay translated the emerging feeling of guilt of French Christians in acknowledging their responsibility in the marginalization and stigmatization of their Jewish neighbors. Indeed, his essay was written in response to a contest organized in 1787 by the Royal Society of Arts and Sciences of the northeastern city of Metz, which he won along with two other candidates; the assignment was to answer the question, "Are there ways to make Jews happier and more useful to France?" That this question, thus formulated, should have been deemed a suitable assignment for a contest is a testament to the social, legal, and economic insecurity suffered by the overwhelming majority of French Jews in the late eighteenth century. Abbé Grégoire's essay developed two main arguments. First, discrimination based on prejudice is socially unprofitable; second, it is not consistent with the humanism and tolerance informing the message of Christ.

Based on these conclusions, with the decree of September 27, 1791, French Jews were granted a new legal and social status, as discrimination against them was officially banned and French citizenship guaranteed. This gave them access to all occupations and land ownership, giving them for the first time the opportunity to fully participate in French political and cultural life. Unsurprisingly, "spurred by the event, Jews themselves did not remain idle. In Paris and Bordeaux, some enrolled in the national guard. They appeared in political clubs in the city of Paris. Those from the Eastern provinces sent delegations to the [national] assembly."[9] Some others embraced the culture and mores of their country to the point of assimilating, by converting to Catholicism or Protestantism, marrying non-Jews,[10] or changing their names. Indeed, beginning in 1808, as the historian Pierre Birnbaum explains,

> The distinctiveness of the names borne by Jews was . . . largely diminished. Their Gallicization, shown as proof of assimilation, rapidly gained increased momentum, even beyond the enforcement of the decree of July 20, 1808 [signed by Napoleon and obliging all French Jews without a stable last name to adopt one], because it was also inscribed in a republican understanding of building a homogeneous citizenry.[11]

Emancipation thus allowed many Jews to gain freedom of movement out of the ghettos and invent news forms of Jewishness. Indeed, their religious practice was also transformed by Napoleon's decision to organize it along the model of the other two official religions (the Catholic and Protestant churches), by establishing an "Organic regulation of the Mosaic religion" in a decree published on March 17, 1808. As a consequence of this new organization, French Judaism has been placed under the responsibility of the Central Consistory, located in Paris and made up of a chief rabbi and lay members. To this day, it has represented Judaism in interactions with public authorities, while regional consistories have kept their autonomy in regulating religious practice and particularly the Kashrut.

It is the Israelite Consistory of France which holds the most central place in the French Jewry. It is in charge of the administrative and financial management of the community, and officially represents the Jewish religion for the French republic, as it oversees the organization of religious practice in the best interests of the community, delivers degrees to the rabbis it has certified, and is consulted when rabbis are appointed at local level (there is one "regional consistory" for every 2,000 individuals identifying as Jewish). Under the royal ordinance issued by King Louis-Philippe on May 25, 1844, it is also vested by the French republic with the power to censure, suspend, and dismiss rabbis at all levels, with the approval of local and regional police authorities (préfets).

These innovations paved the way for the development of a "reformed" Judaism in the nineteenth century, leaving behind the former system of self-organization and internal rules. The historian Shlomo Sand stressed the implications of this evolution as follows:

> Reform Judaism began to flourish everywhere that political liberalism was well established, and at times even helped bring it about. In the Netherlands, Britain, France, and especially Germany, newly established religious communities tried to adapt Jewish practices and tactics to the spirit of enlightenment that had been spread by the French Revolution. Everything in the tradition that was perceived as counterintuitive was modified and imbued with new substance and new expression. Synagogue and prayer observances were changed, and new houses of worship developed invigoratingly original rituals.
>
> Aside from the efforts to modernize community activities, what most characterized the Reform enterprise was the effort to adapt it to the consolidation of nations and national cultures that was then under way. Reform Jews, seeking their place in this process, saw themselves first and foremost as an immanent component of the new collective identities. Hebrew prayers were translated into the increasingly dominant standardized national languages. In addition, Reform Judaism removed from the liturgy all references to redemption that suggested a return to Zion at the end of days. According to the Reform ethos, each Jew had only one homeland: the country where he or she lived. Jews, before being anything else, were German, Dutch, British, French, and American believers in the faith of Moses.[12]

The very fact of suppressing the mention of a "return to Zion at the end of days" is a clear indication of a will to integrate the French mainstream.

The legal emancipation of Jews and their individual integration into the nation-state was also under way in many other European countries, including Germany, Italy, the Netherlands, or the UK during the second half of the nineteenth century, and it was replicated in other parts of the world until the turn of the century. In post-revolutionary France, nationhood mattered more than religious affiliations, and values of humanism, secularism, individualism, and rationality remain extolled in preference to religiosity up to the present day. Of utmost importance to French Jews was the premium put on civil rights, with the issuance of "edicts of tolerance" granting French Jews equal treatment with other citizens.

However, as Alexis Rosenbaum pointed out, the new status obtained thanks to the revolution of 1789 remained problematic, as deeply-rooted prejudices cannot be abolished by a mere decree. Jews are no longer second-class citizens, but distrust continues to prevail where they are concerned—are they really like any other citizen? Their loyalty may at times be doubted, and they can always be identified with the figure of Judas from the Gospels. Let's bear in mind that in the context of emergence of nation-states, a sense of belonging to the nation became of crucial importance, while the unusual blend of insularity and universalism represented by Jews appeared ambiguous, and was rapidly perceived by some as synonymous with anti-patriotic values.[13]

On the one hand, those critical of the new social order brought about by the French Revolution felt threatened by the new status of Jews, especially on seeing the success of some high-profile bankers like Edmond Rothschild under Napoleon III. On the other hand, socialists also perceived these individual achievements as proof that Jews were on the side of the ruling classes and responsible for the social distress of the have-nots: "The stereotype of extremely wealthy Jews controlling nations or bribing heads of state became widely popular. Even the spirit of entrepreneurship was recast as greed by some authors and attributed to Judaism."[14] Vexingly, the overrepresentation of Jews among French philanthropists and their superior degree of generosity to recipients outside of their community of faith did not counter this representation.[15] In the elections of 1848, which were the country's first presidential elections with universal male suffrage, politicians both on the left and the far right of the spectrum scapegoated Jews as "the ideal targets of collective resentment" to massively rally voters against them, particularly among the military, traditional Catholics, the landed aristocracy, small shopkeepers and craftspeople suffering from economic transformation, and the urban proletariat. Meanwhile, in retrospect, a fraction of the conservatives came to view the French Revolution as a successful plot set up by the Freemasons, Protestants, and Jews.

At any rate, the decline of traditional communities accompanying the redefining of Jewishness and the separation between the private and public spheres in French citizens' lives, with religion being relegated and strictly confined to the private sphere, are evolutions that profoundly marked French Judaism. As was noted by the French sociologist Martine Cohen,

> [o]n the ideological plane, the reorganization led to the elaboration of a "Franco-Judaism" where Judaism, now redefined as a belief system and a practice pertaining to the private sphere, was associated with an all-encompassing moral perspective conflating the values of Judaism and those of revolutionary France: the Declaration of the Rights of Man and Citizen was the new Ten Commandments and France an actual "Promised Land." Jewish intellectuals and rabbis, particularly those who founded in 1860 the Universal Israelite

Alliance, were very active at the time in spreading these values for the sake of "regenerating" Jewish individuals with their writings and preaching and by means of a network of schools encouraging vocational training and the command of the French language. . . .[16]

Consequently, French Jews have become so Gallicized and assimilated, like Alfred Dreyfus who became a high-ranking officer, that they felt indebted to France and tended to put their patriotism on display. This was particularly visible during the First World War, when many Jewish generals, as well as other commissioned officers and privates, served and died for the mother country. Even though the use of vernacular languages was actively discouraged among the French, many of whom still had a poor command of the national language, posters in Yiddish could be seen on the walls of Paris, which read,

> France, the country of liberty, equality and fraternity—France who, the first among all nations, granted us Jews the rights of man and citizens—France, where we and our families have found a shelter and a refuge for many years—France is in danger! . . . Brethren! Now is the time to pay our tribute of gratitude to the country that gave us moral emancipation and material well-being.[17]

Thus, Jewish patriotism in France was (and still is, to a large extent) understood as a debt owed to a liberator. Historians have called "Franco-Judaism" this articulation between Jewishness and Frenchness. "The messiah was in fact the emancipation and Paris the New Jerusalem. Jews chosen by God to be 'the light among nations,' were simply the forerunners of French citizens, who would spread the universal message of liberty, fraternity, and equality throughout the world. Being a good Jew meant being a good Frenchman, and vice versa."[18] This was demonstrated by the voluntary enrollment of both French and foreign-born Jews in the French Army during the First World War, with around 7,500 fatalities.[19] In the interwar period, many Jews from Eastern Europe emigrated to France, so that by 1939, close to 130,000 Jews were counted in the city of Paris alone, including 28,500 naturalized French citizens.[20] The French historian Jérémy Guedj remarks,

> If French Judaism in the interwar period had to be encapsulated in one sentence, it would be the following, "French above all else." For the Israelites of the time, who displayed vocal patriotism, France's interests must prevail over any other consideration, including religious ones. They often felt more attracted to their countrymen and women than by fellow Jews hailing from excessively remote places. This does not mean they ignored the denominational ties that united them; but these "brethren" elicited among them very mixed feelings, ranging from attraction to rejection. How to describe the state of mind of French

Israelites? Did they see in them the fellow Jews (the Same) or the foreigners (the Other)?[21]

But the Second World War (1940–1945) tragically reintroduced a dual treatment for Jews in France, with deportations toward Nazi camps and state persecutions under the Vichy regime, which actively supported the anti-Jewish policies of the occupying forces. As the political scientist Michel Winock remarked,

> [i]n the end, it is estimated that the discriminatory laws of 1940–1941 deprived of their livelihood half of the French Jewish population. Social segregation had been organized by the French authorities without any prompting. Banned from jobs in the administrations, schools and universities, the press and publishing houses, the film industry and theaters, banking and the Stock Exchange, French Jews had been turned into pariahs. As for foreign-born or de-naturalized Jews, they were doomed to be sent to the "special camps." The anti-Semitic rage had long been considered a toothless furor; it had now passed into law.[22]

French citizenship, obtained since the Enlightenment, proved elusive to those living in Europe before and during World War II. But the self-help values cultivated by the community were mustered by the Central Consistory even before the liberation of the country by Allied and French forces; though weakened by Nazi occupation in the northern half of the country, it helped small communities as best it could and in 1943, it participated in secret in the creation of the Representative Council of French Jewish Institutions (Conseil Représentatif des Institutions Juives de France, known as CRIF) which was mostly composed of political groups, identifying as Communist or Zionist. Although the Consistory remained the legitimate representative instance with the authorities, it is still flanked today by the CRIF, which speaks for the majority of the Jewish organizations whose mission statements are both religious and political, so that together, they reflect the diversity of the French Jewry in all negotiations with the French republic.

When the state of Israel was officially created, on May 14, 1948, these representative instances of French Jews were now faced with another model of nationhood offered to the Jewish diasporic communities. As the French political scientist Alain Dieckhoff explains,

> Zionism has two dimensions. On the one hand, on the political plane, it does aim to create a new Jew who is active and committed—the polar opposite of the passive, submissive Jew of the diaspora. On the other hand, on the symbolic plane, it is tasked with preserving the legacy of the "Hebrew Jew" among the Diaspora Jews, as the latter genealogically derive from the former. This foundational ambivalence is also found in the identity of the state of Israel. . . . At the

core of the Zionist project is the dogged will to normalize Jewish life, and this normalization implies the establishment and consolidation of a sovereign state. In many ways, this national normalization has been successful.[23]

As a consequence, since the creation of the state of Israel, Zionism has been appropriated by many Jews of the Diaspora as a way to eschew both the push toward assimilation and the recurrent anti-Semitic menace. Even if the stability of the Jewish state has remained under threat since the end of the Six Day War of June 1967, which allowed Israel to claim the Gaza Strip and the Sinai Peninsula from Egypt, the Golan heights from Syria and the West Bank and eastern Jerusalem from Jordan, Jews from the Diaspora are welcome by definition. The pioneer generation of Zionists came mostly from Eastern Europe, followed by those hailing from Arabic-speaking countries; but the coexistence between Ashkenazim and Sephardim has been uneasy.

In France, the decolonization of the country's North African colonies revitalized religious practice and profoundly transformed the Jewish community, as between the early 1950s and the late 1960s, an estimated 240,000 Sephardim were "repatriated" to a "mother country" in which they had no roots.[24] The French sociologist Martine Cohen analyzed this turning point as follows:

> The reconstruction of French Judaism occurred primarily on a social and cultural plane. By a seeming paradox, the creation of the state of Israel in 1948 allowed a new self-definition of Jews in France along the lines of a revalued Jewishness, which they embraced as more modern (reflecting the modernity of the pioneering Kibbutzim), freed from clergy, and bearing the proud legacy of universal prophetic ideals. A hub of intellectual and religious revival was created around the thinkers of the "School of Orsay," namely Emmanuel Levinas, André Néher, Léon Ashkénazi, etc., who spread a modernized Jewish thinking among a wider audience, thanks to the yearly conferences of French-speaking Jewish intellectuals they organized from 1957. Additionally, with the support of American Jewish organizations, the United Jewish Social Fund (F.S.J.U), created in 1949, launched a vast educational and cultural program which pursued in a secular form the educational and philanthropic work of the Consistory. The "community centers" built by the F.S.J.U from the late 1950s were then unique spaces of expression of a Jewish culture and sociability that were gradually taking some distance from religious reference and normativity. They were progressively attended by Jews hailing from North Africa. This new migratory wave, whose successive phases lasted until the 1960s, profoundly transformed the landscape of the French Jewry.[25]

In the end, the French Jewry has a long and rich history which makes it unique among the country's racial and ethnic minorities, with distinct strata corresponding to the country's political and demographic evolutions, which explains why it defines itself along the lines of an Ashkenazi/Sephardic binary to the present day. The recent collective work entitled *Histoire juive de la France*, edited by the historian Anne Sylvie Goldberg[26] and gathering 150 scholars, described the presence of Jews on French soil since the time of Roman Gaul not just as a ghettoized people, passively facing discrimination, persecution, expulsion, emancipation, or even extermination, but as actors of the nation's destiny on the political, economic, social, intellectual, and artistic planes.

More recently, the French Jewry has been faced with more diversity with the rising visibility of Black Jews; but before this point is discussed, it is important to offer a historical overview of the presence of Blacks in France.

BLACK PRESENCE IN FRANCE

It is difficult to give a precise date to trace the arrival of the first person of sub-Saharan African descent on French soil in Europe, but the country became involved in the Transatlantic Slave Trade as early as 1642. As a result, there were Black French subjects, but they were legally defined as chattels, that is, movable objects of private property, under the Code noir of 1685. Paradoxically, though, because France was a Catholic kingdom, all enslaved children, men, and women had to be baptized and receive religious instruction in the Catholic faith. Even in that measure of recognition of their humanity, they were taught that their condition as bondspeople resulted from a divine curse. As the French historian Hélène Vignaux explained,

> It was not long before Africans, or Ethiopians as they were known then, were identified with the descendants of Ham—even though the latter had no kinship ties with Africans. Based on this theory, African Blacks were condemned by God to enslavement, and early Christians had not questioned this situation, in spite of the egalitarian message they meant to propagate. In addition to the so-called "divine will" dooming Blacks to slavery, the color itself symbolized evil, death, and the devil.[27]

Consequently, the lives of enslaved Black French subjects were ruled by an ideology of Providence as well as by the legal provisions of the Code noir, which was enforced in the Caribbean islands from 1687, in French Guiana in 1704, at Reunion Island in 1723, and in Louisiana (with some even more stringent clauses) in 1724. Meanwhile, in metropolitan France, observers could sometimes note in "royal courts or near famous aristocrats, the presence of Black slaves or servants who lent an exotic touch to these secluded spaces where all things rare elicited passionate interest."[28] Indeed, in spite of the Freedom Principle applied on the soil of the "mother country," enslaved Black men, women, and children were taken by their owners to large cities, often beyond the time limit allowed by the state under the "Police des Noirs" which also mandated their registration at the ports of entry. It was not until the mid-eighteenth century that their humanity began to be considered in political and religious circles. Among the famous statesmen who expressed abolitionist views was Necker, the Swiss-born Protestant Minister of Finances of King Louis XVI, who wrote in 1784 (three years after his first resignation):

> France's colonies contain almost 500,000 slaves, and a man's wealth is measured by the number of these poor souls he possesses. . . . We preach a message of humanity, yet every year we put in shackles 20,000 inhabitants of Africa. . . . But would it be an impossible feat if by a general move, all nations agreed to renounce the Slave Trade?[29]

The principles of the revolution of 1789, promising equality among all French citizens, were well understood by the country's Black subjects who, in the Caribbean Sea as in the Indian Ocean, were just as ready for emancipation as French Jews. However, and despite the arguments of the Société des Amis des Noirs, no reference was made to actual slaves in real chains in the Declaration of the Rights of Man and Citizen published on August 26, 1789. Citizenship was not meant to extend to them, essentially out of fear that a massive emancipation of enslaved French subjects would lead to the economic collapse of a very profitable economy (the sugar industry in particular, in the island of Saint Domingue) on which France was dependent. The second argument, common to all defenders of the slave trade and the institution of chattel slavery, claimed that Africans were better off being enslaved by Europeans who allegedly "civilized" them than by Arab Muslims or fellow Africans who were constantly at war with one another (for reasons never explicitly mentioned, as they would have pointed back to the transatlantic trade itself).[30] This argument rested on the notion that Christianizing Africans and their descendants led them to salvation, a contention that did not meet with the approval of all clergy members. Abbé Raynal, an abolitionist Catholic priest, considered it woefully hypocritical: "O benevolent Jesus! Had you foreseen that your sweet doctrines would be bent to justify so much horror? If Christianity thus gave its blessing to the avarice of empires, then its merciless dogmas should be banned."[31] As for Abbé Grégoire, a member of the Société des Amis des Noirs, he advocated for both the granting of civil and political rights to Jews in his 1788 *Essai sur la régénération physique, morale et politique des Juifs,* and the abolition of the transatlantic trade and slavery in two other writings, *De la traite et de l'esclavage* (1789) and *Écrits sur les Noirs* (1808).

Meanwhile, the Black French decided to take up arms to win their own freedom in Saint Domingue or Guadeloupe, the former uprising escalating in a full-fledged independence war involving the United Kingdom and Spain as well as France, while the latter was pitilessly crushed.[32] On February 4, 1794, the Code noir was abolished by decree, and Black French men were recognized as citizens with equal rights to those of the mother country, at least on paper. In reality, the vast majority of those who had not been forced to follow their owners to Louisiana were left to their own devices, with no formal education and no lands to make a living out of. Besides, their emancipation was short-lived, as Napoleon re-established slavery on May 20, 1802, under the pressure of the planter lobby, of which his first wife Joséphine de Beauharnais was a member. Black French subjects were stripped of their citizenship, and those who had become farmers were deprived of their wages and re-enslaved. In metropolitan France, discriminatory measures were implemented against Blacks and "people of color" (gens de couleur) as they were banned from entering the country, while Black officers were excluded from the Napoleonic Army and interracial marriages were forbidden by a memorandum published on January 8, 1803. In all French colonies save for Haiti, Black French men, women, and children would remain enslaved for another forty-five years, until the definitive abolition of the institution was ratified on April 27, 1848, thanks to the efforts of Victor Schoelcher under France's Second Republic.

But at this point in the history of France, this first phase of colonization was already being replaced by a second one, which took place on the African continent (as well as in Southeast Asia). The humanity of Africans was still contested by the racial ideologies and representations of Blackness that shaped the nineteenth century, with so-called scientific racism defining them as an inferior race that White European men had the duty to "civilize." The development of human zoos offers a particularly striking contrast with the idea of emancipation and the values of the Enlightenment that had been extended to White French minorities, since in these itinerant shows, Black colonial subjects were exhibited behind bars in public gardens and paid to act like "savages" for the entertainment and titillation of metropolitan citizens. As the world champion soccer player Lilian Thuram (from Guadeloupe) remarked in a bestselling book on the Black French experience,

> to get an idea of what these zoos meant, imagine a world where very few have the luxury to travel. Therefore, such places represented the epitome of exoticism. In addition to providing an experience of traveling by proxy, they also contributed to educating younger generations, as children could be immersed

in the exotic sceneries that had kindled their imaginations while reading *Dick Sand, A Captain at Fifteen* [by Jules Verne] or *Livingstone's Missionary Travels*. As television did not exist back then, this was the Sunday outing for families; they went there for picnics. All kinds of fantasies could materialize in these spaces where savages were caught unposed, in their half-nakedness, at a time when White people were fully dressed up to their necks, even for sea bathing.[33]

An infamous example of this commodification of African men, women, and children is that of Saartje Bartmann, the so-called "Hottentot Venus" from South Africa who was treated as an object of curiosity under the pretext of scientific exploration and sexually abused with no regard for her psychological well-being. As the French historians Nicolas Bancel, Pascal Blanchard, and Sandrine Lemaire noted, "these zoos, where 'exotic' individuals were exhibited side by side with wild animals behind bars or in pens for the entertainment of an eager audience, offered the most glaring proof of the discrepancy between rhetoric and praxis at the time when colonial empires were in the making."[34] At the same time, the African American musichall artist Josephine Baker built her fame on this thirst for exoticism by complying with requests that she dance topless and without restraint for the pleasure of Parisian audiences.

In the twentieth century, the two world wars led to the first large-scale encounter between Blacks and metropolitan French people, with an unprecedented influx of colonial troops from the country's Caribbean and African possessions. A classic novel accounting for the culture shock is Lucie Cousturier's *Des inconnus chez nous* (1920), where Africans are described as exoticized beings eliciting sexual interest and speaking in broken French, like the well-known tirailleur sénégalais on the ads for the cocoa mix Banania, who embodied African men as childlike and naive. On the political plane, the research published by historian Philippe Dewitte shows how the massive number of war casualties caused by World War I prompted the French government to seek for low-paid workforce in its colonies.[35] However, Africans were excluded out of preference for European job seekers, presumably more assimilable and exempt from the stereotype of laziness cultivated by colonial rhetoric and imagery. As historians Pascal Blanchard and Nicolas Bancel explained, "The only acceptable immigrants are exclusively European . . . so that, at the apex of the colonial rule, at the moment when the myths on natives became embedded in consciences and political praxis, all the rhetoric on undesirable immigration was already inseparable from that on colonized peoples."[36]

The French colonial empire collapsed in the 1960s with the wave of African independences, but the country's economy still needed low-paid manpower that was mainly recruited in North and sub-Saharan Africa, and in the 1970s, the government favored family reunification, partly because it wanted to avoid interracial marriages. New waves of migration came from the African continent, made up mostly of students and asylum seekers. The multiracialism presently observed in France is a consequence of this continuum of slavery, colonization, and legal immigration, even if the latter phase alone appears in discussions of multiculturalism. On the one hand, the presence of Black French men, women, and children has become normalized in representations of the mainstream, as certain occupations are readily associated with persons of African descent (especially in health care, postal services, or the Christian clergy) while transracially adopted as well as biracial children are a common sight on the streets of big cities all over the country. As the French ethnologist Jean Benoist remarked, "every time two human groups interact with each other, even if they kill each other, they always end up being intertwined."[37]

On the other hand, in spite of the multiracialism prevailing in urban environments, members of racial and ethnic minorities in France are still encumbered by the persistent stereotypes and prejudices informing their peers' representations and perceptions of what a French person should look and sound like. This is particularly evident in the uneasiness surrounding the naming of the country's principal minority groups—Jews, Arabs, and Blacks—which is at its maximum in the case of the latter and translates the unspoken guilt vis-à-vis its slaveholding and colonial legacy. The N-word was already problematic enough for Lucie Cousturier to avoid using it in her 1920 novel (mentioned above); to this day, the French word "Noir," although widely used by Black French speakers, is still avoided by White ones, who either prefer its English version or the term "homme de couleur," which was used in colonial times and as such, is the equivalent of "colored" in American English.[38]

Even if French Blacks and Jews do not share the same history, both groups have had an experience of discrimination rooted in exclusionary interpretations of the Bible, as the former supposedly inherited the curse uttered by the patriarch Noah, while the latter similarly were made to pay for the sacrifice of the Son of God by being racialized, chased, dehumanized, and forced to convert to Christianity. Their histories developed in parallel for several centuries, as the majority of the French Jewish population lived in the Hexagon, not in the Caribbean or in the sub-Saharan colonies; but the revolution of 1789 brought the two causes together under the banner of emancipation, and the historian Claude Gozlan notes that during the Haitian war for independence, "the Jewish soldiers embraced the cause of Black slaves' liberation under the commandment of Jean-Jacques Dessalines, who became the first President of Haiti."[39] Finally, the two world wars were tragic landmarks for each of the two groups, which fought to prove or gain French citizenship and also faced the horror of extermination camps. Today, most of these tragedies are denied and minimized in the prejudices and stereotypes faced by Jews and Blacks alike, which makes Black Jewish identities particularly complex in the French context.

RACISM AND ANTISEMITISM THROUGH THE PRISM OF BLACK JEWISH IDENTITY

It is impossible to discuss Jewishness and Blackness without addressing the persistence of antisemitism and anti-Black racism—two issues that have claimed and ruined too many lives yet remain painfully complex to solve. Racism is an intricate concept as it encompasses practices such as segregation, discrimination, physical and psychological violence, representations, and language that, according to the French sociologist Michel Wieviorka, consist in "characterizing a human group by essentializing natural features, associating them with intellectual and moral characteristics that presumably apply to every individual belonging to that group."[40] Furthermore, as the French political scientist Pierre-André Taguieff notes, "Racism, as a modern phenomenon, begins with the dread of blood mixing, the obsession with avoiding to 'taint one's bloodline,' and the desire to keep it 'pure.'"[41] Antisemitism is a brand of racism and as such, the definitions given above may be thought to subsume it, but it is not entirely the case.

Antisemitism designates a set of attitudes of rejection and hatred toward Jews that predates the concept coined by the German journalist Wilhelm Marr in the second half of the nineteenth century.[42] Anti-Judaism, its earlier version, encompasses "the manifestations of hostility towards Jews as persons practicing Judaism. It predates the Christian era, as may be seen in writings by 'pagan' authors who practiced the traditional religions of Ancient Rome and Greece."[43] Then Christian authors sought to dissociate the new religion from its Jewish foundations and this implied rejecting Jews by preaching that the Christian church was the new Israel. Appropriating the concept of Chosen People was seen as part of the punishment God was believed to have meted out to Jews for having failed to recognize Jesus as the Messiah, demanded his crucifixion (according to the Gospels), and refused to adhere to Christianity; the destruction of the Temple and the Diaspora of the Jewish people were read as signs of the latter's fall from grace. The councils and papal decrees and bulls developed and built on these interpretations, fostering recurrent accusations in sermons especially. The social consequences of this anti-Jewish hatred came under the form of discrimination and persecutions, with bans on or abolition of rabbinical jurisdictions, prohibitions on the construction of new synagogues, proselytizing, or interfaith marriages between Jews and Christians. These caused many to convert under duress, or perish in massacres.

The history of Jews worldwide became inseparable from persecutions, as they were a minority everywhere. In the eleventh century, they were accused of having destroyed the Holy Sepulcher (where Jesus is supposed to have been buried between Good Friday and Easter Sunday), and this was used by European Christians as a pretext for retaliatory pillaging and massacres of Jews across Europe. During the first crusade (1096 C.E.) organized by monks and aristocrats, Jews were given an ultimatum between converting and death. In the twelfth century, they were accused of murdering Christian children in magical rituals to make matzoth (unleavened bread consumed for the festival of Pessach to celebrate the Children of Israel's liberation from Egypt),[44] or desecrating hosts.[45] In the fourteenth century, they suffered retaliation for allegedly poisoning wells and causing the Black Plague in Europe.

With the relative loss of influence of Christian churches in Europe in the nineteenth century, anti-Judaism was gradually substituted by a new form of ideological hostility toward Jews, theorized by Wilhelm Marr as the mortal enmity between two racial groups—the so-called Aryan race, which he opposed to the so-called Semitic race, a notion invented in the late eighteenth century in reference to the Biblical forefather Sem, son of Noah, mentioned in Chapter 9 of the Book of Genesis (9:25–27)—a passage where the three sons of the patriarch are mentioned in a curse that dooms Ham's offspring (supposedly, Blacks) to be enslaved by the rest of mankind, in punishment for Ham breaking the taboo of seeing his father Noah's nakedness. Because Kush, a character standing for Ethiopia, is listed among Ham's children, interpretations of this Biblical passage have served as a cultural foundation for the development of racial classifications by European Enlightenment thinkers in the second half of the eighteenth century.

At that juncture and in the nineteenth century, the classification approach of the Encyclopedia morphed into a pseudo-scientific racist ideology. The French author Arthur de Gobineau's work, *Essai sur l'inégalité des races humaines* (1853), set out to establish the existence of human races and develop a scientific theory on the difference among them; it became one of the playbooks of racist thinking in twentieth-century Europe. The starting point of Gobineau's theory is an overtly assumed Christian Eurocentric reading of world history rooted in the Old Testament. In this context, Blackness is portrayed as inherently flawed, due to the so-called curse of Ham, and geographically associated with the African continent (the Biblical text does not mention any dark-skinned groups found in Asia or Oceania); the Semites (descendants of Sem) are identified as Arabs and those who speak Semitic languages like Hebrew, while the descendants of Japhet are supposed to be White people, without any clear geographical—let alone linguistic— definition of the boundaries of this group.[46] Interestingly, not only are Jews, as a group, not spared the implications of the hierarchical logic of racial classification, but the term Semitic rapidly became used to designate them exclusively, rather than the Arabic-speaking Semitic peoples. For instance, the rabidly anti-Semitic French journalist Édouard Drumont, writing in the 1930s, described "the Jew" as "crooked-nosed and thick-lipped, with greed exuding from his hands and general appearance. These are atavistic, hereditary features."[47] Anti-Semitic authors like Drumont regularly depicted Jews as exiles or stateless individuals, even though French Jews had been full-fledged citizens for nearly 150 years when he wrote; this allowed a questioning of their patriotism and facilitated accusations of dual loyalty and treason. The Dreyfus case is the perfect illustration of this ambiguous status.

Indeed, Alfred Dreyfus was the embodiment of the spirit of assimilation displayed by French Jews since the Revolution of 1789. He had a successful career as a commanding officer in the French Army when he was accused of betraying his country at the profit of Germany. He suffered public humiliation and was given a life sentence and a condemnation to forced labor in French Guiana in 1895 before his name was cleared in 1897, notably thanks to a press campaign led by progressives in metropolitan France.

Then, following World War I and the defeat of Germany, antisemitism was further theorized and popularized by Adolf Hitler in his writings and harangues. In these, Jews are dehumanized as a "parasitical race" that brings corruption and decay to the other peoples, metaphorized as all sorts of pests (maggot, fungi, hornets, spiders, rats, leeches, and vampires), and demonized as the "eternal" ferment of division.[48] In contrast, he describes the so-called Aryan race as the pure one that must be preserved from the taint of mixing, particularly with Jews; he put in place a set of laws to that effect soon after he came to power in Germany in 1933. His argument against intermarriage is articulated as follows in his infamous book *Mein Kampf*: "A popular state must therefore not allow marriage to be a perpetual outrage to the race, but instead consecrate it as an institution intended to produce beings in the likeness of the Lord, not monsters who are half-human and half-ape."[49] To achieve these ends, he had anti-Semitic laws (known as the Nuremberg laws) enforced nationwide in 1935, stripping Jews of their German citizenship and forbidding them to date or marry "Aryan" fellow Germans, in order to "safeguard German blood and honor." Extant interethnic marriages were declared null, Jewish-owned businesses boycotted and closed down, and Jewish civil servants and army officers dismissed on account of their origins; in cities like Düsseldorf, Jewish patients were no longer admitted in public hospitals, Jewish students were banned from public schools and universities, and synagogues were burned to the ground. All of this discriminatory legislation set the stage for a massive deportation of the country's Jewish population, defined in racial more than religious terms. Indeed, having three or four Jewish grandparents was enough to be racially designated as a Jew, regardless of one's religious convictions and practice. Whenever a person had a non-Jewish first name, they were forced to add "Israel" if a man or "Sara" if a woman, and all were forced to bear an identity card indicating their Jewish origins while the letter "J" was stamped on their passports.

The consequence of this extreme form of state racism is well-known. World War II claimed close to six million Jewish lives (the Nuremberg tribunal's estimate being 5.7 million) and other groups—Roma people, mentally disabled people, homosexuals—were also marked for extermination to "make room" for the "conquering Aryan race," whose purity and honor they were considered to threaten just because of who they were.

The case of Black victims of Nazism is often overlooked and has been little studied by historians. Yet the French African Studies scholar Catherine Coquery-Vidrovitch[50] as well as the Ivorian-French journalist Serge Bilé[51] mined archives and survivors' oral histories to fill this gap. It should also be noted that the first genocide of the twentieth century was perpetrated in Namibia in 1904 by German colonial troops against the Nama and Herero ethnic groups under the orders of Lothar von Trotha,[52] as part of a conquest enterprise that spanned the 1884–1911 period. In Hitler's Germany, anti-Black racism was embedded into the legal system along with antisemitism. "Today, Blacks and Jews are the victims of fascist terrorism," the Togolese editor-in-chief of the Hamburg newspaper *The Negro Worker* protested in a 1933 column. The 20,000 Black Germans of the time found themselves subjected to the same discrimination as their Jewish fellow citizens: they were stripped of their citizenship, their marriages were annulled and new couples forbidden to wed under threat of being jailed for "race betrayal," eugenics were legalized, biracial Germans sterilized, and Black children excluded from schools. The African American athlete Jesse Owens' gold medals at the Munich Olympics of 1936 did represent a resounding public humiliation for Hitler, but the dictator stuck to his racist ideology all the same. When, in the first year of the war (1939–1940), German soldiers encountered Black soldiers from the Caribbean or African colonies serving in the French Army, Hitler ranted about this presence in the following terms:

> France must be counted as one of these giant states, not only because it is increasingly augmenting the ranks of her army thanks to the resources of the colored peoples of its gigantic empire, but also because it is so rapidly being invaded by the n*** that we can actually talk about the emergence of an African state on European soil. . . . If France continues evolving in this manner for the next three hundred years, the last remnants of Frankish blood will disappear in the Afro-European mulatto state which is presently in the making—an immense autonomous settlement territory stretching from the Rhine to the Congo,

peopled with the inferior race that is slowly being created under the influence of prolonged race mixing.⁵³

In his obsession with race purity, Hitler also blamed Jews and their quest for equality for the presence of Blacks in France:

> While our stupid bourgeoisie . . . are filled with respect for the results achieved by modern pedagogy, the cunning Jew sees it as yet another argument in support of the theory he is bent on forcing into the minds of the peoples, proclaiming equality among men. The decadent bourgeoisie is totally unsuspecting of the sin thus committed against reason; for it is criminal folly to train a being who, in essence, is no more than a half-chimpanzee, until people take him for a lawyer, while millions of representatives of the most civilized race are forced to languish in disgraceful situations. It is a sin against the Maker's will when we allow the most gifted men to suffocate by the tens of thousands in the swamps of the proletariat even as Hottentots and Kaffirs are being trained in the professions. For this is nothing else than training, as with poodles, not scientific culture. . . . This is why France is and remains our most dreadful enemy. That people, which is increasingly regressing to the level of n***, is stealthily jeopardizing the existence of the White race in Europe, because of the support it gives Jews in their effort to attain universal domination. For the contamination caused by the influx of n*** blood on the Rhine, in the heart of Europe, is both the result of the sadistic thirst for revenge of the hereditary enemy of our people and the cold calculation of the Jew, who sees it as the perfect way to introduce race mixing from within the center of the European continent, and lay the foundations of its own domination by infecting the White race with the blood of an inferior mankind.⁵⁴

He justified state racism in voting intermarriage bans by the presumed urgency of saving Europe and preserving the "purity of the Aryan race"⁵⁵ Because the Geneva Convention of July 27, 1929, on the treatment of war prisoners was not applied by the German Army when it captured Black prisoners, the latter were systematically executed. Out of the 77,000 African soldiers serving in French ranks, 30,000 died or were missing in action, according to the research done by Serge Bilé,⁵⁶ who also found that half of the children of German women and Black soldiers were sent to concentration camps, while the other half were forcibly sterilized under the command of Eugen Fischer—a program which was rapidly applied to all of Germany's Blacks.

The period following the genocide seemingly ushered in a new awareness of the falsity of racist ideology and a feeling of horror at the atrocities it had permitted. Compassion and atonement temporarily prevailed over xenophobic and anti-Semitic attitudes, and the concept of race became durably disqualified. "The new generations in the Catholic Church signaled a revision in its positions which led to the declaration *Nostra Aetate,* adopted by Council Vatican 2 in 1965, that officially put an end to the accusation of deicide and the 'teaching of contempt.'"[57] The latter phrase was coined by the French Jewish historian Jules Isaac, Holocaust survivor and co-founder of the Judeo-Christian Friendship, who influenced Council Vatican 2 (1962–1965) in offering a new reading of the Catechism of the Council of Trento.[58] The dampening of antisemitism in French society, however, did not stop it from resurfacing under different names, such as Judeophobia or anti-Zionism. Indeed, Pierre-André Taguieff defines Judeophobia as

> a sweeping, systematic rejection of Jews founded on an essentialized definition of the "Jewish people" or the "Jewish category" (all Jews being expected to embody one single essence) entailing negative passions and informing at least one of the following dimensions, which do not necessarily have a positive correlation with one another: attitudes or opinions (i.e. prejudices and stereotypes, implying negative sentiments), behaviors (whether individual or collective, either political mobilizations or physical abuse), institutional forms (segregation, legal or silent forms of discrimination) and ideological discourses, expressing one worldview or another centered on identifying Jews as agents of evil and providing staunch Judeophobes with modes of validation of their beliefs.[59]

According to this author, the Judeophobic process follows various stages which are starting points as well as outcomes. Although the concept was born in the late nineteenth century, it reappeared in the 1990s to designate forms of rejection or opposition toward Jews as a group and members of a religion, mingling antisemitism, anti-Judaism, and anti-Zionism. Since Zionism designates the political movement whose project was the creation of a Jewish national homeland in Palestine, in order to restore the political autonomy of Jews and protect them against antisemitism, anti-Zionism designates all those who oppose this project or the underlying political doctrine. Originally, anti-Zionists were mostly those Jews who preferred remaining in the Diaspora, such as the activists of the Bund in the early nineteenth century (many of whom had emigrated to the USA). But in the interwar period, the Middle East saw an intensification of both Jewish and Arab nationalisms, with many Arab nationalists embracing anti-Zionist positions. In the wake of the creation of the state of Israel in May 1948, war broke out and many states had to take sides in what proved to be a lasting conflict.[60] But in the present social context in France, it is the concept of antisemitism which is most commonly used in everyday conversation, whether in the media or in the political sphere. Consequently, I will use this concept as well in order to describe as accurately as possible the social reality of the persons interviewed.

Since World War II, French ruling élites seem anxious to heal the country of the legacy of infamous treatment of its Jewish citizens. Holocaust denial has been a crime since the voting of the Gayssot Act of 1990, and antisemitism since the law of 2003, which provides that "an offense preceded, accompanied or followed by anti-Semitic (or racist or xenophobic) statements, writings, images, objects or actions calls for heavier penalties due to this aggravating circumstance."[61] This piece of legislation strengthened the individual protection against all forms of discrimination already guaranteed by the Declaration of the Rights of Man and of the Citizen of 1789. Since then, very few anti-Semites have expressed their views overtly in the French media or political landscape, save Holocaust deniers like Jean-Marie Le Pen, who, since 1985, has maintained and reiterated his belief that gas chambers were "a footnote in the history of World War 2."[62]

The various expressions of anti-Semitic sentiment in modern French history—from the wrongful accusations of treason against Captain Dreyfus in the 1890s (see above) to the rise of pro-Nazi rhetoric in the 1930s—developed a discourse portraying Jews as alien to a French identity that was successively labeled as Gallic, Catholic, European, or even Aryan. At this stage, Jews were dubbed as Orientals and "Asiatics," in a move to make them appear as inherently unassimilable to the French nation. Then, the definition of Jews by the Vichy régime, under German occupation (1940–1945), revolved around a binary antagonism between the so-called Aryan race and a Jewish race explored by the historian and sociologist Samuel Ghiles-Meilhac. Finally, in the wake of migrations of Jewish citizens leaving the country's North African colonies in the early 1960s and popular pro-Israeli demonstrations in May–June 1967, the identity of French Jews emerged in an interplay with other transnational minorities composing the French nation.

Yet it was not until 1981 and the election of Socialist President François Mitterrand that the ruling élites began paying attention to expressions of regional and diasporic cultural demands. In a report entitled *Cultural Democracy and the Right to Differentness,* which he submitted on request of the authorities, Henri Giordan laid out a typology of minority groups in France, distinguishing those emanating from regional cultural ensembles from "minorities with no roots in French territory." Within the latter group, he identified three subcategories, namely, "communities of foreigners and first-generation migrant workers," "refugee communities," and "communities formed essentially by French citizens in transnational cultural situations."[63] This designation applied to three groups to which he said, should be paid special attention—the Jewish, Roma, and American communities. Being thus singled out as foreign, can Jews escape racialization?

To address this question, Sander L. Gilman[64] analyzed ethnological literature on pigmentation (as this phenotypical parameter remains the foremost factor in the Western concept of race) to see how it was applied to Jews. He found that latenineteenth-century authors all agreed that Jews were "black" or "tawny," two colors associated with ugliness, and insisted on the features of the nose, olive skin, thick lips, and protruding jaws to build their case. Such representations of Jews as Black were dominant until the early twentieth century, by which time the successful integration of many Jewish Americans in financial and political circles allowed the group to be included less grudgingly into the White category while retaining some aspects of their ethnic specificity. Historian Nadia Malinovich emphasizes that while the interwar period in the USA saw a reinforcement of institutional antisemitism, with "a broad consensus that Jews formed a distinct race, it was also the moment when Jews from the great waves of immigration also became full-fledged Americans."[65]

Yet, as the journalist Michael Lerner explains, joining the American mainstream implied an erasure of the history of Jews as an oppressed group, since, in a society thus organized around the dominance of the White group, no minority could become White and still identify as an oppressed group.[66] Still, as Samuel Ghiles-Meilhac notes,

> Jews' no longer being discriminated against did not keep them from building individual or collective alliances with Black organizations, particularly the NAACP, to fight segregation. The symbol of such cooperation is the proximity between Dr. King and Rabbi Abraham Heschel. From the late 1960s, disagreements between Jewish and Black activists have become more frequent, especially over Affirmative Action. From the standpoint of some Black activists, Jews had escaped the political and social margins to join the dominant group. Their access to White privilege has been a recurrent argument in the critical or hostile rhetoric wielded by African American spokespersons against Jewish Americans, as exemplified in James Baldwin's text "Negroes are Anti-Semitic Because They're Anti-White."[67]

But however influential racial and ethnic relations in the United States may be on the French context, what remains to be seen now is how Black identity claims are expressed in terms of the articulation between politics and religions in France. How do Black people situate themselves in an assimilationist society which implicitly views non-Whiteness as peripheral or foreign? In 1998, the French soccer team's victory at the World Cup had sent the deceiving signal that the French were entirely comfortable with their multiethnic landscape and the new motto "Blacks, Blancs, Beurs" describing the ethnic makeup of the team as emblematic of a society of Whites, Blacks, and North Africans. But the backlash came quickly, with the far-right leader Jean-Marie Le Pen's unexpected success at the first round of the presidential elections of 2002.

Since then, conservative politicians have been consistently catering to the fears of invasion harbored by Le Pen voters; Nicolas Sarkozy in particular got elected in 2007 thanks to a campaign that successfully combined the utilization of the Jewish minority and the stigmatization of Muslim and other African minorities, designated as "racaille" (scum). Himself the descendant of European Jewish immigrants, he celebrated patriotism in unambiguous terms, when he quipped, "If anyone feels uncomfortable in France, well, they're entirely free to leave a country they don't love."[68] In February 2007, when a participant in a TV panel during a debate asked him if such slogans as "France, love it or leave it" were not likely to encourage nationalistic sentiment, then-Minister of Domestic Security Sarkozy famously responded: "I am the first right-wing politician to say that what we need is chosen immigration. But I am also saying one thing with the utmost conviction, which is that no one is forced to live in France. And when you love France, you respect her. You respect the rules, which means you don't practice polygamy, you don't do female genital mutilations, and you don't slaughter sheep in your apartment; you respect the rules of the Republic."[69] These remarks, implicitly framing Muslim Arabs and Africans, are to be contrasted with the statements, mentioned earlier, by former Prime Minister Manuel Valls and President Sarkozy's successor François Hollande, who, lamenting a wave of departures of French Jews to Israel in the face of a rise in antisemitism and terrorist attacks in France, both asserted that "France without French Jews would no longer be France."

But would France still be the same without its Blacks and Arabs? While the far-right parties are unambiguous about their response to this question, other political players have been less straightforward in public. One exception is Brice Hortefeux, friend, campaign aide, and successor of Nicolas Sarkozy as minister of domestic security, who went further down the same path as Sarkozy, displaying the same disrespect for French Muslims in an off-the-record joke about a conservative party member of North African descent who was praised for eating pork and drinking beer, essentially calling the man a token Arab: "Oh but this is not going to work, he doesn't fit the stereotype at all! You always need one of them. When there's only one of them it's fine. When there are many—that's when problems start!"[70] Thankfully, no French politician today would ever dream of designating Jews as a source of "problems" for the rest of the nation or making remarks on their numbers; but the contrast with Muslims and Blacks is blatant. In February 2011, when attending the annual dinner of the council of Jewish organizations in France (CRIF), President Sarkozy reiterated his appreciation for Jewish identity, in the wake of the brief celebratory allusion to his own humble Jewish origins he had made after his election: "while France has Christian roots, she also has Jewish roots. The presence of Judaism in France was documented even before France became France, even before she got Christianized. . . . Indeed, Judaism is part of the roots of France and every French person, regardless of creed or descent, may be proud of that."[71] Stigmatized minorities could not but note the differential treatment, even if they were not always aware of the political utilization behind such a move.

Although both racism and antisemitism are punishable by law, anti-African sentiment is unabashedly displayed by such esteemed public officials as the late Hélène Carrère d'Encausse, a specialist of the former Soviet Union and the life-appointed Secretary of the French Academy, when she gratuitously blamed African polygamy for the social unrest in the ghettos around Paris in November 2005. When asked if she wished to qualify her comments, she persisted, saying, "those people have come straight out of their African villages. But the city of Paris, and the other European cities, are not African villages."[72] The uproar that ensued was barely over when it was followed in December 2006 by another more insensitive statement, this time from a public figure close to President Sarkozy—Pascal Sevran, the host of a very popular music show aired every Sunday, who wrote in his book *Le privilège des jonquilles*, "the cocks of Black men are the cause of famine in Africa." When controversy ensued, he also persisted in an interview he gave to a local paper, *Var Matin*, "So what? Africa's dying because too many children are born there to parents who can't afford to feed them. I am not the only one to say this. Half of the planet should be sterilized!" Again, the ensuing uproar was not enough to discourage further expressions of anti-African sentiment by politicians in the media, as exemplified by the attorney Sylvie Noachovich, a conservative candidate to the legislative elections of 2007 and a media figure herself. According to the newspaper *Le Canard enchaîné*, she commented on her challenger Dominique Strauss-Kahn in the following terms, "He is said to be a great womanizer. Well, my husband can feel perfectly safe as far as I'm concerned: in my constituency, there's nothing but Blacks and Arabs. The very thought of sleeping with any of them repels me."[73] In October 2010, the famous perfume maker Jean-Paul Guerlain, as a guest on the national channel France 2, answered a question on the making of one of his most successful fragrances by using a racist phrase that he deliberately embraced: "I worked like a n***, well I'm not sure n***s ever really worked, but still—." Yet immediately after the ensuing uproar led him to apologize, Jean-Paul Guerlain soon afterward insulted three employees of the national railroad company (two of whom were Caribbean French and their coworker, Asian French). As they were telling him he had missed his Eurostar train to the UK and needed to board the next train, he seethed, "France is a shithole country, this train company is a shitty company and on top of that, we are served by nothing but immigrants!"

These examples among many, coming from high-profile French individuals, show that although racism is qualified as an offense and not an opinion in France, just like antisemitism, people can make racist statements with a feeling of impunity. While such racist comments recurrently cause outrage, political leaders toy with hot-button identity issues they are not quite sure they can handle. In 2005, a bill drafted by conservative lawmakers aimed to encourage the authors of history schoolbooks to celebrate the "positive role" of the colonization by France of overseas territories, particularly in North Africa. Clearly catering to constituents whose families had been settlers in Algeria, Morocco, or Tunisia, the bill caused anger both within and outside the political sphere, so that then-President Jacques Chirac put an end to the controversy by killing the bill. Similarly, the nationwide debate on French identity launched by President Sarkozy in November 2009[74] sparked so much unease that it fizzled out after several months of "complex-freed" talk online and in prefectures.

When President Hollande came into office in 2012, he proposed that the word "race" be deleted from the text of the French constitution. Yet French legislation against racism and antisemitism is founded on Article 1 of the 1789 Declaration of the Rights of Man and of the Citizen, the preamble to the Constitution of 1946, and article 2 of the 1958 Constitution, which stipulates that "France guarantees the equality before the law of all citizens regardless of origin, race or religion." For candidate François Hollande, during the 2012 campaign, "race has no place in the Republic." This sentence expressed the socialist party's nominee's commitment to antiracism; but in spite of a bill ratified in 2013, the constitutional text has remained unchanged and the political will to combat expressions of race-based prejudice proved a utopian project, given the persistence of race-based discrimination and differential treatment of faith communities, not to mention the persistence of racist rhetoric among elected officials and political leaders. The conservative French member of the European Parliament Nadine Morano, a longtime supporter of Sarkozy, caused an outrage in 2015 when she asserted on a popular TV show, "France is a country of the white race, where we also welcome foreigners."[75] This cost her the backing of her party at the next elections.

The automatic public shaming of those opinion leaders who indulge in racist statements, as well as the type of political sanction mentioned above, could have acted as an effective deterrent to hate speech in French political spheres. Yet the following year, President Sarkozy caused controversy again by stating at a presidential campaign rally in Franconville, in the greater Paris area, "We will no longer be satisfied with an integration model that's broken—we shall demand assimilation. From the day you become French, your ancestors are Gauls." Yet, the French Republic's egalitarian, universalist motto, "Liberty, Equality, Fraternity," already sustains a system of assimilation which melts all racial, ethnic, and religious minorities into a single value system, shaped by French Enlightenment values.[76] Consequently, when Sarkozy demanded that all identify with the Gaulish ancestors, as in French latenineteenth-century schoolbooks, he implied a familiar nationalist reference to a French race, which by definition ignores the (former) colonized subjects—even though he later added the tirailleurs sénégalais (African colonized soldiers who fought in the two world wars) to the galaxy of glorious French ancestors, to counter accusations of rejection of the non-White French. Such rhetoric sounds all the more commonsensic as citizens of North African and sub-Saharan ancestry are routinely stigmatized in the French media and political discourse while also being the most subjected to systemic racism and discrimination, while their Jewish fellow citizens are presumed White.

Understandably, even if self-identifying as Whites, Jews feel concerned by antisemitism. But since the 1980s, the latter is increasingly subsumed by what far-right politicians and media call "anti-White racism," a talking point that has been frequently used since the mid-2000s by a highly popular media provocateur, Éric Zemmour—himself a Sephardic Jew of Algerian descent, who systematically opposes White and Jewish identities to "Arab" and Black ones while peddling "Great Replacement" and "White genocide" theories in his books and TV and radio shows. As Samuel Ghiles-Meilhac notes,

> Jews [today] suffer none of the traditional social discrimination (in trying to access housing, the job market or leisure activities) that some minorities do, in particular those hailing from the former colonial empire of France. This freedom from traditional discrimination therefore tends to equate them, albeit imperfectly, with the White mainstream, which is exempt from discrimination. Additionally, anti-Semitic political rhetoric is unanimously condemned in the public space; even the National Front publicly does so. Finally, the organized Jewish community enjoys a privileged relation with the French state, as is best exemplified by the string of high-profile politicians attending the annual dinner of the CRIF (Representative Council of Jewish associations in France), which shows that the state accepts the Israeli dimension of contemporary Jewish identity.[77]

Conversely, whenever demonstrations are set up to protest anti-Semitic crimes in France, few demonstrators are of North or sub-Saharan African descent. True, even in the 1960s when Rabbi Heschel locked arms with Dr. King in the United States to call for equal rights for racial minorities, French Jews and French Blacks had no such coalitions. This means that as a result, relations between Jews, Blacks, and "Arabs" in France have been shaped by political leaders rather than by the grassroots, and in the last two decades, the former have found an interest in extolling French Jews as a model minority, thereby creating resentment among other minorities which feel unwanted in their own country.

This rejection is unambiguous when leaders with an African, North African, or West Indian background become political figures. The most emblematic illustration was given by Christiane Taubira, an elected official from French Guiana, who was the first Black woman to run for presidential office in 2002 and was appointed Minister of Justice by President Hollande ten years later. She was publicly compared to a monkey by an elected official from the National Front, offered a banana peeling by a child, and satirized on the Facebook page of another elected official from the far-right party who posted a caricature of Taubira featuring her as an avatar of the famous grinning tirailleur sénégalais with a new caption, "Y'a pas bon Taubira" (Taubira, no good). When confronted about the nature of their public statements, the officials concerned claimed they were simply critiquing the Minister of Justice's penal policy and that France's tradition of free speech had always made room for irreverence and caricature. In the same spirit, in August 2020, the rising far-right magazine *Valeurs Actuelles* published a serialized comic strip representing French politicians in past moments of the nation's history; Danièle Obono, a second-generation Gabonese French female member of Parliament from the left-wing party La France Insoumise, appeared in one episode as a topless enslaved woman in chains, with an iron collar around her neck. The magazine was fined twice, in September 2021 and November 2022, but the amounts it had to pay were modest (1,500€ for a racist insult in 2021, 1,000€ in 2022, and 5,000€ in damages).

Even if French politicians, including the President and the Prime Minister, expressed outrage at the racism of the attacks against Ms. Obono, such examples of impunity and lack of recognition of African and North African minorities have led to the emergence of new opinion leaders and organizations in their midst, which advocate the end of racism and race-based discriminations in the country. The ambiguous recognition of French citizens from racial and ethnic minorities and their silencing by the assimilationist creed across the ideological spectrum have given them ample reason to discard the role of silent minorities and get involved in political activism. As the sociologist Leonetti-Taboada explained,

> Faced with the host society's authoritarian assignation of a social or ethnic identity, minority groups have opted for a variety of strategies, ranging from acceptance to rejection to negotiation. These include internalization, ethnic outbidding, circumventing, semantic reversal of stigma, the utilization of assigned identity, assimilation to the mainstream, denial, or group activism.[78]

Reacting to the differences in the media treatment of the various racial and ethnic minorities in France, some Black public figures have carved a place for themselves and tried to launch a national conversation on Blackness in France, such as the biracial comedian and provocateur Dieudonné, who initially contrasted the dearth of films and documentaries on the slave trade and the institution on slavery in the French Caribbean, with the abundance of films and documentaries on the Holocaust and French participation in or against it. The French sociologist Nicole Lapierre explains this argument as follows:

> [h]aving become an epitome, the memorialization of the Holocaust also finds itself vilified, due to its very "success." This leads Dieudonné and the like to indulge in the despicable rhetoric of a competition of memories that results in challenging the legitimacy of this memory, and even the negation of History itself. This is the side effect, or rather, the monstrous product, of the belated but massive recognition of the Holocaust in a Western conscience which also happens to be loath to revisit its colonial legacy.[79]

Consequently, since the early 2000s, Dieudonné has become an infamous icon of antisemitism in France, due to his vehement denunciation of the state of Israel and the plight of the Palestinians, and his deriding of the memory of the Shoah. However, just as public outrage over provocative celebrations of Whiteness by political leaders did not impede the rise of racist sentiment among voters, Dieudonné's legal woes and fines have only further encouraged expressions of anti-Semitic sentiment among his fans. Yet as his popularity and hostility toward Jews have taken on increasing momentum, it is becoming increasingly clear that the Jewish minority is also being utilized by political leaders and the media, which brand it as a sort of convenient model minority to stigmatize North African and Africana minorities as "incompatible" with the Enlightened values of the French Republic, thereby unwittingly exposing French Jews to increased attention from terrorist groups and petty criminals from these other ethnic backgrounds. As Nicole Lapierre notes,

> it would be a mistake to restrict this phenomenon to the viewpoints of the "protagonists." It actually concerns the entirety of the respective societies in which they live. More broadly, tensions and/or conflicts largely depend on the place given to minorities in each society, which is itself unequal, differential, and varying across time. These tensions also result from the (non-)recognition by each culture of the history of the groups currently oppressed or persecuted in the past. Between such groups, neither rivalry nor solidarity can be taken for granted. Depending on circumstances and context, the same prejudice can bring people together and encourage them to struggle or, on the contrary, in response to the mainstream's reactions, it may cause a feeling of injustice and stoke division or even antagonism.[80]

While antisemitism in France has integrated a new international component since the creation of the state of Israel in 1948, Jihadism in Syria has romanticized the plight of Palestinians as an echo to the stigmatization of French

Muslims to recruit among the latter's petty criminals in French jails. Both Mohamed Merah, an Algerian French terrorist who killed four soldiers of North African descent like himself and four Jewish people including three children attending a Jewish school in the southwestern cities of Montauban and Toulouse in March 2012, and Amedy Coulibaly, a Malian French terrorist who killed a French Caribbean policewoman in Montrouge and four customers of the Hyper Cacher store he had taken hostages in January 2015, left recordings explaining they saw themselves as combatants for the Palestinian cause. As Pierre-André Taguieff explains,

> in their anti-Zionist worldview, Israel is seen as the tip of the iceberg. This is a demonizing interpretation of the Jewish state which, although it was created to politically "normalize" Jewishness, is recast as the arch-enemy.
> In "anti-Zionist" propaganda, "Zionism" is indeed fantasized as a world power which is all the more formidable as it is believed to be largely secret—a new avatar of the "Jewish peril."[81]

Just as French Muslims are required to publicly distance themselves from Jihadis in the wake of every single terrorist attack in France, Salam Fayyad, speaking in the name of the Palestinian authorities, had issued a statement in 2012 warning against a weaponization of the Palestinian cause, saying, "[i]t is high time these criminals stopped justifying their terrorist actions in the name of Palestine."[82] Analyzing the reasons behind some young French Muslims' embrace of Jihadi rhetoric couched in pro-Palestinian positions, the French sociologist Farhad Khosrokhavar took the parameter of class into account:

> among inner city youth, radicalization helps sacralize a hatred towards society born from a feeling of economic and social exclusion, injustice, and humiliation; while among middle-class youth, it provides an answer to the lack of authority figures, the tiredness of life, or a form of absence of moral standards.[83]

This insightful analysis helps us better understand the repercussions of the attack perpetrated by the Kouachi brothers against the satirical paper *Charlie Hebdo* in January 2015 in Paris, where eleven cartoonists and journalists were assassinated in retaliation for publishing cartoons of Prophet Muhammad. In the wake of the rampage, French authorities and most French media extolled freedom of speech as a cardinal value of democracy, as well as the French law's protection of the right to blasphemy, dating back to the Revolution of 1789. On the one hand, the shock and horror led to a massive support of the paper which became a symbol of freedom, expressed by the slogan "Je suis Charlie" (I am Charlie). On the other hand, a counter-slogan, "Je ne suis pas Charlie" (I am not Charlie), was observed on social media in early February 2015, at a moment when the French Ministry of Education made class discussions of the attacks and freedom of the press mandatory in all public middle and high schools. Romain Badouard, who conducted the survey, explained that "a minority also voiced a critique of *Charlie Hebdo* for stigmatizing Muslim populations and identified as participants in a more general struggle against racism."[84] Another study showed that in majority-minority neighborhoods, 30 percent of middle schoolers "are not Charlie," for reasons mostly tied to social exclusion:

> Ultimately, the exclusion of some from the realm of "acceptable" opinions is only the reflection—and the consequence—of a spatial exclusion that has been going on for several years. "We have allowed ghetto middle schools to grow everywhere, to protect a form of self-segregation that makes life simpler for everybody," a history and geography teacher denounced in the paper by Louise Tourret. It comes as no surprise that many students who, witnessing the daily burden their families are saddled with, and understanding that their own prospects won't be any brighter, are not too keen to sing the "*Charlie*" kumbaya.[85]

Among these minority students and youth who insist that they "[are] not Charlie," some point to the state-ordered ban on standup comedian Dieudonné's show as contradicting the principle of freedom of speech extolled by the media and politicians' tributes to *Charlie Hebdo*. Their argument, whether or not they support Dieudonné's explicitly anti-Zionist positions, is that the state silences the comedian to punish his antisemitism while it protects or even celebrates *Charlie Hebdo*'s Islamophobia. In reality, the satirical magazine has always thrown vitriol on all religions, not specifically Islam; but its publishing caricatures of Prophet Muhammad triggered the attacks. When the trial around the latter began in 2020, *Charlie Hebdo* published again the same caricatures, in a spirit of resistance and provocation, while President Emmanuel Macron justified the magazine's move, defending the "freedom of blasphemy which is tied to freedom of conscience," and insisting that his role "is to protect all of these liberties" in spite of criticism from other democracies. Shortly after, a history teacher named Samuel Paty was beheaded by a terrorist for using these caricatures as teaching material in a lesson. This further rekindled the debate on the need to defend freedom of speech and freedom of blasphemy.

Therefore, being faced with what they perceive to be a two-tier system, Black and North African minorities tend to emphasize the unemployment, discrimination, and racism they grapple with. As the French sociologist Michel Wieviorka notes,

> [i]n France and elsewhere, the new anti-Semitism is expressed by migrants who are rather underprivileged and discriminated against. This represents a massive change and is even paradoxical, because they commune in the hatred

of Jews with far-right French nationalists who simultaneously hate Arabs and disdain Blacks![86]

This again leads to Jews being scapegoated.[87] The most tragic recent illustration of this was the assassination of Ilan Halimi, a young twenty-three-year-old Sephardic Jew who died in 2006 as a result of anti-Semitic prejudices. A gang of petty criminals, self-identifying as "the gang of barbarians" and led by an Ivorian French Muslim named Youssouf Fofana, decided to lure Halimi with the help of a twenty-year-old White French woman to exact money from him by means of kidnapping and torture, acting on the belief that he must be affluent due to his ethnicity and demanding that his rabbi pay a ransom. Sequestered for twenty-four days in a basement in Bagneux, a town in the greater Paris area, Ilan Halimi was found in a critical state, lying alongside a railroad track, miles away from Bagneux; he died of his wounds in hospital. The crime shocked the entire nation and did not remain unpunished, with the Minister of Justice Michèle Alliot-Marie appealing the initial verdict which she found too lenient. Fofana was eventually sentenced to a mandatory minimum sentence of twenty-two years and in 2009, his twenty-six accomplices (two of whom were minors in 2006) received sentences ranging from six months to eighteen years in jail, as well as two acquittals. For the sociologist Pierre-André Taguieff,

> [u]ndoubtedly, for young men who have known one another since their childhood or teenage years and never had a strong intellectual foundation, gathering into a criminal gang in their "hood" represents one out of many bad options they ended up choosing, as representatives of a generation and a social group plagued by high unemployment rates, academic underachievement, and seclusion in "problem areas" with "tribalized" zones. In this perspective, it makes sense to consider the assassination of Ilan Halimi as a "generational crime."[88]

While these petty criminals became murderers by acting out of anti-Semitic prejudice, organizations promoting Black cultural nationalism occasionally display anti-Zionist sentiments openly, such as Tribu Ka, an Afrocentric group created in 2004 by a French man of Haitian descent who calls himself Kemi Seba. A political and religious movement, Tribu Ka develops the theory of Black supremacy and explicitly rejects Whites, interracial marriages, and the state of Israel:

> Tribu Ka describes itself as a political and religious movement where mythology masquerades as political legitimization and worldview, or Weltanschauung. In this case, it is an all-encompassing theory in which "Kemite" myths depict this people as a superior race, whose historical enslavement allegedly results from a conspiracy plotted by the White races. . . . Members of Tribu Ka preach

ethnic nationalism, more precisely a brand of Pan-Africanism, reject interracial unions to promote endogamy, and embrace the racist-essentialist project of a separate development of each "race." Kemites see integration as high treason and race mixing as sleeping with the enemy.[89]

It is striking to observe a racialist movement stemming from Afrocentrism appropriating Nazi ideology for its own ends, extolling racial purity by preaching anti-miscegenation and the genetic inferiority of "leukodermas" (i.e., Whites), and accusing Jews of having introduced the idea of the Triangular Trade and the enslavement of Africans by popularizing an anti-Black reading of the episode of the curse of Ham. According to Tribu Ka, Zionist ideology is at the root of a conspiracy dominating politics in France and in all Western countries. They demand reparations from the latter to fund a massive back-to-Africa movement, which is clearly reminiscent of Marcus Garvey's project in the early twentieth century and shows an influence of the Nation of Islam, whose current leader Louis Farrakhan[90] is known for his anti-Semitic positions.

Of course, Dieudonné's anti-Semitic provocations as well as the agit-propaganda of the fringe group Tribu Ka have been repressed by French national authorities. Tribu Ka, which came to prominence thanks to its media exposure, was dissolved by a presidential decree drafted by then Minister of Home Security Nicolas Sarkozy and signed by thenPresident Jacques Chirac on July 28, 2006. It re-emerged under another name but was dissolved again. Its leader Kemi Seba is now based in Benin, of which he has become a citizen and where he created a Pan-African organization. The French government is now considering stripping him of his French nationality in response to his anti-French discourse. In 2014, the nationwide ban on Dieudonné's one-man show "Le Mur" (The Wall) led to a public showdown between the comedian and then Prime Minister Manuel Valls (from the socialist party). Thus, governments across the political spectrum have displayed a stronger political will to crack down on antisemitism than on other manifestations of racist prejudice or anti-Muslim prejudice. The French sociologists Véronique de Rudder, Christian Poiret, and François Vourc'h noted in 2000 that

> [r]acist activities have developed almost unhampered within French society, under the mantle of good conscience offered by the so-called "republican model" . . . [which amounts to] a system of intimidation forbidding minority groups to launch any social protest movement, while providing them with no means to combat the inequality and oppression they suffer.[91]

Responding to an interviewer, Kemi Seba reformulated the same observation, but with an anti-Semitic conspiracy theory twist:

Authorities say, "whoever assaults a Jew is assaulting France," but when racist attacks are launched against our people, I don't hear of anyone coming to comfort the families. What this tells me is that this country is in the hands of Zionists, not Black people. And it's a good thing for us to understand that this country is not ours but belongs to those who have ruled the world for many, many years. We're talking about the Zionists today, but they are none other than the imperialists of yore.[92]

Systemic racism being more difficult to handle than scapegoating another minority group, anti-Zionism seems to provide more and more members of Black and North African minorities in France with a tempting explanation to their predicament. However, the phenomenon of Black antisemitism remains difficult to assess, as neither the French police, nor the Human Rights National Consultative Commission (CNCDH), which publish jointly a yearly report on the matter, have any legal tool to identify Black individuals as either the perpetrators or the victims of racist actions.[93] This is further complicated by an ethnic factor of a part of the French Jewry, which Alexis Rosenbaum described as follows:

[French] Jews also mostly hail from North African countries, which facilitates comparisons that fuel envy and hypersensitivity to differential treatment. Additionally, among the younger generations, conspicuous consumption of branded clothing, technological knickknacks, and the like plays a crucial part in obtaining social recognition, which only reinforces the momentum of the relative frustration mechanisms. . . . The hypothesis of relative frustration shows . . . to what extent the system of exacerbated comparison encouraged by modern societies may fuel anti-Semitism and lead to bouts of individual rage whenever people become convinced that Jews occupy a more desirable position on the social ladder ("they are constantly whining about how much they suffered, but the truth is, they control everything," etc.).[94]

Over the past decade, anti-Semites have become increasingly open about their resentment, and the rise in profanations of synagogues, Jewish cemeteries and schools, individual attacks, and verbal abuse, killings, and terrorism has even inspired copycats in search of media attention, including teenagers with little interest in politics. In January 2014, a catchall mass demonstration organized by fifty organizations to protest the Hollande government's policies in employment, fiscal and ethical matters, including the passing of the law on same-sex marriage, the alleged "Islamization of France," and the restriction of Dieudonné's freedom of speech, the following anti-Semitic slogans were heard: "Jew, France is not yours," "Down with pedophile-criminal-Zionist-Satanic Europe," "Hollande and the CRIF: Which of the two is the puppet?"[95]

But ethnic and racial relations in France may change with the new activism of the country's Asian minorities, which had so far been an example of silent, "unproblematic" integration and recently voiced their exasperation with the lack of protection offered to them by French authorities when they are the victims of theft, abuse, and assault in the greater Paris area. One protester from the majority-minority town of La Courneuve stressed that popular representations of Asians in films and the media are also part of the problem: "We feel as if any joke is acceptable whenever Asians are the butt [an allusion to a racial slur heard on the national TV channel France 2 comparing Asians to Pikachu]. This fans the flames of racism, because it shows that people are allowed to do anything they want with us."[96] French Asians' malaise suddenly gained media visibility after the shooting by police of a Chinese-born father of two in March 2017, which triggered reactions from the Chinese embassy and the Asian-French community, whose demonstration against racism organized on September 4 in Paris was accompanied by a TV ad made by the comedian Frédéric Chau and entitled "Safety for all."

This took place in the wake of other historic protests in the ghettoized communities of the greater Paris area, caused by instances of police brutality. The first such incident dates back to October 2005 in Clichy-sous-Bois, when two teenagers (Zyed Benna, of North African descent, and Bouna Traoré, of sub-Saharan African descent) died in an electricity transformer while running away from a police patrol, and apparently were not succored by the policemen; during the subsequent unrest in their hometown, a tear gas hand grenade was thrown into the entrance of the mosque by policemen who had been pelted with stones. Urban uprisings ensued in several cities of the greater Paris area throughout the month of November.[97] In July 2016, a young man of African descent, Adama Traoré, died in unclear circumstances while being arrested by police in Beaumont-sur-Oise, another greater Paris town with a majority-minority population, leading to protests explicitly inspired from the Black Lives Matter movement. In February 2017, riots in the greater Paris area followed the brutal arrest in Aulnay-sous-Bois of Théo Luhaka, yet another young man of African descent, whose beating and raping with a Billy club by three policemen were captured on a smartphone and sent to the media; in January 2024, after pleading they acted in self-defense, they received light sentences and were all acquitted of rape charges although the young man is now permanently disabled as a result of the arrest. Lastly, in late June and early July 2023, the filmed lethal shooting of sixteen-year-old Nahel Merzouk for allegedly refusing to comply caused even more intense urban unrest across the country, with more damages in eight days than during the three weeks of uprisings of November 2005.

Yet, racialized minorities in France also express their views otherwise than by protesting more or less violently. Since the 1980s, several grassroots organizations were created to demand social justice and an end to racism. The most historic one is SOS Racisme, an unofficial branch of the socialist party which was created in the early 1980s. More recent organizations, such as Devoir de mémoire or Les Indigènes de la République, focus more on the need for national reconciliation over France's colonial past as well as gender issues in both the mainstream and Muslim minorities. The most emblematic is the CRAN (representative council of Black associations), which was founded in 2005 by Patrick Lozès[98] to federate 150 Black organizations scattered over the French territory. Explicitly inspired from the NAACP, it is still actively fighting race-based discriminations targeting Blacks in France. One of its co-founders, Professor Pap Ndiaye, pointed out in his now-classic book on Blacks in France[99] that the push to eliminate the notion of race from the French Constitution unfortunately had no effect on the persistence of racism, which is why the CRAN lobbied in favor of introducing ethnic and racial statistics in France so that race-based discrimination may be measured more scientifically. He also advocated the implementation of a French-style affirmative action program (which he called "positive action" instead of the usual mistranslation "positive discrimination") as another means of improving social mobility.

Black French activism is also inclusive of religious groups. Religious activism is also seen in more constructive initiatives by faith-based communities in France, be they Muslim, Christian, or Jewish. Because these events are more consensus-based than sensational, they draw less media attention; but they still combine patriotic and religious values in interesting ways. Social players are members of clubs, organizations, and faith-based groups, which encourage them to participate in gatherings and sensitize other groups to antisemitism, racism, and discrimination thanks to ecumenical cooperation and interethnic coalitions designed with the representatives of the other communities concerned. Besides, some organizations play an active part in intercommunal dialog, particularly between Muslims and Jews or between Blacks and Jews. For instance, organizations such as the Alliance judéo-noire, created in 1994, the Amitié judéo-noire (Judeo-Black friendship) in 2004, the Amitié judéo-musulmane de France (AJMF), and la Fraternité judéo-noire 2007 were created in order to consolidate relations between Jews and Muslim and between Jews and Blacks. To better understand how African or Caribbean converts or born Jews articulate their Jewishness and Blackness within or outside of these organizations, let us first delve into an analytical description of their diverse profiles and experiences.

NOTES

1. Alexis Rosenbaum, *L'antisémitisme* (Paris: Bréal, "Thèmes & Débats de Société" series, 2006), 16.
2. "Deux mille ans de présence juive en France," *Le Monde juif*, 1 no.144 (1992): 18, accessed July 31, 2023, https://www.cairn.info/revue-le-monde-juif-1992-1-page-17.htm
3. Edgar Morin, *Le monde moderne et la question juive* (Paris: Seuil, 2006), 26.
4. Elisheva Carlebach, "La communauté juive et ses institutions à l'époque moderne," in *Aux origines du Judaïsme,* eds. Jean Baumgarten and Julien Darmon (Paris: Actes Sud et Editions des Liens qui libèrent, 2012), 359.
5. Rosenbaum, *L'antisémitisme,* 22.
6. Carlebach, "La communauté juive," 360.
7. Pierre-André Taguieff, *L'antisémitisme* (Paris: PUF, 2015), 28.
8. Henri Grégoire, *Essai sur la régénération physique, morale et politique des Juifs* (Metz: Devilly, 1789).
9. Michel Winock, *La France et les Juifs, de 1789 à nos jours* (Paris: Editions du Seuil, 2004), 16.
10. Winock, *La France et les Juifs,* 32–34, 37.
11. Pierre Birnbaum, "Décrets sur les noms juifs, 20 juillet 1808," accessed November 25, 2016, http://www.archivesdefrance.culture.gouv.fr/action-culturelle/celebrations-nationales/2008/vie-politique-et-institutions/decret-sur-les-noms-des-juifs.
12. Shlomo Sand, *The Invention of the Land of Israel: From Holy Land to Homeland,* trans. Geremy Forman (New York and London: Verso, 2012), 167.
13. Rosenbaum, *L'antisémitisme,* 25.
14. Rosenbaum, *L'antisémitisme,* 26.
15. See Céline Leglaive-Perani, "De la charité à la philanthropie: Introduction," in Céline Leglaive-Perani, ed., *Le "moment" philanthropique des Juifs de France (1800–1940), Archives juives* 1, no. 44, Paris: Les Belles Lettres (2011): 4–16, accessed August 7, 2023, https://www.cairn.info/revue-archives-juives1-2011-1-page-4.htm.
16. Martine Cohen, "Les Juifs de France. Affirmations identitaires et évolution du modèle d'intégration," *Le Débat* no. 75 (May–August 1993): 101–2.
17. Quoted in Michel Winock, *La France et les Juifs, de 1789 à nos jours* (Paris: Editions du Seuil, 2004), 171.
18. Kimberly A. Arkin, *Rhinestones, Religion, and the Republic: Fashioning Jewishness in France,* Stanford: Stanford University Press (Stanford Studies in Jewish History and Culture series, 2014), 22.
19. Winock, *La France et les Juifs,* 174.
20. See Nancy Green, "Juifs d'Europe orientale et centrale," accessed November 25, 2016, http://www.histoire-immigration.fr/des-dossiers-thematiques-sur-l-histoire-de-l-immigration/juifs-d-europe-orientale-et-centrale.

21. Jérémy Guedj, "Les Juifs français face aux Juifs étrangers dans la France de l'entre-deux-guerres," *Cahiers de la Méditerranée* [on line], 78 (2009), posted on line on February 15, 2010, accessed November 1, 2016, http://cdlm.revues.org/4637.

22. Winock, *La France et les Juifs,* 224.

23. Alain Dieckhoff, "Le sionisme et l'État d'Israël face au judaïsme: la continuité incertaine," in Baumgarten and Darmon, eds., *Aux origines du Judaisme,* 432.

24. Valérie Assan and Yolande Cohen, "Circulations et migrations des Juifs du Maghreb en France, de la veille de la Première Guerre mondiale aux années 1960. Introduction," *Archives Juives*, 1, 53 (2020): 4–15, accessed August 5, 2023. DOI: 10.3917/aj1.531.0004. URL: https://www.cairn.info/revue-archives-juives-2020-1-page-4.htm.

25. Cohen, "Les Juifs de France," 103.

26. Anne Sylvie Goldberg, ed., *Histoire juive de la France* (Paris: Albin Michel, 2023).

27. Hélène Vignaux, *L'Église et les Noirs dans l'audience du Nouveau Royaume de Grenade* (Montpellier: Presses Universitaires de la Méditerranée, Voix des Suds series, 2009), accessed November 11, 2016, https://books.openedition.org/pulm/496.

28. Pascal Blanchard et al., "Depuis 1685, Trois siècles de présences en France, Introduction," in *La France noire* (Paris: La Découverte, 2011), 16.

29. Quoted by Liliane Crété, *La traite des nègres sous l'Ancien régime* (Paris: Perrin, 1989), 260.

30. Jean Meyer, *Esclaves et Négriers* (Paris: La Découverte / Gallimard 1986), 36–37.

31. Quoted in Crété, *La traite des nègres,* 260.

32. Crété, *La traite des nègres,* 265.

33. Lilian Thuram, *Mes étoiles noires, de Lucy à Barack Obama* (Paris: Editions Philippe Rey, 2010), 165.

34. Nicolas Bancel, Pascal Blanchard, and Sandrine Lemaire, "Ces zoos humains de la République coloniale," *Le Monde diplomatique*, August 2000, 16.

35. Philippe Dewitte, *Les mouvements nègres en France, 1919–1939* (Paris: L'Harmattan, 1985).

36. Pascal Blanchard and Nicolas Bancel, *De l'indigène à l'immigré* (Paris: Gallimard, 1998), 35.

37. Jean Benoist, "Le métissage: biologie d'un fait social, sociologie d'un fait biologique," in Jean-Luc Alber, Claudine Bavoux, and Michel Watin, eds., *Métissage Tome II. Linguistique et anthropologie.* Actes du Colloque International de Saint-Denis de La Réunion, April 2–7, 1990 (Paris: L'Harmattan, 1992), 13–22.

38. See Philippe Dewitte, *Les mouvements nègres*; Jean-Pascal Zadi, *Tout simplement noir,* feature film, 90 minutes, 2020; Charlotte Causit, "'Je n'aime pas qu'on me dise 'black': Pourquoi, en France, le mot 'noir' reste tabou," *France info,* posted on June 12, 2020, updated on September 1, 2021, accessed October 1, 2023, https://www.francetvinfo.fr/france/je-n-aime-pas-qu-on-me-dise-black-pourquoi-en-france-le-mot-noir-reste-tabou_4003111.html.

39. See Claude Gozlan's preface to Elvire Maurouard, *Juifs de Martinique et Juifs portugais sous Louis XIV* (Paris: Editions du Cygne, 2009).

40. Michel Wieviorka, "Introduction," in Michel Wieviorka, ed., *Le racisme, une introduction* (Paris: La Découverte, Poche / Essais, 1998), 7–12, https://www.cairn.info/le-racisme-une-introduction--9782707128669-page-7.htm.

41. Pierre-André Taguieff and Michel Wieviorka, in *Le Racisme-Le Multiculturalisme, Cahier du CEVIPOF* no. 20 (1998): 44.

42. He developed a conspiracy theory in a racist tract entitled *The Victory of Judaism over Germandom* (Bern: Rudolph Costenoble, 1879). See https://www.jewishvirtuallibrary.org/wilhelm-marr, accessed August 17, 2023.

43. "Les juifs en Europe. L'antijudaïsme médiéval, de 610 à 1492," https://www.herodote.net/610_a_1492-synthese-24.php, accessed August 17, 2023.

44. See Bouillet and Chassang, *Dictionnaire universel d'histoire et de géographie*.

45. This is the name given to the unleavened bread used in the Catholic church for the ritual of the consecration re-enacting the sacrifice of Christ on the Cross. See Bouillet and Chassang, *Dictionnaire universel d'histoire et de géographie*.

46. *Bonkanda w'Ecole w'efe* (Bongandanga: CBM, 1920), 11.

47. Édouard Drumont quoted in Michel Wieviorka, *L'antisémitisme expliqué aux jeunes* (Paris: Editions du Seuil, 2014), 13.

48. Hitler's speech at the Berlin Sportpalast, January 30, 1942. Jewish Virtual Library website, accessed August 28, 2023, https://www.jewishvirtuallibrary.org/hitler-speech-at-the-berlin-sports-palace-january-30-1941.

49. Adolf Hitler, *Mein Kampf*, trans. J. Gaudefroy-Demombynes and A. Calmettes (Paris: Nouvelles éditions latines, 1982, t.2, La Bibliothèque électronique du Québec, Collection Polémique et propagande, Volume 3: version 1.2), 56.

50. Catherine Coquery-Vidrovitch, *Des victimes oubliées du nazisme. Les Noirs et l'Allemagne dans la première moitié du XXème siècle* (Paris: Le Cherche Midi, 2007).

51. Serge Bilé, *Noirs dans les camps nazis* (Paris: Editions du rocher, 2005).

52. Namibia was annexed in 1884 by Germany, then became part of the Dominion of South Africa under British rule from 1915 to 1961; the tutelage of the independent Republic of South Africa went on until 1990. The genocide perpetrated in the early twentieth century claimed the lives of the native insurgents and their families, an estimated 65,000 Hereros and close to 20,000 Namas.

53. Hitler, *Mein Kampf*, 106, 477.

54. Hitler, *Mein Kampf*, 439–40.

55. Hitler, *Mein Kampf*, 56.

56. Bilé, *Noirs dans les camps nazis*.

57. Rosenbaum, *L'antisémitisme*, 34–35.

58. See Carol Iancu, "Les réactions des milieux chrétiens face à Jules Isaac," *Revue d'Histoire de la Shoah* 1, no. 192 (2010): 157–93, accessed September 3, 2023, https://www.cairn.info/revue-d-histoire-de-la-shoah-2010-1-page-157.htm.

59. Taguieff, *L'antisémitisme*, 70–71.

60. Rosenbaum, *L'antisémitisme*, 88–89.

61. In 2015, in a statement he made on the site of the former deportation camp in Aix-en-Provence, then-President François Hollande instructed the Minister of Justice (Christiane Taubira from French Guiana) to draft a legislative text making it an

aggravating circumstance for any offense to be inspired by racism or antisemitism, whoever the offender may be.

62. In an interview he gave on April 2, 2015, on cable news channel BFM TV and Radio Monte-Carlo, Jean-Marie Le Pen refused to apologize for his past statement and reiterated it instead as follows: "What I said was consistent with my thinking, which is that gas chambers were a detail in the war, that is, unless you consider it was the war which was a detail of the gas chambers." The Paris criminal court decided that Le Pen was guilty of denying a crime against humanity and sentenced him to a fine of 30,000 euros in April 2016.

63. Henri Giordan, *Démocratie culturelle et droit à la différence* (Paris: La Documentation française, 1982), in Samuel Ghiles-Meilhac, "Les juifs français sont-ils (devenus) des Blancs comme les autres?" *Juifs d'Europe: Identités plurielles et mixité* [online] (Tours, France: Presses universitaires François-Rabelais, 2017), 31–32, accessed June 27, 2021, http://books.openedition.org/pufr/16086. ISBN: 9782869067257. DOI: https://doi.org/10.4000/books.pufr.16086.

64. See Sander L. Gilman, *L'Autre et le Moi. Stéréotypes occidentaux de la race, de la sexualité et de la maladie* (Paris: Presses Universitaires de France, "Littératures européennes" series, 1996), 207–40.

65. Nadia Malinovich, "What's the Color of a Jew? Les Juifs, la blanchitude et le multiculturalisme aux États-Unis à l'époque contemporaine," in Michel Prum, ed., *La place de l'autre* (Paris: L'Harmattan, 2010), 42.

66. Michael Lerner and Cornel West, *Jews and Blacks: A Dialogue on Race, Religion and Culture in America* (Penguin Books, 1996), quoted in Malinovich, "What's the Color of a Jew?," 47.

67. Ghiles-Meilhac, "Les Juifs français sont-ils (devenus) des Blancs comme les autres?" *Juifs d'Europe: Identités plurielles et mixité* [online] (Tours, France: Presses universitaires François-Rabelais, 2017), accessed June 27, 2021. http://books.openedition.org/pufr/16086. ISBN: 9782869067257. DOI: https://doi.org/10.4000/books.pufr.16086.

68. Speech to the new members of the UMP (conservative) party, April 23, 2006.

69. Nicolas Sarkozy, guest of the show "J'ai une question à vous poser," broadcast live on TF1 channel on February 5, 2007.

70. Editorial board, "Brice Hortefeux définitivement relaxé pour ses propos sur les Arabes," *Le Monde,* November 27, 2012, accessed on May 30, 2017, http://www.lemonde.fr/politique/article/2012/11/27/brice-hortefeux-definitivement-relaxe-pour-ses-propos-sur-les-arabes_1796614_823448.html.

71. Quoted in Judith Waintraub, "Nicolas Sarkozy souligne les 'racines juives' de la France," *Le Figaro*, February 9, 2011, accessed on May 30, 2017, http://www.lefigaro.fr/actualite-france/2011/02/09/01016-20110209ARTFIG00725-nicolas-sarkozy-souligne-les-racines-juives-de-la-france.php.

72. http://www.lemonde.fr/societe/article/2005/11/16/le-ministre-de-l-emploi-stigmatise-la-polygamie_710615_3224.html#Ot5aRL1BExLeMyxE.99.

73. Quoted in *Le canard enchaîné*, June 13, 2007.

74. See Céline Jannot, Sandra Tomc, and Marine Totozani, "Retour sur le débat autour de l'identité nationale en France: quelles places pour quelle(s) langue(s)?"

Revue de Linguistique et de Didactique des Langues (2011): 44, accessed May 31, 2017, https://lidil.revues.org/3139.

75. Nadine Morano, on Laurent Ruquier's show *On n'est pas couché,* France 2, September 26, 2015.

76. See Emmanuel Todd, *Le destin des immigrés. Assimilation et ségrégation dans les démocraties occidentales* (Paris: Seuil, 1994).

77. Ghiles-Meilhac, "Les Juifs français," 39.

78. Isabelle Taboada-Leonetti, "Stratégies identitaires et minorités," *Migrants-formations* no. 86 (1991): 54–73.

79. Nicole Lapierre, *Causes communes. Des Juifs et des Noirs* (Paris: Stock, series "Un ordre d'idées," 2011), 17.

80. Lapierre, *Causes communes,* 17–18.

81. Taguieff, *L'antisémitisme,* 29.

82. Salam Fayyad, accessed October 17, 2016, http://www.lexpress.fr/actualite/societe/tueur-au-scooter-les-hommes-du-raid-en-action-a-toulouse_1095906.html.

83. La sociologie de la radicalisation: entretien avec Farhad Khosrokhavar, http://ses.ens-lyon.fr/articles/la-sociologie-de-la-radicalisation-entretien-avec-farhad-khosrokhavar-291659, accessed October 23, 2016. See also Khosrokhavar, *L'islam des jeunes* (Paris: Flammarion, 1997).

84. Romain Badouard, "'Je ne suis pas Charlie.' Pluralité des prises de parole sur le web et les réseaux sociaux," *Le Défi Charlie. Les médias à l'épreuve des attentats,* 2016. https://hal.science/hal-01251253. Published on January 5, 2016, accessed October 7, 2016.

85. Aude Lorriaux, "30% des collégiens des quartiers populaires ne sont pas vraiment 'Charlie,'" accessed October 23, 2016, http://www.slate.fr/story/107191/collegiens-charlie-etude-afev.

86. Michel Wieviorka, *Le racisme,* 95.

87. Yves Chevalier, *L'Antisémitisme. Le Juif comme bouc émissaire* (Paris: Éditions du Cerf, 1988).

88. Pierre-André Taguieff, *La Judéophobie des modernes, Des lumières au Jihad mondial* (Paris: Odile Jacob, 2008), 47.

89. Stéphane François, Damien Guillaume, and Emmanuel Kreis, "La Weltanschauung de la tribu Ka: d'un antisémitisme égyptomaniaque à un islam guénonien," *Politica Hermetica,* no. 22 (2008): 113–15.

90. He claimed that Jews played a key part in the Transatlantic Slave Trade and the slaveholding system. See Robert Singh, *The Farrakhan Phenomenon: Race, Reaction, and the Paranoid Style in American* (Washington, DC: Georgetown University Press, 1997).

91. Véronique de Rudder, Christian Poiret, and François Vourc'h, *L'inégalité raciste: l'universalité républicaine à l'épreuve* (Paris: PUF, 2000), 186.

92. "Entretien avec Kemi Seba, Fara de l'ex-Tribu Ka. Ancien du Parti Kémite et de la 'Nation of Islam,'" accessed October 16, 2016, http://www.voxnr.com/cc/tribune_libre/EEypZyZZyZUmORMJLo.shtml.

93. See Édith Bruder, *Histoire des relations,* 219.

94. Rosenbaum, *L'antisémitisme,* 60–61.

95. "Jour de colère: quenelles et saluts nazis dans les rues de Paris," *Huffington Post France,* January 27, 2014, accessed October 23, 2016, http://www.huffingtonpost.fr/2014/01/27/jour-colere-quenelles-saluts-nazis-rues-paris_n_4671985.html. See also Maxime Vaudano, "À Paris, une manifestation attrape-tout contre François Hollande," *Le Monde,* January 26, 2014, accessed on June 5, 2017, http://www.lemonde.fr/societe/article/2014/01/26/a-paris-une-manifestation-de-colere-attrape-tout-contre-francois-hollande_4354734_3224.html.

96. See http://www.francetvinfo.fr/faits-divers/en-seine-saint-denis-le-ras-le-bol-de-la-communaute-chinoise-ici-tout-le-monde-a-subi-au-moins-une-agression_1730965.html, accessed October 22, 2016. The Chinese French community in particular were said to be exasperated by the increase in the frequency and violence of the attacks they suffered.

97. See Gilles Kepel, *Terreur dans l'Hexagone* (Paris: Gallimard, 2015).

98. Patrick Lozès, "Les 'Noirs' de France, une invention utile?" discussion with Jean Boulègue, Jean-Pierre Chrétien, Agnès Lainé, Patrick Lozès, Pap Ndiaye, Marc-Olivier Padis and Nicolas Masson," *Esprit* 6, no. 335 (June 2007), Paris: Éditions Esprit, 86.

99. Pap Ndiaye, *La Condition noire: essai sur une minorité française* (Paris: Calmann-Lévy, 2008).

Chapter 2

Self-Identification or Quest of Jewishness

Have the Hebrew people actually existed? Archaeologists are still struggling to uncover any material proof of the crossing of the Red Sea, and even of the Exodus to Egypt and the existence of Moses, for that matter. Some even suggest that the authors of the Bible may have heavily borrowed from ancient Egyptian texts.[1] Still, Jewish people nowadays are all supposed to be direct descendants of the Hebrews, on the basis of the Biblical genealogy of the twelve tribes of Israel, and they all identify as members of the same people. As the historian Esther Benbassa puts it, "Jews have cultivated a self-representation built around their religion as well as myths. This narrative has allowed even converts to Judaism to define themselves as part of the same cultural and religious entity, these two dimensions being inseparable from each other."[2] Likewise, a segment of Black Jews and Africans claiming to be Hebrews perceive themselves through the prism of Hebrew ancestors, whom they consider to be Black people.

AFRICAN GROUPS CLAIMING HEBREW ANCESTRY

At first sight, when evoking the history of the Hebrews, Black people do not come to mind, for Jews, the descendants of Hebrews by all claims, are generally perceived as White people. However, Black Jews have existed for a long time, and among them, African, Americans, and Caribbeans have claimed a Biblical heritage. The best-known are Ethiopian Jews, who are often designated by the derogatory term "Falasha" (meaning exiles) but prefer calling themselves "Israel," that is, the House of Israel. Since the 1980s, the media have sensitized public opinion to their existence by covering the rescue operations Solomon or Moses, whereby the successive Israeli governments organized their repatriation (Aliyah) in Israel, where they became the most recent wave of newcomers to be assimilated into the Hebrew state's Melting Pot. Their challenges have been documented and analyzed by several scholars, among whom Daniel Friedmann[3] and Lisa Anteby-Yemini.[4]

Less famous African Jews are the Lemba people, who live in South Africa and Zimbabwe. Their history is still patchy, but the scholars who specialize in the study of their culture mention a migration to South Africa from Yemen via a sea route. They live separately from the neighboring ethnic groups, as is emphasized by the South African anthropologist Magdel Le Roux: "[t]heir uniqueness, however, lies in that they keep themselves separate from other people, regard themselves as an offshoot of the Yemenite Jews, have a religion which stems from Abraham and came from a city called Sena."[5] Having preserved their oral traditions, practicing endogamy and circumcision, eating neither pork nor animals slaughtered out of the Kosher ritual, never mixing meat with dairy products, they define themselves as Israelites with Semitic ancestry.

Their identification claims were eventually validated by the DNA tests carried out by Spurdle and T. Jenkins in 1996[6] as well as those made in 2000 by Mark G. Thomas, Tudor Parfitt, and others[7], all of which tend to demonstrate the Lemba's Semitic origin. Magdel Leroux explains that the DNA testing of samples of groups of Ethiopian Jews, Lemba, and White Israelis have revealed that Ethiopian Jews are similar to the rest of the Ethiopian population whereas Lemba prove closer to Semitic genetic markers, in particular those of the descendants of an ancient caste of Jewish priests tracing its roots to Moses' brother Aaron, namely, the Cohens. Indeed, Dr. Karl Skorecki, a specialist of human genetics, showed that a particular mutation of chromosome Y that is found among 80 percent of the Cohenim assembled for the ritual prayer at the Wailing Wall also appears among the Lemba.[8]

Other communities of African Jews investigated by researchers include the Igbo of Nigeria[9] and the Danites of the Ivory Coast, both of which claim Jewish origins dating back to Biblical times. The emergence of the former, in particular, has elicited considerable interest among White Jewish scholars and rabbis, whose work has documented a phenomenon of racial appropriation of the forefathers of Judaism. This is particularly clear in Jeff Libermann's documentary film, where an interviewee called Mariam Akwa Ibo asserts, "do you think they [Hebrews] were White? They were Blacks, Avraham (Abraham) was Black, even Ya'acov (Jacob) was not a White man, I think you get my point."[10] Not only do they see Biblical figures as racially similar to them, but they also point to their ancestral dietary traditions, as another female respondent did: "as a child, my father taught us we do not eat these fishes without scales, how did he know that? We don't eat pigs, how did he know that? Even the way we kill our animals is a Kosher way."[11] The French ethnologist Édith Bruder explains,

[a]ccording to oral tradition, their [Igbo] ancestors came from Israel via the ancient trade routes; the ruling clans claim to be descendants of the Levites and the name Igbo/Ibo allegedly is an alteration of Ivri/Ibri/Hebrew. Nowadays, the Igbo compare their customs and traditions, funeral rituals, circumcisions, ritual slaughtering of animals, endogamy and marriage rites to those of the ancient Israelites.[12]

In one of the first autobiographical slave narratives in 1789, Olaudah Equiano, the most famous Igbo man to date, had already drawn these parallels, which struck him when he became Christianized:

[w]e practiced circumcision like the Jews, and made offerings of festivals on that occasion in the same manner as they did. Like them also our children were named from some event, some circumstance, or fancied foreboding, at the time their birth. [. . .] I have remarked that the natives of this part of Africa are extremely cleanly. The necessary habit of decency was with us a part of religion, and therefore we had many purifications and washings; indeed almost as many, and used on the same occasions, if my recollection does not fail me, as the Jews. Those that touched the dead at any time were obliged to wash and purify themselves before they could enter a dwelling house. Every woman too, at certain times, was forbidden to come into a dwelling house, or touch any person, or anything we eat.[13]

Additionally, the Igbo's Supreme Being is called Chukwu Abiama, which they say literally means "God of Abraham." The fieldwork carried out by Édith Bruder shows similarities between ancient Judaism and the Igbo's traditional beliefs prior to British colonization. Their identification to the Hebrew people is based on one of the versions of Igbo myths—that of the Nri clan, which claims that it traces its roots to the tribe of Gad—thus making the claim that they are part of the Lost Tribes of Israel. Édith Bruder explains that the recent discovery in the region of Aguleri of an onyx stone bearing the name of Gad engraved in ancient Hebrew is considered as crucial evidence by the Igbo.[14] Indeed, they see it as proof that they are descendants of the tribe of Gad, based on an interpretation of *Exodus* 39:6: "And they wrought the onyx stones, inclosed in settings of gold, graven with the engravings of a signet, according to the names of the children of Israel" (American Standard Version).

However, the more than one million Igbo who claim to be Jewish after centuries of Christianization are not recognized by the state of Israel. Daniel Lis notes, "[f]or Judaizing communities in Nigeria, it must have been even more frustrating that the connection of the Igbo to the Jews was not generally recognized by Israel's Supreme Court and Chief Rabbinate and that a number of Igbo in Israel who had converted there under an ultra-orthodox rabbinical court were being expelled back to Nigeria in 2007!"[15]

Meanwhile, the Yoruba, another well-known ethnic group of Nigeria, also claim an Israelite origin for themselves. According to the German historian Dierk Lange, "From a comparative analysis of Ọyọ dynastic tradition and ancient Near Eastern history, it appears that Israelites migrated to West Africa subsequently to the fall of the Assyrian Empire, and that their descendants survive as the core people of the present day Ọyọ-Yoruba. Indeed, Ọyọ tradition reveals that the ancestral Yoruba were mainly composed of Israelites, who, in the course of their history, became influenced by Assyrian views of past events."[16] Analyzing the myth of the Lost Tribes of Israel, Lange makes links between these claims and the history of migrations in West Africa, oral traditions, and the onomastic evidence in the lists of Central Sudanic kings, and concludes:

> Moreover, it appears from the traditions of Kanem-Bornu, Hausaland, and Yorubaland that, although numerically not very important, the Israelites had the greatest cultural influence of all the different national groups which found their way to West Africa. . . . A word should be said about the Israelite component of these ancient Near Eastern immigrants. Though numerically the Israelites from the northern state seem to have been weak, their cultural influence was considerable. In Kanem, the dynastic hero Sef/Sargon is credited with descent from the biblical patriarchs, beginning with Adam and ending with Abraham, and the unity of the different immigrant and local clans was ensured by a national shrine, the Mune/Manna, which the Imam Ibn Furt'ū claims to be identical with the Sakina of King Saul.[17]

The Danites of the Ivory Coast, also known as Dan Yacouba, are another African community of self-identified Jews; over two million strong, they claim to be members of the tribe of Dan and one of the ten Lost Tribes of Israel. Less well-known, they gained recent media exposure thanks to the broadcasting of David Szerman's documentary film on the Sunday morning Jewish program on French television.[18] Szerman gave an account of the fieldwork he carried out among them with two French-Israeli rabbis, Haim Rosenfeld and Abraham Sellem. In the interview he gave on French television to explain the making of his film, the filmmaker explained that the three of them asked the gatekeepers of local traditions, including "witch doctors," about animist rituals in order to trace possible parallels with Hebrew rituals predating the destruction of the Temple, or Canaanite or Assyrian rituals. They ascertained that the Danites believe in one invisible God, whom they call "Atanaï" (which sounds very close to the Hebrew name of God, Adonaï) and that their holy day is Saturday, which they call "Saabaa," that is, "Day of Sacrifice" or "Day of Awe," during which it is strictly forbidden to do any work. Observing rules of family purity, they practice endogamy and circumcision differently from the neighboring groups in the Ivory Coast. An uncircumcised man is not allowed to marry a Danite woman and cannot have a say in the decisions made for the community.[19]

Two of my interviewees, members of a Danite family based in the Paris area, gave a striking testimony at the conference organized by the International Society for the Study of African Jewry at the Museum of Jewish History in Paris in November 2015:

SHEMA ISRAEL ADONAI ELOHENOU, ADONAI EHAD

This prayer, as well as other blessings, have been familiar to us from our infancy; we have heard and recited them in French and in our mother tongue. We are Jews from the Ivory Coast, in West Africa, and our home town is called Lakota.

For as long as they could remember, our parents and grandparents had customs that distinguished them from other families in the village. For instance, on Fridays before noon, all the women in our large family left the fields to make Shabbat.

During meals, men ate separately from women, with their heads covered with their takis (taliths) throughout the meal. During the holiday of the great fast, we stayed up all day for the great prayer without eating or drinking or even talking to one another, and we also wore torn clothes. We were circumcised by our father, who explained that this had been done for generations and generations, from father to son.

The meat we consumed was from animals whose throats had been slit in such a way they did not suffer, dying "immediately," with no blood left in the meat because it had been soaked in salt and then washed several times, or processed over fire to be made kosher.

Menstruating women were separated from the rest and did not cook, and it was the same for those who had just delivered a baby. All women also used to cook for the next two days, and everyone abided by the ban on field labor for two days in a row, during which strangers in need could pick the crop from our fields.

All of these customs and prayers, all of the rituals I have not mentioned, offer ample evidence that our cultural and religious origins are to be found elsewhere. For us, there was never a shade of doubt about this.

I can still hear my grandmother saying, "we have not always lived in this village; our forefathers came from a very faraway place, and our teachings come from my grandmother who also received them from her grandmother. They were passed down from one generation to the next, through oral transmission."[20]

Clearly, the Danites were aware of their differences with their neighbors, and they identify with the Jewish people although some of them converted to Christianity. Yet, like the Lemba and Igbo, their religious and cultural similarities with the ancient Hebrews are dismissed, as David Szerman lamented on a sarcastic tone: "Israeli TV did not even condescend to watch the film. Of course, why should they? There's nothing vulgar about it, no anti-religious rant, but on the contrary, two million Africans who declare they're Hebrews and proclaim their love for Israel. Why should it even matter to them?"[21]

These remarks must be situated against the backdrop of the difficulties experienced in Israel by the Ethiopian "repatriates" who, after being welcomed as exiles returning to the Promised Land and presented as such to Western media, were then perceived as a social burden and a challenging group to integrate into Israeli society. One of the respondents of Lisa Anteby-Yemini, an Israeli Ethiopian Jew, described in these terms the racism he experienced: "[w]hen will they stop calling us 'Ethiopians'? I've been in Israel for thirty years and all my children were born here, and they are still calling us Ethiopians. When will we be Israelis?" Lisa Anteby-Yemini noted, "[i]n the field of health care, Ethiopian immigrants were until recently classified as an at-risk group (due to a high rate of hepatitis B and AIDS), which caused the 'Blood Scandal' in 1996, when it was revealed that their blood donations were discarded without their knowing."[22] In spite of the efforts made by Israeli governments to facilitate their economic and social integration, the growing disillusionment of the most famous community of Black Jews combines with the authorities' indifference to the claims of other African groups to make any other Black community's "return to the Promised Land" a highly unlikely prospect.

However, across the African continent, such groups keep claiming or asserting their sense of belonging to the Hebrew people, among which the Tutsis of Rwanda-Burundi, the Zakhor movement of Timbuktu in Mali, the Abayudaya of Uganda, the House of Israel community in Ghana, the Beit Yeshourun of Cameroon, or the Kasuku community of Gathundia in Kenya, and the list goes on. These Africans returning to Judaism often reach out to the state of Israel to point out the similarities of their customs with Jewish practices of Kashrut, circumcision, or other aspects of the Halakha, although they are usually met with indifference, save for a few Israeli and US individuals who are willing to visit them.

The reason for this outreach is undoubtedly the extraordinary media coverage of the "return" of Ethiopian Jews, even though the first mass movement of migration of Black Jews to Israel actually dates back to 1969, when Black Hebrew Israelites, a group of African Americans led by Ben Ammi Ben-Israel (a.k.a. Ben Carter) and claiming to be the descendants of the tribe of Judah, were given land to settle on in the Negev desert, a recently annexed Syrian territory. Their narrative is that their ancestors emigrated to Africa following the destruction of the Temple in Jerusalem, only to be later enslaved in America. In 1966, the angel Gabriel appeared to Ben Ammi in a vision, telling him to return to the land of his ancestors, that is, Israel. Three years later, answering this call, he led to Israel around four hundred fellow African Americans, mostly from Chicago. During their trip, they stopped in Liberia where they discarded their Western outfits as badges of their ex-slave status, embracing traditional West African garb instead. They took on Hebrew names, embraced polygamy, a diet proscribing meat, dairy products, eggs, and sugar, and a communal way of life based on the Torah and the teachings of Ben Ammi, who died in 2014. They are currently estimated at over three thousand and while their Jewishness is not officially recognized, as Liron Shimon explains,[23] after two decades of legal battles with the Israeli state, the latter eventually granted them resident status. The documentary made by Ben Schuder and Niko Philipides, *The Village of Peace,* gives a detailed account of their religious and social experience in what is known as the Dimona community, while John L. Jackson Jr.'s work *Thin Description* offers an in-depth analysis of their ideology and practices.[24]

Long before them but in a similar fashion, a community of Black Hebrews had developed in Harlem in the 1930s, combining Black nationalism with an appropriation of the history of the Hebrew people. Studies by Howard Brotz[25] analyze this important community of African American Jews within the broader frame of the groups that organized in the interwar and Depression era to find a way out of the "American dilemma" of Black double-consciousness and achieve moral, cultural, and political autonomy.

In addition to all these groups of self-identified Jews who observe the commandments of the Halakha yet elicit as much questioning and doubting as interest, there also exist African ethnic groups which claim to have Jewish origins but do not practice Judaism. This is certainly attributable to the reactions of Christian missionaries who, on discovering the customs and rituals of these ethnic groups, assumed that they were descendants of the mythical Lost Tribes of the House of Israel. The South African anthropologist Magdel Le Roux found that at least five ethnic groups were designated as such by colonial missionaries, including the Khoikhoi, the Zulu, the Satho-Tswana, the Xhosa, and even the Dutch Boers.[26] Likewise, the French anthropologist Georges Balandier pointed out in his classic study of the Kingdom of Kongo:

> The early chroniclers pointed out the larger number of circumcised males and wondered about the origins of this practice. Pigafetta emphasizes the universality of this custom: "This tribe practices circumcision in the manner of Jews." Father Bernardo de Gallo in the report dating from 1710, makes the same observation while describing the collective demonstrations that accompanied the reappearances of the circumcised males: "others practice the circumcision of

children or young boys and celebrate it publicly. And certain whites allow this. The latter belong, perhaps, to the race of traitors [Jews]."[27]

Yet, besides the egregiousness of circumcision as a shared cultural element, other aspects are also emphasized to buttress the thesis of African Jewishness. During a conference organized at the town hall of the sixteenth arrondissement of Paris by AM-I-FA[28] and the local chapter of the B'nai Brith, I met a fellow Congolese named Mireille, who, after introducing herself to me as a Protestant pastor, added confidently, "we Bantus are Jews, this is why I am here." The Bantu, as described by the anthropologist Tidiane N'diaye, are

> a group of peoples who speak relatively germane languages, from the south of Cameroon down to South Africa, including central and east Africa. Bantus are divided into two main linguistic branches, the eastern and the western one. Eastern Bantus migrated across the high plateaus to Zimbabwe and Mozambique and further, to South Africa. Western Bantus have settled in the forest and the savannah as far west as Angola and as far south as Namibia and Botswana.[29]

Historians of the African continent agree on the existence of a phenomenon known as the great dispersion of the Bantu, which they say began at the beginning of the formation of the Sahara Desert, from 5,000 B.C.E. The findings made by paleontologists and anthropologists have allowed them to identify traces of the presence of Bantu types across the Sahara from the Mesolithic period. The ancestors of the Bantu lived in the Upper Nile region, between the seventeenth and twenty-first parallels. Distant cousins of the modern Sudanese, they inhabited the kingdoms of Kush, Napata, and Meroe by the seventh century B.C.E. Many studies have been published on the Bantu, particularly those conducted by Théophile Obenga, a disciple and colleague of the famous Afrocentric scholar Cheikh Anta Diop.[30]

Due to their popularity, the Internet is rife with content claiming to demonstrate the link between Bantu and Jewish identities, as well as the theory of a falsification of Biblical history. A Google search with the keywords "Jew" and "Bantu" yields unambiguous results, with webpages bearing titles such as "The Bantu are the ancient Hebrew Jews," or "The biblical Israel is Black and Bantu, Jews are converts." Long before social media facilitated the propagation of such theories, *Zaïre Actualité,* a monthly magazine from the Democratic Republic of Congo, bore the following headline: "The Twelve Tribes of Israel Identified at Last! Hebrews are Authentically Black."[31] Linguistic parallels are frequently resorted to in order to demonstrate the validity of the thesis, with little to no attention paid to the history of either the Hebrew language or the Bantu language extolled as its matrix, as if the latter had not received any influences from Western missionaries circulating Biblical concepts among the population they were Christianizing.[32]

These claims have found renewed legitimacy with the new searches of 117 inventoried sites carried out in the Lovo Massif (Democratic Republic of Congo, near the Angolan border), including twenty decorated caves, that the archeologist Geoffroy Heimlich[33] and his team have cross-dated between the thirteenth and eighteenth centuries, that is, the period of the Kingdom of Kongo. Congolese authorities are considering requesting that the Lovo Massif be listed as part of the UNESCO's world heritage sites. Among the findings and research hypotheses are some observations made in 1962 by two Belgian scientists, Raymaekers and van Moorsel, concerning traces of paleo-Hebrew alphabet in the most ancient paintings in this cave art: "out of the 22 signs making up the ancient alphabets (Phoenician, Moabite or Paleo-Hebrew), seventeen identical ones are found in Iberian and Congolese cave art."[34] Following these hypotheses, which gesture toward a link between Hebrew and Kongo ethnicities, Rabbi Shimon Roth Ikala, who identifies as a scholar of Central Africa and speaks Lingala as well as French, contends on his videos on social media that the exodus of the Hebrew people out of Egypt occurred in two separate directions—one toward the Land of Canaan in Israel, and the other towards sub-Saharan Africa, particularly the Congo Basin. This hypothesis is also considered by other scholars, such as Jaap van Stageren: "Since the times of Abraham, North Africa has imbibed pagan as well as Hebrew customs. At the same time, Jewish and Egyptian groups went up the Nile towards African territories."[35]

Likewise, the French ethnologist Maurice Dorès noted that

> [t]he reality of the [Jewish] people depends on no biological or even familial determination. The Talmud specifies that the people led by Moses into the desert was made up for one third of the Semitic offspring of the descendants of Abraham, another third, of descendants of Jethro, Moses' father-in-law, the ancestor of the Bedouins, and the last third, of a variety of peoples that Egyptians had subjugated into slavery. This people became organized into twelve tribes, several of which were probably Black, such as the tribe of Dan.[36]

Additionally, archaeological discoveries in the Democratic Republic of Congo seem to suggest an ancient Egyptian presence or influence there: almost a century after a gold statuette of Osiris was found on the banks of Lualaba river in 1918, a vase was discovered in 2009 in the village of Kakulu in western Kasai that is identical to the four canopic jars found in pharaohs' graves and used to preserve their internal organs (liver, lungs, stomach, and bowels), as well as a green stone used by ancient Egyptian queens for make-up.[37] The Kananga museum in Kasai is encouraging further research in hopes of debunking the commonlyreceived understanding of the ancient Egyptian civilization as having flourished without any Black African cultural influences. Meanwhile, hypotheses abound in Congolese circles to suggest that the ancient Egyptians were Black Africans and the Baluba ethnic group of the DRC have Hebrew origins, as Tshimanga Mujangi Shambuyi contends in a recent book.[38] Another author, Moïse Rahmani, notes that the Baluba call themselves Bayuda (which means "Jews" in Lingala), which indicates that they came from the kingdom of Judah.[39]

Next to the DRC, in post-genocide Ruanda, the Tutsi group's need for reconstruction is also expressed in the form of a collective identification to the Jewish people, partly due to the similarity between the two experiences of persecution and genocide. Under the Tutsi head of state Paul Kagame, the country has developed tight bonds with the state of Israel,[40] while a growing number of Tutsis practice Judaism, particularly festivals, arguing that these are rooted in their own culture and traditions.

By the same token, many cultural features, mores, or culinary customs observed in African societies are also given a Biblical origin, as is contended in a contribution entitled "Black Mentality and Biblical Mentality" whose author, the Cameroon-based Jesuit priest Jean-Claude Bajeux, wrote, "The Black man felt at home in the Bible. . . . The Black reader of the Bible rejoices to find a civilization with the same pace as his own."[41] He particularly emphasized the functioning of kinship groups, circumcision, the importance granted to the meaningful naming of children and adults, and the value given to poems and songs in African cultures. A pastor named Ake Dieudonné also endeavors to list all the comparisons to be made between Hebrew and African cultural practices, by quoting from the Bible several rituals, customs, and family names that can still be found in present-day Africa, particularly in the Ivory Coast. Among these are the payment of a bride price, circumcision, the shaving of the head when one has lost a parent or relative, the offering of libations, sexual abstinence imposed on menstruating women and new mothers, levirate marriage, or the washing of hands on returning from a burial.[42] Such identification to the Biblical world causes many African and Caribbean people to believe that they have Hebrew ancestry.

Guy Roger, a Seventh-Day Adventist pastor of Caribbean descent, recently recorded a talk entitled "Africa, the Black Man and the Bible" in which he stated the following beliefs:

> first, the Bible was written so that Africans may know that God is their God; second, the people of Israel is a Black people and third, we Caribbean descendants of slaves probably include descendants of the lost tribes of the House of Israel. This is why we said several times, "but this was meant for the Jews, and we are not Jews, we are not Israelites" (I make the distinction between Israelites and

Israelis) and who are we? We are all too willing to describe ourselves as pagans or converted pagans.[43]

Such constructions fall under what Vincent Wimbush calls Scripturalization, which

> may (typically) come to be represented as canonical or natural regimes of thinking and speaking and acting. But they may in turn inspire or provoke and even help structure refractions, differentiation, alternatives, mimetics, resistances—other complex, denaturalized, and unstable (de-/re- constructive) practices, rituals, formations, and forms of conscientization [which Wimbush calls] "scripturalizing." The latter may be evident in (mis)uses and (mis)readings of languages and objects, texts, and signs, as well as the arrogations of other languages, texts, signs, objects, and so forth. In short, . . . [s]cripturalizing dynamics and work are carried out in complex relationship to—in imitation of, within, and around the edges of, in resistance to—scripturalization.[44]

According to Édith Bruder,

> [i]n most of these groups, a process of identity reorganization that had been underlying since the colonial period was reinforced and accelerated by the existence of the Falasha and the outcome of their situation. When, in the early twentieth century, Jacques Faitlovitch declared the Falasha were Jews, he launched the beginnings of an identity redefinition and a probable line of Jewish descent for a Black African group. He thus demonstrated, so to speak, that a black-skinned group could be Jewish while practicing a marginal form of Judaism and being unaware of rabbinical practices. By conflating Jewishness with Africanness, the process of recognition of the Falasha which established their kinship with the global Jewry had just created the concept of "Black Jew." Their transfer from Ethiopia to Israel in 1980 and 1990 as they fled the Ethiopian regime's persecutions, coupled with the worldwide interest elicited by these spectacular events, acted as a trigger in African societies that were already leaning towards Judaism. The images of this modern-day Exodus with Biblical connotations gave them proof of the existence of a mythical African Jewish community with mysterious roots that eventually reconnected with the Promised Land.[45]

The French ethnologist Maurice Dorès concluded:

> It thus seems that we are witnessing the emergence of a Black Jewish cultural identity, in the same way as we speak of American Judaism or Moroccan Judaism. It is a new branch of the Jewish people that rests on ancient foundations.[46]

Yet, these remarks leave unaccounted for the many similarities observed between African customs and Jewish traditions: have Africans been influenced by the Bible during their contacts with colonizers, or do Biblical texts reflect earlier African cultural traits, which may or may not have been recorded in written form? Magdel Le Roux echoes these questions:

> [w]hat confuses the situation is that many other indigenous groups in Africa have many manners and customs with a Semitic resonance. Where did they get this from? Are they descendants of the lost tribes? Or is there any evidence of a more general religion that existed earlier throughout the world?[47]

In all likelihood, African cultural practices preceded the reception of the Bible. This is the worldview that appears in Afrocentric theories, which, in the wake of Cheikh Anta Diop's, appropriate Biblical founding myths to confirm the hypothesis of the preexistence of Black civilizations. Among these, Kemitism is a Pan-African movement that emerged in the 1970s in the USA and calls for a return to the values, beliefs, and religious practices of ancient Egypt, which is represented as the Black African matrix of all monotheistic religions.[48] The late Jean-Philippe Nioussérê Kalala Omotunde, in particular, significantly popularized this approach among Francophone readers and audiences in the Caribbean islands, African countries, and the Diaspora by means of conferences and televised interviews.[49] Consequently, Kemitism appears in their understanding and interpretations of the Bible.

THE BIBLE THROUGH AN AFROCENTRIC PRISM

According to the African American Afrocentric scholar Molefi Kete Asante, "[a]frocentricity proposes a cultural reconstruction that incorporates the African perspective as a part of an entire human transformation."[50] Afrocentric theories extol Africa as the cradle of humanity and African civilizations, especially that of ancient Egypt, as the matrix of Western civilizations, particularly ancient Greece. In this perspective, the revision or revisiting of Biblical history holds a central place. A major Afrocentric scholar who worked on ancient Egypt, the Senegalese researcher Cheikh Anta Diop, argued that pharaohs were Blacks and Hebrews were the offspring of interracial mixing between Blacks and Whites.[51] He wrote about them:

> [t]he Semitic world was born during protohistory and resulted not from a biological mutation, but from a racial mixing between Blacks and Whites meeting in Western Asia. It becomes a mystery every time we try to understand it without taking into account these two components and presenting it as a sui generis reality. Archeological facts confirmed by the myriad testimonies contained in Semitic literature itself (Biblical Hebrew, Arabic, Aramaic, etc.) confirm that all of the present-day habitat of the Semites was initially occupied, from

prehistory to the onset of the historical period, by Blacks who did not vanish, but mixed with a White element that had come from elsewhere.... These White tribes mingled with the Canaanite Negroid natives to produce the branch of Northern Semites. These ancient Semites were much darker-skinned than some present-day Semites, as is shown by reproductions of figures and engravings of the time. They were Othellos of sorts.[52]

Holding a degree of chemistry as well as philosophy, Cheikh Anta Diop used the carbon-14 dating method to shed light on the sketchy history of Black Africa. He worked on the mummies of pharaohs kept in the laboratory of physical anthropology of the Musée de l'Homme in Paris, and eventually concluded that the rate of melanin he found under the skin of ancient Egyptians is in sufficient quantity to demonstrate that the latter were darker skinned than Europeans.[53] Additionally, for him, Western civilization was crucially influenced by the civilization developed by Africans in the Nile Valley; he blamed Europeans for deliberately falsifying world history and misleading Africans about the reality of their contribution to world civilizations. When he defended his doctoral dissertation in 1947 at the Sorbonne university in Paris, he earned his degree without honors and was forbidden to publish his research in the colonies of France; but he nevertheless created a laboratory of carbon-14 dating in Dakar, Senegal, to keep combating the prejudiced view that African peoples have no history. In 1974, he organized an international conference in Cairo with the support of UNESCO, whose then-Director General Matar Mbow said that "the Western participants admitted that it was fair to consider Egypt and its inhabitants as African in essence."[54] Although contested to this day, Cheikh Anta Diop's findings are frequently cited by his disciples and by Afrocentric movements as restoring the truth about the continent and its rightful place in world history, and this logically includes an examination of the African cultures in, or of, the Bible.

Regarding Jews, he wrote, "we must examine the genesis of the Jewish people—how it was born, how it fostered the piece of literature that is the Bible, where the offspring of Kam, the ancestor of Blacks and Egyptians, has allegedly been cursed. What is the presumed historical origin of such a curse?"[55] Starting from the episode of the entry in Egypt of the Hebrews (then numbering 70 people) up to the exodus of their 600,000 descendants after four centuries of enslavement, Cheikh Anta Diop investigated the prophetic character of Moses, whom he believed to have been influenced by the Egyptian religious and cultural environment in which he had been born and grown up. For him,

> Moses lived at the time of Tell-el-Amarna, where Amenophis IV (a.k.a. Akhenaton, ca. 1400 BCE) attempted to renew the primitive Egyptian

monotheism which was fading under the clerical apparatus and the corruption of priests. Akhenaton seems to have tried to reinforce political centralism in the immense empire that had just been conquered, by backing it with religious centralism: the empire needed a universal religion. It can be surmised that Moses was sensitive to this religious reform, and became, from then on, the champion of monotheism in the Jewish milieu. Monotheism in all its abstraction was already alive in Egypt, which itself had borrowed it from Meroitic Sudan, the Ancient Ethiopia. In the climate of insecurity surrounding the Jewish people in Egypt, a God that could promise a more stable future represented a matchless moral support. Thus, after the initial reluctance, that people, who does not seem to have known monotheism until then, contrary to the belief of those who say it invented it, nevertheless developed the concept to a fairly considerable degree.[56]

Following Cheikh Anta Diop, the Afrocentric American scholar Molefi Kete Asante insisted on the monotheistic character of hymns sung in the praise of the Egyptian gods Aten and Amen:

[t]he later Hymn to Aten, from Amarna, begins, "Father of the gods who created Mankind, who made the animals . . . and all the plants that sustain the cattle . . . Lord of the rays of the sun that give light. . . . " The earlier hymn to Amen says, "Holy God who created himself, who made every land, created what is in it, all people, herds and flocks, all trees that grow from the soil." Both hymns to African deities fit the monotheistic theology of the Jewish, Christian, and later Islamic traditions, with the idea of one Supreme Creator. However, it is not possible to infer from this that Akhenaten's Aten worship was unique even in ancient Africa. It did not vary that much from traditional Egyptian beliefs. Thus, our Akhenaten appears more consistent with the established contours of Egyptian theology and ultimately related to the monotheism of Origen and the rise of Christianity in Egypt.[57]

Historians disagree on the origins of monotheism, as Mario Liverani pointed out: Bible specialists have agreed for a long time now that monotheism emerged after a long evolution, but they still disagree over the exact historical moment when it appeared. We thought long ago, following Renan, that monotheism resulted from a conditioning wrought by environment, by experiencing life in the desert with its immense, empty spaces. Later on, and still recently, we thought it was a consequence of what was called the monotheistic revolution of the heretic Pharaoh Amenophis IV. . . .[58]

Regarding Moses himself, Grégoire Biyogo notes: "The name *Moshe* itself is not of Hebrew, but Egyptian origin: Mose, saved from the waters coming from the root *oshi* (water)."[59] In the same line of reasoning, Messod and Roger Sabbah, two brothers from a rabbinical family, further assert:

The legend of Moses, the prince saved from the waters, was borrowed like many others from Mesopotamia and Egypt. Moses had to be born among the Hebrew people and become miraculously an Egyptian, raised by Pharaoh's daughter to be the "head of her household" and study the wisdom of Egypt . . . Moshe (Moses) means in Egyptian, "the son birthed by the great God (Ra)." . . . Moses saved from the waters echoes the legend of the godly child borne by the Nile River. This tradition was part and parcel of Egyptian tradition. Each year, on New Year's Day, the flooding of the river was believed to bring back the godly child, the solar child conflated with the young king who was said to regenerate every year.[60]

This version of the figure of Moses is found in all Afrocentric theories, particularly those of the French Caribbean historian and theologian Pierre Nillon,[61] who focused his research on demonstrating the Africanness of Moses. His first argument, based on Biblical verses and classical historians like Herodotus, is that since Moses was born, raised, and educated in Egypt, then he must be an Egyptian; and since the Torah as well as classical historians described Egyptians as Blacks, then Moses was Black as well. His second argument is a comparative exegesis of thirty-three Biblical passages and texts about the Egyptian Pharaoh Akhenaton, which leads him to conclude that the character of Moses replicates that of Akhenaton. Here are the most significant analogies: both of them were Egyptian royalty (*Exodus* 2:10, 19 and *Acts* 7:21); each of them married a foreign, light-skinned woman (Nefertiti, daughter of a priest named Ay, and Zipporah, also the daughter of a priest named Reuel, *Exodus* 2:16, 21); after repudiating Nefertiti, Akhenaton married a Nubian (or Ethiopian) woman named Kiya, while Moses, after repudiating Zipporah, married an Ethiopian (or Nubian) woman whose name is not mentioned (*Numbers* 12:1); both men were the first in their lineage to break away with polytheism and extol monotheism for all mankind (*Exodus* 20:2–3); before Akhenaton's rule no deity named Aton had been worshiped, and before Moses' leadership no one in Egypt knew any god called Adonai (*Exodus* 3:13–15 and 5:2); finally, Akhenaton showed his people the "didactic name" of the god Aton on two stone cartouches nine years into his rule, while Moses also presented his people with two stone tables containing the testimony of God (*Exodus* 32:19).[62]

Understandably, these arguments are highly controversial, particularly among faith-based organizations. The Afrocentric publisher Anibwe, who sold me the book cited above, told me that Nillon's first book had been censored by Jewish, Muslim, and Christian organizations. Yet he is not the first to have doubted the existence of the man and authenticity of the Scriptures that man is said to have authored; Voltaire for instance wondered, "[i]s it really true that there was a Moses? If a man who was obeyed by Nature itself had ever existed among the Egyptians, shouldn't such extraordinary events have made up the major part of the history of Egypt?"[63] The Jewish philosopher Spinoza shared similar doubts, according to the historian Philippe Abadie: "from the seventeenth century, with Spinoza and his Theologico-Political Treatise (1665), a critical approach of Scriptures emerged, which questioned Moses' authorship of the Pentateuch and, by ricochet, the existence of the man and the historical accuracy of the events narrated in the Book of Exodus."[64] Likewise, Messod and Roger Sabbah assert that "the many similarities between the Bible, oral tradition, commentaries by sages and the history of Egypt testify to the existence of a primary Hebrew Torah, which is now lost but revealed the history of Yahuds. They cultivated their past to the point of worshiping it, and in order not to fall into oblivion, they narrated in their sacred text the story of their exodus from Egypt as they experienced it on the fall of [the city of] Akhet-Aton. Evolving from one century to the next, adjusting to the dominant rulers and deities, the Torah gradually became the Mesopotamian history of the Hebrews. . . . The original Torah was the history of ancient Egypt as narrated by the Yahuds."[65] Nowadays, the question remains moot, as seen in the title of the exhibit "Moïse, figure d'un prophète" (Moses, a prophetic figure) organized at the Museum of Art and History of Judaism (MAHJ) in Paris, where the question of Moses' actual existence was implicitly posed.

But whether Moses was a fictional or historical character and Hebrews were or weren't a distinct people, it remains that Judaism was born of these founding myths. By the same token, Black Jews emerged not from Afrocentric Egyptology or a possibly dark-skinned Moses, but from Hebrew tradition and particularly the Torah, whose roots they often claim to be African, either because they consider Hebrew forebears to have been Black (especially Zipporah or the Queen of Sheba), or because they detect an African presence or influence within ancient Judaism. Indeed, Black identity in Biblical texts is not just perceptible in the story of Moses, but dates back to that of Noah in *Genesis*. If Biblical genealogies are considered as historical, all Black people are supposed to be Africans and descendants of Ham, Canaan, or Kush (*Genesis* 10:6–17). In a famous passage that was abundantly commented on and used in colonial ventures, Ham, Africans' purported ancestor, was cursed in the person of his eldest son Canaan, as well as the latter's offspring, who were condemned to be "a servant of servants" unto the descendants of Ham's brothers Sem and Japhet: "And he said: Cursed be Canaan; A servant of servants shall he be unto his brethren. Blessed be the Lord, the God of Shem: And let Canaan be their servant. God shall enlarge Japheth, And he shall dwell in the tents of Shem; And let Canaan be their servant" (*Genesis* 9:25–27, *Hebrew—English TANAKH The Jewish Bible*).

The myth of the curse of Ham served to justify the enslavement and colonization of African peoples and countries by dominant Others (see chapter 1), as is analyzed by the French sociologist Shmuel Trigano: "for more than a thousand years, the enslavement of Black populations was justified by this passage from the Book of Genesis. Arabs, Europeans, Americans from the New World have found in it the symbolic resources necessary to assign Blacks to a status of inferiority and subjugation."[66] Analyzing the meaning of the word "Ham," he develops: "Ham, *Hom*/heat and *Hum*/brown are very close. There is also *Mefuham*/charred, as black as coal. According to a Talmudic commentary, Ham came out of the ark *Mefuham*/charred."[67] Cheikh Anta Diop also wondered, "[w]here did the name Ham originate, and were may Moses have found it? Where else than in his native Egypt, where he was born, raised, and grew up until Exodus? Indeed, we know that Egyptians used to call their country Kemit which means 'Black' in the Egyptian language. It is bit natural, then, to find the Hebrew word Kam meaning 'heat, black, charred.'"[68]

As for the link between a dark skin and slave status, Shmuel Trigano contrasts the meanings of the words "servant" and "slave." Observing that the Hebrew word *eved* is translated as "slave" with reference to both the Hebrews' status in Egypt and Moses' relation to God as His "servant," Trigano points out, "it would never come to mind that we should translate this description as 'the slave of God.' So why is the word 'slave' used when referring to Canaan?"[69] This leads him to infer from the interpretations about the curse of Ham that "[t]he 'Black' category thus began to designate ethnic groups specifically labeled on the basis of color, that is, race much more than on the basis of the Biblical text. On the contrary this dimension was non-existent, so to speak, in the Bible and rabbinical Judaism."[70] However, if we confront this assertion with the Biblical texts and the Talmud, a very different interpretation of the curse of Ham, Hamites, and Black people connects their skin color with bondage. In the feature film *Go, Live and Become,* when the Ethiopian-born protagonist has to debate a fellow student named Michael Leibovici on the theme, "What color was Adam?" the White student starts the debate with these words: "Adam was created in God's image and the skin color that was chosen was white. In the beginning we were all white, but after the Flood, Noah and his sons came out of the Ark. Noah cursed the offspring of his son Ham and mentioned by name his grandson Canaan: 'Cursed be Canaan, he shall be a slave unto his brothers' . . . Kush, Canaan's eldest son, inherited an additional curse: among the descendants of Ham, some were to be black skinned. And it was so: Kush became black and he begot the Kushim, who are the black people of Africa. This is how the descendants of Ham became slaves and Blacks."[71] Admittedly, the connection between slavery and the ideology of the curse of Ham is traceable in the Bible, as is highlighted by Cheikh Anta Diop:

> [i]f the Egyptian people caused so much suffering to the Jewish people, as the Bible says, and if the Egyptian people is a people of Negroes descended from

Ham as the same Bible says, then we can no longer remain ignorant, in spite of the legend of the drunken Noah, of the historical causes of the curse of Ham which originates in the Jewish literature that is entirely subsequent to that period of persecution. Indeed Moses, in the Book of Genesis, has the Almighty say to Abraham in a dream, "Know of a surety that thy seed shall be a stranger in a land that is not theirs, and shall serve them; and they shall afflict them four hundred years; and also that nation, whom they shall serve, will I judge; and afterward shall they come out with great substance." (*Gen.* 15:13–14) Here is the historical root of the curse of Ham. It is not by coincidence that the curse affecting Ham, the father of Mizraim, Put, Kush, and Canaan, bears only on Canaan, the inhabitant of the land that the Jewish people have coveted their entire history.[72]

In these lines, Diop sounds clearly skeptical as to the authenticity of Moses' authorship of the Biblical texts attributed to him. In a conference entitled "Kushites in the Hebrew Bible," Kevin Burrell elaborated on *Isaiah* 18:2 and 7:2, *Chronicles* 14:9–15 and 16:8, and *Psalms* 68:29, 31 to show that although the Kushites—who were Israel's allies in wartime—were a powerful people due to their military superiority, they were not represented as such in the Bible, for Israel is supposed to owe its salvation to Yahweh alone. He concluded:

[f]or the biblical writer, Israel's salvation is affected not by reliance on a foreign army but by Yahweh Himself. So, to wrap up, the theology surrounding the topical image of mighty Kush surely pushes a militant giant in the Hebrew Bible. Numerically, technologically, abundant in horses and chariots and even physically in *Isaiah* 18; but none of this matters much theologically except to highlight Yahweh's superior power over Kushites and all imperial powers. Kush may be greater than Israel. But he's no match for Israel's god. Here again I wish to emphasize that the Hebrew Bible is a religious text and as such, its representation of Kushites is laden with religious concerns. Specifically, its theology is concerned with the exaltation of Yahweh and his people of Israel, the exaltation of the nations, insofar as the nations are to be exalted, is accomplished only in the context of submission to Yahweh and His chosen people Israel.[73]

What emerges from the doubts expressed by Cheikh Anta Diop and Kevin Burrell is the political usefulness of the ideology of the curse of Ham as resulting from the enslavement of the Hebrew people in Egypt: it likely fostered the notion of a deity intervening in human affairs and siding with the Hebrews to punish their former (Egyptian) oppressors durably, by dispossessing their descendants of their own land—that is, Canaan. Consequently, Abraham, in order to be seen as the father of Hebrews (as well as Arabic-speaking peoples) had to be a descendant of Sem, while Nimrod—whose name comes from the Hebrew word *morad,* meaning rebel—had to be one of

Ham's, since he triggered God's anger by erecting the tower of Babel. Thus it seems logical that God should have chosen Abraham and promised that his abundant posterity would settle down in the land of Canaan, the cursed heir of Ham. In all subsequent texts in the Bible, Ham's descendants, among whom are the Canaanites, the Amorites, the Hittites, or the Kushites, only appear as servants or subalterns. The Book of Genesis (16:1–3) assigns a Canaanite origin to Hagar, the Egyptian maidservant that Sara used to give a child to Abraham in her place. Although the Scripture does not specify Abraham's skin color or Sara's, Jewish commentators did not balk at inserting a racial classification in their reading of the text. One of the leading figures of the Talmud, Rashi, building on the fear shared by Abraham and Sara on their arrival in Egypt, speculated on the skin tone of ancient Egyptians in these terms: "you are comely. But we are now among a people of black-skinned men, brothers of the Ethiopians, who are not used to seeing a comely, [light-skinned] woman."[74] There is little doubt that in Rashi's mind, Egyptians, as descendants of Ham, were Blacks. In the New Testament, the only significant mention of Ham's descendants occurs in the dialog between Jesus and the Canaanite woman, related as follows in the Gospel according to Matthew:

> Leaving that place, Jesus withdrew to the region of Tyre and Sidon. A Canaanite woman from that vicinity came to him, crying out, "Lord, Son of David, have mercy on me! My daughter is demon-possessed and suffering terribly." Jesus did not answer a word. So his disciples came to him and urged him, "Send her away, for she keeps crying out after us." He answered, "I was sent only to the lost sheep of Israel." The woman came and knelt before him. "Lord, help me!" she said. He replied, "It is not right to take the children's bread and toss it to the dogs." "Yes it is, Lord," she said. "Even the dogs eat the crumbs that fall from their master's table." Then Jesus said to her, "Woman, you have great faith! Your request is granted." And her daughter was healed at that moment. (Matthew 15:21–28, *The Holy Bible,* New International Version)

The episode narrated above is said to have taken place in the territory of Sidon, which the Bible designates as the first-born of Canaan (*1 Chronicles,* 1:13). It is therefore significant that the female protagonist of the scene is presented as a Canaanite woman, for this automatically situates her as a descendant of Ham. Indeed, her dialog with Jesus necessarily implies prejudices linked to the ideology of the curse of Ham, which account for his disciples' urging him to send her away without hearing her plea, as well as Jesus' insulting comparison of Canaanites with dogs—a slight which the woman seems to be used to, since she accepts it in her response and refers to Jews as "masters." The master/dog dyad seems to barely conceal a master/slave dyad, with the Israelites, descendants of Sem, acting as masters to the Canaanites, descendants of Ham, who are doomed to be slaves on their own territory, following God's promise to Abraham: "But thou shalt go to thy fathers in peace; thou shalt be buried in a good old age. And in the fourth generation they shall come back hither; for the iniquity of the Amorite is not yet full" (*Genesis,* 15:15–16, *Hebrew—English TANAKH The Jewish Bible*). Indeed, in this passage, God deprives the offspring of Canaan of their territory to offer it to the descendants of Abraham, thus legitimizing the colonization of the Canaanites on their own land (*Genesis,* 17:1–8) for He does not consider their iniquity to be "full." Quite probably, the nature of their "iniquity" is linked with the sin committed by Ham and the curse afflicting his descendants.

Talmudic literature is filled with references to the curse of Ham. In the Talmud of Jerusalem—Taanith 1.64d (Yerushalmi Krotoschin 1865)—Rabbi Hiyya ben Abba said that "[t]hey had the privilege of being saved [from the Flood]. We have been taught that Ham, the dog, and the crow all misbehaved. Ham became black, the dog became particular in the way it copulates, and the crow is different from other creatures." Likewise, in Berakhot R. 36,7, he said, "Ham and the dog copulated on board the ark, which is why Ham became black, and the dog copulates in public." In the Talmud of Babylon Sanhédrin 108b (Babylonian Talmud edited by Isidore Epstein), we can read: "[o]ur rabbis taught us that three copulated on board the ark and all three were punished—the dog, the crow, and Ham. The dog was sentenced to be kept on a leash, the crow to expectorate, and Ham was afflicted in his skin." Two additional versions may be found, which allege that Ham castrated or sodomized his father. Rabbi Huna, citing Rabbi Joseph, asserted that Ham was told, "[y]our offspring shall be *ugly* and black." Finally, in Noah [73b], the Zohar reads, "[i]n showing his nudity, Noah caused Canaan to be dominated; for, because he was a righteous man by virtue of the secret of the alliance, Ham castrated him. In effect, we have learnt that he had rejected the alliance [that is, circumcision]" (Zohar I, éd. Verdier 1981).

Haïm H. Cohn, an emeritus Vice-President of the Supreme Court of the state of Israel, gave useful details on the status of slaves at the time of the Talmud, and compared the unequal treatment of Hebrew and Canaanite bondspeople: "[t]he major difference between the Hebrew slave and the Canaanite slave is that the Hebrew slave has a fixed period of slavery. In the case the court of Hebrew slave sold by the court, 'he shall work for six years, and in the seventh he shall go free.' . . . The Canaanite slave on the other hand, is a slave in perpetuity."[75] The curse of Ham probably accounts for the Canaanite's lifetime bondage. David Malki emphasized this elements in the Jewish collective memory in his book on Talmudic scholars:

> This is what happened with Rabban Gamliel. He had invited the Elders to share his meal and his servant Tabi was standing beside them and waiting on

them, which prompted Rabbi Elazar Ben Azariyah to exclaim, "Woe unto you, Canaan, for causing the misfortune of your descendants, whether they be innocent or sinners. It would have been fairer for Tabi to sit at this table while I stood waiting on him." Indeed, Tabi, the Canaanite servant of Rabban Gamliel, was known for his righteous way of life; and Rabbi Elazar said these words in the early second century of the Christian era, at a time when slavery was common all over the world. We would be hard pressed to imagine anyone, anywhere else, saying such things at a banquet gathering the well-to-do. These words remain remarkable, even if it may be surmised that Rabbi Elazar was actually aiming a barbed comment at Rabban Gamliel for allowing Tabi to keep serving him.[76]

What is striking in this anecdote is not so much the words spoken as the rabbi's justification of a man's enslavement by the Biblical ideology of the curse of Ham, regardless of the banality of slavery at the time. This connection appears even more clearly in the recommendation made by Maimonides, the medieval luminary of Judaism, in the following passage:

> [t]he sages have enjoined us to keep as one's domestics poor Jews and orphans rather than slaves; it is better to employ the former so that the descendants of Abraham, Isaac, and Jacob should derive the benefit and one's fortune, and not the descendants of Ham. He who increases the number of his slaves increases sin and iniquity in the World from day to day, whereas the man who employs poor Jews in his household increases merits and religious acts from hour to hour.[77]

This leaves little doubt about the automatic link between Ham's descent and slave status. The Biblical text does not specify the race of Ham and his offspring, even if the mention of the "blackness" of their skin is explicit, probably because scientific racism was not yet part of Judeo-Christian culture. The word and the ensuing racialist and racist theories did not appear until 1555, to reach their apex in the nineteenth century, as is explained by the sociologist Jan Nederveen Pieterse:

> [t]he curse of Canaan was destined to have a long and notorious career. In the early Church of Augustine the curse of Ham or Canaan was regarded as an explanation of slavery, but not of blacks, simply because slavery at the time was "colourless." The association of the curse of Canaan with blackness arose only much later in medieval Talmudic texts. In the sixteenth century it became a Christian theme and by the seventeenth it was widely accepted as explanation of black skin colour. From here it was but a small step to the interpretation of the curse of Canaan as an explanation of and of justification for the slavery of black African.[78]

Tudor Parfitt's analysis is even more eloquent:

As the exploration and subjugation of western Africa continued and as European commercial and imperial interests changed and developed, and as attitudes toward slavery softened and changed, so an explanation for the history, or non- history, origins and relative status of different African peoples became more urgently required. The Hamitic theory was there to help out. Ethnographers and theologians now started to argue that the biblical Ham and his progeny—the Egyptians and others—were in fact white, thus claiming the wonders of ancient Egypt for Europe's racial ancestors. A discourse now developed in which only Ham's youngest son, Canaan, was black at all; it was only his offspring that populated sub-Saharan Africa and who were cursed. "Hamites" now began to refer to a variety of light-skinned peoples who included the ancient Egyptians, Phoenicians, Canaanites, Ethiopians, and Israelites. The Hamitic hypothesis became a vital tool in the task of differentiating between African societies and in the critical colonial task of rewriting African history.[79]

The ideology of the curse of Ham is still perceptible in contemporary Jewish culture, particularly in the use of the word "Kushi." Although the sociologist Shmuel Trigano, quoting numerous Biblical texts, contends that it also means "comely" (*Song of Songs*) as well as designating the color black ("Can the Kushi change his skin, or the leopard his spots?" *Jeremiah,* 13:23). "Kushi" is identified with "black" or "Ethiopian."[80] Indeed, the word "Kush" comes from a Hebrew root meaning "dark" and the term "Kushite" commonly designates the Ethiopians, as the alleged descendants of Kush, son of Ham. Nowadays, in informal language, the word participates in the Othering and racializing of the Israelis of Ethiopian descent, which, as the anthropologist Lisa Anteby-Yemini explains, "is first made manifest in the language of the host society, which sometimes designates them as 'skhorim' (Blacks) and even calls them 'Kushim' (n- word)—terms . . . associated with the former Barya captives, and thus doubly insulting."[81] The Canadian ethnologist Gabriella Djerrahian explains that the term was first used to designate the Mizrahim, i.e., Jews from the Middle East, who were perceived as the first "Black" Jews in Israel, and then the Ethiopians.[82] According to her,

> [i]t is difficult to offer an unambiguous translation, as in Israel, this designation may refer to individuals racialized as "Black" whether Jewish or not, and occupying a lower social status in comparison with the hegemonic group. It may combine the dual connotation of the term "black" and the n- word to refer to segments of the population that also occupy a lower social position, but may also refer to the color black, as in *ouga kushit,* i.e., "chocolate cake." However, in popular parlance, *kushi* rather corresponds to the n- word in English.[83]

Likewise, in a film made by Mushon Salmona, *Une jeunesse israélienne,*[84] when one of the three protagonists who is of Ethiopian descent is called "Kushi," the slur is translated from Hebrew into French by the N-word in the subtitles. Finally, Ahmadiel Ben Yehuda, a member of the Black Hebrew Israelite community of Dimona in Israel, reacted unambiguously to the use of the word by a rabbi:

> [t]hose who dare suggest that the new chief rabbi didn't understand the negative context of the word are again, in denial, or in league with the worst of the haters and bigots. I can agree that there is little contemporary or historical or cultural relevance about sixteenth century Ashkenazi European culture, but to claim—as did Yaacov Lozowick—that he is victim of "his complete disconnection from the broader cultural universe of most Israelis" is ridiculous. "Kushi" is a derogatory term. Even Israeli children are well-versed in the finer points of connotation, where the acceptable usage of kushi/m begins and ends. Any African who has found himself in certain Jewish neighborhoods knows this well.[85]

Israeli children's familiarity with the "finer points of connotations" alluded to in this passage are reflected explicitly in the testimony of Hortense Bilé, an Ivorian-born respondent who lived in Israel in her teenage years. When she played with her schoolmates, the latter often sang a Hebrew singsong that said, "Kushi bambo, bili, bili, bambo," which literally means, "Black, dirty, very, very dirty."[86] This could be shrugged off as harmless children's racism, but it nearly caused a diplomatic incident, according to Bilé, whose father was the Ambassador of the Ivory Coast in Israel at the time. Consequently, the word expresses anything but Black beauty and rather conveys racist contempt. The memory of this slight did not stop Hortense Bilé from converting to Judaism much later and preach love for Israel in AM-I-FARAFINA, the community organization she created, whose acronym means "friendship between Israel and Africa" (see chapter 5).

Like Bilé, many African and Caribbean men and women have converted to Judaism or were born Jewish, which transforms the image of contemporary Judaism in France by infusing an increasingly transnational dynamics in it. The next chapter will describe their experiences, their embrace of Judaism, their position in the French Jewry, and their self-definition as Jews and Blacks vis-à-vis the Torah and the tenets of Jewishness.

NOTES

1. Messod and Roger Sabbah, *Les secrets de l'exode, l'origine égyptienne des Hébreux* (Paris: Éditions Jean-Cyrille Godefroy, 2000), 65.
2. Esther Benbassa, "Enquête sur le peuple juif," *L'Histoire* no. 343 (June 2009): 18.
3. Daniel Friedmann and Ulysses Santamaria, *Les enfants de la Reine de Saba: les Juifs d'Ethiopie (Falachas), histoire, exode, intégration* (Paris: A.M. Métailié, 1994).

4. Lisa Anteby-Yemini, *Les Juifs éthiopiens en Israël: les paradoxes du paradis* (Paris: CNRS Éditions, CRFJ—Centre de recherche français de Jérusalem, série "Hommes et sociétés," 2004); *Les Juifs d'Éthiopie de Gondar à la Terre promise* (Paris: Albin Michel, 2018).

5. Magdel Le Roux, *The Lemba, a Lost Tribe of Israel in Southern Africa?* 2nd edition (Pretoria: Unisa, University of South Africa, 2015), 25.

6. A. B. Spurdle and T. Jenkins, "The origins of the Lemba 'Black Jews' of southern Africa: evidence from p.12 F2 and other Y-chromosome markers," *Am J Hum Genet* 59, no. 5(November 1996): 1126–33.

7. Mark G. Thomas, Tudor Parfitt, Deborah A. Weiss, Karl Skorecki, James F. Wilson, Magdel le Roux, Neil Bradman, and David B. Goldstein, "Y Chromosomes Traveling South: The Cohen Modal Haplotype and the Origins of the Lemba—the 'Black Jews of Southern Africa,'" *The American Society of Human Genetics*,February 11, 2000.

8. Magdel Le Roux, *The Lemba*, 63.

9. Daniel Lis, *Jewish Identity among the Igbo of Nigeria, Israel's "Lost Tribe" and the Question of Belonging in the Jewish State* (Trenton, NJ: Africa World Press, 2015).

10. Mariam Akwa Ibo in Jeff Liberman, *Remerging: The Jews of Nigeria*, documentary, 2012.

11. Dr. Jane Deleosa, Nigeria state legislator, in Jeff Liberman, *Remerging: The Jews of Nigeria*, documentary, 2012.

12. Édith Bruder, "Judaïsme africain, Tribus Perdues et traditions orales," in Joëlle Allouche Benayoun, *Actes du 32e congrès de Généalogie juive Tome 3 / Volume 3 Mondes séfarade, proche-oriental et africain Volume 3: Sephardic, Middle-East and African areas*, 2012, 441–46.

13. Olaudah Equiano, *The Interesting Narrative of the Life of Olaudah Equiano, or Gustavus Vassa, the African*, 172 in Daniel Lis, *Jewish Identity*, 17.

14. Édith Bruder, "Judaïsme africain."

15. Daniel Lis, *Jewish Identity*, 145.

16. Dierk Lange, "Origin of the Yoruba and The Lost Tribes of Israel," *ANTHROPOS* 106 (2011): 592.

17. Dierk Lange, "Origin of the Yoruba," 584.

18. David Szerman, "Les Danites de Côte d'Ivoire," *La Source de vie*, broadcast on France 2 on June 16, 2013.

19. David Szerman, "Les Danites de Côte d'Ivoire. Qui sont-ils?" interview by Manton Gouine, accessed December 29, 2016, http://mantongouine.free.fr/index.php?option=com_content&view=article&id=139:les-danites-de-cote-divoirequi-sont-ils&catid=1:actualites&Itemid=8. Updated on November 16, 2013.

20. Isaac and Péniel Yayir Kohen, "Une famille juive en provenance de la Côte d'Ivoire," paper read at the International Conference *Juifs d'Afrique et d'ailleurs, L'essor du judaïsme en Afrique, dans la diaspora africaine et en Asie au XXe siècle* held by ISSAJ at the Musée d'art et d'histoire du Judaïsme (MAHJ) in Paris, France, November 10–11, 2015.

21. David Szerman, interview cited above.

22. Lisa Anteby, "Peau noire, masques blancs," 112.

23. Liron Shimoni, "Les Hébreux noirs du désert," *Jerusalem Post,* French edition, February 26, 2013, accessed January 26, 2017, http://www.jpost.com/Edition-fran%C3%A7aise/Israel/Les-H%C3%A9breux-noirs-du-d%C3%A9sert-304581.

24. Ben Schuder and Niko Philipides, *The Village of Peace* (Affinity Vision Entertainment, USA, 63 minutes, 2014); John L. Jackson, Jr., *Thin Description: Ethnography and the African Hebrew Israelites of Jerusalem* (Cambridge, MA: Harvard University Press, 2013).

25. Howard Brotz, *The Black Jews of Harlem: Negro Nationalism and the Dilemmas of Negro Leadership* (New York: Free Press of Glencoe, 1964).

26. Magdel Le Roux, *The Lemba,* 20–24.

27. Georges Balandier, *Daily Life in the Kingdom of the Kongo: From the Sixteenth to the Eighteenth Century* (Sydney, Melbourne, Auckland, and London: Allen & Unwin, 1968), 215.

28. AM-I-FARAFINA is a community organization of Black Jews in France. It is discussed in chapter 5.

29. Tidiane N'Diaye, "Les Bantous: Entre dispersion, unité et résistance," Pambazuka News website, November 13, 2012, https://www.pambazuka.org/fr/governance/les-bantous-entre-dispersion-unité-et-résistance, accessed January 10, 2017. See Théophile Obenga, *Origine commune de l'égyptien ancien, du copte et des langues négro-africaines modernes. Introduction à la linguistique historique africaine* (Paris: L'Harmattan, 1993), and Isidore Ndaywel è Nziem, Abraham Constant Ndinga Mbo, and Tharcisse Tshibangu Tshishiku, *Hommage à Théophile Obenga—Afrique Centrale et Égypte pharaonique* (Paris: Éditions du Cygne, 2020).

30. Théophile Obenga, *L'Afrique dans l'Antiquité—Égypte ancienne—Afrique noire* (Paris: Présence Africaine, 1973); *Les Bantu, Langues-Peuples-Civilisations* (Paris: Présence Africaine, 1985).

31. Bavua Ne Longo, "Les douze tribus d'Israël," *Zaïre actualité,* no. 15 (July 15–31, 1991).

32. "Les Hébreux sont authentiquement de la race noire," 8.

33. Geoffroy Heimlich, *Le massif de Lovo, sur les traces du royaume de Kongo, vol 1* (Oxford: Archaeopress and G. Heimlich, 2017).

34. Paul Raymaekers and Hendrik van Moorsel, quoted in Heimlich, *Le massif de Lovo,* 30.

35. Jaap Van Slageren, *Influences juives en Afrique. Repères historiques et discours idéologiques* (Paris: Éditions Karthala, 2009), back cover.

36. Maurice Dorès, *La beauté de Cham: Mondes juifs, Mondes noirs* (Paris: Ballard, 1992), 30.

37. Laurent Buadi/AfricaNews, 22/07/10 / AfricaNews: La découverte au Kasaï d'un vase des Pharaons signifie-t-elle que les anciens rois d'Egypte auraient vécu en RDC ? - Congoforum.be

38. J. O. Tshimanga Mujangi Shambuyi, *Baluba et leurs origines juive et égyptienne antique* (Kinshasa: Éditions CODEKOR, 2019).

39. Moïse Rahmani, *Juifs du Congo: la confiance et l'espoir* (Saint-Gilles, Belgium: Institut Sépharade européen, 2007), 151.

40. J. R. Beloff, "Rwandan Perceptions of Jews, Judaism, and Israel," *Journal of Religion in Africa* 52, no. 3–4 (2022): 243–68, https://doi.org/10.1163/15700666-12340230.

41. J. C. Bajeux, "Mentalité noire et mentalité biblique," in Léonard Santedi Kinkupu, Gérard Bissainthe, Meinrad Hebga, eds., *Des prêtres noirs s'interrogent: 50 ans après* (Paris: Karthala, 2006).

42. Dieudonné Ake, *La vérité sur les Hébreux noirs d'Afrique et les Khazars de Palestine* (Ouragan du Midi, 2022), 65–72.

43. Pasteur Guy Roger, Thorigny sur Marne, (9) L'Afrique, l'homme noir et la Bible _ guy roger — youtube. Retrieved on September 12, 2020.

44. Vincent Wimbush, "Introduction: Scripturalizing: Analytical Wedge for a Critical History of the Human," in Vincent Wimbush, ed., *Scripturalizing the Human: The Written as the Political* (New York and London: Routledge, 2015), 1.

45. Édith Bruder, "Judaïsme africain."

46. Maurice Dorès, "La Bible et l'Afrique," FJN Internationale (feujn.org), accessed November 30, 2016, http://feujn.org/spip.php?article326.

47. Magdel Le Roux, *The Lemba*, 15.

48. See Sarah Fila-Bakabadio, *Africa on My Mind: Histoire sociale de l'afrocentrisme aux États-Unis* (Paris: Les Indes savantes, 2016).

49. Nioussérê Kalala Omotunde, *Cosmogénèse Kamite,* Tome 1 (Baie-Mahault, Guadeloupe: Anyjart, 2015); *Cosmogénèse Kamite: comprendre le grand livre céleste,* Tome 2 (Baie-Mahault, Guadeloupe: Anyjart, 2015); *Cosmogénèse Kamite: Le mystère des Divinités africaines transmuées en Saints chrétiens,* Tome 3 (Baie-Mahault, Guadeloupe: Anyjart, 2017).

50. Molefi Kete Asante, *The Afrocentric Idea*, revised and expanded edition (Philadelphia: Temple University Press, 1998), 18.

51. Cheikh Anta Diop, *Antériorité des civilisations nègres: mythe ou vérité historique?* (Paris: Présence africaine, 1967).

52. Cheikh Anta Diop, *Parenté génétique de l'égyptien pharaonique et des langues négro-africaines* (Dakar, Abidjan, and Lomé: Les Nouvelles Éditions Africaines, 1977), 29–30.

53. *Kemitiyu*, documentary film made by William Ousmane Mbaye, 2016, broadcast on TV5 Monde on November 26, 2016.

54. *Kemitiyu.*

55. Cheikh Anta Diop, *Nations nègres et culture.*

56. Cheikh Anta Diop, *Nations nègres,* 44–45.

57. Molefi Kete Asante, "Akhenaten to Origen: Characteristics of Philosophical Thought in Ancient Africa," *Journal of Black Studies* 40, no. 2 (November 2009): 301–2, 10.1177/0021934707312814 http://jbs.sagepub.com hosted at http://online.sagepub.co.

58. Mario Liverani, *La Bible et l'invention de l'histoire, Histoire ancienne d'Israël* (Paris: Bayard, 2008), 278.

59. Grégoire Biyogo, "Aux origines kemites des hébreux (sémites)," published on September 5, 2016, accessed January 30, 2017, http://afrikhepri.org/aux-origines-kemites-des-hebreux-semites/.

60. Sabbah, *Les secrets de l'exode,* 450–54.
61. Pierre Nillon, *Moïse l'Africain. La véritable histoire de Moïse* (Paris: Menaibuc, 2001); *La Véritable Bible de Moïse* (Paris: Anibwé, 2009). See also the writings and conferences of the late Jean-Philippe Omotunde, who popularized Afrocentrism and Kemitism among French-speaking audiences.
62. Nillon, *Moïse l'Africain; La Véritable Bible de Moïse,* 64–68.
63. Voltaire in Philippe Abadie, "Moïse (1/7): Le point de vue des historiens," S.B.E.V. (bible-service.net)
64. Abadie.
65. Sabbah, *Les secrets de l'exode,* 538.
66. Shmuel Trigano, "La figure biblique de Ham: Un essai de clarification."
67. Trigano, "La figure biblique de Ham."
68. Cheikh Anta Diop, *Nations nègres et culture,* 46.
69. Trigano, "La figure biblique de Ham."
70. Trigano, "La figure biblique de Ham."
71. Radu Mihaileanu, *Live and Become,* Elzévir Films, 2005.
72. Cheikh Anta Diop, *Nations nègres et cultures,* 45–46. The translation of *Gen.* 15:13–14 is from https://mechon-mamre.org/p/pt/pt0115.htm.
73. Kevin Burrell, "Kushites in the Hebrew Bible," videoconference on the YouTube channel of the Archaeological Research Facility, UC Berkeley, accessed August 19, 2021, https://www.youtube.com/watch?v=4w21n0QPunE. Aired on May 20, 2021.
74. Rashi, Genesis 12,11 in Sabbah, *Les secrets de l'exode,* 301.
75. Haïm H. Cohn, *Human rights in the Bible and Talmud* (Tel Aviv: Galei Zahal Tel Aviv University, Series Editor: Tirza Yuval, English translation, 1989), 59–60.
76. David Malki, *Les Sages de Yabneh, Le Talmud et ses Maîtres-II,* translated from Yiddish by Edouard Gourevitch (Paris: Editions Présences du Judaïsme, Albin Michel, 1983), 38–39.
77. Maimonides in Salo Wittmayer Baron, *A Social and Religious History of the Jews, High Middle Ages, 500–1200:* volume IV, *Meeting of East and West* (New York: Columbia University Press, First Printing 1957, Second Printing, 1960), 196.
78. Jan Nederveen Pieterse, *White on Black, Images of Africa and Blacks in Western Popular Culture* (New Haven and London: Yale University Press, 1992), 44.
79. Tudor Parfitt, *Black Jews in Africa and the Americas* (Harvard University Press, 2013), 30–31.
80. Trigano, "La figure biblique de Ham."
81. Anteby-Yemini, *Les juifs éthiopiens en Israël,* 497.
82. Gabriella Djerrahian, "Le discours sur la *blackness* en Israël. Évolution et chevauchements," *Ethnologie française* 45, no.2 (2015): 335, 336.
83. Djerrahian, "Le discours sur la *blackness* en Israël," n3, 339.
84. Mushon Salmona, *Une jeunesse israélienne,* Film, 2007.
85. Ahmadiel Ben Yehuda, "Israel's rabbinate reflects country's racist streak," posted online in August 2013, accessed January 28, 2017, https://972mag.com/israels-rabbinate-the-rot-of-racism-and-a-return-to-african-roots/77476/.

86. Comments made in public by Hortense Bilé during the questions and answers following the paper given by Dr. Shalva Weil, "Colour Gradations and Degradations among Ethiopian Jews in Israel" at the ISSAJ conference held at the Musée d'art et d'histoire du Judaïsme (MAHJ) in Paris, France, on November 10–11, 2015.

Chapter 3

Patterns of Conversion of Africans and West Indians to Judaism

From Christian to Jew

Studies of conversions have traditionally focused on Christianity and Islam to such an extent that there are scarcely any studies of conversions to Judaism. Sébastien Tank-Storper's sociological work is an exception that has set the stage for any scholar interested in mining that field in France. This chapter aims to continue clearing this path from an intersectional perspective, by describing the religious itineraries of African and French West Indian converts who were mostly Christians prior to becoming Jews. Here, I will analyze the motives behind their conversions as well as identity-related issues and their negotiations with the receiving institution, namely, the French Jewry.

The word "conversion" is to be understood both in the sense of the Latin verb *convertere,* which means "to turn towards," and in the sense of bifurcation, whose Latin root *bis-furcus* evokes something splitting into two and implying change, a choice between two options and a re-routing at a crossroads. The French sociologist Loïc Le Pape notes,

> conversion appears as a prime example of bifurcation. Indeed, there is a more or less lengthy sequence of action that begins with a spiritual quest, then materializes in the training of the convert by a religious institution, and ends with a specific ritual—a baptism, a ritual bath, or a religious incantation. The outcome of this sequence of action is only partly predictable, since not everyone desiring to convert necessarily obtains the necessary go-ahead from the clerics in charge of training the candidates.[1]

These remarks will be exemplified throughout this chapter, in the life stories collected among the respondents. Yet both notions—a change in religions and a bifurcation—imply that converts previously experienced a religion before embracing a new one. The spiritual voyage from a Christian identity and worldview to a Jewish one is thus always an individual one. However, I will delineate the specific ways in which conversion connects non-native Jewish men and women to the French Jewry, as well as the patterns of identity reconstruction that they implement as they change religions. The goal is to gain an insight into the choices and motivations of these believers who embraced Judaism and Jewishness and measure the impact of their conversions on their personal statuses and social lives in France.

Sébastien Tank-Storper has shown how conversions to Judaism give a premium to the institutional dimension, and how the choice and recognition of a person's conversion revolve around the social and political stakes of Jewishness and its transmission to the next generations. The parameters defining Jewishness are linked to memory, culture, ethics, politics, family, and nation, which makes the confrontation between the institutions and the candidates to conversion a locus of conflict and imposition of norms. Indeed, religious authorities' entitlement to normatively shape the practices of believers makes it necessary for anyone studying converts to first explore the path to conversion, as it determines the person's mode of identification to Judaism. Therefore, I will discuss both the host institutions and the converts, on the basis of semi-guided interviews, life stories, and analyses of documents on Judaism.

But before I do so, the very notion of conversion to Judaism must be addressed in the Bible and the history of Judaism, for it is usually considered that it is impossible to convert to Judaism due to the predominance of lineage. However, Abraham may be considered as the first convert, for God's calling impelled him to leave his birthplace of Haran, which the Bible designates as a place of idolatry. His example is said to have inspired many to embrace monotheism (*Genesis* 12:5). The second most emblematic figure of convert in the Bible is undeniably Ruth, from the land of Moab, whose famous lines to her mother-in-law Naomi read, "And Ruth said, 'Do not entreat me to leave you, to return from following you, for wherever you go, I will go, and wherever you lodge, I will lodge; your people shall be my people and your God my God'" (*Ruth,* 1:16. The Jewish Bible with a Modern English Translation and Rashi's Commentary). These words are a testament to the willpower and steadfastness that must be exemplified by a convert, as well as the latter's desire to belong to an entire people. Likewise, the Scriptures also suggest that the Queen of Sheba converted to Judaism out of love for King Solomon and bore him a son named Menelik (a.k.a. Ibn El Hakim), whom Solomon later acknowledged as his offspring, this legitimizing the Ethiopian dynasty claiming him as an ancestor.[2]

Besides, the Bible claims that the Hebrew people spent 400 years as slaves in Egypt and that they were joined by Egyptians when they left for the land of Canaan. This points to the highly probable existence of intermarriage, which sheds a new light on the concept of *ger* defining the status of foreigners, as Shmuel Trigano discusses:

> the condition of the ger designates the descendants of the erev rav, the "great multitude" that joined Israel when they left Egypt. They are not tied to Israel by lineage, but by the Law, the Sinai covenant as well as the memory of bondage in Egypt. Gerim are believed to be the descendants of the non-Hebrew slaves who merged with Israel when they were freed from Egypt. Their presence in Israel— as distinct from the separation of the Levites—is intended to morphologically inscribe in togetherness the excision of Israel out of Egypt, so that Israel's coming out of Egypt should not cause it to be self-centered.[3]

The status of the foreigner conflated with the convert is developed in these terms by Haim Hermann Cohn:

> [t]here is no such thing as "conversion" in the Bible; according to the Biblical law, every stranger is "converted" automatically; by the very fact that he is a stranger, he is a "convert." The process of conversion was only devised at the time of the Talmud, and only for "righteous strangers"; in other words, conversion was meant only for those strangers who wished to stop being strangers and wanted to become Jews; they no longer wanted to be strangers and foreigners, but wanted to become what we today would call naturalized, so that they would be accepted as if they had been naturally-born Jews. (. . .) When a person has been converted in accordance with Jewish law, there is no difference between him and any Jew; from then on he is considered to be as if he is one of the descendants of the patriarch Abraham, and in most cases he is given the name Abraham son of Abraham.[4]

This proves that throughout the history of the construction of Judaism, there have been spiritual guides who encouraged converts to continue embracing the culture, religion, and people. In the Talmud, Rabbi Elazar ben Pedat asserted that the *raison d'être* of the exile imposed upon the Jewish people is to enrich it with the presence of more converts (Treaty Pessa'him p.87/b). Maimonides, a leading figure of medieval Judaism, gave his stance on conversion in the following terms: "while we have the duty of respecting our parents and obey our prophets, our most pressing obligation concerns the converts living among us: that of loving them."[5] It thus seems undeniable that there were conversions to Judaism at the times when the Bible was written, so it is not surprising to see this tradition being continued up to the present day. Since the present study is focused on the conversions of African, Caribbean, and even African American people, it will analyze the pull factors that attracted them to Judaism and the conditions of their reception in Jewish institutions.

To begin with, "converting to Judaism is feasible but not easy"[6] as Rabbi Pierre-Yves Bauer points out. Second, candidates have to choose among the many different denominations of modern-day Judaism. On the one hand, the Israelite Consistory of Paris claims to uphold an Orthodox version of Judaism and sees itself as the most or only legitimate institution; its conversion requirements are notoriously and deliberately deterrent. On the other hand, the so-called "modernist" stream includes Reform Judaism and conservatives, also known as Masorti, as Martine Berthelot explains:

> Reform Judaism has created liberal Judaism and progressive Judaism, which are both very accepting of ideological and societal change. [. . .] Reform Judaism includes (1) Liberal-Progressives and (2) Masorti-traditionalists. Although to varying degrees (more liberal for the former, more conservative for the latter), these two branches do not consider the Halakha to be God-ordained and constraining, and thus believe that it should be adjusted to modernity, the new socio-historical contexts, and the ethics of the times. Both branches work in favor of liberalism, progress, and gender equality in particular, whether in terms of doctrine or religious observance. The religious praxis is partial for the liberals, and ore codified among the Masorti.[7]

Sébastien Tank-Storper completes the description as follows:

> Traditionalist in terms of liturgy and religious practice, Masorti Judaism self-describes as progressive on issues like individual liberties or gender equality. In contrast, the so-called orthodox branch explicitly insists on its attachment to tradition, Rabbi Joseph Caro's 1565 *Shoulkhan Aroukh,* and the sacredness of the Halakha. Two major branches can be observed: on the one hand, Haredi or ultra-orthodox Judaism, and non-Haredi orthodox Judaism. The former advocates a strict separation not only between Jews and non-Jews, but between Jews who abide by the Law and those who don't (including liberal Jews). Haredi Judaism is not built around central institutions, for each group coalesces around a yeshiva (Talmudic school) or a particular rabbinical personality. The latter branch is characterized by more moderate separatism, whether with respect to non-Jews, non-orthodox Jews, or the state of Israel. It is also more structured around institutions—the official Rabbinate of Israel or France's Central Consistory are historically closer to this branch of Judaism—and more open to compromise.[8]

In France, the Central Consistory of Paris, currently chaired by Rabbi Joël Mergui, claims to represent Orthodox Judaism in its compliance with the Halakha and be the sole authority for determining whether converts may be accepted. However, as the historian Richard Marienstras argued, nowadays "the Consistory, which theoretically 'represents' all Jews actually only expresses the views of certain segments of religious Judaism. It does not contain them all, which implies a formal, institutional, and financial limitation."[9] Likewise, the sociologist Chantal Bordes explains that

> [d]espite its evolution towards a stricter form of Judaism, the Consistory is not recognized. The leadership of Consistorial authorities is weakened by the emergence of synagogues with different proclivities. One the one hand, Lubavitch or ultra-orthodox synagogues are on the rise, and on the other hand, Liberal communities are more and more appealing to more educated believers, among whom intermarriages with non-Jews in particular are numerous.[10]

Scholars therefore seem to agree that the Consistory is on decline, but in spite of this, it remains quite attached to its—contested—monopoly in the management of petitions for conversion to Judaism in France.

Still, even if conversions to Judaism are not encouraged, they are still possible and offered by all branches, from liberal to Masorti to Orthodox to ultra-Orthodox. The Consistory's website reads,

> A community that is not open to others is doomed to go extinct. Each year, petitions from all regions of France are sent to the Consistory of Paris, and we put all our energy into welcoming and guiding the seekers in their quest. An applicant's success is also the success of the conversion department. Petitions are very diverse in nature. Some come from children of mixed (exogamous) marriages; others from non-Jewish spouses; others still, from people having no known Jewish ancestry. Every situation is considered with utmost care.[11]

Understandably, the website will not state in explicit terms how the recognition of the Central Consistory's certificates by the official Rabbinate of Israel facilitates that institution's ability to deny the right of Return (Aliyah), a literally vital stake for families in case of anti-Semitic persecutions; nor will it specify that the children of mixed marriages that it mentions may well have attended Talmud-Torah classes for all their childhood and teenage years, but still be under pressure to ask for conversion on turning eighteen. In spite of the importance of access to the right of Return, there are undeniably conversions within the Masorti and Liberal branches, and these do not include the Jews for Jesus movement,[12] which is considered to be outside of the Jewry due to their dual Judeo-Christian identity and their insistence on believing and preaching that Yeshua (Jesus) is the Messiah of the Jewish people, whose divine election they also recognize.

In spite of the lack of encouragement with which petitions for conversion are systematically met, Black converts or would-be converts are received by the Central Consistory as well as in the Masorti and Liberal branches. Consequently, among my interviewees were converts from Africa, the Caribbean, or North America who either had been accepted or were still in the process of conversion in one of these branches, as well as Jewish-born Black respondents who hailed from Ethiopia or were born to one Jewish parent, so that a diversity of origins and experiences is analyzed in the sample. It is important to point out that converting to Judaism in France, as opposed to African countries where oral tradition is given priority, implies a strong command of written tradition; this means that any convert must be educated to even begin the process. Indeed, they must first send a letter of intent to explain their reasons for converting; then, attend services very regularly within a given community; and finally, sit a final exam before a committee made up of three rabbis. All of my respondents had graduated from high school and had educational levels ranging from second year of college to completion of a doctoral degree. A majority had been formerly exposed to Biblical texts as Christians—there is no Muslim person among them—either as Roman Catholics or as Protestants, essentially in Evangelical and Pentecostal churches.

Some of their conversion journeys reflect a religiously diverse family background, as in the case of Marah, a Congolese-born Frenchman who was born in a Protestant family from the Church of Christ in Zaire, but has Muslim uncles; he had joined an Evangelical church before eventually converting to Judaism. As for Caroline, her spiritual quest began in her teenage years: "around the age of thirteen, I switched from Catholic to Protestant, and then I was without any religious affiliation. I did comparative readings on Islam, Judaism and Christianity, and I drew my own conclusions from these" (Caroline, 30, interview given in 2010). Many respondents from the subgroup of converts came from homogeneously Christian families, either Catholic or Protestant. Among them, Hanna, a woman from the Caribbean who was aged sixty-four when I interviewed her in 2009, had to overcome the opposition of her Catholic family, who even called upon their local priest to try to discourage her.

There are three types of converts, according to the French sociologist Danièle Hervieu-Léger:

> The first one is the individual who "opts for a new religion," whether because they explicitly reject an initial religious identity that had been inherited and claimed, in order to take on a new one, or because they discard an imposed religious identity that they had never embraced. The second type of convert is the person who never belonged to any given religious tradition, and undertook a more or less lengthy journey to discover one that suits them and which they ultimately decide to incorporate. . . . The third type of convert is the "re-affiliated" individual, or "insider convert," that is, the person who discovers or rediscovers their religious identity, which they had so far experienced in a superficial manner, or with minimal involvement, in a purely conformist way.[13]

CONVERTS' MOTIVATIONS

It is therefore time to explore the reasons that impelled these African or Caribbean converts to opt for Judaism. What were the catalysts, and how did they reach out to the Jewish world? The fieldwork has allowed me to identify several motives of conversion and thereby distinguish five categories of converts.

The first one is made up of people in a spiritual quest, who have followed four types of approaches. First, many respondents have quoted the chronological precedence of the Jewish religion, explaining that they had chosen to embrace it while attempting to consolidate a pre-existing faith. Marah, mentioned above, had been a preacher in an Evangelical mega church. The catalyst for his conversion to Judaism was provided when he discovered and understood a passage from Paul's *Letter to the Romans* (11:16–24) which reads:

> For if the first fruit be holy, the lump is also holy: and if the root be holy, so are the branches. And if some of the branches be broken off, and thou, being a wild olive tree, wert graffed in among them, and with them partakest of the root and fatness of the olive tree; Boast not against the branches. But if thou boast, thou bearest not the root, but the root thee. Thou wilt say then, The branches were broken off, that I might be graffed in. Well; because of unbelief they were broken off, and thous standest by faith. Be not highminded, but fear: For if God spared not the natural branches, take heed lest he also spare not thee. Behold therefore the goodness and severity of God: on them which fell, severity; but toward thee, goodness, if thou continue in his goodness: otherwise thou also shalt be cut off. And they also, if they abide not still in unbelief, shall be graffed in: for God is able to graff them in again. For if thou wert cut out of the olive tree which is wild by nature, and wert graffed contrary to nature into a good olive tree: how much more shall these, which be the natural branches, be graffed into their own olive tree?

While preparing a sermon on this passage, he made the decision to be grafted into the root, that is, convert to Judaism through the Consistory of Paris (Marah, interview given in 2010). As for Myriam, a Masorti convert who was born a Catholic, this is how she described her journey:

> I kept wondering about the origin, where it came from, what was the source of the Christian religion; At one point, when growing up, as I had been a Catholic by birth, I looked into other religions, including Islam, and I dug deeper by reading the Qur'an, but I never felt the urge to convert to Islam. On the contrary, the more I discovered about Judaism, the more I felt something while reading the texts and watching the documentaries. I always felt this closeness, due to the

fact that it [Judaism] is at the root of everything. . . . By nature, I feel the urge to find the source of everything. So at one point, I told myself, "Here I am, am I going to find something deeper in Judaism?" . . . That's why I took the final step. (Myriam, 33, BA, interview given in 2010)

The second subgroup of converts in the category of spiritual seekers comprises those for whom a life crisis or comparable existential problems have catalyzed a conversion to Judaism. A female respondent born in Martinique and a convert in the Orthodox (consistorial) branch under the name Hanna explained her choice as follows:

I have been Jewish for five years. I am from Martinique. I am a form of anomaly, because I converted very late in life, at sixty, and my family didn't go along. You know, in life you make choices, after giving them a lot of thought, and to begin with, if you want to be a Jew you must be very brave, you must be very persistent, and have a lot of conviction. You can't come in dragging your feet and saying, "well today the weather is good so I'm going to be a Jew." Now that's not going to work. . . . I was not familiar with Judaism before, I discovered it because I was seeking for something. I had just suffered the loss of my husband at the very same time I went on retirement. I was a jurist, I worked for the Inspection of Finances department. As I was going through a lot, really, I was wondering why, and asking myself lots of questions. The Catholics couldn't give me any answers. And then one day it dawned on me just like that, I understood that Jews have something special, and I began buying books. And one day the young lady who was selling these books to me told me, "you know, we can't leave you struggling on your own, you need someone to guide you," and she put me in contact with a Rabbi. . . . It is a completely personal quest, and I wouldn't advise anybody to do what I did, because it's tough to be Jewish. (Hanna, 64, interview given in 2009)

The third subgroup of spiritual seekers includes those for whom the unplanned discovery of books on Jewish spirituality, or the viewing of films and documentaries on the Holocaust, or encounters with Jewish mentors have prompted a process of identification with the Jewish people. This is the case of Guershon Nduwa, a native of the Democratic Republic of Congo, who sought out a spiritual mentor while a student in Cameroon:

Before I went to Israel, I was a student in Yaoundé, where I met Rabbi Leon Ashkenazi. He was friends with the President of Cameroon. He often spoke about spirituality on television, and he really piqued my interest. I asked for an appointment so I could meet him in person, and it was an uphill battle because he had bodyguards. I fought for an entire week because I was determined to see him. And finally they told him, "there's a gentleman out there who's been waiting for five days to see you" and he said, "let him in." So I got to meet him and tell him that I felt attracted to Judaism and that I had a strong desire to be part of the Jewish people. He said to me, "converting is fine, but you have to have three rabbis. I only come to Cameroon every now and then, and there are no rabbis the rest of the time. So even if you study hard, your conversion won't happen, simply because you need three rabbis, and from different countries on top of that. How are they going to supervise your studies if one is in Cameroon, another one in Nigeria and the third one in the Congo? I would advise you to go to Israel, where I could be your supervisor." (Guershon Nduwa, 51, interview given in 2015)

Likewise, Caroline, born into a Catholic family, embarked on a spiritual quest that led her first to Evangelical churches and then to Islam, where she said she found no adequate answers. She found those in Judaism, particularly in Maimonides' writings:

Actually the one book that really turned me around in a decisive manner was Maimonides' *Guide for the Perplexed*. This book is fundamental to me and to my understanding of my faith. When I read Maimonides, I moved on to the next stage, which was to become a Jew through the process of conversion. I enrolled at the Consistory of Paris, and since then I have been studying to be admitted. (Caroline, 30, interview given in 2010)

The love of Judaism and the Hebrew language are also mentioned by others as reasons for converting. Among these is Albert, a fifty-year-old French man of Togolese descent, who used to pastor an Evangelical congregation of around a hundred members. Attracted to the Hebrew language and civilization, which he studied at the Sorbonne, he decided to renounce his Christian faith to convert to Judaism. He went to Israel, asked for conversion, and became a rabbi. His congregation did not follow him down that path; only his wife and around twenty of his congregants attend the synagogue of Les Ulis, in the greater Paris area.

Finally, a more mystical subgroup of spiritual seekers say they have responded to a divine calling in becoming Jewish; among them are several former pastors of Holiness-Pentecostal churches. For instance, Ofer, a native of the Democratic Republic of Congo who holds a doctoral degree in theology, embraced Judaism following a series of dreams. Shortly after arriving in France, while a preacher in Congolese Evangelical churches, he had three significant dreams:

I dreamed that I was on a bus with, on my left, the Jewish people and on my right, the non-Jews, and I stood in the middle holding the Israeli flag, raising it high in the air and shouting three times, "Reunification, reunification, reunification." I did not wake up then and had a second dream, in which I was taking a walk in a Jewish section of town and suddenly found myself in front of a house in which a Rabbi was teaching an audience of Jews. I was struggling to get in, and it was difficult to enter, so I got around the building to get through the back door and fraudulently listen to the teachings given by the Rabbi. At the end of the service, I followed two women that had come out of that house and gave them my business card, telling them I wanted to be part of their gatherings from now on. Two days later, I dreamed that I was taking part in a group chat between the Liberal and Orthodox branches, and I eventually found the answer that bridged the gap between the two branches. (Ofer, 30, interview given in 2009)

Conversions triggered by a mystical belief in dreams as vectors of a calling are very frequent in Christian circles, especially in Evangelical and Pentecostal churches, but less common among converts to Judaism. Yet, for Ofer, these dreams were highly significant and decisive in his choice to embrace Judaism. He now worships at a Liberal synagogue in the greater Paris area.

The second category of converts is distinct from these examples of individuals actively searching for Judaism, insofar as it gathers African respondents who have been immersed in Israeli culture and decided to embrace Judaism as a result. They either grew up there as children of diplomats or migrated to Israel as students or interns, and even as they remained attached to their African origins, they naturally embraced the religious culture as they gradually adopted Israel as their new homeland. They define it as the country that revealed Judaism to them and instilled in them a deep feeling of religious belonging, thanks to lived experience in Jewish communities.

Yann, a native of Congo Brazzaville aged thirty-four when I interviewed him, provides a good illustration of such a discovery of Judaism through immersion in Israeli life:

> I was living like a Jew but I did not want to mingle with the Orthodox religious branch. In Israel people are free to choose whether to pray or not to pray, to wear a kippah while not going to the synagogue. This is liberty in the democratic sense of the term. This is the way I used to live my faith. I would associate with Christian evangelical circles, but I felt like a Jew. . . . I would wear a kippah, fast on the Day of Kippur, and observe all the great holidays. I was lucky, because I stayed with an Israeli host family who adopted me like a child, so I really experienced Judaism on a daily basis. It was up to me whether to take the necessary steps to actually become a convert. I had decided not to, because to me it wasn't a priority. But when I came to France, I felt something worse than vacuum inside, and I told myself that I don't feel at home here. I cried and I called my host family to tell them I needed to return home. But they said, "you spent money on your studies, you should stay there." So I decided to convert, I wanted this to go fast. (Yann, 34, interview given in 2009)

This testimony is enlightening because the strong sense of belonging expressed by this convert is focused on the experience of finding a new home in Israel and embracing Judaism as a result of homesickness. It is significant that he did not feel the need to officially convert to Judaism as long as he was able to practice Judaism within an inclusive Israeli environment (which he defines in political terms, as "democratic"), but that it became urgent to become visibly Jewish upon arriving in France, because in that new country, the combination of Blackness and Jewishness in one individual was so unthinkable that the only way to keep his sanity was to opt for conversion. It is worth emphasizing that those converts who, like Yann, came to Judaism via life experiences in Israel are often late converts, for they typically begin the process in France, to join a minority group of the Diaspora, rather than in Israel where Judaism is part of the mainstream.

The third category is composed of individuals who claim to have Hebrew origins and therefore refuse to go through the conversion process. They identify as native Jews but are in need of religious legitimacy, as their right of Return under the Aliyah law has yet to be affirmed by religious authorities. Indeed, "Beta Israel" Ethiopians (also known as Falashas) whose families had settled in France before the repatriation operations of the 1980s and 1990s (Operation Moshe, Solomon, or Joshua) have not benefited from these and now have to go to Ethiopia in order to prove their Jewishness, a constraint they object to.

I indeed met Ethiopian Jews who had lived in France for a very long time but refused to be forced to convert in order to prove the legitimacy of their Jewishness. For example, Dov had this to say:

> My grandmother is a Yemeni Jew; she lived in Israel and then they returned to Ethiopia. I have lived in France from the time I was four. My mother worked for the United Nations and my father had an administrative job. Here in France I was reunited with an Ethiopian uncle, and it is with him and thanks to him that I am learning my family history. I have done a lot of talking with my parents and I have yet to return to Ethiopia and see where my house is; once this is done, then I will go to Israel, because if you want to go there you need to be legitimate. (Dov, 38, interview given in 2009)

Having lived as Jews all their lives, bearing Jewish first and last names, these converts are placed in the paradoxical situation of being native Jews who need to prove their legitimacy in two successive stages: first by going to Ethiopia to obtain their certificate of Jewishness there, and then by going to Israel as refugees. This represents a contrast with the "Refuznik" Jews of the former USSR, who were never forced to return to Russia to ground their claims to Aliyah but on the contrary, were helped in their visa requests by the pressure exerted on the USSR.[14]

By the same token, other African groups claim to have Hebrew ancestry and belong to the Jewish people also refuse to go through the process of conversion. Among these are Igbos from Nigeria, Danites from the Ivory Coast, Lembas from South Africa, or Black Hebrew Israelites. For instance, Claudine, who is of French Caribbean and African American descent and was raised in the Baptist church, had lived in metropolitan France since the 1980s when I interviewed her; she identified as a Black Jew (see chapter 2) and worshiped at the Synagogue Copernic in the sixteenth arrondissement of Paris, but refused to go through conversion. A young Danite who came to France at age five with his family from the Ivory Coast was aged twenty-six when I interviewed him; he and his nine siblings are well known in Black Jewish circles in France as "the Kohen brothers." He and his family, considering they have always complied with Jewish traditions and identified as Jewish, refuse conversion but used to worship in French synagogues. All these individuals from various groups that claim historical Jewishness struggle to be accepted within one of the Jewish communities of France, exactly like the other Black Jews I have met (see chapter 4).

The fourth category of converts is made up of partners in interracial marriages (see chapter 6). As in the case of those who lived in Israel, daily life with a Jewish spouse gradually led some of them to embrace Judaism. Others focus more on transmitting Jewishness to their offspring; several women respondents decided to convert before marrying their partners in order to save their children the hassle of conversion, or, if they have grown up as Jews, they either submit to the conversion process in hopes of marrying a (White) Jew or insist on forcing their partners to convert to Judaism before marriage. This group includes biracial Jews, whether native or converts.

While her case is slightly different, Hortense is part of this category because she converted to Judaism out of motherly love, as her son had developed a passion for Judaism after attending Talmud Torah classes with his best friend:

> It was during the holiday of Kippur. Before Kippur I used to tell everybody, "I am just here to accompany my son and better understand, as a mother, what he has to do with respect to Kosher food; given that he wants to do his bar-mitzvah, I want to have a better understanding." I wasn't intending to aim for conversion, and I said it to the Rabbi. Then came the period of Rosh Hashanah. . . . So I had to attend the festival of Rosh Hashanah every morning at seven, and somehow I felt a calling. I have to say that at the moment of the sounding of the Shofar for Rosh Hashanah, when I heard that sound, I felt something stirring in me. I can't tell you exactly what it was that I felt, but it was like a calling—and then the solemnity of the worship services, the kavvanah, I must say it's really the

kavvanah, that's what really attracted me in Judaism, I loved the way he says the prayers, I loved the explanations, I loved the sermons given on Shabbat to explain the Parasha that would be read afterwards, the next day and everything. So yes, Kippur with the sound of the shofar, there was something inside of me, a voice inside that made me understand that I had found my home, I didn't need to look anywhere else, because I had found what I was looking for and I could stop seeking. I had already begun to take Hebrew classes with my son, and I began to take Judaism classes to understand Judaism. Actually, I don't know how to explain it to you, maybe it was a mother's love for her son that was rewarded. I had just wanted to accompany him and I got into Judaism, now I'm in it heart and soul and I have no regrets. (Hortense, 60, interview given in 2010)

A fifth and last category gathers Africans who chose to convert to Judaism because they subjectively identify as Hebrews as a consequence of their ethnicity. Indeed, today in many African countries, several ethnic groups claim to be authentic Hebrews (see chapter 2). Consequently, people who have grown up with these references may choose to reconnect with their roots by converting to what they consider to be their ancestors' religion—following Hervieu-Léger's third type of convert, described earlier in this chapter. For instance, Josué, a forty-five-year-old convert of Cameroonian origin, justified his joining the Lubavitch Orthodox community by contending that his ethnic group claims to belong to the Hebrew people, even though his family worships at a Baptist church. This is how he explains it:

In Cameroon, I belong to an ethnic group that considers itself as descending from Hebrews. It is the Douala ethnic group, from a very specific region. My grandmother always told me that we are Christians, but our true religion is Judaism. I have lived in France for 35 years now. I was on a spiritual quest; I had many Jewish friends and I had resolved to place an official request. I went to lots of synagogues as a visitor, but the fruit was not ripe yet. The catalyst was in 1994 and I began attending the Consistory in 1997 and I learnt the Torah. I began the conversion process in 1997 but it is a slow process: it lasted nine years. (Josué, 45, interview given in 2009)

In these cases, conversion is seen as a confirmation of their subjective identification with the Jewish people. Likewise, converts from the Caribbean often cite an imaginary genealogy that is reinforced by a genealogical search. For instance, Dine, a native of Guadeloupe, explained that her decision to convert to Judaism came from the results of her genealogical search, which indicated that her White ancestors were Jewish, not from Brittany as she had believed so far.

Besides these five classes of respondents, I have also interviewed people who identify as Jewish but do not practice or convert to Judaism, or even identify with the Jewish people, which they often consider as "phony Jews"—the "real" ones being Black Hebrews, according to them. For example, Yann told me:

> I kept looking at the Jews from Ukraine and Russia, with their White skins and blue eyes—how surprising! I said, "these can't be real Jews." To me they could not be the real Jews, it was too surprising, it just can't be—or else I haven't read the Bible! I haven't read the story of Moses, then! Moses must have been born somewhere, right? . . . I have no scientific explanation, but to the best of my knowledge, the Hebrews lived four hundred years in Egypt, so they had time to get a little tan with the sun. Even if they had been White before, four hundred years is enough to be a little Black. So how did *these* guys embrace Judaism? How is it that back in Ukraine, Russia, Poland or Hungary, they embraced Judaism? How did they do that, I wonder. It is more obvious that in Africa, Jews were a bit more tanned, and dark-skinned. (Yann, 34, interview given in 2009)

Likewise, Aurélie, a female respondent with Ivorian and Senegalese parents, identifies as Jewish on account of her Pullo (Fulani) ethnic background, and while worshiping in Reform synagogues in Rouen (Normandy), she sees no point in converting to Judaism. While Yann, the male respondent quoted above, did submit to the process that she considers unnecessary, there are many other Black French persons who are simply claiming a Jewish identity on social media, without joining any practicing or cultural community pertaining to the French Jewry. Given their prior Christian identities and the various reasons underlying their identification to Judaism, conversion processes among them are diverse and their responses often hint at the necessity of accounting for their former Christian references within Jewish circles, whether they like it or not.

A CHRISTIAN OR A JEWISH IDENTITY?

Christian identity implies the belief that Jesus is the only Son of God and the Messiah, or Savior of humankind. This dogma, which was consolidated in the Nicene Creed in 325 C.E., caused anti-Judaism in many European countries with Christian monarchs, who ordered Jews' forced conversion to Christianity, or their expulsion or even their slaughter, under the accusation that Jews had caused the death of Jesus at the hands of the Romans (see chapter 1). By the same token, Africa, as well as other colonized continents, was Christianized before and after the Triangular Trade, sometimes by force, and missionaries naturally transmitted this brand of antisemitism to the new Christian converts. Judaism does not recognize Jesus as the Messiah, let alone the Son of God, and has no special place for him even if he is now the best-known and most beloved Jew in the world. Most Jews are still expecting the coming of a Messiah whom they do not identify as Jesus, while Christians, for over two thousand years, have believed that the Messiah has already come in the person of Jesus, and saved humankind, provided his godly nature is acknowledged. Therefore, it is understandable that African and Caribbean Christians converting to Judaism may have difficulties discarding the belief in Jesus as Messiah and Savior of humankind.

Hence, their identification to the Jewish people is complicated by their Christian baggage in three major ways. One is marked by uneasiness, as in the case of Florence, a Caribbean French thirty-two-year-old woman, now a member of the Reform Judaism movement. She confessed that she was apprehensive of the way her former Christian identity would be received. But her fears were appeased at the door of the synagogue, when she heard an American female rabbi sigh "Jesus!" in English, to complain about the rain outside (Florence, 37, interview given in 2011).

Doubts about the possible Christian identity of Black Jews are also linked to the case of the Falash Mura—Ethiopian Jews who underwent conversion to Christianity in 1800 and are often caught in between their Christian identity and their Jewish roots. Although officially considered as non-Jews, many of them emigrated to Israel between the 1990s and the early 2010s, and had to show evidence of their complete conversion to Orthodox Judaism to obtain full citizenship. Indeed, they are frequently suspected of being missionaries seeking to convert their Ethiopian neighbors to Christianity. Don Seeman has shown how Falash Mura individuals who converted to Pentecostal Christian denominations currently occupy a minority position vis-à-vis both the Beta Israel and the Israeli mainstream.[15]

Bearing this in mind, during the interviews, I mentioned the 2005 feature film *Live and Become*,[16] inspired from the experience of the Beta Israel Ethiopian Jews, whose rescue operation is used by a desperate Christian widow to save her nine-year-old son from starvation and death by having him take the place of a dead Jewish boy (with the consent of the latter's mother) so that he may leave his home country for Israel. The character, renamed Shlomo, has to face several challenges, including transracial adoption, as he learns to live with his new family, classmates from the Talmud-Torah, and Israeli society in general. My respondents' reactions to his story seem to echo their own experiences, as well as concern with an amalgam between themselves and the Falash Mura. For instance, Hannah, an Ethiopian woman who was part of the repatriation scheme, said:

> When it came out, my daughter told me, "Mom, go and watch this film!" and I said, "No, anything but, because I'm not sure they tell the truth." To my knowledge, a good many Ethiopian Jews did not watch *Live and Become,* because I

know my history better than *Live and Become*. *Live and Become* is not about a Jew, but a young Orthodox Christian who becomes Jewish because his mother told him to leave, convert, and have a better life in Israel—and that's what happened. . . . When Operations Solomon and Moshe took place, many Orthodox Christians came along with the Ethiopian Jews to Israel, just as there were Russians who did the same thing just to land in Israel. That is an existential problem, for sure; but for whom? (Hannah, 54, interview given in 2013)

As for Guershon, he explained that he had disliked the passing of a Christian child for a Jew:

I did watch the film, but I'm not crazy about it, because it's a very stereotypical film. There are too many stereotypes: they show a Christian kid who was saved by Judaism, and that's not accurate. It's about a Black kid who is cast as a Christian. When you think about it, for someone like me who lived in Israel, it's exaggerated. This is extreme caricature, and that's very dangerous. For my part, that's not the way I see Judaism. He shouldn't have been a Christian child. The children who were taken to Israel were *Jewish* children who left Ethiopia. (Guershon, 45, interview given in 2009)

These two responses concur in criticizing a story which tends to invalidate the Jewishness of the Beta Israel by presenting the rescue operations concerning them as demonstrating the hospitality of the state of Israel, whereas the Aliyah concerns all Jews of the Diaspora. Indeed, the right of Return automatically grants Israeli nationality to any individual recognized as a Jew when they apply for immigration. It is the legal translation of the bond between the Jewish people worldwide and the state of Israel, embodying a fundamental principle of the Hebrew state, namely, the guarantee of a safe haven for Jews from all countries.[17]

However, for some of the respondents who used to be Christians before their conversion—unlike my Ethiopian interviewees—a measure of ambivalence may exist at times; this is the second main finding about converts' complicated stance. For instance, I was told by a Jewish colleague that a Black convert, although validated by the Consistory of Paris, once forgot in the synagogue after worship service a bag that contained several flyers of Jews for Jesus, which prompted the people who returned the bag to automatically assimilate him to one of them. Another convert told me at the end of our interview that for him, the Messiah expected by the Jews would arrive on the Second Coming of Christ, announced in the Book of Revelation.

Finally, for some respondents who identify as Jews, Christian identity may also be associated to Jewish life in an explicit manner. Such is the case of Emeka and Alo, both of them Igbos from Nigeria who live in France, used to be Evangelical Christians before embracing Judaism, and are members of the Jews for Jesus movement. On the day I interviewed Emeka, he was visibly upset on arriving. When I inquired about the reasons for his anger, Emeka explained to me that he had just walked out of the meeting of the French Federation of Black Jews (FJN, see chapter 5) because its president, Guershon Nduwa, had demanded that he renounce his faith in Jesus, if he was serious about being Jewish and being recognized by the state of Israel—which was out of the question for him (Emeka and Alo, 33 and 27, interview given in 2013).

In effect, where African and Caribbean converts are concerned, pre-Jewish identity mainly revolves around the person of Jesus and former beliefs or teachings about him. Whereas Jews usually reject Jesus as a result of the persecutions suffered at the hands of Christians, Black converts who were previously socialized in the Christian faith seem to struggle with the obligation of renouncing their attachment to Jesus. Consequently, when I ask them what Jesus represents for them, their answers reveal a certain hesitation regarding the place he should hold. Hortense, an Ivorian-born convert, described Jesus

> as a prophet and no more. [I see him] as someone who came to revolutionize religion, for Judaism was losing its soul. . . . Jewish people were really lost as regards all the teachings they had received, and the miracles from the Almighty, they were no longer practicing. You must see this in relation to the chronology of the Bible, every time the Almighty came back to His people's rescue because He chose this particular people to actually embody the mystery of His Word. So every time, He sent someone to redeem them. So for me, Jesus is a prophet, who came to revolutionize things and remind the people that the Almighty is eternal. (Hortense, 60, interview given in 2010)

Responding to the same question, Marah, the former Evangelical preacher who is now a rabbi and the head of the Jerusalem-based Yeshiva Botsina Kadisha, answered as follows:

> This is a question that many people ask me. You have to know that the invaluable information that I got about Jesus from Judaism—information from the Talmud and elsewhere . . . have long remained secret for fear of retaliation. But Judaism knows the character very well. Now my personal understanding of the character is that I no longer consider him to be the sole intermediary between me and God. I learnt and understood that we can talk to God directly. . . . Judaism says a very important thing, which is that the reason why there have been Jesus and Mohamed is that there was a specific goal, namely, preparing the world to understanding the coming of the Messiah. But you can't say overnight that because we know someone's going to come, then that must be him, you just can't do that. It is necessary to ingrain into people's minds the notion that a person is going to come; now, for spiritual and religious reasons Jesus is perceived as a Jew that revolutionized the world and he's an essential figure of Judaism

because he allowed the people to understand what the Torah is about, because he was not a Christian himself, he was Jewish. I do not deny his mystical abilities, he did several things, which I recognize. But the messianic function is not the same in Christianity, for me he is an essential figure who lived an incredible life. (Marah, 27, interview given in 2010)

As for Albert, another former pastor, he explained:

We can read in Hosea, Chapter 2, Israel in its entirety is the son of God . . . and you can find it again in *Hosea* Chapter 11 verse 1, Israel in its entirety is called by God the son of God . . . then if you look at *Deuteronomy* 14 verse 1, the whole of Israel is addressed here: "you are children of God." Now we must consider, if we are Christians, that there is a way of speaking in the East which is called metonymy, that is, expressing what is small in terms of what is big, and what is big in terms of what is small. In other words, if you want to speak of the entirety of Israel for example, you can pick a specimen who is Jesus, and when speaking of Israel, you will say that the whole of Israel is the child of God, but you can just as well call Israel the Son of God. When you use this phrase, you are speaking of the entire household; it's the same as if I had a cup of tea and said, "I drank a cup of tea," well it's not actually the cup that I drank, for the cup is just the container, but I drank the tea that was in it. This is metonymy and it is very common in their way of writing; those who wrote saying that he [Jesus] is the Son of God were not liars, since he is a part of Israel and Israel in its entirety is called the Son of God. I believe you know the verse from *Hosea* Chapter 5 that says, "Let my first-born son go, so that he may worship me," well Israel is that first-born. Well you find this again in *Romans* 8, verses 29 to 30, Christ is the first-born who must lead the rest in the image of His Son. So when they write in that way, they pick up things in the Old Testament and they say, "Here you are, this is materialized in Christ." While in fact it is not Jesus alone who is the Son of God, but any person who is a Jew is the son of God, the twelve tribes of Israel are called sons of God. (Albert, 52, interview given in 2015)

Although these respondents are not part of the Jews for Jesus movement and no longer consider Jesus to be the Messiah, let alone an incarnation of God, their perception of Jesus suggests a form of affection and sympathy for the person he was, contrary to the native-born Jews who, having had no exposure to Christian teaching, express unmitigated rejection of Jesus. Today, as exegesis scholar Sébastien Doane explains,

Saying that Jesus is the equivalent of God is considered blasphemous by Jews and Muslims. In their eyes, this way of presenting Jesus puts him on the same plane as God and makes him God's equal. This way of designating Jesus is not congruent with their understanding of the oneness of God. It is therefore a stumbling block in the interfaith dialog among the three monotheistic religions.

Jews and Muslims are willing to acknowledge Jesus as a wise man or a prophet, but making him God's equal is a great scandal.[18]

I had the opportunity to ask Dr. Gilles Bernheim,[19] the former Grand Rabbi of France, why Jesus, the universal Jew who is so revered around the world, does not contribute to Jewish pride but is rather rejected by Jews, and if, without being seen as the Son of God, he could have been a prophet or even an important rabbi in his people. Countering the outrage expressed by the mostly Jewish audience in response to my question, Rabbi Bernheim answered in a benevolent tone that the question was less naïve than it seemed, and proceeded to explain that Jews' rejection of Jesus was due to the circumstances in which his teachings were imposed upon Jewish minorities across Europe, in a climate of violence, massacres, and forced conversions which could not but foster hatred and loathing for the figure of Jesus.

More surprisingly, not only do my convert respondents depict a less negative image of Jesus, but some even say he played a part in their conversion. For example, Sarah—the African wife of Albert, the former pastor—who was initially reluctant to follow her husband's choice, eventually did so because she heard Jesus' voice tell her that she should go with her husband to the synagogue because the Jesus in whom she had faith was also a Jew himself. In this case, Jesus, while having no status in the contemporary Jewry, can be seen as a bridge between these converts' former Christian identity and their new Jewish one.

However, after conversion, the frontier between the two legacies appears to be clearer, albeit not entirely solidified. Indeed, having experienced Christianity from the inside and having relatives who still identify as Christians, African, Caribbean, and African American converts do not necessarily feel the need to reject Christianity. Besides, it must be pointed out that Judeo-Christian dialog began before these converts embraced Judaism, as it started after World War II under the aegis of Protestant churches.[20] The budding sense of guilt of some European intellectuals after the Holocaust began to be documented fostered a new attitude among European Protestant churches, advocating a rejection of anti-Judaism as well as atonement for the sin of the Holocaust. The exchanges[21] that took place in Germany in 1961 between Protestant Christians and Jews led to the expression of an official declaration of the then World Council of Christian Churches, that "anti-Semitism is a sin against God and mankind," that the covenant between God and Jews is a perennial one, and that the Christian theology of the substitution of Jews by Christians as the Chosen People should be discarded.[22]

The rapprochement with the Catholic church was materialized in the form of a text entitled "The Gifts and the Calling of God are Irrevocable."[23] It included three particularly significant elements, namely an emphasis on the

Jewish roots of Christianity, and the shift from the banality of anti-Judaism to its condemnation, as well as that of the Christian claim that the church is the new people of God, born of a new covenant canceling the "old covenant." The Biblical covenant between God and Jews is now still considered valid by virtue of the forebears, among whom Apostle Paul is even presented as the precursor of Judeo-Christian relations. The new document, elaborated for the fiftieth anniversary of the Conciliar Declaration *Nostra Aetate* of 1965, is a sum of "reflections on theological questions about Catholic-Jewish relations. These usher in the shift from mutual monologs to dialog, which demands mutual respect between the two religions," explains historian Menahem Macina, who was born Catholic but embraced Judaism without renouncing his Christian faith. In his writings, Jews and Christians are described as "two irreductible elects" and "the two faces of the same mystery." He sees Jewish and Christian identities as inseparable, and considers the rebirth of Israel as a nation as "the ultimate stage of the incarnation of divine design."[24]

Consequently, it is understandable that African and Caribbean converts with Christian baggage may remain open to interfaith dialog and sensitive to the Christian teachings they received prior to embracing Judaism, whether these persist in their new religious identity or undergo criticism. Ofer, a musician and former pastor of an Evangelical church, has not renounced his Christian culture, since he leads a Gospel band that sings both Jewish and Christian themes, both in French and in Hebrew. Yet the Christian heritage and particularly the notions of Christian doctrine received in the past are now reassessed and critiqued through the new Jewish concepts that they acquired through conversion and the study that it necessarily implies. Myriam gave a good example of this critical distance:

> I think that I needed a structure, though, perhaps because I was raised and educated in a Catholic institution, so I also felt like living my faith with other people and especially practice collectively, because for me it's a way of expressing my faith in another way than by prayers. . . . Here there are other people, shared meals, parties, get-togethers and lectures, there are so many things. Had I been all by myself I would not have cultivated as I do now my relationship with God. (Myriam, 31, interview given in 2009)

These remarks emphasize a rejection of the individualistic nature of mainstream Catholicism in France and, conversely, a need to be part of a close-knit community, even if the dominant discourse is adverse to ethnic enclaves. As for Caroline, who converted in the Consistory of Paris, she stressed the lack of consistency of Catholic prayers:

For example, [I'm thinking of] the Catholic prayers that were written by emperors and that are based on nothing. When I think in depth about what people say, for instance in one of the Catholics' prayers they say, "Holy Mary, mother of God"—well, in my understanding of God, He doesn't have a mother. (Caroline, interview given in 2010)

Hortense is also critical of her Catholic past when she contrasts her former religious practice to the new one:

I must say I was a Catholic Christian before. From the age of seventeen I refused to take communion, because I did not understand the meaning of communion. What is communion all about in reality? It's about sharing. But among the Christians, the meaning of it wasn't really given, they said it was about receiving the body of Jesus. I couldn't wrap my mind around that, so I asked several priests but never got accurate answers. In reality, communion is the sharing of bread. Sharing means breaking all that is negative in us. When you share with other people you don't know, you bring them positivity, which is love. Here you didn't need to have gone through First Communion. I wasn't Jewish, but I broke bread with them. I saw how children, even very young ones, share and hand out the food, and we Christians don't have that. There is wine, or grape juice, for the priests, and I could watch them drinking it; the Protestants also share, though not in the same way. And that was not sharing, it was distribution and that was it. On the contrary, here it is about sharing your bread, and feeling what you are doing. All of this—a dot, then a comma, make a semi-colon—led me to conversion. And then I had my mind very much set, I don't mean I thought that Jews are very good or very evil, you have a mix of both everywhere. But whatever I rejected in Christianity and whatever I accepted in Christianity, is understood more in depth among Jews. They express things in a deeper manner. (Hortense, interview given in 2010)

Moshé's testimony is also critical of a key dimension of Catholicism: "when I used to pray as a Catholic, we had too many intermediaries, and I had enough of that. Instead of talking to God directly, you asked His servants" (Moshé, interview given in 2010). This view is shared by Micheline, who spends her time between France and the Ivory Coast:

When I was a Catholic, I didn't quite feel at home: I was told about Jesus, and the Virgin Mary, I was told that Jesus is the Son of God, born of a virgin, and these were notions I was struggling with, I couldn't wrap my mind around them. After getting baptized, I went to Mass but I felt like an outsider, because I had no answers to my questions. I asked several priests to explain me certain things but none of them was helpful. So there came a time when I stopped going to church. When I came to France, I broke all ties with the Church. (Micheline, interview given in November 2020)

These respondents concur in emphasizing their new understanding of the New Testament as well as rituals that they used to practice when they were Christians, clarifying these religious practices and concepts. They insist on the centrality of the communal experience in their chosen religious identity.

Conversely, other interviewees who still identify as Christians but are experimenting with Judaism are led to a gradual immersion in the Jewish world, if not to actually becoming Jews themselves. Claudine, a forty-year-old native of Guadeloupe, was raised in the Catholic tradition, but has opted for Evangelical Protestantism. However, she increasingly attends synagogues because she has recurrent dreams and visions drawing her toward the Jews. She used to ask herself existential questions, wondering why she was on earth and why she faced psychological issues and inhibitions that she couldn't overcome. She began to find answers in the Bible:

> I see myself constantly in dreams, either in a big room or in a party with Jews, it happens all the time, really all the time. These are dreams I keep having. The vision I had also is that I was in a big garden in an estate, with a table around which stood many Jews wearing kippahs, and I was getting into a covenant with the Jewish people, that is, I was getting married. From then on, I told myself, "Why not get closer to that suffering people?" So that's how I got closer, by associating with some community organizations, trying to accompany them, particularly in protests against antisemitism. So, I began getting into Christian organizations which are like me, into activism for Jews. Because of all the visions I've got, I felt I couldn't sit idly by and remain on the side. It's as if this had been imposed on me, in some sort of way, since I began having these visions and dreams, I understood I had to get involved on that level as well. . . .
>
> I found myself like Moses, looking at a tree that's never consumed, and then the Lord came out of it with the hammer like a very harsh judge, telling me, "It's irrevocable!" I said a prayer and a little later I went to a seminar that was organized by an association of Messianic Jews. They had a book there on the table which showed the very same vision I had had, so you can imagine my surprise. I saw that same vision on the book cover, so I looked at the title and it was *The Irrevocable Calling*. I went to a Rabbi to understand the meaning of this, and he told me that all of those who have had this irrevocable calling had a calling for Israel. So now I am committed to Israel. (Claudine, interview given in 2015)

For the time being, this respondent says she does not feel the need to convert to Judaism, but that she believes she must "accompany the Jews" to act upon what her visions tell her. Given the recurrent nature of her dreams and her increasing ties with Jewish milieus, it seems quite likely that she will eventually convert to Judaism.

Once admitted as converts, Africans and Caribbeans become integrated in Jewish communities on the basis of identity parameters which are considered as constitutive of ethnicity, namely: the ideology of Hebrew ancestry by matrilineal descent, the Bible as a shared history, Kosher food, circumcision, a special link to the territory of Israel, Hebrew first and last names, and the memory of the Holocaust.

The Ideology of Hebrew Ancestry by Matrilineal Descent

The notion of a common ancestry suggests that all Jews have a common ancestor—Abraham, who lived in an undetermined Biblical past—and dispersed around the world after several invasions and destructions of the Temple. Today, under rabbinical law, the Jewishness of a person is determined by that of their mother. This has consequences for any convert; but it is especially true of Black ones, whose Otherness is more visible. How do Black converts position themselves vis-à-vis this ideology of matrilineal descent in a context of rising interest in genealogical research? The historian Nadia Malinovich explains:

> it is misguided to associate Jewishness to any specific race or ethnicity. This is even reinforced by the possibility of converting to Judaism: even if Jewishness does not boil down to a religious identity, this dimension of Jewishness still distinguished it from other ethno-racial categories. Hence reality makes it even more vexing to answer the age-old question, "Who is a Jew?"[25]

Still, because Jewishness strongly implies verifiable ethnicity markers, French converts find legitimacy in communities by seeking for authenticity within the ideological frame of Hebrew ancestry. Consequently, even after conversion, they often strive to further validate their claim to Jewishness by aiming to prove their Jewish origins, whether real or mythical. Dina, a woman from Guadeloupe, gives a good example of this process:

> I couldn't understand what I was feeling inside. It began at a very young age and it has taken significance in my life. And I realized that I felt a very strong interest in Jews, when I hears about the Holocaust and Israel in history classes, my strongest desire was to learn Hebrew while I was just entering sixth grade but I was told that Hebrew is a dead language and you must learn Latin. . . . When I realized that in my family there were people who were converts and were assimilated, I realized that the history of Guadeloupe is actually very rich, because we were told that our ancestors were from Brittany, but they were not the only ones. It's untrue, completely untrue. This is when I realized that History had tried to give me an identity which is not our own. So today I do this work also for my family, when I went back I told them, "excuse me but I'm going to teach you something: our ancestors, a part of whom we've found but we can't go further in

the past, well they were navigators and I'm convinced they were Jews." Today my goal is to talk about it and testify so that everybody may understand what their identity is. And that is something very important for me. (Dina, testimony given at the conference of the FJN, 2010)

Indeed, there have been studies that demonstrated the presence of Jewish settlers in the French Caribbean, including two books by Elvire Maurouard, one of which, entitled *Les Juifs de Saint-Domingue (Haiti)*,[26] showed that Jews fleeing repression in metropolitan France found refuge in Saint Domingue, while the other, *Juifs de Martinique et Juifs portugais sous Louis XIV (Français)*, documented the presence of Jews in Martinique in the context of sugar cane trade. The existence of such historical evidence has reinforced the motivation of some converts like Dina, who see it as an opportunity to carve a place for themselves in the ideology of Hebrew ancestry and emulate their fellow Jews' passion for genealogical research. In Dina's case, genealogy is used to justify the apparently inexplicable attraction she felt for the history of Jews and Israel as well as her desire to learn Hebrew, and it seems to offer a means to supplement the lack of Jewishness implied by the convert status. For converts, the Bible also looms large in collective and individual self-representation.

The Torah or the Bible as a Frame of Reference for Identity

The Bible, considered as the founding myth of Israel and the Jewish people, is a core element of ethnic pride due to its universal dimension. But paradoxically, it also entails a form of ethnic exclusiveness which seals off the group to all those who are not deemed to have Hebrew ancestry—namely, the "goyim," those who are not part of the covenant between God and his Chosen People. This worldview explains the difficulty of converts of whatever race in obtaining acceptance, let alone integration, in Jewish communities. In the early twelfth century, an Italian contemporary of Maimonides named Obadiah had confronted these same issues after converting from Islam to Judaism. He was concerned that, as a person whose ancestors were not Jews, it was inappropriate for him to recite the numerous liturgical phrases referring to "our God and God of our ancestors," "Who has chosen us"; he therefore asked Maimonides if he should change the wording of these when saying them in public or even in private. This is what Maimonides answered him:

> You should say all this in the prescribed fashion. Change nothing; rather, it is appropriate that you recite the blessings and prayers just as they are recited by

those born as Jews, both when you are engaged in private prayer and when you are serving as the prayer leader.

The basis for this is that Abraham our Father taught the masses, enlightened them, and made known to them doctrinal truth [i.e., monotheism] and [the fact of] God's unity. He rejected idolatry and abolished its practices, and he gathered many under the wings of the Divine Presence. He provided them with instruction and guidance. He charged his descendants and subsequent "members of his household" with keeping the ways of the Lord forever, as Scripture states, "For I have singled him out, that he may instruct his children and his posterity to keep the way of the Lord [by doing what is just and right]."

Therefore, throughout the generations, whoever converts to Judaism and whoever confesses the unity of the Divine Name, as it is prescribed in the Torah, is counted among the disciples of Abraham our Father, peace be upon him. They are all members of Abraham's household, and he it is who brought them back to the good.

. . . As a consequence of your having come under the wings of the Divine Presence and having attached yourself to Him, there is no distinction between us and you, and all miracles performed for us have been performed, as it were, for both us and you. Thus is it said in the Book of Isaiah, "Let not the foreigner say, who has attached himself to the Lord, 'The Lord will keep me apart from His people.'" There is no difference whatsoever between you and us.[27]

The difficulties encountered by Obadiah in the twelfth century certainly find an echo today among African and Caribbean converts to Judaism, especially since access to their own histories tends to include more blind spots, as was emphasized by Dina in the testimony transcribed above.

Among Black Jews, there is a tendency to appropriate the Bible by identifying the Hebrew people as non-White and even Black (see chapter 2). Ofer, a former Evangelical pastor who is now a member of the Reform Judaism movement, asserts that "as a rule, every Black person is a Jew, whether they know it or not" (interview given in 2009). For such respondents, whether born Jews or converts, the consciousness of belonging to the Jewish people, or the subjective or mythical identification with the Biblical Israel, are justified by Judaism being the source of Christianity and Islam. Biblical figures identified as Black are also extolled, particularly Zipporah, the wife of Moses. Marah, the former Evangelical pastor who is now a rabbi in Israel, explains:

It is possible to be both Black and Jewish, because the religious reference in Judaism is Moses, and he married a Madianite. Zipporah was not blonde and blue-eyed, and she wasn't either a woman with a tan and pale eyes. She was a Kushite, a Black woman. So, if Moses, the religious reference of Judaism, who is at the root of the laws we practice today, married a Black woman, then their children were mixed-race. This means that the question of color and religion is baseless, and you can see that from the very beginning. (Marah, interview given in 2010)

It bears repeating that these respondents have such reasonings because the presence of Blacks is documented in the Bible. Besides, the archetypal figure of Ruth is seen as an inspiration that justifies the various models of conversion. Albert, another former pastor who told me he had converted and become a rabbi in Israel, identifies with her in the following terms:

I have also felt an attachment to the land [of Israel] and to the [Jewish] people. And I see that as accomplishing in my life the verse from *Ruth* 1:2, their people is my people, and their God is my God. (Albert, interview given in 2015)

Like Albert, many Black converts also embrace Israel as part of their religious experience and expression.

Black French Converts' Relation to Israel

In effect, Israel holds a very important place in African Christian religiosity. In Evangelical and Pentecostal churches in the two Congo, for instance, members greet one another saying "Shalom" and commonly bear Biblical first names like David, Ezekiel, Jeremiah, Elijah, or Sophonias. The names of churches or holy sites—New Jerusalem, Noah's Ark, Rehoboth, Bethel, Gethsemane, synagogue of all nations—also refer to the Bible. Pilgrimages to Israel are organized by many African churches, as is illustrated by the feature film *James' Journey to Jerusalem*,[28] which tells the story of a pious young African whose village pools their resources to send him to Jerusalem so that he may tell them about the idealized holy city on his return. Under the aegis of the International Christian Embassy Jerusalem (ICEJ), an Evangelical Protestant organization "founded in 1980 as an evangelical response to the need to comfort Zion, following the commandment found in the Scriptures, in *Isaiah* 40:1–2,"[29] three hundred Evangelical Protestants from the Ivory Coast, entirely funded by the State, attended the annual Christian celebration of the Festival of Tabernacles in Israel in October 2019, just before the COVID pandemic. This love of African Evangelicals for Israel is analyzed by the French historian Sébastien Fath as follows:

[o]ne of the singular characteristics of sub-Saharan evangelical Protestantism is its Judeophilia, which is particularly perceptible in the field of Christian/Gospel music. The analogical proximity between the theodicy of the Hebrew people's enslavement and liberation from Pharaoh, and the experience of former African slaves, has fostered shared sensitivity and sympathy.[30]

Further in his study, Fath synthesized his conclusions on what he calls African Evangelical Zionism, in the wake of fieldwork in South Sudan, Burkina Faso, the DRC, and Madagascar, analyzing as follows the references to Israel that he observed in Evangelical worship spaces:

> [t]hus, thousands of African Evangelical denominations, missions, and organizations have appropriated Hebrew names. . . . New prophetic independent denominations are also keen to use a Jewish frame of reference, like for instance the two Kenyan networks of prophetic churches, the Jerusalem Church of Christ and the African Israel Church Niniveh. Hebrew names and concepts such as Ebenezer, Rehoboth, Bethel, Evenou Shalom, Maranatha, El Shaddaï have become common currency in these African Evangelical Protestant milieus. . . . In Evangelical worship, prayers for Israel and peace in Jerusalem are also frequently offered. In the scenography and decoration of services, many elements are borrowed from the Jewish frame of reference, such as the menorah (the seven-branch candelabrum) or flags of the state of Israel in worship spaces, among others. . . . Another clue is given by onomastics and first names, which are commonly borrowed from the Jewish frame of reference. . . . Many Evangelical Protestant families in African countries and the diaspora have members named Solomon, David, Rebecca, Sara, Jacob, Daniel, Ruth, Esther as well as less familiar names such as Nahson.[31]

The philo-Semitism, or Judeophilia, of African Christians may also be observed in the popular enthusiasm for the Kabbalah, which consists in appropriating Kabbalistic interpretation techniques to prophesy, particularly in Pentecostal and Evangelical African churches, whose pastors, bishops, and prophets are increasingly seen wearing the kippah or talith or blowing the shofar. This mystical trend is currently gaining momentum in African Christian milieus, which leads other African Evangelical churches to act as gatekeepers of Christian orthodoxy and denounce it as witchcraft under another name.[32]

If African Christians profess such love for Israel, it is all the more so for Black converts, as is evidenced by the interviewees: "I've been to Israel seven times now. Israel is the motherland, like a second home for me" (Moshé, interview given in 2009). When I asked Myriam why she wanted to go to Israel, she answered, "because that's where it all began" (Myriam, interview given in 2010). Yann, who spent eight years in Israel as a student, said:

> For sure, I liked it very much in Israel. I liked everything, the lifestyle, the homeland, the freedom, the state of Israel, the culture of the country, the people, the open-mindedness. I walked the streets telling myself, "Wow, now *that* is a country!" From the moment I set foot in Israel, I felt, as they say, *welcome back home* [in English], I felt at home, I felt I was a part of this tiny piece of land. (Yann, interview given in 2009)

For this respondent, Judaism is redefined as a chosen homeland, an Israel outside of the state of Israel, and he describes his conversion as an attempt to return "back home," a place where Black Jewish identity would no longer be problematic. As for Guershon, he waxed lyrical about his time in Israel when he said at the convention of the FJN:

> At least Israel is a place where we, Blacks, can find a refuge. . . . When I went there last August, I felt lyrical sometimes. I was so happy to feel at home that sometimes I felt like doing stupid things out of provocation, for example going to a restaurant, placing an order and not paying, just because I'm a Jew in Israel. (Guershon, testimony given at the convention of the FJN in 2010)

Israel appears in these representations as a place where Black Jews are welcome and legitimate; however, Black Jews' idealization of life in Israel is nuanced by natives of Israel. During the time allocated for questions and answers at the convention of the FJN, I asked the following question to Daniel Limor, a (non-Black) Israeli activist advocating for Ethiopian Jews and then Vice-President of the FJN: "When listening to Guershon's presentation and yours, I feel that he and you have two different perceptions of the reception of Black Jews. Guershon describes Israelis as open-minded and French people as narrow-minded, but listening to you, we get the impression that narrow-mindedness is rather prevalent in Israel. Is this correct?" This is what he answered:

> Unfortunately, in Israel there is no open-mindedness. I have to say this, it's not a question of open-mindedness at all, unless, maybe, you were blond and blue-eyed, and I'm a bit ashamed to have to say this. . . . I envy Guershon when he says he goes to Israel and feels great and all that, but that is subjective. I am quite familiar with the issues faced by Ethiopian Jews who have been in Israel for a long time now but are not accepted yet. I have to say it as it is, it was never easy and it's not going to be easy, but it's not a reason to refrain from going to Israel, on the contrary, you should. If you're a Jew, you're stubborn. . . . There is no open-mindedness in general, quite the contrary. . . . I agree that you can't just say "I want to become a Jew" and that's enough for you to become a Jew. You have to go through a process. . . . Then again, the rabbinical institution should be more welcoming and empathetic. I mean, they shouldn't treat people as if they were beggars coming here to ask for a favor when they ask to be accepted as Jews. That is not right but unfortunately that's the way it is. (Daniel Limor, convention of the FJN, 2010)

Hannah, an Ethiopian Jew who benefited from Operation Moshe and now lives in France was in a better position to compare her experiences in Israel and in France. This is what she told me: "in Israel I am left in peace, and I can feel confident living my religion; in fact, Israel is the ideal place" (Hannah, interview given in 2010).

It is useful to compare the situation of Black Jews in France and in other countries, particularly Israel, where they are now fully part of the nation's self-representation. There, they belong to the same streams of Judaism, namely, (ultra-)Orthodox, Reform, and Conservative. Conversions are observed in each of these, but contrary to France, religious jurisdiction in Israel is associated with citizenship. Indeed, official recognition by the state of Israel of conversions outside the Orthodox denomination is only possible "as a directive (thus without a legal foundation): conversions obtained outside of the country are recognized by the [Israeli] Interior Ministry, while those obtained in Israel are validated only if they have been supervised by an Orthodox institution."[33] The Israeli socio-cultural anthropologist Michal Kravel-Tovi, borrowing a concept from Michel Foucault, shows how conversion processes in Israel pertain to the "biopolitics of belonging," insofar as the secular state depends on Jewish religious authorities to facilitate the production of good citizens. Even though she does not dwell on the matter of race, her description makes it perceptible as a factor in conversion processes in Israel, as when she mentions Russian immigrants being selected for state-subsidized conversions because they represent racially desirable bodies congruent with the majority Ashkenazi norm, whereas "[n]ot surprisingly, the work of the committee reinforces a highly stratifying logic, establishing the greatest barriers to citizens from the third world or developing countries."[34] This is because racialized candidates' desire to become Jewish is found suspicious and problematic: "The committee members believe that applicants will often exploit conversion in order to receive citizenship, including the economic and civilian benefits for which new olim are eligible." Michal Kravel-Tovi, *When the State Winks: The Performance of Jewish Conversion in Israel* (2017), 80. As recently as December 2021, the rejection of a young Ugandan Jew's conversion made the headlines, with explicit titles chosen by the progressive daily *Haaretz*, "This Jew by Choice Is Testing Israeli Top Court's Landmark Ruling on Conversions" and *The Jerusalem Post*, "Pride and prejudice: The State of Israel vs Yosef Kibita."[35] The young man, a student hailing from the well-researched community of Abayudaya in Uganda, wanted to see his Jewishness acknowledged by the Israeli state tribunals. After undergoing a first conversion in Uganda in 2008 at age eighteen and moving to Israel in 2017, he applied for citizenship under the Law of Return in 2018. He was ordered to go through conversion again in a recognized Masorti community in Israel, in order to obtain recognition from the Israeli Interior Ministry; but this certification was denied shortly before his visa expired, prompting petitions and formal protests by the Masortis.[36] This tends to prove that even in Israel, Black Jews' legitimacy is not a given, contrary to that of European immigrants.

Following the fieldwork I had conducted in the USA in 2012 among African American Jews, I had concluded:

> While Black Jews in France tend to have an idyllic view of Israel in their construction of their Jewish identity, the attitudes of African American Jews are more ambivalent, shaped by their experiences of race-based discrimination as well as by the political choices of the State of Israel. Tanya, a biracial respondent of Sephardic descent, hammered out her answer to this question: "Israel is building Nazi camps in Palestine." When I asked her if she had ever been to Israel, she said, "No, and I don't feel like going there. I'm not interested." When I asked Tifferet if there were any aspects of Jewish life that she found negative, she replied, "I hate Israel." When prompted to explain her answer, she told me that she had been there on a high school trip to a kibbutz and that she had been called "Kushi," which was often unpleasant.[37]

This racial slur was also mentioned by Caroline, an African woman who converted at the Consistory of Paris and now lives in Israel after making Aliyah. When I asked her if the term was racist or not, she gave a more nuanced answer:

> When certain people use it, yes, such as people from Hasidic milieus who only live among themselves. But I know a Yemeni mother, whenever she sees me, she hugs me tight and calls me "my little Kushi, my little Kushi" and she loves me to the moon and back, when she says it there's nothing racist to it. (Caroline, 40, interview given in November 2020)

The Africanist scholar Steven Kaplan, who taught comparative religion at the Hebrew University of Jerusalem, analyzed the racial discourse surrounding Ethiopian immigrants in Israel, explaining how

> [their identification] as black frequently places them (explicitly or by implication) at one end of a bipolar opposition with their (allegedly) white Israeli co-citizens. This "whiteness" of veteran Israelis, like the "blackness" of Ethiopians is not a mere description of pigmentation, but rather a designation which carries with it numerous social and political associations. By identifying themselves as whites, Jews in general and Israelis in particular are attempting to transform their historical role in Western and particularly European culture as the "Other" and the "Outsider." This whiteness of Israelis is part of their positioning themselves in the world as neither Asian nor Middle Eastern, but as Western, European and white. In contrast to Ethiopian Jews and other Jewish Israelis, other groups—most notably Israeli Arabs—do not figure as part of the

colour spectrum and are thus rendered invisible in discussions which ignore their existence.[38]

Even though Black Jews in France are aware of the existence of racism in Israel, the country is inseparable from their identification to the Jewish people. While French Jews in general have either a religious or a Zionist position toward Israel, Black French Jews, whether converts or born Jews, Israel is an actual homeland, to the point that some even become involved in Zionist movements, like Yann:

> I often hear people speak unfavorably of Zionism, but I am a Zionist and always will be. You're asking me if there are unpleasant aspects about life in Israel; well, without being a fanatic I'll tell you, why don't they leave Israel alone, then we'll see Israel's vocation. (Yann, interview given in 2010).

The terms used by this respondent are fraught with political and emotional significance, especially as he identifies as a Zionist and started a political career. They point to two important elements: on the one hand, a transnational definition of Jewishness, centered on adhesion to the political values of the state of Israel, and on the other hand, an implicit, veiled critique of the way in which Blackness is experienced by newcomers on the French soil (see chapter 7). The will of French Black Jews to belong to the Jewish people by embracing the state of Israel is also apparent in the names they choose for themselves, as will be discussed next.

JEWISH FIRST AND LAST NAMES

First and last names represent a means of asserting Jewish origins, as Joëlle Bahloul points out: "the family name, which bears elements of ethnicity, is completed by the first name, giving rise to a whole range of distinction strategies."[39] Blacks who are native-born Jews naturally have Jewish first and last names, such as Emanuel Yerdai, Hannah, David, Myriam, Abraham; so do Danites, with last names such as Yair Kohen and first names such as Ismaël, or Peniel. Igbo respondents have Igbo names, but they stressed their religious meanings: for instance, Chukwu means "supreme God," Alo Chukwu, "the notion of God," Chukwuka, "God is the mightiest," Chukwuma, "God knows all," or Chukwuyem, "God gave me." Biracial interviewees also bear Jewish first and last names, and thus say they do not need to prove their Jewishness because they are immediately identified as Ashkenazi or Sephardi.

Names are so important in the parameters of Jewishness that conversion always implies a name change, and the names chosen by African and West

Indian converts are particularly fraught with meaning. These names testify to the circumstances of their conversions and tell something about the history of this process. Indeed, they display a need for identity reconstruction linked to their yearning to symbolically situate themselves in the Biblical genealogical representations. Hence, female converts typically chose the names Zipporah (an emblematic Biblical figure, for she was Moses' wife) or Ruth, identifying to her experience as a convert, or Esther, celebrating her willpower. Hannah, Leah, Rachel, Sarah, or Shulamith are also favorites. Male converts proceed in the same manner, with first names such as Moshe, which was very often borne, or Guershon, the son of Moses, mentioned in the Bible, whose name means "foreigner."

Also noticeable was the name Pinchas, a descendant of Aaron the priest, mentioned in the Bible for assassinating a prince from one of the tribes of Israel. The interviewee who had chosen this name was a former pastor; he "killed" his Christian identity to become a Jew. This is how he explained it to me:

> What I like in this name and this Biblical figure, is the fact of being empowered to become what you were not supposed to become. . . . Pinchas is the one who was clear-sighted enough to make the right choice, to the point of overthrowing what was established by nature, and this speaks to me because of both my past and my ambition.

This particular interviewee, who is now a rabbi, can also explain the Biblical significance of his birth name:

> My initial first name, that my parents gave me, is already a Hebrew name, which is mentioned twice in the Torah. . . . In the Pentateuch, you have what is called "the waters of Marah" [*Exodus,* 15:22–27]. When the children of Israel came out of Egypt, they found a stream and tried to drink from it, but the water was bitter. Moses put his rod in it and it became fit to drink. And all the studies of that episode say that by that time, God had already given Moses a number of laws, even before he gave the Ten Commandments. It is a very important and meaningful moment in the history of Judaism, this episode of the waters of Marah. So because I already have a Hebrew first name, people are used to calling me by this name. The second mention is by Ruth's mother-in-law, Naomi. When she and Ruth returned to Israel, after leaving the country where they had been, she said, "Do not call me Naomi, call me Marah, for I feel the bitterness of having left my country." [*Ruth,* 1:3–6] These are the two junctions where you find this name in the Torah. So, the name that is in the Torah, I don't mind people calling me by that name. (Marah, interview given in 2010)

As for Claudine, the woman from Guadeloupe quoted earlier who had recurrent dreams, she said that God had changed her last name, calling her Lévy:

> In my dream He called me Claudine Lévy; I heard His voice and it's God calling me Claudine Lévy. Is it something about my origins? I don't know, but I know that with the colonization of the West Indies there were some Jews who got there. Anyway, what matters to me is the present, and I committed myself until I have something more precise to do. I talked with a rabbi about this, and he told me that Levi is the one who accompanies, and I received confirmation of this name because every year I go to the South of France for seminars, and every year I sign up for the workshop entitled "Communication with the Roots of our Faith"—that is, the Jewish root. I had opted for a trailer to sleep in because there were no more rooms left. They had put signs everywhere with the names of tribes, because there were many people camping; and I got assigned a trailer which exactly bore the sign "Tribe of Levi." That's what I mean when I say certain things are precise and don't happen by chance: it means now I have to step in, and it's up to me to pray to know what I am supposed to do. (Claudine, interview given in 2015)

Albert, who is now called Abraham, also stressed the notions of continuity and return to the roots behind the choice of a Hebrew name:

> You know, it's when Jews came to France that they were forced to take local first names. That's how the first name "Abraham" became "Albert" in French. When I converted, I decided to go back to the origin of the name "Abraham." In fact I have had a Jewish name from the start, I didn't even need to change my first name, because when I told them that my first name is Albert, they kept answering, "Abraham." . . . As my name is Abraham and we didn't know what name to give to my wife, someone was inspired and said, "Sarah," This inspired us in turn, and she took it as her conversion name. (Albert, interview given in 2015)

As for Moshe, a man from Guadeloupe who joined the Masorti, he chose his name in reference to the circumstances of his conversion:

> I chose this name because some time ago, when I was already engaged in the process of conversion, I attended the synagogue in Versailles and worshipped and talked with the members there. . . . At that time there was a wave of Ethiopian Jews who were going to Israel. The secretary of the synagogue, or janitor if you prefer, who saw me regularly and knew I was on my way to conversion, used to say: "The Black guy is called Moshe, so you'll be Moshe." She said this to me twenty-seven years ago, and this has stuck with me. (Moshé, interview given in 2009)

Understandably, the significance attached by the Black converts themselves to their Hebrew names is central in their understandings of their Jewishness, and is closely tied to identity markers related to the Hebrew language.

Converts' Relation to the Hebrew Language

The French sociologist Pierre-Jean Simon analyzed the importance of language as a marker of ethnicity as follows:

> No doubt, language is, in many cases, an extremely important tenet of ethnicity. It plays the dual role of keeping the group closed to outsiders by setting up a barrier of understanding excluding larger groups, and maintaining the group's inner cohesion thanks to mutual understanding, which is a very strong factor of preservation of the members' consciousness of belonging to a collective that is united by a pact and separated from the rest.[40]

These remarks apply all the more to the Hebrew language as it is defined as sacred. It may therefore be expected of Black converts that they should have developed a special relationship with Hebrew. Albert, who converted at the Consistory, gave the following answer to this question:

> I fell in love with the language, which I have translated and am now teaching to people who struggle with Hebrew. It is also what led me to visit the land of Israel and discover this land. At first I went there just to pray, and then I developed a bond with the land and the people. (Albert, interview given in 2015)

I can testify to the depth of this respondent's attachment to the Hebrew language. He was a guest speaker at a conference organized by the Black Jewish organization AM-I-FA and the Ben Gurion chapter of the B'nai B'rith in May 2016 at the Paris city council of the sixteenth arrondissement. When he delivered his talk to share his experience as a former pastor turned rabbi, he gave it both in French and in Hebrew.

As for Myriam, she was in the process of conversion with the Masortis and learning Hebrew when she accepted to be interviewed; this is what she had to say:

> For me, learning the language proves two things. It has to do with the Scriptures: I want to understand what I am reading. The problem is that Hebrew texts are translated into French, while in Hebrew, words may be interpreted in a variety of manners but never entirely accurately. (Myriam, interview given in 2010)

Consequently, the need to learn the language is perceived as inseparable from their religious training and contributes in their presentation of their Jewish selves to their fellow White Jews, whose cultivation of memory and suffering also becomes their own legacy.

Memories of the Holocaust and Slavery among Black Jews

It would be unlikely to claim to belong to the Jewish people without cultivating the memory of the Holocaust in one way or another. Among the respondents, particularly those who are biracial or adoptees, the transgenerational trauma is apparent. For instance, Rébecca, who was seventeen when I first interviewed her, has an Ashkenazi father whose parents are survivors of the Holocaust and a mother from Martinique, whose ancestors were enslaved; she contrasted in the following terms the significance the two legacies have for her:

> I feel closer to the memory of the Holocaust than to that of slavery because the legacy of slavery is more remote in time, whereas that of the Holocaust is more recent, as my grandfather often tells me about it. My grandfather was deported to Auschwitz, while my mother never mentions slavery. (Rébecca, interview given in 2011)

Rébecca's interest for the Holocaust was uncommon. She collected newspapers from the 1930s and 1940s and cited as her favorite films Steven Spielberg's *Schindler's List* and Roberto Benigni's *Life is Beautiful*. The following analysis by the anthropologist and psychologist Yoram Mouchenik provides a useful framework to understand this behavior:

> The Holocaust may be seen as the paradigm of the place of collective trauma in identity construction, and particularly the transgenerational transmission of trauma. While building their personalities, Jewish teenagers are confronted . . . with the massive and oppressive perception of the historic event known as the Holocaust, namely, the attempt to exterminate all of the Jews of Europe during the Second World War. I thus contend that it is partly in the confrontation with the multiple representations of a terrifying collective event, that some have considered as "unthinkable"—the deportation, torture, and murder of a great part of Europe's Jewish population—that certain aspects of the identity construction of every Jewish teenager are consolidated. This identity if therefore largely complicated, since the transgenerational transmission of identity also integrates the historic and immeasurable parameter of the genocide, which, under some circumstances, takes up all the space, so that access to identity becomes associated with the constitution or transmission of a trauma.[41]

In the case of Black Jews, the trauma of slavery may also be associated with that of the Holocaust. The next chapter will offer discussions of the positions taken by Caribbean respondents vis-à-vis the two legacies.

To conclude the present chapter, it may be observed that an original identity has gradually taken shape beyond the diversity of individual experiences, in a process that mingles Jewish ethnicity and religious identity, Christian baggage and Jewish religious practices, African value systems preserved in the diasporic experience, and cultural values underlying Jewish religious life in France. This leads us to address the next question, which is the insertion of Black Jews within the French Jewry.

NOTES

1. Loïc Le Pape, "'Tout change, mais rien ne change.' Les conversions religieuses sont-elles des bifurcations?" *L'enquête sur les bifurcations. Les sciences sociales face aux ruptures et à l'événement* (Paris: La Découverte, 2010), 9782707156006. http://www.editionsladecouverte.fr/catalogue/index-Bifurcations9782707156006.html. hal-01077023.

2. See Joseph Halévy, "La légende de la reine de Saba," *École pratique des hautes études, Section des sciences historiques et philologiques. Annuaire 1905* (1904): 5–24. DOI: https://doi.org/10.3406/ephe.1904.2491. See also Robert Beylot, *La Gloire des Rois, ou l'Histoire de Salomon et de la reine de Saba* (Turnhout, Belgium: Brepols, 2008).

3. Shmuel Trigano, "La logique de l'étranger dans le judaïsme. L'étranger biblique, une figure de l'autre?" *Pardès* 2, no. 52 (2012): 95–104.

4. Haim Hermann Cohn, *Human Rights in the Bible and Talmud* (Tel Aviv: MOD Books, 1989), 53–54.

5. Maimonides quoted by Rabbi Benjamin Blech, "Épouser une convertie," accessed August 22, 2022, https://www.aish.fr/print/?contentID=442723973&section=/israel/monde_juif.

6. Rabbi Pierre-Yves Bauer, "Le processus de la conversion au judaïsme," accessed January 27, 2012, http://www.viejuive.com/2007/12/le-processus-de-la-conversion-au.html.

7. Martine Berthelot, "Approche des grands courants actuels du judaïsme religieux et laïc en Occident," in *Juifs de Catalogne: Et autres contributions à l'étude des judaïsmes contemporains / I altres contribucions a l'estudi dels judaismes contemporanis* [online] (Perpignan: Presses universitaires de Perpignan, 2011), accessed March 1, 2022. DOI: https://doi.org/10.4000/books.pupvd.1396.

8. Sébastien Tank-Storper, "Trouble dans la judéité. Mariages mixtes, conversions et frontières de l'identité juive," *Ethnologie française* no. 4 (October 2013): 591–600.

9. Martine Hovanessian and Richard Marienstras, "La modification des Juifs de France," *Journal des anthropologues* 72–73 (1998): 93–106.

10. Chantal Bordes, *La condition juive en France*, 94.

11. See the website of the Consistoire central: Conversion—Consistoire de France.

12. Franck La Barbe, "Les juifs pour Jésus," in Anne-Laure Zwilling, Joëlle Allouche-Benayoun, Rita Hermon-Belot, and Lionel Obadia, eds., *Les minorités religieuses en France. Panorama de la diversité contemporaine* (Paris: Bayard, 2019).

13. Danièle Hervieu-Léger, *La religion en miettes ou la question des sectes* (Paris: Calmann-Lévy, 2001); Danièle Hervieu-Léger, *Le pèlerin et le converti. La religion en mouvement* (Paris: Flammarion, 1999), 121–24.

14. See Pauline Peretz, *Le combat pour les Juifs soviétiques, Washington-Moscou-Jérusalem, 1953–1989* (Paris: Armand Colin, 2006).

15. Don Seeman, *One People, One Blood: Ethiopian-Israelis and the Return to Judaism* (New Brunswick, NJ: Rutgers University Press) 2010. See also Don Seeman, "Pentecostal Judaism and Ethiopian Israelis," in Nadia Marzouki and Olivier Roy, eds., *Religious Conversions in the Mediterranean World* (London: Palgrave-MacMillan, "Islam and Nationalism" series, 2013), 60–76.

16. Radu Mihaileanu, *Live and Become,* Elzevir Films, 2005.

17. Bill approved by the Knesset; the bill and explanatory documents were published in the legislative package No. 48 of 12 Tamouz 5710 (May 27, 1950), 189, accessed October 27, 2019, http://www.akadem.org/medias/documents/1-Loi-retour.pdf.

18. Sébastien Doane, "Fils de Dieu, Les évangiles appliquent ce titre à Jésus. Mais, savez-vous que d'autres textes de la Bible apposent ce titre à d'autres personnages?," Chronique du 13 avril 2012, accessed October 25, 2019, http://www.interbible.org/interBible/ecritures/mots/2012/mots_120413.html.

19. Chief Rabbi Gilles Bernheim, "Le modèle paulinien, cadre nécessaire et difficile du dialogue judéo-chrétien," Lecture given in the locale of the Judeo-Christian Friendship of Paris West, rue Jouffroy d'Abbans, on January 23, 2017.

20. Alain Massini, Chair of the "Commission Chrétiens et Juifs" of the Fédération Protestante de France. The text was first published in 2004 on the website of the French Protestant Federation, where it can no longer be found. This version comes from the (now closed) website Rivtsion and posted on Academia.edu, by M. R. Macina, on May 17, 2019.

21. The Commission Chrétiens et Juifs is home to widely different tendencies. While Lutheran-Reformed members approve of this text, they also cohabit with more Evangelical-oriented churches that are closer to the American Evangelical movement, as well as others that subscribe to the declaration "Un unique Christ pour tous," which insists on the centrality of Jesus Christ as the only path to salvation.

22. The theology of substitution contends that the Jewish people was stripped by God of its title as Chosen People and replaced by the Christian church, identified as the "new Israel."

23. The document, which was written in collaboration with Jewish authorities, was presented by Cardinal Kurt Koch, chair of the Papal Committee for religious relations with Judaism, by Father Norbert Hofmann, S.D.B., secretary of the abovementioned dicastery, by Rabbi David Rosen, international chair of interfaith affairs for the Jerusalem branch of the American Jewish Committee (AJC), and by Prof. Edward Kessler, founding director of the Woolf Institute in Cambridge, UK. The text, entirely

translated into French by the Catholic press agency Zenit in Rome on December 11, 2015, was posted by Prof. Edward Kessler at the Vatican and the Zenit Agency on the website Academia.edu on April 11, 2018.

24. Menahem Macina, *Chrétiens et juifs depuis Vatican II. État des lieux historique et théologique. Prospective eschatologique* (Avignon: Éditions du Docteur angélique, 2009).

25. Nadia Malinovich, "What's the Color of a Jew? Les Juifs, la blanchitude et le multiculturalisme aux États-Unis à l'époque contemporaine," in *La place de l'autre*, ed. Michel Prum (Paris: L'Harmattan, 2010), 52.

26. Elvire Maurouard, *Les Juifs de Saint-Domingue (Haiti)* (Paris: Éditions du Cygne, 2008); *Juifs de Martinique et Juifs portugais sous Louis XIV* (Français) (Paris: Éditions du Cygne, 2009).

27. Quoted in Eliezer Diamond, "Halakhah, Theology and Psychology: The Case of Maimonides and Obadiah the Proselyte," in *Hakol Kol Yaakov,* The Joel Roth Jubilee Volume Series, The Brill Reference Library of Judaism, Vol. 61 (Leyden: Brill, 2021): 5–8, accessed August 17, 2022, https://doi.org/10.1163/9789004420465_002.

28. Ra'anan Alexandrowicz, *James' Journey to Jerusalem,* feature film, Lama Films, 2004.

29. PR, "Pèlerinage: 300 chrétiens protestants évangéliques ivoiriens en Israël pour prendre part à la Fête des Tabernacles," accessed October 25, 2019, https://news.abidjan.net/h/664582.html.

30. Sébastien Fath, "Afrique subsaharienne et sionisme évangélique," L'enjeu mondial, published in January 2017, accessed October 25, 2019, https://www.sciencespo.fr/enjeumondial/fr/odr/afrique-subsaharienne-et-sionisme-evangelique.

31. Sébastien Fath, "Le sionisme évangélique africain. Impact géopolitique d'une identité narrative," proceedings of the conference "Juifs et protestants, 5 siècles de relations en Europe" organized by P. Cabanel at the Musée d'Art et d'Histoire du Judaïsme, 2021. hal-03100482, p. 10.

32. For example, a websearch carried out on March 2, 2024, on YouTube using the French keywords, "kabbale" and "églises africaines" yielded thirty-five video and live broadcasts by Christian "revival" churches warning against the influence of this mystical approach and accusing it of introducing magic and witchcraft into Christian churches.

33. Tank-Storper, "Qui est juif?," 39.

34. Kravel-Tovi, 80–81.

35. Judy Maltz, "This Jew By Choice is Testing Israel's Landmark Ruling on Conversions," *Haaretz,* June 27, 2021, https://www.haaretz.com/israel-news/2021-06-27/ty-article/.highlight/this-jew-by-choice-is-testing-israels-landmark-ruling-on-conversions/0000017f-e51c-d9aa-afff-fd5c97ed0000; Judy Maltz, "Appeal to Grant Israeli Citizenship to Ugandan Convert Rejected," *Haaretz,* January 5, 2022, https://www.haaretz.com/israel-news/2022-01-05/ty-article/.premium/appeal-to-grant-israeli-citizenship-to-ugandan-convert-rejected/0000017f-f659-d318-afff-f77b823c0000, and David Breakstone, "Pride and Prejudice: The State of Israel vs Yosef Kibita," *The Jerusalem Post,* June 9, 2021, https://www.jpost.com/israel-news

/pride-and-prejudice-the-state-of-israel-vs-yosef-kibita-657105, consulted on March 17, 2024.

36. "Ugandan Jew Threatened With Deportation After Interior Ministry Ruling," *Masorti Matters Blog,* December 13, 2021, https://masorti.org/ugandan-jew-threatened-with-deportation-after-interior-ministry-ruling/, consulted on March 17, 2024.

37. See Aurélien Mokoko Gampiot, "Black Judaism in France: An Example of the Intersection Between Religion and Ethnicity," in Joëlle Allouche and Harriet Hartman, eds., *Contemporary Jewry* 36, Special Issue No. 3, "Transformation and Evolution in the Jewish World: Judaisms and Judaicities in Contemporary Societies" (2017), http://rdcu.be/tGYG.

38. Steven Kaplan, "Black and White, Blue and White and Beyond the Pale: Ethiopian Jews and the Discourse of Colour in Israel," *Jewish Culture and History* 5, no. 1 (2002): 51–68, DOI: 10.1080/1462169X.2002.10511962, 63.

39. Joëlle Bahloul, "Noms et prénoms juifs nord-africains," *Terrain* 4 (March 1985), posted online on July 23, 2007, accessed November 1, 2019. http://journals.openedition.org/terrain/2872; DOI: 10.4000/terrain.2872.

40. Pierre-Jean Simon, "Eléments de la bretonnité," Sociology Masters lecture, University of Rennes 2, France, 1996/1997.

41. Yoram Mouchenik, "Réflexion sur l'identité chez l'adolescent juif," *Champ psychosomatique* 1, no. 25 (2002): 119–128. DOI: 10.3917/cpsy.025.0119.

Chapter 4

Black Jews' Insertion in the French Jewry

In France, Black Jews are not a separate community from the French Jewry: to this day, there is no community of Black Hebrews or Israelites with a distinct claim to Jewishness, but rather individuals who identify as Jews from birth or following a conversion. Of course, Blacks are not the only ones converting to Judaism, as many people of European, American, or Asian descent also do.[1] The specificity of Black Jews in France is that they have felt the need to gather in order to become visible to Jewish institutions. In a country where race is not easily discussed but the unspoken norm is White, including in Jewish milieus where racial ambiguity can be observed, what difficulties are Black Jews confronted with?

At first sight, Black Jews are not distinct from their fellow White Jews, as they share the same values, beliefs, commandments, and ethnicity markers. Yet, a deeper investigation of their experiences raises the following questions: how do converts and native Jews find their place and express their integration in the French Jewry? How are they perceived by non-racialized Jews and how do they, in turn, perceive the latter?

As discussed in the previous chapter, conversion to Judaism entails an identification with the Jewish people and a total immersion into a Jewish community and the global Jewry:

> Conversion must indeed be understood as the encounter between specific individuals and a specific belief system, but it seems more accurate to frame the relationship thus created as one of reciprocal identification. Conversion implies the constitution of an exclusive identity. It is not merely an adhesion to values or salvation methods. It is inseparable from a process whereby the convert espouses the contents of the belief system and, by extension, the institution bearing this system . . . a process of assimilation in the fullest sense of the term, a reciprocal incorporation. The process observed in a conversion is a dynamic process of symbolic appropriation serving a better self-understanding

and involving a personal transformation. It is a process of identifying oneself to the Other and the Other to oneself.[2]

To what extent does this analysis by the French sociologist Sébastien Tank-Storper apply to Black converts to Judaism?

It appears that, once conversion obtained, the process of identification of the Other to the self and of the self to the Other may be observed in the acceptance and welcome offered by Jewish institutions; however, as regards identification with the Jewish people, their new sense of belonging is hindered by instances of rejection by fellow Jews and Jewish institutions as well as French Jewish milieus.

Converts, as well as individuals seeking to convert or refusing to do so because they already consider themselves Jewish, position themselves in relation to already existing branches of Judaism. In France, the important reform of Judaism following the minority's emancipation in 1791 (see chapter 1) resulted in a plurality of branches that often experience tensions with one another—namely, Reform, Masorti, Orthodox, or Lubavitch. Like all other Jews, Black converts or native Jews can choose among these various branches, and their reasons for opting for one in preference over the others is worthy of discussion.

Understandably, the answers given to this question vary according to their positioning. Myriam, who converted within the Masorti movement, said:

> In fact, when I did my research, I had initially opted for the Reform movement, but I chanced upon the Masortis. I visited their website and read lots of articles on politics, topical issues in Israel, the Halakha, and various opinions pieces on topical issues and so on. I realized that this was in line with my worldview and my way of thinking. It strengthened my will to convert. I also exchanged about it with people—there are lots of intellectuals, there are writers, journalists, historians, and tons and tons of books. Then, what I liked about them is they insist on dialog among religions, they have exchanges with different Christian congregations and Muslim groups. They have meetings to talk with one another, there was one at the synagogue and another one in a Catholic church, and yet another one in a Muslim prayer room. They [Masortis] give a lot of importance to relations with others. Of course, we have our own activities and communication networks, but we shouldn't keep to ourselves until we find ourselves in a ghetto, because that's not the point. There are people from different cultures, different origins and branches, Reform, orthodox and all the rest, and we must be welcoming to all, that's the point. (Myriam, interview given in 2009)

The first motive put forward in this testimony is learning, which is a very recurrent element in the responses I have obtained. For example, when I asked Claudine "Lévy" (see chapter 3) what she liked about Jewish milieus, she spontaneously retorted, "the teachings." Then, Myriam's appreciation of the diversity of origins and social backgrounds was also emphasized as a prime motive by the respondents who had chosen the Reform and Masorti movements. Finally, interfaith dialog was also mentioned several times as a reason for opting for the Masorti and Reform Judaism movements, as this was seen to demonstrate their open-mindedness and willingness to share. Hortense Tsiporah was categorical in her assessment:

> When I did my conversion, I chose the Reform movement, because they're open-minded. We never could have organized the Rosh Hashana seder as we did [i.e., with non-Jewish guests] anywhere else, never ever. With others—let me tell you, they would never have accepted for a community organization to have a say in such a holiday—because it's an important holiday—and in the organizing of a Rosh Hashanah seder. (Hortense, interview given in 2015)

Consequently, the Reform Judaism movement is often preferred by Black converts over the Orthodox branch embodied by the Israelite Consistory of Paris, which they deem too inflexible and rigid. Moshe, who converted in the Reform Judaism movement but is now part of the Masortis, explained how he moved from one branch to another:

> As the Consistory kept saying no, I told myself it was useless insisting with them. So, I tried the Reform Judaism movement of France, which is an important synagogue as well; I studied and after three years, I was converted by the rabbi of the French Reform Judaism movement. Then, I left them to worship with the Masortis. I feel so at home with the Masortis! It's a conservative, tradition-minded movement. They apply the laws, men and women don't mingle, and I was welcomed there. (Moshe, 45, interview given in 2009)

As for Rébecca, she has to deal with the fact her mother is not Jewish:

> The Reform Judaism movement accepted me as a Jew although my mother is not Jewish. The Reform Judaism movement is not like the Consistory, there are women rabbis, men and women worship in the same space, women are equal to men. Everything a man can do, women do as well as regards rituals. To be honest, personally I don't feel represented by the Consistory, I don't feel too comfortable with the dogmatism they want to force upon you, knowing that you don't necessarily have to convert in order to feel Jewish. Jewishness is important without necessarily having to go through the religious obligations, all the dos and don'ts. I don't feel comfortable first because we're separated from men and often women are relegated to a tiny balcony, from which they can't follow the service. I don't see the point of going to a place of worship if you can't follow what's going on. I feel useless and I don't see the point of being there in fact. On the contrary, I feel like going to a Reform synagogue, there is a real community

there, a real sense of sharing, and you simply feel welcome, you see. (Rébecca, interview given in 2020)

Guershon said he waited for seven years at the Consistory until he converted within the Reform Judaism movement. As several respondents pointed out already, the Consistory of Paris holds an Orthodox position, holding fast to traditions and systematically discouraging applications for conversion; however, many Black candidates to conversion opt for this branch, because it stands for legality and legitimacy in their eyes. As a result, among my convert respondents, many more are members of the Orthodox than the Masorti or Reform Judaism movements. Landry, a native of Cameroon whose Jewish name is Enoch, explains why he converted within the Consistory of Paris: "in fact it was my choice, I have nothing against Reform Judaism, but to begin with I really wanted to do things the right way in my religious practice" (Enoch, 34, interview given in 2017).

Beyond the diversity of branches of Judaism in which they worship, as was explained in the previous chapter, Jewish identity entails ethnic parameters that function as processes of identification or Othering. Among these are markers of what Fredrik Barth called "ethnic boundaries."[3] I wanted to understand how Black converts and native Jews handled the implications of racialization or non-racialization as possible such boundaries in Jewish spaces.

In his analysis of the rhetoric around French Jews' perceived, assigned, or claimed Whiteness, the sociologist Samuel Ghiles-Meilhac[4] posits an identification to the mainstream as a dominant group that is free from discrimination. He first points to the so-called emancipation of French Jews under the French Revolution, which granted the status of Israelite French citizens. This was a major turning point in the construction of France as a modern nation, as in previous centuries, French Jews' refusal of assimilation through forced conversions to Christianity caused them to be massacred or cast out of the country. This placed Jews in a tragic dilemma: either they must stop being Jewish, by putting down roots unreservedly in the host nation (and thus following a principle of total assimilation or radical loss of distinctiveness), or they must leave the homeland (by forced emigration), unless they were willing to accept discrimination, stigmatization, and social exclusion."[5] With the decree of September 27, 1791, French Jews were granted a new legal and social status, as discrimination against them was officially banned and French citizenship guaranteed. This gave them access to all occupations and land ownership, giving them for the first time the opportunity to fully participate in French political and cultural life. Some embraced the culture and mores of their country to the point of assimilating, by converting to Catholicism or Protestantism, marrying non-Jews, or changing their names. (See chapter 1.)

In the next two centuries, the various expressions of anti-Semitic sentiment in modern French history—from the wrongful accusations of treason against Captain Dreyfus in the 1890s to the rise of pro-Nazi rhetoric in the 1930s—developed a discourse portraying Jews as alien to a French identity that was successively labeled as Gallic, Catholic, European, or even Aryan. At this stage, Jews were dubbed as Orientals and "Asiatics," in a move to make them appear as inherently unassimilable to the French nation. Then, Ghiles-Meilhac explores the definition of Jews by the Vichy regime, under German occupation (1940–1945), which revolved around a binary antagonism between the so-called Aryan race and a Jewish race. Finally, in the wake of migrations of Jewish citizens leaving the country's North African colonies in the early 1960s and popular pro-Israeli demonstrations in May–June 1967, the identity of French Jews emerged in an interplay with other transnational minorities composing the French nation. Yet it was not until 1981 and the election of Socialist President François Mitterrand that the ruling élites began paying attention to expressions of regional and diasporic cultural demands. In a report entitled *Cultural Democracy and the Right to Differentness,* which he submitted on request of the authorities, Henri Giordan laid out a typology of minority groups in France, distinguishing those emanating from regional cultural ensembles from "minorities with no roots in French territory." Within the latter group, he identified three subcategories, namely, "communities of foreigners and first-generation migrant workers," "refugee communities," and "communities formed essentially by French citizens in transnational cultural situations."[6] This designation applied to three groups which, he said, should be paid special attention—the Jewish, Roma, and Armenian communities.

Consequently, in the context of the French Jewry, an ethnicization of social interaction may be observed, which mandates the study of Black Jews, as their inclusion in it seems to materialize the color line. Hannah, an Ethiopian Jew who was part of the first generation of repatriates to Israel, told me, "I had never seen any White Jews before; for me Jews could only be Black" (interview given in 2011). But among White Jews who encounter Black Jews, doubts as to the Jewishness of the latter are expressed openly, often with little regard to the offensiveness of such comments, as the concept of micro-aggression tends to be unknown in France, save among racial activist circles which are often accused of being Americanized and "woke." Still, Black Jews are sensitive to the idea that Jewishness entails Whiteness in France. As Enoch put it, "in fact, I think that those who are known as Ashkenazim and Sephardim have been so brainwashed into believing that you have to be White to be a Jew that they ended up persuading themselves that it's a fact. I call that the Pavlovian reflex" (Enoch, interview given in 2017).

This response emphasizes the concept of race, which, according to the French sociologist Pierre-Jean Simon, naturalizes a shared origin and sense of belonging while implying impassable boundaries among the various groups. The salience of ethnicity ultimately depends on the way in which people self-identify and define "others." The taboo on crossing these boundaries is what fosters racism, because unquestioning loyalty to the group forbids exploration of any other group. Conversely, such exploration is made possible by learning a different culture from one's birth culture—via processes of assimilation or acculturation—a positioning that Pierre-Jean Simon calls ethnicism.[7] The French Jewry displays instances of such processes, where the Black Other is welcomed and crossing racial boundaries is possible, but it also displays racist attitudes that assign Jews to a straitjacket of Whiteness and thereby prevents any exchange with racialized Jews, including Black Jews.

When asked what they appreciated about the French Jewish landscape, the respondents emphasized welcoming attitudes, hospitality, the sense of sharing, and acceptance. Myriam said:

> Yes I like it, because in the community I am now a part of, I was extremely lucky. As I was coming to the faith at my own pace, I had a positive reaction from people because I got there slowly, did things little by little, and got integrated. . . . People got used to seeing me around, sitting next to me and chatting, so they ended up trusting me. . . . I've really had a warm welcome and this makes me very happy, it helped me a lot. (Myriam, 33, interview given in 2009)

Hospitality is frequently mentioned as a quintessentially Jewish value. Caroline, who is a member of an Orthodox synagogue, developed this point as follows: "I think I was lucky, I am quite pampered and really adopted by my community. Maybe this is because I am articulate and I have a good job" (Caroline, interview given in 2010). When describing how they became integrated in their respective communities, respondents often said, "I was lucky," which indirectly points out that they are aware not all Black Jews have had a positive experience (as will be discussed further).

The feeling of community, expressed in synagogues and community centers, was also emphasized as an important factor of individual and collective well-being. I was able to witness what they meant by this at a Rosh Hashana seder, a meal organized in 2015 by the Black Jewish community organization AM-I-FA (described in chapter 5) at the synagogue of AJTM (Reform Judaism) in Paris, where Jews and non-Jews, Blacks and Whites were seated side by side in a friendly and warm atmosphere where the significance of the food and rituals was explained to all and traditions and songs shared by the older members of the community.

Friendship is a notion that respondents also mentioned spontaneously to describe their integration in Jewish milieus. Marah, for instance, related his conversations with a five-year-old boy:

In the synagogue where I worship, Abner is my best friend. Abner is five, and when I take a seat, he always comes and sits down next to me.... Then one day he was really puzzled, and he asked me, "But d'you really like being Black?" I looked at him and said, "yeah, I love being Black." So he looked at me and said, "Well, I love being White."

"Really, how is it you love being White?"

"Because it's pretty."

So I said, "So Black isn't pretty?"

He goes, "yeah" and he says, "Why d'you like being Black?"

I answered, "Because we Blacks are strong."

He said "that's not true!"

What I found interesting is that from that moment, a relationship was created in which a child coming with his questions received answers with the words of a child. And from then on, at every Shabbat, every Friday evening or Saturday morning, when he enters the synagogue, his first reflex is to check whether there's an empty seat next to me, and if there's already someone, he does everything he can to get them to move. (Marah, FJN convention, 2010)

While the story of this transgenerational friendship born of a discussion of racial representations was told to move an audience that was already inclined to racial inclusiveness, it is nonetheless revealing of a perception of Black worshipers as intruders in the French Jewish landscape. The child's gaze reflects a White norm which is unspoken among adults—especially in a country where it is considered patriotic to be colorblind—but remains perceptible in the inquisitiveness of their behavior, as will be discussed further.

Some of my respondents asserted that acceptance by their fellow White Jews is such that the latter no longer pay attention to their skin color and simply consider them as persons. This is especially true of those who are teenagers or grew up in their synagogues, but an older respondent, Myriam, embraces this typically French understanding of colorblindness:

I grew up outside of Paris, in a small town where I was the only Black person in my primary school, so the way others look at me is really something I don't pay attention to anymore, because from as far as I can remember it's something I've always lived with.... It's funny, just a few days ago I talked about it with people who told me, "Oh really, I forgot you are Black." People who know me say the same thing, "you are not Black, you're Myriam and that's it." So, after some time, color simply disappears, you know! It's not something I wear on my sleeve. This being said, I am a Togolese, born and raised in Togo, I love Africa and I have African friends from various origins, but I'm not going to designate people as "So-and-So who's Black," "So-and-So is Black," I'm Black, period. (Myriam, 33, interview given in 2009)

Likewise, Éthan, a young Ethiopian Jew, explains that because he grew up in his community, his differentness is not seen anymore: "I have worshiped in my synagogue for as long as I can remember, and I never had people glare at me or any other type of discrimination. I grew up in my community, so I think they don't see me as Black" (Éthan, 24, interview given in 2011).

Family is also put forward as evidence of acceptance by respondents who were raised as adoptees by White Jewish parents. I met several such interviewees; Rabbi Rivon Krygier, who is at the head of the Masorti community in France, has two Black children who were too young to be interviewed. Others have also mentioned warm welcomes in the frame of interracial marriages, which I discuss in chapter 6. Yet, because multiracialism is not socially recognized as a factor of identification of families in France, the country's Jewry does not have organizations comparable to the Boston-based Jewish Multiracial Network, which pushes for a better recognition of "Jewish diversity through empowerment and community building with Jews of color and Jewish multiracial families" who are aiming to "lead a movement that makes Jewish racial/ethnic diversity fully embraced in American Jewish life"; or Be'chol Lashon, a think tank founded by sociologists Gary and Diane Tobin, which "celebrates and prioritizes diversity as a Jewish value by uplifting the historic and contemporary racial, ethnic, and cultural diversity of the Jewish people."[8]

In the realm of cultural practices, several similarities between African and Jewish traditions are worth mentioning, as they make it easier to live as a Black Jew. The first one, circumcision, holds great importance in Judaism. Regardless of their religious upbringing, almost all African men are circumcised. Therefore, the question of circumcision does not pose as much of a problem as with other converts, even if there is a bloodletting ritual for male converts who are already circumcised. Certain respondents have cited this tradition to assert their identification to the Hebrew people, such as Josué, a native of Cameroon who is now part of a Lubavitch community: "sometimes I think we are Jews thanks to our birth culture. I see the difficulties of the other new converts, Europeans in their forties or fifties, in getting circumcised, whereas we Africans are done with that already" (Josué, 52, interview given in 2010). The second similarity mentioned by the respondents concerns African culinary habits, which are very close to the Kashrut as regards the preparation of meat in particular, as Josué stresses: "sometimes I wonder if our parents did not practice this kosher ritual. They slaughtered animals and let them shed all their blood, and then they made sure they washed them thoroughly, because Africans don't usually eat their meat rare, they insisted on their food being well-done" (Josué, interview given in 2010). These two important cultural elements are often cited to demonstrate the Jewishness of Africans, or the Blackness of Hebrews.

An attachment to the specificity of certain rituals was also mentioned by some respondents as facilitating integration, as in the case of Moshé: "the synagogues of the fifteenth arrondissement [of Paris] are mostly Ashkenazi, while I was used to Sephardic rituals, which I was already practicing . . . Among the Sephardim, I feel at home" (Moshé, 45, interview given in 2009).

Unsurprisingly, the spiritual benefits of conversion have also been emphasized by the respondents. Caroline, a former Catholic, says she acquired an entirely new idea of God:

> It is a new proximity with Hashem, as a Jew I have a better understanding of my relation with Hashem and what I am supposed to do as a Jew. I mean that in daily actions, practice and all that, I no longer see God in a certain way, and this has led me to behave differently, actually. (Caroline, interview given in 2010)

Micheline says she found answers to her questions:

> the question I used to ask myself about Jesus has become pointless now. Back in the day, when I prayed at home, I used to ask myself: "Whom should I address, Jesus or god?" Today I no longer have that problem. And the teachings and explanations I receive, too—before, I used to ask, "does God hear me, does God exist?"—well, today I don't have doubts anymore, for me God is for real; in the past, when I prayed, I always had a doubt, but now it is not a problem for me anymore. At some point I felt guilty of abandoning Christianity, but today, thanks to the teachings I have been receiving for over ten years now, I know for certain that God exists, and I have no doubts left in me. (Micheline, 52, interview given in November 2020)

Finally, the personality of the rabbi matters to the respondents, both as a celebrant of religious services and as a community organizer within his synagogue. The acceptance of Black aspiring converts or members by Jewish milieus is often contingent on the benevolence of the rabbi toward them, as he is the one welcoming them, accompanying their progress, advising, instructing, helping, and protecting them from prejudice in Jewish circles. Little can be achieved without the rabbi's blessing.

Besides, no matter how hard Black Jews try to blend in, if their White fellow Jews' attitudes betray doubts about their legitimacy, then their identification to the Jewish people becomes problematic. When asked what they disliked about the Jewish community, the respondents frequently cited prejudice and rejection, which they said were expressed in several ways.

First came institutional rejection, particularly the strictness and narrow-mindedness of the Consistory. Two biracial women respondents spoke about this point in detail. The first one has a Sephardic mother and a father from Guadeloupe; she speaks Hebrew fluently, having lived in Israel from the age of thirteen until she returned to France at thirty. While she was recognized as a Jew in Israel, in France she was requested to go through conversion, as she had no ketubah (certificate of Jewish marriage) to show the Consistory as proof of her belonging to the Jewry. But the lack of such a document is due to the Consistory's refusal to consider her father's petition for conversion thirty years before, which precluded any religious ceremony (Liana, interview given in 2012). The second biracial interviewee has a non-Jewish mother from Martinique and an Ashkenazi father; but contrary to the former respondent, who accepted to convert, she considers herself a full-fledged Jew although her father is her only Jewish parent, and told me she refused conversion both in her first interview at seventeen and in the second one, ten years later. Her testimony is similar to those of respondents who described being immersed in a Jewish way of life in Israel: "I don't need a conversion to identify as a Jew, because I was raised in Judaism: my entire family on my father's side, especially my grandparents, uncles, and cousins are Orthodox Jews" (Rébecca, 17, interview given in 2011). Contesting the authority of the Consistory to grant or deny recognition, she has opted for the Reform Judaism movement. Likewise, the Yayir Kohen family struggle to obtain recognition, as Danites from the Ivory Coast who attend Orthodox synagogues but have faced numerous instances of prejudice and micro-aggressions there.

The Consistory is not exempt from criticism from within the French Jewry: Rabbi Rivon Krygier, the head of the Masorti branch, made the following remarks in the interview he gave me:

> the Consistory has become increasingly radical over the past thirty years. There are several sub-entities within the Consistory. There's the Beth Din, that is, the legal body of rabbis, which is a bit under the influence of the Israeli rabbinate, which is itself very hostile to modernization. But does that mean that it will be rejected by a majority of Jewish families? Some will, others won't. We a part of many other Jewish institutions than the Consistory. It's been a long time since the Consistory lost its monopolistic leadership position in the [French] Jewish community, it's just a "church," if you will, among others, a very large denomination which is the biggest in France and is able to have weight. But we would like to have more brotherly and respectful relations. We are not too happy with the current situation, but it doesn't stop us from thriving and living our Judaism as we see fit. (Rabbi Rivon Krygier, interview given in 2012)

Although conversions made by the Masorti and Reform Judaism branches are not recognized by the Consistory, regardless of race, many converts have decided to do without the latter's blessing and Black Jews are no exception. Hortense expressed her choice in a political tone: "because anything extreme defaces a human being and has a negative feel to it, I steer clear of extremes and that's why I chose Reform Judaism. I am not an ultra-liberal, but I'm a liberal" (Hortense, interview given in 2010). Yaakov shared his experience of repeated micro-aggressions:

> Well, just opposite my place, there's an Orthodox synagogue, and just the thought of entering it brings back so many bad memories. I was asked to show my ID, say who I am and why I want to enter. Then they told me they would make a copy of my ID and call me back to tell me if I can enter. They did that all the time. But the first time I went to the Reform synagogue, I just breezed through, no questions asked. (Yaakov, 30, interview given in 2020)

Secondly, respondents insisted on the feeling of rejection caused by the expressions of disbelief of their fellow Jews, who made them feel out of place as Black worshipers, rather than realize the racial homogeneity of their own communities. Guershon put it in the following terms: "In France, unfortunately, it is not yet a given. We face some difficulties, especially when we become curios. People wonder how come we're Jewish. We have to help our White fellow Jews to move on and leave the surprise behind" (Guershon, interview given in 2009). Shulamite, an Ivorian-born convert, said she had gotten used to the staring: "it's no different from stepping into a church where there's no one Black but you. So even if there are hostile stares, I don't see them, I'm like a fish in water" (Shulamite, interview given in 2009).

But given the importance of sharing one's faith with a Jewish community—a point that many cited as one of the pull factors of Judaism—in spite of their bravery and forgiveness, Black converts face unusual hurdles in being integrated in Jewish communities. Guershon Nduwa, the founder of the Fraternité Judéo-Noire (FJN), wrote about race in uncommonly plain terms for a French person:

> The assumption in the French Jewry is that officially, color is invisible. Only colorless [sic] Jews have rights. This utopia looks like self-delusion from the standpoint of people of color, who have to testify every day about their belonging to the community, simply because they do not share the same phenotype with their fellow Jews of European descent.[9]

Not only does the Ashkenazi/Sephardi binary, prevalent in the French Jewry, leave no place to the possibility of Black Jews, but prejudice also exists within this binary, according to the French historian Esther Benbassa. She contends that while the Sephardim are a majority in the French Jewry since the 1960s, they are treated condescendingly by the Ashkenazim, who used to call them "Black" in a derogatory manner. Conversely, among Sephardim, she writes, "families frowned upon any union with an Ashkenazi. But there was a worse prospect, namely marrying a Sephardi from North Africa, which would cause the family to mourn their child. Jews are not immune to (imaginary) notions of superiority of one group over another."[10]

As Katya Gibel Mevorach noted,

> people identified as being "of color" and who are thrust under the limelight are usually Jews by choice, conversion or adoption, as a testament of the capacities for integration of Jews as a people. At any rate, it is the *elision* of Jews of color—from the Maghrib, Ethiopia, Yemen or India—which reinforces the notion that being a Jew and being a person of color are two distinct phenomena. People don't stare in the same way at Whites wishing to join Judaism.[11]

Thus, it should not come as a surprise to hear that Jews from sub-Saharan Africa or the Caribbean islands are also confronted with race-based prejudices. Enoch said that a friend of his, who was adopted by an Ashkenazi family, was once told in his own synagogue that he was "too dark-skinned to be an Ashkenazi" (Enoch, interview given in 2017). As for Alice, who considers herself a Jew on account of her Fulani origins and worships at a Sephardic synagogue in Rouen, this is what she had to say:

> It's fairly complicated but it's mostly Sephardic people who have a problem with people of color. They sort of look down on us and make us feel as if we're not quite welcome. . . . What makes Judaism so strong is that it's a people who are really united and deep into sharing, but it remains an exclusive club. Many things are done for the community, but there's little outreach. There's not much open-mindedness. Of course, most Sephardim are Arabic-speaking Jews and many were born in North Africa before they came to live in France, but they are prejudiced against Arabs, let's face it. You can see clearly how Blacks [sub-Saharan migrants] are treated in North African countries nowadays. Ashkenazim are less prone to be aggressive, I remember we used to celebrate festivals together in Paris for Hanukkah. . . . It's different, it's another atmosphere, they are more welcoming, they smile to you. . . . A Sephardic Jew feels the need to say that *he* is the real Jew, and they claim to be more Jewish than the Ashkenazim. It's funny how among them it's also different as far as women's condition is concerned, their women are less free than on the other [Ashkenazi] side. (Alice, 40, interview given in 2020)

Evidencing the tendency—commonly found in Jewish milieus—to essentialize a given Jewish ethnic subgroup on the basis of one's personal experience with one's community or family, Marah's testimony tended to tip the scales in favor of Sephardim:

> My personal experience proves the contrary: during my conversion I was given a cold shoulder by Ashkenazi communities, so it led me to join the Sephardim. And in the first synagogue I found, I met a very fatherly rabbi, who trusted me,

and even wrote the preface of my book. So I would rather tend to say that there's a cheerfulness among the Sephardim, a way of living your Judaism which leads you ever more to live the Torah from the inside, and that speaks to me more than the "Shalom, shalom" side [superficial greeting] and the Ashkenazi way of favoring intellectualism, where each person finds their pleasure but in the way they think about things. (Marah, 37, interview given in 2020)

Whichever side they take, the duality between Ashkenazim and Sephardim characterizing the French Jewry represents a barrier to the successful integration of Black Jews, as many of them remain aware that they are not perceived as belonging to either of the two groups. This is why they complain of the racist attitudes of their White fellow Jews. As the French sociologist Pierre-Jean Simon notes, racism

> avails itself of whatever differences may exist in the anatomy of human groups, as elements of "visibility," but these do not seem absolutely necessary, for it can make them up out of thin air. . . . Its principle is to create and maintain an unsurmountable, inegalitarian difference so that certain human groups may be arbitrarily banned forever from joining others.[12]

Consequently, the French Jewry, while itself combating antisemitism, is still struggling to transcend the boundaries created by race and ethnicity and integrate racialized individuals who remain defined by their phenotype, even after jumping through the hoops of the conversion process in the Orthodox branch. Expressions of race-based rejection can be traumatic, as in the case of Hanna, a Martiniquan woman who converted with the Consistory: she was banned from her community with the assent of the rabbi (whom I will refrain from naming out of respect for his reputation) because of the pressure exerted by the other women members, who complained of her body odor. As mentioned earlier, rabbis play a key role in the integration of converts—especially visible ones like Blacks—by introducing them to the rest of the community; but in this case, the rabbi became an agent of exclusion.

A third expression of prejudice described by the respondents was paternalism, perceived as a form of racism cloaked in good feelings, the alternative to the glares. In this context, the Black worshiper as Other is treated like a permanent dependent, in need of a tutor because they can never take initiatives. On the basis of the assumption that Black people need to be taught everything, fellow Jews will volunteer to provide information, mentoring, and unsolicited help in deciphering prayer books and understanding rituals. The common stereotype of the Black Other as less intellectually able is the cause of a number of the uncomfortable situations narrated by the respondents. Josué, a Cameroonian convert and a member of the Lubavitch, explained:

the first times I worshiped in my Lubavitch synagogue, I had a lot of people glaring at me. They often came to check if I was following properly in my prayer book. After they had done this a number of times and seen that I was always on the right page or even helping other people who were lost, they eventually left me alone. (Josué, 52, interview given in 2010)

As for Hortense Tsiporah, she reminisced the following event:

One day I was at the synagogue of the Tournelles, where women worship from the balcony and the men downstairs. On the third day, they told me to stay downstairs and seated me almost in front of the rabbis. And then while we were saying the prayers, sometimes I looked up and I could see some of the women gripping the railing to see [laughs] if what I was reading was actually Hebrew. Since they [the rabbis] say the prayers very fast and don't announce the page numbers, I was following and turning the pages just when we were supposed to. And then I heard one of the women say, "it's really Hebrew." (Hortense, AM-I-FA meeting, 2017)

Unsurprisingly, African and Caribbean worshipers tend to be overzealous to counter the paternalistic attitudes of their White fellow Jews.

A fourth aspect of prejudice is that Black Jews also experience rejection in response to their Jewish first and last names, whether they are converts or sons and daughters of Jewish parents (whether adopted or biological). Several respondents have been outraged to face negative reactions when saying their names, particularly the Yayir Kohen siblings, who are Danites from the Ivory Coast. In an open letter, the leaders of AM-I-FA denounced specific acts of discrimination suffered by one of them in hopes to raise awareness in the French Jewish community:

after spending Shabbat at his elder sister's . . . in Sarcelles, [he] went to the Great Synagogue Paul Valéry wearing his talith and his kippah on his head. The name "Yayir," meaning "you shall light the path" has been borne by many generations and in thousands of families of the Dan people of the Ivory Coast as well as other sub-Saharan countries. The security agents immediately began grilling him: "What business do you have here?" "I'm here to attend the service." "Show us your ID." "It's Shabbat so I don't have it on me." "What's your name?" . . . "Your address?" "I live in the eighteenth arrondissement." "So why are you here?" "I am spending Shabbat at my big sister's." "Name and address of your sister?" "Sarah Yayir Kohen, she lives on this street." "What's your father's name?" "Djessia yayir Kohen." "Are you Jewish?" "Yes." "Where do you worship usually?" "Montmartre." "Do you speak and read Hebrew?" "I can read, but I can only speak a little Hebrew." "Have you ever been to Israel?" "Yes, with Taglit in 2015." "Follow us," they said, and they led him away from the CCTV. "Phone number?" He gave it to them. "Your email address?" He gave it to them. "Your Facebook handle?" He gave it to them. They checked and realized he was telling the truth, but they still called the police. When they came, they frisked him in a most humiliating way but found nothing. The policemen, noticing the kippah on his head, said they were surprised that there existed Black Jews and left, saying out loud that this was a case of racism. Yet in spite of this thorough search, which gave no results, the security guards did not let him in to pray. [The young man] just said "thank you" in a calm voice and left, feeling hurt, humiliated, dishonored and bleeding from an inner wound that was already there but had lain dormant until then. They rubbed red pepper on the pre-existing wound, for he suffered similar humiliation all his childhood, and now he says they have killed his *neshama*, his soul.[13]

This example is illustrative of the painful integration of Black Jews in Jewish communities that are not used to their presence. The questions asked by the security agents reveals between the lines the ethnic parameters of Jewishness: Jewish first and last names, the command of Hebrew, a stay in Israel, regular attendance at a synagogue. But the racial element seems to cancel all the ethnic ones. Even if Black worshipers have Jewish last names to show, they remain confronted with distrust. For example, in an interview given in July 2020, another of the Yair-Kohen brothers, who was born in the Ivory Coast and now works in the Paris area as a consultant for business creators, described an unpleasant experience he had while at work, advising a future entrepreneur. The customer, who was Jewish, blurted out, "So you are supposed to be Mister Kohen? Are you sure? Can you show me your ID, I can't believe you can bear the name Kohen." After checking the ID, he went on questioning Ismael, trying to check if he really practiced Judaism, "So you're Jewish, huh? Do you observe Shabbat? What does Shabbat mean for you? Can you recite a blessing for me?" "And he went on and on," he explained; "As I was at work, I refrained from raising my voice, but otherwise I would have asked him to leave my office." This was not an isolated incident, for he concluded: "this is an anecdote that's replicated with many other Jews and even non-Jewish people." The Yayir Kohens, a family of twelve siblings who migrated to France from the Ivory Coast and have always identified as Jews and practiced Kosher rituals, have suffered recurrent acts of discrimination from security at the entrance of synagogues. Even when wearing the kippah and the talith, they are systematically asked by other Jews if they are real Jews or if they are wearing a costume, only to be denied entrance under the pretext that they might be terrorists. Such expressions of race-based prejudice often crystallize around the use by Black Jews of ritual garments and objects. Hortense Tsipporah told me about a similar experience that she had with her son: although she had decorated the room in which her friend's daughter was to celebrate her bat mitsvah, she and her son were searched at the entrance of the synagogue of La Roquette (Paris) when they tried to join the friend and her family. Although the search gave no results apart from a talith, tefillin, and her son's kippah, they were denied entrance. She explained:

> When they [her Jewish friend's family] heard we had been sent off, they banded together. They begged me to come back, and I said, "I'm not coming back." ... Then they asked me to come back for the seudat [a meal ending the Shabbat or religious festivals], saying, "come on, you organized the whole thing and even the seudat, you have to come." I said no, I'm not going to come and be told I'm here to grab some food—you know, because we're Black, they will say we came just for the food. I was not having any of this. So, I did not go back there. (Hortense, interview given in 2010)

Hortense was all the more disgusted with that experience as she had converted to Judaism precisely so that her son might not need to prove his Jewishness. At a conference organized by the International Society for the Study of African Jewry in November 2015 at the Museum of Jewish Art and History in Paris (just before the terrorist attacks) on the theme "Jews from Africa and elsewhere," two of the Yayir Kohen brothers gave the following testimony:

> We had never thought that our being Jews would mean conflict in France, particularly with our own Jewish brethren. We moved to France in 1996 with our brothers and sisters, to join our father who had settled here previously. Everything we had deemed natural ends up being a problem. Indeed, only here in France did we realize that it could be a problem for a Black man to wear a kippah, as we were repeatedly asked by fellow Jews the same question, "Are you really Jewish or is this a costume?"[14]

Emeka, an Igbo from Nigeria who also identifies as a Jew, told me an anecdote that happened to him when he had recently settled in the Paris area. Riding the Paris metro with his kippah on his head, he ran into a group of three Jewish men who were also wearing the kippah. Excited to see White Jews for the first time, he said, he ran up to them to introduce himself, but froze in his steps when they ignored his greeting. These testimonies tend to prove that the visible markers of Judaism—kippah, Magen David, tefillin, or talith—are not sufficient to grant Black Jews legitimacy in the eyes of their White fellow Jews. Unsurprisingly, the Orthodox branch is very often designated as the culprit of such micro-aggressions. The respondents identifying as members of the Reform or Masorti movements who shared negative experiences with me often pointed out that the security agents or believers with prejudiced attitudes were from Orthodox synagogues.

Likewise, respondents who are members of synagogues affiliated with the Consistory also lamented the indifference of their White fellow Jews and resulting acts of discrimination or distancing within the synagogues. In this respect, the Consistory is often blamed for not raising enough awareness about the existence of Black Jews in France. Unfortunately, all my attempts to obtain an interview with Rabbi Joël Mergui, the current President of the Consistory, have been in vain so it is not possible to have his take on the matter.

Whether or not they are acknowledged by White instances or fellow Jews, micro-aggressions play an important part in the daily religious experience of Black Jews. In their responses, there are recurrent mentions of systematic frisking at the entrances of synagogues, long stares, expressions of doubts or even in-depth questioning about their Jewish faith or practice, and indifference expressed by the following words and phrases: "you are here, but no one sees you"; "nobody talked to me"; "are you sure you're Jewish?" or "you are here just for the food." Yet, in spite of such slights, African and Caribbean Jews, whether native-born or converts, insist on identifying with the Jewish people and express pride in belonging to a religion which also nurtures them. As Micheline put it with humor, "I love Jews, I don't know how to explain it but even if at times they play dirty tricks on us [laughs] I love Jews" (Micheline, interview given in 2020). In this identification with White Jews, markers of Jewish ethnicity are appropriated, so that they identify as both Black and Jewish.

A fifth element revealed by the fieldwork is the importance of the Biblical episode of the curse of Ham (see chapter 2) in complicating the integration of Black Jews. Both on the FJN website and in the interviews he gave on French radios, the organization's founder Guershon Nduwa insisted on this passage to deconstruct it; therefore, I decided to insert this point in my questionnaire. The responses show three types of reception of this myth. One group of respondents celebrate the descendants of Ham, as exemplified by Dov, an Ethiopian Jew:

> The first pharaohs were Black men, Nubians. Who gave Moses his power and knowledge? Kushites did. Who created the greatest kingdom on Earth, where everyone was highly civilized? The descendants of Ham, who, by excellence, is a Black man. So it can be said that the Black man invented what we call civilization. And yet we have always been part of History. . . . The actual Jew is the Black man. Our identity was stolen, which is quite normal, because we went through a war. Back in the day, when you went through war, they would go as far as to erase your very existence and rub your name off the walls. What we see nowadays is the result of that, with people forgetting that we come from something big—the greatest city. So we have an identity problem, and that's why I am interested in it. (Dov, 38, interview given in 2009)

The second group is made up of respondents who reject the myth and object to it, as does Guershon Nduwa:

> It's the monotheisms, and especially Christianity, that introduced a dichotomy which in turn contributed to racism incrementally and gradually. Then Islam popularized the thesis of the curse of Ham as the alleged ancestor of Blacks, which eventually was used by enslavers to justify slavery. But nowhere does the Bible say that Ham was Black.[15]

The last group of interviewees believe, like Caroline, that they have been cleared of the curse by converting to Judaism:

> Then there's the story of Ham, because there's the curse. It's not a question of whether or not I believe in it, it's the Torah and the Talmud that mention it, so it's not about whether you want to believe in it or you don't. . . . But then, I don't think that when you are a convert the curse still applies to you. . . . From the Talmud, we know that Ham is the ancestor of Blacks; I never exchanged about it, I just read or heard comments on the Internet, but I never had an opportunity to exchange about it, no. Anyway, it would be like a provocation, a Jew can never talk to me about it, as we are forbidden to embarrass or offend a Jewish brother or sister. To be honest, I don't think that the curse would still follow me after conversion. (Caroline, 30, interview given in 2010)

Yet I did meet respondents who complained of having been offended by explicit or implicit references to the curse of Ham. Enoch shared with me that the father of his ex-girlfriend, expressing his rejection of their relationship, called him a descendant of Ham (Enoch, 24, interview given in 2017). Finally, some respondents—usually the youngest—had nothing to say about it because they had never heard of this passage from the Book of Genesis.

The need felt by most Black Jews to address the myth of the curse of Ham in their daily religious experience may seem revealing of a colonial issue that remains unsolved, regardless of its mythical nature. Indeed, its presence is still demonstrable in modern-day Jewish subjectivities: a *siddur* (prayer book) published in 2003 introduced the *Meshaneh Habriyot* blessing in the following terms: "when seeing a Black person or someone whose features are abnormal by birth, or when seeing an elephant or a monkey."[16] Only Black people from within the Jewry can be cognizant of the existence of such a blessing.

I was personally made aware of the persistence of such beliefs after giving a talk on Black Jews in France at the university of Turku, Finland. After our panel had been closed, I asked two other speakers, both of them eminent scholars of Judaic studies, whether Blacks were mentioned in Biblical Judaism. One answered she had not researched this question, while the other immediately referred to the curse of Blacks through their ancestor Ham. In response to his exposé, the woman scholar put her hand on my shoulder, only to be imitated by her colleague. I did not pay special attention to the gesture, but my other Jewish colleagues did; when they later began speculating on the branch the two speakers belonged to, they ruled out the possibility of their being Lubavitch, telling me, "if they had been Lubavitch, they would never have touched you, but both of them did."

This gave me a deeper insight into the underlying meaning of casual physical interaction with a Black person in the most Orthodox branches of Judaism. It also illustrates the analysis offered by Shmuel Eisenstadt and Bernhard Giessen on the ways in which any religious community constructs its sense of self in interacting with the Other, who may be a fellow member but will be perceived as "simply unalterably different, and this difference conveys inferiority and danger at the same time. Strangers are frequently considered as demonic, or as endowed with a strong and hostile identity which threatens the existence of primordial communities."[17] This observation is corroborated by the recent fieldwork conducted by the US anthropologist Kimberly Arkin on the schooling of young Sephardic French Jews in Orthodox Jewish schools in the greater Paris area; she observed and recorded how a female religion teacher told seniors at Beit Sarah that wine touched or even looked at by a non-Jew was no longer Kosher and therefore unfit for consumption: "If a *goy* so much looks at my glass, I can't drink it; I throw it out. Others might [drink it], but I would rather be safe than sorry."[18] This observation implies that at least some Orthodox Jews profess an ideology of separatism from non-Jews which helps them construct a self-perception of Jewishness as a saintly or sacred identity. Analyzing the processes of socialization or identity construction among the students of these Orthodox schools, Arkin noted that

> many of these same students appealed to an entirely different mode of identity construction—not to nature, but to the sacred or transcendent realm (divine blessing, the Halakhah)—as a way of explaining their invocation of an unchangeable Jewish essence. Where primordial identities are understood as always already constituted, identities rooted in the sacred or transcendent often foreground the constant spiritual and ritual work required for belonging.[19]

This self-identification suggests an elective ideal that discredits non-Jewish Others. However, when the Other is also Jewish but Black, this person finds themselves assigned to an identity which functions as a stigma in the eyes of their White fellow Jews. The CanadianAmerican sociologist Erving Goffman famously defined stigma as a visible or invisible feature that is apt to profoundly discredit its bearer, not in and of itself, but because of the way it is recognized as discrediting in interactions with other individuals.[20]

This made all the more valuable the respondents' answers to my question on their personal reaction of the myth of Ham. This is what Caroline had to say:

> Yes of course, it's sad because it would mean that Jews can legitimately be racist; but Jews still have obligations towards the rest of mankind. As Jews, we are still supposed to love the children of Ham and the foreigners. We shouldn't forget that non-Jews are creatures of Hashem [God] also. So we should not forget that no matter our color, black, green or yellow, we still have an ethics to abide by. This is really the main cause of backlash for us when we treat people wrong; because it gives cause for complaint to all those who are covert anti-Semites; whereas if we respect ourselves and one another, they have nothing to criticize. All too often I hear things like "some Jews are racist," "Jewish people mistreated me," "my boss is Jewish, and this is what he did to me." Of course, it doesn't make it okay for others to be anti-Semites. So not giving them any cause for complaint is an advantage for us, that's what I think. (Caroline, interview given in 2010)

Contrary to Caroline, who shifted the question from acknowledging anti-Black prejudice to countering antisemitism while identifying Blacks as "others," Emeka, one of the Igbo Jews for Jesus I interviewed, chose to admonish White Jews in these terms:

> No, Blacks are not cursed, God did not curse Black people, but God cursed Israel, God cursed Jewish people. Because in spite of what God did, by making the Jewish people get out of Egypt, they still strayed away from Him. You're asking me if Black people are cursed. Well, let me ask you just one thing, is there any peace in Israel, and can their children go to school normally? No. Aren't they the ones who are cursed? Now, all around the world, you almost need a policeman for every Jew—doesn't this look like a curse to you? (Emeka, 33, interview given in 2013)

Clearly, a certain degree of self-denial is perceptible among those who accept the notion that Blacks are cursed and hope to be saved by conversion to Judaism, while a reversal of the stigma (as analyzed by Erving Goffman) is noticeable among those for whom being the posterity of Ham is a positive identity. As for Alice, she chose to revisit history and question the rejection of Blacks that she witnessed among Jews:

> Often, in Jewish milieus, people feel quite comfortable saying that Jews are Semites . . . Why is it so hard for Jews to admit that a part of their Semitic identity actually comes from race mixing? Because it's true that Blacks mingling with Caucasians produced the Semitic origin of Jews and Arabs. What I find sad today about mankind is that whether you talk about Judaism, Christianity or

Islam, you get the impression that Blacks have no place in any religion. I don't understand why there's so much contempt towards Black people, I really don't get it. Because if you go back in history, when you talk about Jews getting out of Egypt, you cannot be speaking of Jews as we know them today. Of course they were Black Jews, and there are descriptions on the black stone tablet [perhaps a reference to the Mesha stele] which say clearly that they were Kemites, which means Blacks. And then there was a derivation of the term Kushi, from the Land of Kush, and I don't understand why this entire dimension of history got erased. (Alice, 40, interview given in 2020)

This response shows that the attractiveness of Afrocentric theses among Blacks in France who seek a positive narrative about African civilizations predating White ones (see chapter 2) may also be observed among Black Jews.

Among the issues complicating the integration of Black Jews in the French Jewry is the very designation "Black Jews," because in emphasizing race, it suggests that the Jewish norm is White. How should they call themselves? At the convention of the Fraternité Judéo-Noire (FJN), Marah called for the discarding of the term "Black Jews" in the following terms:

Black Jews—well, I hope that in the near future the term "Black" will go away and we'll just be Jews, period. Otherwise, maybe, if we need to define those Jews coming from Africa, the Caribbean, or who are pan-African, the let's say, "the children of Zipporah." (Marah, FJN convention, 2010)

This suggestion reveals two major elements. First, it shows one more time the insistence of Black Jews on belonging to historical Judaism via descent. The episode of Moses' marriage to Zipporah (*Numbers* 12:1) is an important and recurrent feature whenever the respondents address their modes of identification to the Jewish people.

Then, even if the term "Black Jews" tends to be commonly used, it still causes discomfort on three levels. First, just after I had introduced my research to an Ethiopian Jew prior to interviewing her, she corrected me, saying, "I am not a Black Jew, I am a Beta Israel." Although Ethiopian Jews are often designated as Falashas, which means "exiled," they refuse to be called as such, due to the word's negative connotation, and insist on self-identifying as Beta Israel (the House of Israel). Secondly, other interviewees also objected to being identified as "Black Jews," like Shoshana, an Ivorian-born convert who joined the Orthodox branch:

Let me tell you something first. I feel uncomfortable with these designations. It's a very Jewish thing to always add something to Jewish identity: Moroccan Jew, Tunisian Jew, Spanish Jew, Black Jew. Why don't you find these labels in other religions? People here never talk about Black Muslims, Italian Muslims, Black

> Christians or fill-in-the-blank Christian. . . . I am Jewish, period. (Shoshana, 27, interview given in 2009)

Dov, whose family is Ethiopian, shared the same position:

> Something I really dislike is that people keep talking of Black Jews, Moroccan Jews, Portuguese Jews. No! Because if you're a Jew, you're a Jew. When you're a Muslim, there are no Black Muslims or Arab Muslims. (Dov, 38, interview given in 2009)

These Jewish believers are seemingly trapped between the French ideal of universal colorblindness and the self-identification practices existing in the French Jewry, where national origins remain important.

The third cause for tension around the term "Black Jews" is the tone sometimes used by their fellow Jews to designate them. One of my interviewees, who asked for total anonymity, shared with me a personal experience:

> I attend Midrash classes, and one day we were each introducing ourselves on request of the instructor. After I had introduced myself, the instructor added, "*He* is a Black Jew," and I did not understand why he needed to specify this, especially since my classmates who are also Jewish were not gratified with such a comment on top of introducing themselves.

On the one hand, these believers consider themselves to be full-fledged Jews; but on the other hand, they feel singled out by their White fellow Jews who either ignore them or racialize them as Black in order to introduce distance and barriers.

Such instances of rejection and perceived discrimination kindle inner tensions, which translate in two ways: some renounce the Jewish faith while others persevere. The former have been a minority among my respondents, in part because I sought out individuals identifying as Jews rather than ex-Jews, but even those who still did had stories to share. An Ethiopian Jewish interviewee told me that her Ashkenazi husband had eventually become an atheist out of disgust for the racism suffered by his multiracial family, and that their children had become supporters of the anti-Zionist Black comedian Dieudonné. Another respondent, Enoch, explained that he knew a young biracial woman with a Sephardic mother and an Ivorian father, who

> couldn't take it anymore. It was too much, she didn't last more than six months, and then she had enough. Whenever she entered a synagogue, people made nasty comments and did all they could to make her ill at ease. Yet she did everything right, she did the Shabbat right, she had her head covered, she did all she was

supposed to. She finally gave up and it's a shame, she's disappointed, disgusted, and has completely stopped practicing. (Enoch, 24, interview given in 2017)

Likewise, Liana, whose mother is Sephardic while her father is from Guadeloupe, told me that her mother not only ended up divorcing him when she understood he would never be allowed to convert to Judaism, but she actually renounced her Jewish faith out of disappointment. Meanwhile, Liana's father became a Buddhist (Liana, interview given in 2012). Finally, Ismaël Yayir Kohen, whose family is well-known in Black Jewish circles, told me that his father had suffered so many slights that he no longer worships in synagogues but prays at home; as a matter of fact, I have never been able to obtain an interview with him.

Nevertheless, many other Black Jewish believers persist in their faith despite more or less severe micro-aggressions—which does not mean that they suffer in silence instead of denouncing the rejection. In reaction to the discriminatory searches at the entrances of synagogues, they usually send letters to the Consistory, which sends back a letter of apology in response. This what Hortense described: "I wrote the Consistory, I wrote the Chief Rabbi of Paris, I wrote the President of the Board of Administrators, and they wrote back with apologies like 'some people can be overzealous,' and that was all. Then he [the security guard] also apologized" (Hortense, interview given in 2010). However, it must be said that many respondents feel increasingly impatient of such formal apologies, whose only effect is to temporarily appease tensions until the next racist incident happens.

In reaction to attitudes of rejection in synagogues, Black Jews also opt for strategies akin to the African American concept of John Henryism, that is, outperforming their White fellow Jews in their religious practice. Hortense/Zipporah gave a good example of this:

> I can honestly say that everywhere I have been, at conferences, in synagogues where they don't know me, they have noted that I sing very well, while they can't sing. They are reminded that they were born in the culture, but they haven't learned vocally, but I know all the prayers, even the prayers women don't say, I know everything. So, they are surprised, and pleasantly surprised. When demonstrations are organized to support Israel or denounce an anti-Semitic attack, I am always present. So the people I meet in demonstrations are happy and then when they hear me sing, they tell me, "You know it all!" and they hug me. (Hortense, interview given in 2010)

She is not the only one to seek excellence in the recitation and singing of prayers, attendance to worship services and community demonstrations on the streets or other public places, where they are seen bearing all the identity markers (kippah, Magen David, tzitzit, tefillin, and talith), and draped in the Israeli flag while the rest of the crowd is less conspicuously Jewish.

Faced with the barrier created by the ideology of matrilineal descent and often intent on identifying with their White fellow Jews, Black Jews tend to either engage in genealogical searches or craft Jewish origins for themselves.[21] Their need to find a stable pace for themselves in the French and global Jewry is so acute that many feel that Jewish ancestry is absolutely necessary to demonstrate the legitimacy of their sense of identification to the Jewish people. Dina, a convert from Guadeloupe who was accepted by the Consistory, explains:

> I left Guadeloupe some time ago. . . . Everything began because the Inquisition persecuted all these Jews, whether they were Portuguese or Italian or from some other country. They emigrated not only to North Africa, but also to the Caribbean islands. When I researched my genealogy on my mother's side, I began to trace de family names for which there was no specific place mentioned, and I realized that the family name that came from our great-great-grandfather came from northern Italy. Continuing my search, I found others who came from Tunisia. . . . Our ancestors, part of whom have been rediscovered but [for whom] we can't go further back in time, were navigators, and they are Jewish. (Dina, testimony given at the FJN convention, 2010)

Genealogy proves so central to Judaism and Jewishness today that Black Jews, whether converts or native Jews, invest in searches to confirm their intuitions or feed their imagination. Some scrutinize their genealogy in parallel with their conversion process, as Dina did. African converts often put forward a mythical or imaginary genealogy to assert their historical belonging to the Jewish people. Marah, who is a native of Congo and was admitted by the Consistory, emphasized the subjectiveness of this sense of belonging:

> There are also cases such as mine, where you suppose you have Jewish ancestry that you cannot prove because Africa doesn't have an administrative culture that allows you to go back to the year 1700 or 1800 to prove your genealogy. I have an unproven genealogy that is complicated to justify . . . Being a Congolese and a Jews are not incompatible, quite the contrary: my [Kongo] ethnic origin allows me to feel close to Judaism. (Marah, interview given in 2010)

Among my African interviewees, Cameroonians from the Bassa, Beti, and Douala ethnic groups have all emphasized their alleged belonging to the Jewish people, while an Angolan said to me assertively that all Bantus are Jews (see chapter 2). Under these circumstances, these respondents' perseverance in seeking conversion in spite of all the deterrents is also partly due to their firm belief that they already belong to the Jewish people thanks to their ethnic group. A conversion then legitimizes or at least confirms their sense of belonging to the Jewish people, even if it may be based on speculation.

Likewise, the frequency of interracial marriages among Black Jews is also partly attributable to the importance of descent in Jewish milieus. On the one hand, the question of transmission of Jewishness to the children and therefore the latter's affiliation to the Jewish people is presumably settled by marriage with an Ashkenazi or Sephardic partner (see chapter 6). On the other hand, however, the American anthropologist Katya Gibel Azoulay, who herself experienced the situation of persons born of Black-White Jewish parents, stresses that things are not so simple for native-born Black or biracial Jews:

> An "interracial" child of a Black parent and a Jewish parent can always and often will be designated as both Black and Jewish. Membership (ascriptive or voluntary) in one or both communities manifests the experiental dimension of race and the complexity of giving Jewishness meaning in a secular world. Considering what happens at the intersection of these two different frames of reference as a "context of being" brings into relief questions of alienation, subjective positions, and social experiences, as well as the place of history and memory as a cornerstone for cohesive identities (as opposed to the fragmentation suggestive of a postmodernist model).[22]

In the contemporary French Jewry in particular, cultivating the memory of the Holocaust is so central that historian Esther Benbassa entitled one of the chapters of her book *Suffering as Identity,* "French Jews' Conversion to the Religion of the Holocaust." In a socio-political context where the memories of the slave trade and the Holocaust are regularly pitted against each other, biracial respondents have often expressed that they feel directly concerned, having actually inherited the trauma. For example, Laure's father and grandparents personally experienced the viciousness of antisemitism:

> My father was a hidden child—well, first, my grandfather was born in Romania and arrived in France when he was nine and lived in poverty. He slept on the streets, so everything I hear about today echoes his experience, for he was undocumented. He got the French citizenship but was stripped of it by the Vichy regime. He was born in 1915 and my grandmother was born in 1920 in France. My great-grandmother was a storeowner, so she had a little money. You know, those Jews who succeeded in life were those who spoke some French and knew how to build a network. My father was born in 1941 and as you can guess, it was not the best year for having or expecting a baby. Everyone on my father's side, I mean all the men, enrolled in the army along with his father. So, they left the women and children behind, and they went to Switzerland. Switzerland left its boundaries open for some time, provided you had a child under one year old. It was my father's case, so they were able to escape to Switzerland. My grandparents had to stay in relocation camps that were funded by a charity, and

my father was sent to live for 4 or five years at a Swiss pastor's and returned to France in 1945. (Laure, 54 years old, interview given in 2020)

But aside from biracial Black Jews with Ashkenazi family, my respondents have often paired the memory of the Holocaust with that of the Transatlantic Slave Trade, emphasizing the parallels between the persecutions suffered by both groups and also mentioning the presence of Black detainees in Nazi concentration camps. French historian and African studies specialist Catherine Coquery-Vidrovitch[23] authored a book on Blacks as forgotten victims of Nazism and Ivorian journalist Sergé Bilé[24] also published his research on Blacks in Nazi concentration camps, where he shows that concentration camp detainees also included Africans, Caribbeans, and African Americans. From the interviewees' standpoint, this knowledge legitimizes their feeling of solidarity with Jews as victims of Nazism, because not only were the persecutions comparable, but the two groups that are so often seen as competing for victim status actually shared the same spaces. Claudine, who is of Martiniquan descent, said, "I feel concerned [by the memory of the Holocaust]. Blacks too were victims of the Holocaust: people must read Serge Bilé's book on Blacks in Nazi camps" (interview given in 2010). Alice pleaded for a more comprehensive approach of the Holocaust:

> Commemorating the Holocaust is a good thing, but many people get forgotten, because it was not only Jews who got killed in this horrible war and this cleansing. They eliminated disabled people and homosexuals, as well as people of color, ultimately, in these concentration camps, and communities of Roma people too, it wasn't only Jews. Yet they [Jews] had this ability to get to work on their memory, which Africans were not able, or not allowed, to do. (Alice, 40, interview given in 2020)

For Hortense, "slavery and the Holocaust are one and the same, it's all about human hostility" (Hortense, interview given in 2010). Likewise, Ofer, a former preacher, chose to preach that "whether we talk about slavery or the Holocaust, our duty is to refuse to transmit hatred to the next generations" (Ofer, 30 years old, interview given in 2011). Yet Moshe, who was born in Guadeloupe and is therefore a descendant of enslaved Africans, notes a lack of transmission on the Caribbean side: "people make a lot of noise around the memory of slavery, but in the Antilles, people never address the question: it's a taboo" (Moshe, forty-five, interview given in 2009). Significantly, none of the respondents mentioned Jews' presumably greater ability to empathize with other victims of crimes against humanity and race-based discrimination, but rather insisted on Blacks' inclination to do so.

In conclusion, nearly all of the persons interviewed, except the teenagers and the members of the Masorti and Reform Judaism movements (who are not exempt from discrimination, though), have stressed that their integration to the French Jewry was or had been a painful process. Faced with indifference, rejection, outright racism, or doubts on the possibility of their Jewishness, my respondents adopted various individual strategies aiming to simultaneously protect themselves and transform the mentalities of their White fellow Jews: "I pretend not to notice"; "they need some more time to get used to us again"; "it makes me laugh"; "I began calling them out for their racism"; "well, they're only human, nobody's perfect"; "people need to evolve" were recurrent statements in the fieldwork. In their quest for a better integration, many move from one synagogue to another, while others have opted out of their synagogues or communities to pray at home; a third group have decided to remain in their synagogues and simultaneously denounce the slights they are suffering, by becoming involved in community organizations, which is their ultimate form of reaction to racial prejudice within Jewish milieus.

NOTES

1. See Sébastien Tank-Storper, *Juifs d'élection. Se convertir au Judaïsme* (Paris: CNRS Editions, 2007).

2. Tank-Storper, *Juifs d'élection*, 17–18.

3. Fredrik Barth, "Les groupes ethniques et leurs frontières," in Philippe Poutignat and Jocelyne Streiff-Fénart, eds., *Théories de l'ethnicité* (Paris: PUF, 1995), 203–49.

4. Ghiles-Meilhac, "Les juifs français."

5. Pierre-André Taguieff, *L'antisémitisme* (Paris: PUF, 2015), 28.

6. Henri Giordan, *Démocratie culturelle et droit à la différence* (Paris: La Documentation française, 1982), in Ghiles-Meilhac, "Les juifs français."

7. Pierre-Jean Simon, "Ethnisme et racisme, ou l'École de 1492," *Cahiers Internationaux de Sociologie* XLVIII (January–June 1970): 119–152. Simon distinguishes "ethnism," as a form of classification based on cultural criteria, from racism which is a form of classification based on natural criteria, stressing that both racial and cultural modes of classification differ in terms of their degrees of permanence.

8. http://www.jewishmultiracialnetwork.org/who-we-are/and https://globaljews.org/, accessed March 18, 2024.

9. Guershon Nduwa, "De l'invisibilité des Juifs noirs en France," accessed July 21, 2008, http://www.fjn-123.fr/spip. php?article48 quoted in Mokoko Gampiot, "Black Judaism in France," 324.

10. Esther Benbassa, "Être séfarade ou pas," *L'Express,* December 19, 2007, accessed June 27, 2021, http://www.lexpress.fr/actualite/societe/etre-sefarade-ou-pas_474041.html.

11. Katya Gibel Mevorach, "Les identités juives au miroir de l'héritage du racisme aux États-Unis," *Pardès* 44, no. 1 (2008): 120–21, https://www.cairn.info/revue-pardes-2008-1-page-119.htm, consulted March 3, 2024.

12. Pierre-Jean Simon, *La Bretonnité, une ethnicité problématique* (Rennes, France: Éditions Terre de Brume presses universitaires de Rennes, 2006), 13.

13. AM-ISRAËL-FARAFINA, open letter, "Stop au racisme antijuifs-Noirs-Métisses (*sic*)- Basanés," Paris, April 3, 2017.

14. Testimony by three of the Yayir Kohen brothers at the conference entitled "Juifs d'Afrique et d'ailleurs. L'essor du judaïsme en Afrique, dans la diaspora africaine et en Asie au XXe siècle," organized by ISSAJ (The International Society for the Study of African Jewry) in Paris, at the Musée d'Art et d'histoire et du judaïsme, November 10 and 11, 2015.

15. Guershon Nduwa, "Les Noirs sont-ils les descendants de Cham, le maudit?" accessed October 12, 2010, http://www.fjn-123.fr/spip.php?article160.

16. For a more recent reference which also discusses the connotations of the term "Kushi" in modern Hebrew, see Tal Kra-Oz, "Israeli Chief Rabbi Calls African Americans 'Monkeys,'" *The Tablet,* March 21, 2018, accessed September 10, 2022, https://www.tabletmag.com/sections/news/articles/israels-chief-rabbi-calls-african-americans-monkeys.

17. Shmuel Eisenstadt and Bernhard Giessen, "The Construction of Collective Identity," *European Journal of Sociology / Archives Européennes de Sociologie / Europäisches Archiv Für Soziologie* 36, no. 1 1995: 78–9 http://www.jstor.org/stable/23999434.

18. Kimberly A. Arkin, *Rhinestones, Religion, and the Republic: Fashioning Jewishness in France* (Stanford: Stanford University Press, Stanford Studies in Jewish History and Culture series, 2014), 156.

19. Arkin, *Rhinestones,* 135.

20. See Erving Goffman, *Stigma: Notes on the Management of Spoiled Identity* (Englewood Cliffs, NJ: Prentice Hall, 1963).

21. See Aurélien Mokoko Gampiot, "La quête des origines chez les Juifs noirs en France," in Joëlle Allouche-Benayoun, ed., *Mondes Séfarade, Proche-Oriental et Africain,* Vol. 3, 2014.

22. Katya Gibel Azoulay, *Black, Jewish, and Interracial. It's Not the Color of Your Skin, but the Race of your Kin, and Other Myths of Identity* (Durham and London: Duke University Press, 1997), 32.

23. Catherine Coquery-Vidrovitch, *Des victimes oubliées du nazisme. Les Noirs et l'Allemagne dans la première moitié du XXe siècle* (Paris: Le Cherche Midi, 2007).

24. Serge Bilé, *Noirs dans les camps nazis* (Paris: Éditions du Rocher / Le Serpent à Plumes, 2005).

Chapter 5

Black Jewish Organizations in France

THE FÉDÉRATION INTERNATIONALE DES JUIFS NOIRS (FJN) AND AM-ISRAËL-FARAFINA (AM-I-FA)

Personal dissatisfaction due to attitudes of rejection have gradually given rise to a collective protest movement, with Black Jews organizing to raise awareness within the French Jewry. Two organizations have become prominent over the past decade: the Fédération internationale des Juifs noirs (FJN), or international federation of Black Jews, and Am-Israël-Farafina.[1] The FJN was founded by Guershon Nduwa, a native of the Democratic Republic of Congo who was born in 1965 and discovered Jewish culture while growing up in Israel, where his parents were diplomats. He converted to Judaism after meeting with Leon Ashkenazi, a famous rabbi known as Manitou, during the latter's stay in Cameroon; then he learned Hebrew and attended courses at the Hebrew University of Jerusalem. He moved to France in 1995 and spent seven years waiting in vain for his conversion to be validated by the Consistory, after which he joined the Mouvement juif libéral de France (MJLF), which is part of the Reform Judaism movement. His mentors were Rabbis Daniel Farhi, one of the founders of the MJLF, and Rivon Krygier, who was the leader later took the leadership of the first Masorti synagogue in Paris. His personal experience and his growing awareness of the difficulties faced by Black Jews in France, both in and outside of the Jewry, led him to join activist movements. The first of these was the Alliance judéo-noire (Black-Jewish alliance) created in 1994 by Abdoulaye Barro, a native of Burkina Faso (West Africa) who was the first to initiate a rapprochement between Jews and Blacks in France. In 1995, the organization took a new name, "Juifs et Africains," under the leadership of the philosophers Abdoulaye Barro and Shalem Coulibaly and the ethnologist and filmmaker Maurice Dorès.

In 2004, he co-founded the organization Amitié judéo-noire (Black-Jewish friendship) with filmmaker and actor Cheikh Doukouré, physician Yves-Victor Kamami, and the ethnologist and filmmaker Maurice Dorès, in a context where many organizations were created by minority groups such as the Indigènes de la République, Devoir de mémoire, or Conseil Représentatif des Associations Noires de France (CRAN). Nduwa had been the secretary of the latter organization before he founded the Fraternité Judéo-Noire in 2007 with Lawrence Mordekhai Thomas, an African American Jewish academic, Emanuel Yerday, an Ethiopian Israeli, David Lharrar, an Ethiopian Frenchman, and Alexandre Feigenbaum, an Ashkenazi antiracist activist and emeritus professor at the national institute for agronomical research. In 2013, the FJN changed its name to Fédération Internationale des Juifs Noirs, with Guershon Nduwa as President, Daniel Limor (an Israeli) as Vice-President, Lawrence Mordekhai Thomas as secretary, and Christine Yaltonsky as coordinator and treasurer. The new FJN aims to liaise among Black Jews all over the world and has its headquarters in Nigeria. Nduwa explains that he chose that country because it is home to large numbers of Igbo Jews.

In 2013, another organization was born out of a split in the FJN, due to charges of embezzlement brought against Nduwa: Am-Israël-Farafina. It is chaired by a woman, Hortense Tsiporah Bilé, who was born in the Ivory Coast and lived in Israel as a diplomat's daughter like Guershon Nduwa. Her organization is defined as Zionist, pro-Israel, and aiming to facilitate rapprochements between Israel and African countries, as the name shows: A-M are the first two letters of the word "amitié," which means friendship in French, while "am" means "people" in Hebrew; I stands for Israel and F-A for Farafina, which is the name of Africa in Bambara, one of the languages of Mali in West Africa. Members are used to calling it AM-I-FA. Due to the life experiences of their founders, both organizations critique the lack of integration of Black Jews in France and work for their recognition within the French Jewry.

The two organizations have the same mission statement: making Black Jews visible and their voices heard within the Jewish diaspora and particularly the French Jewry, and fighting against racism and discrimination within French Jewish institutions and French society. Both claim a religious identity, without explicit ties to a particular branch of Judaism; but their common emphasis on revealing the existence of race-based discrimination in Jewish milieus is a testament to Black Jews' will to speak for themselves. When I asked Guershon Nduwa why he had founded his organization, he answered:

The creation of the Amitié judéo-noire was essentially rooted in cross-cultural dialog. With the rise of anti-Semitism in Black milieus, we needed a structure that could bring them closer to one another. Then, the organization morphed into a political movement, which I could no longer relate to. But this is not the reason why I founded the Fraternité judéo-noire. *This* organisation is about the community only. When you look at the United States, Israel, and the United Kingdom, you realize that representing Black Jews is a non-issue; while in France, it poses a problem. But we have a place and we want to play a part just like the Jews from North Africa and Eastern Europe. We refuse to be seen as an eternal minority. (Guershon Nduwa, interview given in June 2009)[2]

All the branches of Judaism coexist within the FJN and AM-I-FA, insofar as their members may worship at synagogues from the Consistory, the Lubavitch movement, the Masorti or Reform Judaism movements, or even be Jews for Jesus and non-Jews. The Torah and Talmud are the books of reference. Many of the members speak Hebrew and teach it to both members and non-members, organize trips to Israel for both spiritual revitalization and language immersion for Hebrew learners. Their religious practices are centered on the Kashrut: they shop at Kosher supermarkets or order from Kosher catering businesses under the control of Jewish religious instances. However, Black Jews from sub-Saharan African cultures emphasize African culinary practices' similarities with the Kashrut, particularly the ritual slaughtering of animals and insistence on hygiene in the processing and cooking of food to further demonstrate the validity of identification claims between their ethnic groups and the Jewish people.

Food is a particular locus of identity claims and recognition, as observed by the French sociologist Séverine Mathieu: "the kitchen as a unique space of memory and transmission holds a special place in the transmission of Judaism." During her fieldwork, dishes or preparations were labeled as Jewish when presented by her respondents:

> Most of the time, "Jewish dishes," or dishes identified as such, appeared on the tables (of Ashkenazi or Sephardic families alike). . . . [T]o create spaces allowing them to maintain a link with a secular form of Judaism, respondents have resorted to individual "operations of bricolage," and what is done in the kitchen also involves such operations.[3]

When Black Jews come from countries where the food consumed has little to do with Mediterranean culinary customs, they express a similar need to implement "operations of bricolage." Whether converts or native Jews, many African Jews seek to share and enhance the cuisines they were raised with, in spite of the difficulties encountered in finding African foodstuffs in Kosher grocery stores supervised by the Beth Din; but cross-cultural reluctance also creates obstacles. Guershon Nduwa gave me the example of fried locusts, which are a very common delicacy in the Great Lakes region of Africa:

> There is nothing more Kosher than locusts, they are designated in the Torah as very Kosher food. When I returned from spending holidays in the Congo, I brought back some locusts and offered a few to the rabbi of my synagogue. They all refused to have them because they distrust anything they don't know. (Guershon, interview given in 2013)

Appropriating the concept of Pan-Africanism in the FJN's manifesto, Guershon Nduwa pleaded in favor of a diversification of the Kashrut in France thanks to Black Jewish organizations like his own:

> Keeping a Kosher diet on a daily basis implements an economic cycle in which we Africans are compelled to squeeze certain foods that belong to Pan-African culture but that the mainstream forces here in France have not made Kosher in their understanding of the concept. True, merguez [a spicy beef and mutton sausage, very popular in the North African couscous dish], falafels and couscous are not unsavory, but we want to be able to enjoy our own typical Pan-African food while respecting the Halakha. Pan-African identity has other specificities, whether they be physical, culinary or educational, but France sorely lacks adequate responses to these specificities. This is why the FJN, in its community outreach, hopes that in the next ten years, stores, shops and facilities allowing the Pan-African Jews to live their specificities while strictly abiding by the Kashrut.[4]

Back Jewish organizations pursue a double goal. On the one hand, they aim to help Back Jews in France to live as Jews recognized by the Consistory on a par with members of other Jewish ethnicities (namely, Sephardim and Ashkenazim). On the other hand, they combat racism and discrimination within the French Jewry as well as the rising antisemitism expressed in the broader French society. These activists ask for dedicated spaces where they could meet, organize training sessions and cultural and intellectual exchanges with other Black Jews from France and elsewhere, in order to stop being unseen and anonymous. In the long run, they also aim to contribute to Jewish museums outreach, by giving the public access to archives on the little-known histories of Black Jews. The positions of the FJN and AM-I-FA reveal a need to address the articulations and intersections of race and ethnicity with Jewish matters. More importantly, it is also because these organizations took control of the information and its circulation that the issues faced by Jews of African and Caribbean descent have been receiving more publicity over the past ten years.

AM-I-FA is active from within the structures of the Reform Judaism branch, particularly the Paris-based Alliance pour un judaïsme traditionnel et moderne (AJTM) led by Rabbi Gabriel Farhi and aiming to combine Halakhic principles with the evolutions of an increasingly globalized world. As Hortense Tsiporah Bilé, AM-I-FA's founder and President, is a member of AJTM, it partners with the latter to give exposure to its activities. Bilé teaches Talmud-Torah classes, which gather children from age seven every Sunday in the facilities of ATJM's community center. The learning objectives are centered on reading Hebrew, studying Jewish holidays, cantillating prayers, and the Parasha, in preparation for the bar mitsvah or bat mitsvah.

Both organizations also express a need of exposure within the global Jewry, particularly in Jewish institutions and media. Their strategies include attending the communities that they consider to be more inclusive, such as the community center of the greater Ermont-Eaubonne (CCEE) located in Saint-Leu-la-Forêt, in the Paris metropolitan area, where the members of FJN often go to celebrate Pessah and Sukkot. This center has a synagogue for rituals and festivals and also offers a vibrant and diversified range of cultural activities in connection with the city. The CCEE is committed to welcoming all Jews, whatever their opinions or religious practice, and offering them a space in a spirit of togetherness and mutual help. The members of AM-I-FA often celebrate Sukkot in the Paris apartment of Rabbi Gabriel Farhi (AJTM), where they can come with non-Jewish friends. I have had the privilege of being invited both at the CCEE and at Rabbi Farhi's home for Sukkot.

However, the FJN, striving for a better inclusion of its members in Jewish cultural and religious life, aims to play a role in it by calling for a community center or synagogue for Blacks in the greater Paris area, in spite of the French dogma of colorblindness. Ruth, a member of the FJN, said, "Oh yes, I am all for it, I can't wait, and I'm trying to get my folks involved to help raise funds. I hope that that project will be fulfilled and grow, especially if the Consistory is in charge. I insist on that synagogue being under the control of the Consistory, so we'll be Orthodox Black Jews. It's doable, otherwise we'll always be considered by the other Jews, whether non-Black of White, as something that doesn't belong. We should be seen as full-fledged Jews, like anyone else. We have to be under the control of the Consistory and practice an Orthodox ritual, because that's how we'll earn our recognition among the rest" (Ruth, 30, interview given in 2010). The founder of the FJN, Guershon Nduwa, said that the planned synagogue "will of course be open to our fellow Jews of all walks of life. The Jewish community is too confined to Ashkenazim and Sephardim. Since we are neither one nor the other, what are we supposed to do?" (Guershon, interview given in 2010).

The interviewees expressed a diversity of viewpoints regarding the need for a Black synagogue:

if the point is to avoid being glared at, I am all for it; but if it's about getting together only with other Black folks and being in a ghetto, then I don't want any of that. (Yann, interview given in 2009)

I find it interesting to push for a Black synagogue for us to become visible. Because it makes sense, there are twelve tribes of Israel and each tribe has its own way of life, so it's a good thing to have a Black synagogue. Now, is it important to have a Black synagogue? We can have a synagogue, period, where everyone, every people, every color, every tribe will stop being alien to one another. Because we used to be scattered by the multitude, but today we are part of the multitude; everywhere you go, to India or wherever, you see Black folks. (Dov, interview given in 2009)

Some time ago I didn't get the point of the synagogue we wanted to created, but now I understand better, because Black people need to be given their identity back. Because people don't need camo unless they're at war. It doesn't have to be especially for Blacks [in English], everyone must feel welcome, Ashkenazim, Sephardim, Blacks or others. It's about recognition. (Moshe, interview given in 2009)

I have mixed feelings about that Black synagogue. I'm not going to leave my home to move into a Black ghetto. At first, I wasn't favorable to it, because we had to give people the time they needed to get used to Black folks, so for me, we are drawing back instead of seeking integration. (Shoshana, interview given in 2009)

The need to create a Black synagogue or community center is clearly being expressed in reaction to the rejection and discrimination suffered by many believers. Yet, Rabbi Rivon Krygier confesses that

it would be shameful for the Jewish community. It would mean that we are incapable of integrating Blacks, it would be like a synagogue for homosexuals, that would mean we're incapable of integrating homosexuals so they are forced to go found their own synagogue. If we do that, to me we're admitting our failure. I think we shouldn't lock ourselves up in a ghetto. (Rabbi Rivon Krygier, interview given in 2012).

Hannah, an Ethiopian Jew, echoes this view in the following terms:

creating a synagogue only for Black Jews would be a way of corralling them and rejecting them even further, it's a way of turning them away from their Jewishness. No offense, but in Israel, Black Jews are welcome in all synagogues. When I lived in Israel, whenever I felt like going to a synagogue I did so, no matter what religious brand worshiped there. I know that as an Ethiopian, and as a Black woman, I am labeled from the onset because I'm different, even if I'm Jewish, I know I'm different. . . . I won't attend such a synagogue, as I told you. Those Black Jews who do that are hurting themselves; I believe that the vast majority of these people haven't lived in Israel. It would be better if they went to Israel, then they would better frame the issue. They really should go to Israel, and then they would realize that there's no specifically black synagogue over there. Staring at folks is a universal problem—if you're Black in a country of Whites, you'll be stared at, and if you're White in a country of Blacks, you'll be stared at just the same. (Hannah, interview given in 2012)

Nevertheless, although both organizations' founders did live in Israel, they object to the identity controls and frisking at the entrances of synagogues, which they claim apply more systematically and insistently to Black worshipers. In a highly recurrent manner, their quest for recognition also involves the objectives defined by the FJN and AM-I-FA, namely, denouncing the hostile stares directed to them in synagogues, sensitizing their fellow White Jews to the possibility of Blacks worshiping in synagogues, criticizing the extra-lengthy conversion process and spiritual training for Black candidates, challenging the unwelcoming attitudes of the owners of specialized bookstores and Kosher grocery stores, and contesting the systematic searches at the entrances of synagogues. The most recent illustration of this struggle was when a young Danite was searched in front of the synagogue in Sarcelles in 2015. The outrage caused by this incident was such that AM-I-FA's leaders decided to write an open letter to all Jewish authorities in France (the Presidents of the Consistory and the CRIF, or Representative council of Jewish organizations in France, the Chief Rabbi of France, the ambassador of Israel in France, the President of the BNVCA [Bureau national de vigilance contre l'antisémitisme], and the rabbi of all French synagogues) to denounce racism in French Jewish milieus. The content of this letter, entitled "Stop racism!," caused a shock among the latter, who are all the more sensitive to accusations of racism as their community has suffered more than others of racial hatred, especially during World War II; even though it is common to hear in France that it is human, after all, to be racist because everyone wants to stick with their own kind. As the French sociologist Ida Simon-Barouh noted, "Equally strong is the idea that staying within the community is a necessity in order to preserve oneself and avoid ignorance and faux-pas, and all the clashes stemming from the inevitable impossibility to communicate one's culture, as well as the mutual misunderstandings that nothing but a shared identity can deflect."[5] But when the Black Other, albeit a fellow Jew, enters the realm of that shared identity, barriers appear, as in the case of a young Danite.

The incident described in the letter was the frisking that he had to go through at the hands of the Jewish security guards standing at the entrance of the synagogue Paul Valéry of Sarcelles, in the greater Paris area. His feeling of humiliation was conveyed unambiguously in the following terms:

once again, a Black Jew has been inflicted shameful contempt at the hands of fellow Jews, and this is one time too many! Of course, it is necessary to ensure the safety of all by having security guards search the bags of a stranger before allowing them into a synagogue. But the racist, hateful and inhuman doings of a few are beyond the acceptable. I am indeed using the words "racism" and "hatred" rather than "zeal," which is all too often used to cover up for such shameful, nefarious and inhuman behavior on the part of our White Jewish brothers, every time the problem is tentatively addressed in a case-by-case manner and denied with excuses.[6]

This example is indicative of the positioning of community organizations when responding to racist aggressions within French Jewish communities. Deborah Feldman, the author of the autobiographical work *Unorthodox*, "[a]fter reflecting on the Holocaust and historical persecutions against Jews, came to the conclusion that 'Judaism has always considered that it was too vulnerable to have debates on the injustice and discrimination happening in its own community.'"[7]

I was also surprised, when I was invited by AM-I-FARAFINA to listen to the testimony of Enoch, a new member hailing from Cameroon, to discover that the meeting rapidly turned into a healing session of sorts, where each participant shared their own experiences of humiliations in Jewish circles, and which resulted in their deciding to go as a group from one synagogue to another to force White Jews to acknowledge their presence. The President of the organization, Hortense Tsiporah Bilé, exhorted her followers in these terms:

> From now on, we should go to one another's synagogues and go to synagogues we're not used to, but go there in groups of three, four, five, ten, so that they'll see Black folks showing up like UFOs. Then they'll realize it's not just one UFO turning up, but several. We're done with the talking, now we've got to force acceptance. (Hortense Tsiporah, after Enoch's testimony, 2017)

Long before AM-I-FARAFINA did, it was the FJN which expressed its will to carve a place for itself in the French Jewry, when it organized in 2010 a convention with an explicit title, "How to durably include Black Jews in the French Jewry and worldwide?" This question largely manifests the need perceived by Black Jews to blend into the global Jewry, yet this perception is so strong that Marah, then one of the members of the FJN, expressed his discomfort with the formulation of the title: "there is one word that makes me uncomfortable. . . . That word is 'durably.' When you speak of duration, it means you are somehow thinking of a time limit. Well, I say no, we shouldn't be asking this question, because the right question is, 'How to forever include

Black Jews in the French Jewry and worldwide?'" (Marah, FJN convention, 2010).

For Black Jews, community organizing is strongly tied to their quest for recognition as full-fledged Jews and their identification with the Jewish people as a whole. They display a dual loyalty, both to their assigned racial identity which they cannot renounce, and to their Jewish religious identity which is inherited in certain cases and acquired through conversion in others. Whether they are protected in their communities like Ruth (with, nonetheless, a fear of going to other synagogues) or unwelcome in all synagogues like Enoch, they know for certain that it is never a problem for their fellow Jews to worship in safe spaces in Ashkenazi-only or Sephardic-only communities.

In order to build a consensus among Black French Jews around the question of visibility, the creation of a Black Jewish community center and synagogue appears to be the natural outcome of their quest for a safe space which they can't find in Ashkenazi or Sephardic communities. Already, all the experiences of frustration resulting from rejection, discrimination, and doubts on individuals' right to belong are being handled by community organizations as a rule, as the French sociologist Gilles Verbunt made clear:

> it is not surprising to see individuals retreating rather than confronting tensions, and it is very tempting to (re)turn to the comfort provided by an all-encompassing entity—whether it is a nation, a denomination, a cult, or ethnic community—whose intrinsic function is to lift all doubts on identity and whose cultural norms (language, mores, values and institutions) are well established. It is the circle within which everything falls back into place and which provides presumably unquestionable landmarks. Here, members will be restored to the identity cocoon they believe existed in olden times, and feel supported by an entire community.[8]

Thus, feeling that organizing makes them stronger, they are empowered to demand plurality beyond the Ashkenazi/Sephardic binary, which they consider obsolete. When Guershon Nduwa, the head of the FJN, was invited to the radio show "Mémoire d'un continent" on Radio France Internationale, the Africanist scholar Elikia M'bokolo asked him the following questions: "What does [Africans'] Judaism consist in? Where does their religion come from? In the case of biracial individuals, it's understandable, but in the case of Africa, we don't get the impression that outside of Ethiopia there are any hubs." This is the answer he gave:

> You are right, we must begin with historical parameters. Those who read the Bible already know that Moses had married a woman called Zipporah, who was a Black woman. The Scriptures are unequivocal on that point, since Moses' sister had mocked her brother's choice, asking, "why marry a woman of a different

color?" After which, Miriam was immediately stricken with leprosy, which is interpreted as a punishment from God. This is to tell you that in reality, the history of Judaism has been a history of race mixing for a long time. Now today, even if you discover us as a brand-new community, we are not new. There are Jews in this country who came from Ethiopia before their return to Israel, there are Jews who are converts, there are Jews who were born of a contact between Ashkenazi or Sephardic Jews with Black peoples in general. All these strands make up the tapestry, so that you can't just speak in terms of duality between Ashkenazim and Sephardim, but rather speak in terms of the unity of one people beyond this or that skin color.[9]

It is worthy of notice that the race mixing resulting from Moses' marrying a Black woman is claimed as evidence of Africana peoples' right to identify with the historical past of the Jewish people. It also bears repeating that the Bible does mention Blacks. At the dinner organized by the FJN in January 2012, which I attended, Joël Mergui, the President of the central Consistory of France, freely made a comment on this point as he underlined that one would be hard-pressed to find any mention of Ashkenazi or Sephardic forebears in the Bible, whereas it is much easier to find mentions of Blacks. As for Yann, this is how he answered my question on the mentions of Blacks in the Bible:

> To anyone telling me the contrary, I will say, "why don't you go back to study your Talmud and Torah?" I don't know much about Talmud, I don't know much about the Torah, but the little I know is Judaism, the Hebrew people, for all I know the Hebrews lived some place on Earth. The Torah was given to the Hebrews, and that wasn't in Hungary or in Czechoslovakia, right? In Egypt, and Egypt is not in America, right? It's in Africa, that's all, and I don't need any other proof. Africans received the Torah, Africa received the Torah before taking it to Israel, I don't need any other proof. People reproduced that in films, but I was expecting to see the Jews a bit more tanned, well, black, actually. (Yann, interview given in 2010)

What is expressed here is a feeling of pride in being Jewish and the claim to a positive self-identity in which Jewishness and Blackness are mutually inclusive. However, what hinders their identification to the French Jewry is that racial markers are used to establish and maintain a frontier between the assigned category in which their fellow Jews place them and the one they claim for themselves. While they insist on being outside of the Ashkenazi/Sephardic binary, they tend to be classified as Sephardim by whoever is willing to recognize them as Jews. At a dinner organized by the FJN on January 6, 2011, the French sociologist Shmuel Trigano designated Black Jews as Sephardim although just an hour before, the organizer Guershon Nduwa and his other guest Shlomo Mula, an Israeli member of parliament representing the Ethiopian Jewish community, had each stated clearly that they were neither Ashkenazi not Sephardic. Some Ethiopian Jews living in France may be pressured to fit into the binary, such as Hannah, who told me that she identifies as Sephardic because her rabbi told her that African Jews are Sephardim (Hannah, interview given in 2011).

This proves that beyond the religious factor, the issue of ethnicity is also raised, in the definition offered by the French sociologist Pierre-Jean Simon:

> a set of relatively objective, or at least objectifiable, features that are shared by a number of individuals, allowing them to perceive themselves and be seen by others as a distinct community. Ethnicity also designates their consciousness of belonging to the latter. It is what makes you a member of an ethnic community, in your own eyes as well as those of the other members of your group (self-identity) and in the eyes of the outsiders to your group (hetero-identity), and makes you feel acceptance, pride—sometimes to the point of conceit (a positive identity that may be vindicative and aggressive)—or on the contrary, a sense of shame (negative identity.) You are aware of sharing with others one of the myriad singular ethnic identities, among which one may quote Jewishness, Quebecois, Breton, Vietnamese or Japanese identities.[10]

Consequently, as the French sociologist Denys Cuche explains, what matters is to study not so much

> the cultural content of identity, but rather the mechanisms of interaction which, by using culture in a strategic and selective way, maintain or challenge the collective "boundaries." Contrary to a widespread belief, long-standing, continuous relations among ethnic groups are not necessarily conducive to an eventual meltdown of cultural differences. Instead, these relations are very often organized with a view to preserving cultural differences, and they even occasionally result in emphasizing these differences, as a consequence of the (symbolic) patrolling of identity boundaries.[11]

Equally important is the Canadian sociologist Danielle Juteau's remark that "[e]thnicity is constructed rather than natural, but it is nonetheless real and not imaginary; it remains a concrete, albeit imaginary, reality. This is the foundation of its durability and its capacity to mobilize individuals in both the past and the present."[12]

Hence, despite the difficulties encountered by their members, the organizations offer them an identification to the Jewish people that includes the ethnic markers listed above, including Biblical ancestors, the Hebrew language, Israel, Jewish first and last names, Kosher food, all of which play a very important part in asserting their Jewishness. I will now discuss their inclusion in the French Jewry, in order to better grasp where and how they express their views, and what networks they belong to.

In France, Jewish communities are not a monolithic bloc with identical expectations and needs; they are characterized by their plurality, as I already emphasized earlier. Although ethnic statistics are not collected in France, it is estimated that the country is home to around 650,000 Jews. For the same reason, it is very difficult to give an estimate of the number of Africans or African-descended individuals identifying as Jews, even if Guershon Nduwa, the founder of the FJN, claims that there are 250 families hailing from the Caribbean and (for the most part) sub-Saharan Africa in the greater Paris area, half of them converts. Nduwa told me that he received calls from many other French regions, particularly from the large cities of Marseille, Lyon, and Lille. Many among them, being denied recognition as full-fledged Jews, look for compensation by contacting Black Jewish organizations. It is the will to find their place in the French Jewry that pushes them to join the latter in reaction to the rejection and slights. For example, Caroline admitted that she had initially doubted the need for a Black Jewish organization, until she experienced racial discrimination firsthand:

> It is really important to sensitize people to the sociological fact that there are Black Jews, so that other Jews may realize it, deal with it, and react differently. Because it's a real tragedy for a Jew to be rejecting another Jew, it's a tragedy. . . . I had just been on holidays in New York City for a few days when I went to a synagogue, thanks to a woman who was Jewish and took me along to pray in her community. . . . We were upstairs in the balcony and then two people noticed my presence and came upstairs to tell me that this was a synagogue for non-Blacks only so I had to leave the place, and that's what I did. It was particularly unpleasant. In fact, the organization's name in the first place was fraternité judéo-noire [Black-Jewish brotherhood] and I contacted them. I was glad to find them because this is a place where you feel some sense of unity. Of course, my community treats me very well, but it's always comforting to know that you are not alone being a Black Jewish woman. So yes, I am a member of the organization, because we have everything to gain in being recognized as a group just like the Ashkenazim and Sephardim, and to have places of worship where all Black Jews will receive a warm welcome. (Caroline, interview given in 2010)

Likewise, Ruth explains,

> I have no issues with my community. Problems begin when I get out. To be honest, I'm sometimes scared to go to other synagogues. When Guershon reported the infamous experiences of the Black Jews who were denied entry into a synagogue, and I had the same thing happen to me, well it makes me understand with a much greater sense of urgency the necessity for us to have a place of worship. (Ruth, interview given in 2010)

As for Enoch, he was still without a synagogue he could call home when he testified to the other members of AM-I-FA:

> I have attended four synagogues so far, four large synagogues, and it will soon be four years since I converted. Every time it's the same problem. People don't trust me—they always keep me at bay. That's the real issue, and I moved from one synagogue to another due to these integration problems, which persist because people distrust us. I even met some rabbis who were honest about it, they told me, "If you don't stay, then people won't trust you." And I answer, "I've been attending for one year and people still doubt me!" Once I went to a demonstration and I felt happy because at last I could see Black Jews, and that's always comforting. I sent a desperate letter to your organization [AM-I-FA] because I felt so confused, I couldn't find a synagogue and that was not easy, it was really hard. (Enoch, testimony given in 2017)

What these testimonies make clear is that whether or not they are implicit, racial preconceptions actually inform the acceptance or rejection of newcomers in synagogues, so that a non-White convert has to face additional difficulties compared to a White person. This is paradoxical insofar as Maimonides, one of the luminaries of the Jewish faith, recommended accepting converts on an equal footing with native-born Jews, as is reminded by Rabbi Jacky Milewski:

> Abraham being the father of all converts, a proselyte may blend in among the biological descendants of Abraham. Maimonides also adds that all the miracles accomplished in favor of Israel were also intended to benefit the future proselytes, as their entry into the Jewish people had been planned beforehand and G . . . performed His miracles with the converts in mind as well as the Jews. Thus, proselytes are part and parcel of the community of Israel. They are associated with the Jewish people's historical past.[13]

However, the tendency to distance oneself from converts and consider them inauthentic seems a recurrent phenomenon, not just in the case of Judaism. As the Canadian anthropologist Géraldine Mossière explained,

> converts bear the stigma of presumed psychological weakness. No matter how often they insist on their free will and emphasize that their choosing to free themselves from the religion inherited from and transmitted by their group testifies to their autonomy, converts still appear primarily as the victims of an oppressive dialectics between the Other and the Same. The burden of proof is theirs to demonstrate the authenticity of their choice.[14]

In the case of Black Jewish converts, their dogged will to identify with the Jewish people is nonetheless inseparable from their struggle for visibility.

The planned Black synagogue points to their necessary solidarity in their individual struggles to practice their religion without racial discrimination. At the collective level, thus, their relations with the broader French society are mediated by the FJN and AM-I-FA, even if not all Black Jews are members of either organization. Each is self-funded, thanks to member subscriptions and donations from sympathizers. They communicate with city councils, particularly when they organize special events such as concerts, lectures, or garden parties. For instance, in May 2016 I was invited to a conference organized by AM-I-FA and the Ben Gurion chapter of the B'nai B'rith, where Hortense Tsiporah Bilé hosted representatives of the Ivorian Danite community as guest lecturers in one of the lecture rooms of the town hall of Paris' upper-class sixteenth arrondissement.

These actions aim to publicize their cause by both revealing the existence of Black Jews in France and facilitating their individual and collective integration in French society. They manifest their agency in transforming the way they are represented and interact with their fellow Jews. From their perspective, militancy means achieving visibility and normalcy within the French Jewry and the broader French society in the long run. Hence, they have evolved from being safe spaces or havens to lobbies pushing back against the gatekeeping prevailing in the French Jewry as well as the racism and antisemitism at work in French society.

To achieve their goals, they have set two interrelated objectives. The first is to create a system of inclusiveness by sensitizing Jewish authorities to the increasing diversity of the contemporary Jewry and the presence of Black members in it. The second is to celebrate all that can unite them—religious holidays, demonstrations, protests, and commemorative marches. Because their Jewishness is sapped by the indifference and rejection of their fellow White Jews, they insist all the more on being a part of the community and its collective self. This does not imply a denial of their Blackness; but in reaching out to their fellow Jews, they are confronted with a mirror image of their quest to redefine Jewishness along parameters enhancing both Black and Jewish identities. Indeed, being the signs of the diversity of the French Jewry, they also participate in the construction of self-representations and representations of the Other. For example, many Black Jews speak Hebrew, and even Yiddish in Guershon Nduwa's case, and teach these languages to other Jews, whether members or non-members of their organizations. Some are committed to the Zionist cause, while others actively promote cooperation between their home countries in Africa and the state of Israel. The best illustration is given by Marah Saday, a native of the Democratic Republic of Congo, who did his Aliyah in 2012 and became a rabbi in Israel, creating a yeshiva named *Botsina Kadisha-Eliezer Programme* in Jerusalem. In 2011, he had run for President in the DRC, for the first time, as a candidate of the Congolese socialist party.

The members of the FJN and AM-I-FA hail from African francophone countries (Benin, Congo-Brazzaville, the DRC, Cameroon, the Ivory Coast, Senegal, Chad, and Togo), African anglophone countries (Nigeria, Ghana), African lusophone countries (Angola, the Cape Verde islands), Ethiopia, Caribbean islands (Guadeloupe, Martinique, Haiti), French Guiana, Brazil, the United States, Canada, and Israel. They include psychologists, attorneys, financial experts, medical doctors, economists, teachers, but also administrative agents, realtors, trade representatives, domestic workers, and workers in the hospitality sector. Most have lived in at least three countries, and their transnational experiences allow them to compare their religious and social integration in France and in other countries.

AM-I-FA has close ties with the Ben Gurion chapter of the B'nai B'rith in France, the Epbomi organization representing the Danites of the Ivory Coast, and Noesis, a London-based hip hop band. The FJN is also present in Israel; the representative of that branch, an Ethiopian Jew called Avraham Lincoln, announced in January 2018 that

> [t]he new federation will follow three main lines of action, namely, assistance to Black Jews in Israel, the recognition of Israel in the francophone community, and leadership training for Jews residing on the African continent, so that they may "become the ambassadors of Israel." To achieve that aim, he wants to facilitate their access to higher education and incite them to build closer ties with the authorities.[15]

Both organizations have created partnerships with other Jewish community organizations, based in France and overseas. Among these, UPI SAR EL, a civil volunteering organization, often sensitizes FJN members to the importance of supporting rear bases in Israel.

The two organizations have also built interfaith connections. For instance, AM-I-FA collaborates with David School, a Christian group of Gospel singers and musicians. As for Islam, while both organizations reject its radical branches, they also express a willingness to engage into dialog with certain Muslim authorities. In 2011, the national periodical *Le monde des religions* published an article on a meeting between Guershon Nduwa and Abdelaziz Gnabaly, an Imam at the mosque of Saint Denis (greater Paris area), to show that Black Jews and Muslims did not ignore one another and felt a need to discuss their places in their respective religious communities.[16]

Black Jews are conscious of being a minority within a minority group; yet as French Jews are becoming part of the mainstream in the global Jewry, they may tend to reflect the dominant/subordinate binary in their interactions with

Black Jews. In this sense, Blackness as a racial identity becomes, as Daniel Fabre explained, "the consciousness of belonging to a group that stands out thanks to specific cultural practices and that, considering that its differentness is denied, perceives struggles at all levels as a means of achieving a new society where these differences would be acknowledged."[17] As such, what Pierre-Jean Simon would designate as a "combative and vindicative neo-ethnicity"[18] provides the grounds on which community organizations help redefine and circumscribe the racial issue faced by Black French people and offer responses to it, by collecting individual testimonies and life stories. They function as bridges, mediators, and negotiators among Black Jewish believers who share similar experiences in Jewish communities and in French society at large. They also offer interpretations of the Torah which insist on specific episodes, such as Moses' marriage with Zipporah, presented as a Black woman, or on the theory of the Lost Tribes of Israel, which Danites, Lembas, Ibos, or Ethiopians may adhere to.

Consequently, the FJN and AM-I-FA have become pivotal in the evolution of the racial issue in the French Jewry and society. Many Black Jews are tired of anonymity and have joined these organizations to act for the improvement of their individual and collective lot, feeling the duty to act for change. This is how, over the years, the project carried by the FJN and its members has morphed into a larger, more constructive transnational endeavor by including African Jews living on the African continent. They express a desire for change without rejecting traditions, as was explained to me by Guershon Nduwa:

> We're not creating a community, we're simply saying that we're not visible. We're simply saying, "How can that be? We're right here, and no one sees us. Is there a problem?" Why are we seen in the United States, in Israel, in London, but not here? Here, we're in an abnormal situation, in fact. We're not creating a community that will exclude people; we're putting into place structures that will allow everyone to be visible. We've got to break the isolation. The Jewish community is too confined to just Ashkenazim and Sephardim. But we're neither one nor the other, so what are we supposed to do? What we're trying to do is to break open this dangerous binary. Our visibility implies taking part in society, and by this I mean that institution-wise, Black Jews must be visible, community-wise, Black Jews must be visible, and nation-wise, Black Jews must be visible. When you go to certain Jewish institutions, you get the feeling that the Jewish community is only contained in these people. We are demanding visibility for ourselves, since we all have the same abilities. The CRIF [Representative Council of French Jewish Institutions], the Consistory, the Jewish Students' Union of France—we need to be visible in all of these. We are unseen, even though we've been around for a long time. (Guershon Nduwa, interview given in 2009)

The two organizations have two joint objectives: first to gain recognition from the established Jewish authorities (the Consistory, CRIF, and FSJU) and secondly, to become politically visible in the social and religious landscape. Black Jews are not a recent phenomenon, since many lived and practiced their religion in the shadow. The data I collected during my fieldwork suggest that they have been present in France since the 1970s, but Guershon Nduwa says that the database of the FJN goes back to 1957. Both organizations have a significant ability to mobilize and attract members around activities with a strongly integrative and rewarding value, such as concerts, lectures, festive meals such as that of Rosh Hashanah at the AJTM community center or the garden party held in the home of one of the members of the Ben Gurion chapter of the B'nai B'rith to celebrate AM-I-FA's second anniversary (I was invited to both events), gatherings for religious holidays, testimonies, the making of films, including a documentary made in 2018 for the BBC by Nadir Djennad where both Nduwa and Bilé were interviewed, and frequent appearances on TV and radio shows[19] thanks to Guershon Nduwa's media exposure. A regular guest of Radio J, Radio France Internationale, and Africa No. 1, he was also published in the magazine *Tribune juive* and on the CRIF's website, besides posting very regularly on social media (Facebook page, WhatsApp group chats, Instagram) and daily on the FJN's website (http://feujn.org/). Nduwa claims that it grew from 25,000 subscribers in 2010 to 60,000 today. It is undeniable that the two organizations' activities have earned Black Jews an unprecedented level of attention from the media and scholars, even if the general public is hardly aware of their presence. The rise of modern means of communication, especially social media, has largely facilitated their improved social visibility, not only in France but also in the global Jewry. Conferences organized by scholars who study African Jewish communities, or by Black Jewish organizations themselves, afford greater exposure to publications on Black Jews and a constant dialog between members and the researchers analyzing their narratives and evolutions. Among the needs addressed by the organizations, marriages, particularly interracial ones within the French Jewry, are particularly recurrent among both men and women. The next chapter will discuss this uphill battle.

NOTES

1. The two organizations have already been discussed in Aurélien Mokoko Gampiot, "Les Juifs noirs: Fédération internationale des Juifs Noirs (FJN) et Am-Israël -Farafina," in Anne-Laure Zwilling, Joëlle Allouche-Benayoun, Rita Hermon-Belot, and Lionel Obadia, eds., *Les minorités religieuses en France. Panorama de la diversité contemporaine* (Paris: Bayard 2019), 847–63.

2. Paula Haddad, "L'espoir d'un centre communautaire judéo-noir en France," *Jerusalem Post* French edition, accessed June 30, 2009, http://www.fjn-123.fr/spip.php?article181

3. Séverine Mathieu, *La transmission du judaïsme dans les couples mixtes* (Paris: Éditions de l'Atelier, 2009), 77.

4. Guershon Nduwa, *Manifeste des juifs noirs* (Orthez, France: Publishroom Factory, 2016), 129–30.

5. Simon-Barouh, *Juifs à Rennes,* 123.

6. Open letter by AM-ISRAËL-FARAFINA, "Stop au racisme anti juifs-Noirs- Métisses (*sic*)- Basanés," Paris, April 3, 2017.

7. "'Ultra-orthodoxy is an issue for us all,' says the author of Unorthodox. Translations of her book have multiplied since the worldwide success of its adaptation into a series by Netflix in Spring," AFP, *The Times of Israel*, July 16, 2020.

8. Gilles Verbunt, "Culture, identité, intégration, communauté: des concepts à revoir," *Hommes et Migrations* no.1180 (October 1994): 8.

9. Guershon Nduwa, interview by Elikia M'Bokolo, *Mémoire d'un continent,* Radio France Internationale, August 16, 2009, audio.

10. Pierre-Jean Simon, "Ethnicité," *Vocabulaire historique et critique des relations interethniques,* cahier n°2, Pluriel Recherches (1994): 14–20.

11. Denys Cuche, *La notion de culture dans les sciences sociales,* Grands repères, 4th edition (Paris: La Découverte, 2010), 113.

12. Danielle Juteau, "L'ethnicité comme rapport social," *Mots* 49, no. 1 (1996): 104.

13. Jacky Milewski, *Naissance d'une identité: Conversion au Judaïsme dans l'œuvre de Maïmonide* (Paris: Safed éditions, 2004), 23–24.

14. Géraldine Mossière, *La conversion. Retour à l'identité, Théologiques* 21, no. 2 (2013): 7–16. https://doi.org/10.7202/1028460ar.

15. https://fr.timesofisrael.com/la-federation-des-juifs-noirs-ouvre-une-antenne-en-israel/.

16. Aïssata Ba, "L'alliance noire d'un imam et d'un rabbin," *Le monde des religions* (January–February 2011): 16–17.

17. Daniel Fabre, "Les minorités nationales en pays industrialisés," in Condominas and Dreyfus-Gamelon, eds., *L'anthropologie en France. Situation actuelle et avenir* (Paris: Editions du CNRS, 1979), 293.

18. Pierre-Jean Simon, "Aspects de l'identité bretonne," *Pluriel* 19 (1979): 23–43.

19. See for instance Freddy Mulongo, "Nduwa Guershon, premier rabbin noir de la région parisienne?" May 22, 2009 at 11:44 am, Radio Réveil FM International; Guershon Nduwa, "À la rencontre des juifs noirs," interviewed by Elikia M'Bokolo, *Mémoire d'un continent,* Radio France Internationale (RFI), April 2, 2017; or "Guershon Nduwa de F.J.N-Religions du monde," Radio France Internationale (RFI), January 31, 2010.

Chapter 6

Interracial Marriages

I would like to begin this chapter with an anecdote which was related to me by Brigitte, a Sephardic Jewish woman whose parents were Tunisian born. In her teenage years in France, she was attracted to Black boys and was thinking of marrying one when she grew up. But her mother used to thwart her projects by saying, "My daughter can only marry a Jew, and there are no Black Jews." Serendipitously, one day when her mother had just repeated her favorite warning one more time, the news on television showed Ethiopian Jews being repatriated to Israel. Brigitte immediately drew her mother's attention to what she was seeing, "See, Mom? On TV, they're talking about Blacks who are Jewish!" But her mother only switched off the television set in response.

This anecdote is revealing of the way French-speaking Jews consider marriage. Indeed, the mother's prescriptive attitude shows how the transmission of Jewishness is prioritized and organized through marriage. This definition of transmission precludes the existence of Black Jews, who are perceived as an anomaly. This is the only explanation to the mother's denial of the existence of Black Jews even in the face of evidence. The importance of genealogy is so central to the transmission of Jewishness that interethnic marriages are always a source of tensions, even among White Jews, and interracial marriages even more so. Hence the interest of exploring the Biblical roots of the construction of the matrilineal transmission of both Judaism and Jewishness.

INTERRACIALISM IN THE BIBLE AND TALMUDIC TRADITION

Although interracial intimacy is documented in Biblical texts, race mixing was not viewed favorably among the founders of Judaism. To being with, Abraham—considered as "the father of all nations" among Jews, Muslims, and Christians—is part of the descent of Sem, whom the Book of Genesis presents as blessed by God Bible while Ham's was accursed. As a counterpart to the curse of Ham, God forbade any intermarriage between the descendants of Abraham and those of Ham living in Canaan. As is well known, God initially promised to give Abram a posterity as innumerable as the stars in the skies, and changed his name into Abraham so that it meant "father of a multitude" (*Genesis* 17:1–8); but as his wife Sara was ageing and childless, she urged him to use her Egyptian servant (or slave) Hagar to have a child by her—his first son, Ishmael. Yet for God's promise to be fulfilled, Abraham had to have a child by Sarah, his Hebrew wife, instead of a descendant of Ham, so that his actual heir may be an unmixed offspring, pure of any Hamite streak. Eventually, prompted again by Sarah, Abraham stripped Hagar of whatever privilege she may have enjoyed and repudiated both her and Ishmael (*Genesis* 16:1–16).

Later, before he passed away, Abraham made sure his son Isaac did not wed a Canaanite woman, by arranging his marriage with Rebekah, the daughter of a relative of his, so that God's promises may be accomplished in his descent (*Genesis* 21:1–13 and 24:1–5.) When Isaac's wife gave birth to twins who allegedly embody the separation between peoples and nations (*Genesis* 25:23), Jacob was chosen as the ancestor of the blessed people (*Genesis* 28:1). Significantly, he was applauded not only for usurping his brother's birthright and Isaac's blessing, but also for marrying two women belonging to his parents' extended family; while Esau had not only renounced his birthright for a "mess of pottage" (in modern English, a dish of lentils) and been deprived of his father's blessing, but also made the "wrong" choice of wedding Hamite women (*Genesis* 26:34–34 and 28:1–5.) Clearly enough, the ideology of the curse of Ham's descent is visible in these marriage prescriptions and taboos—an Israelite was not supposed to marry a Hamite.

Yet in the following generation, Jacob's son Joseph, who was sold into slavery by his brothers and settled down in Egypt, married an Egyptian woman and eventually brought his whole extended family to that country, to save them from famine. The Bible says that seventy of them entered the country and after four hundred years in bondage in Egypt, there were six hundred thousand of them, not counting the women and children. If kings such as Solomon—of whom the Bible says he had 700 princesses as wives and 300 concubines who were all foreign (*1Kings* 11:1–3)—felt free to mix with women from neighboring or faraway regions in spite of the Torah's prohibition of such unions, it is highly unlikely that the common Hebrew man made it a point to marry only members of his own tribe in a period preceding the formalization of Judaic precepts.

Indeed Moses, the great lawmaking prophet of Israel who received the Ten Commandments, had to face criticism from his brother Aaron and his sister Myriam after he married Zipporah, a Cushite woman (*Numbers,* 12:1). While the Scripture does not describe her as "black" or dark-skinned, she is identified as a Cushite, a term usually reserved for Ethiopians and linked to the genealogy of Ham, as Kush was the latter's son and the elder brother of Canaan (the only named target of Noah's curse). To this day, in the Hebrew language the word "Kushi" is still known to be a racial slur against Blacks.

The famous French rabbi Rashi (1040–1105 CE) observed in his Talmudic commentaries of the episode of Zimri and his Midianite concubine Kozbi (*Numbers* 20–25) that Moses' marriage to Zipporah was frowned upon by the children of Israel as an illicit union. Indeed Zimri, who was a prince of Israel, challenged Moses to declare his choice unacceptable while he too had a dark-skinned, non-Hebrew partner: Zimri grabbed Kozbi "by her braids" and brought her before Moses, asking him, "Is she allowed or forbidden? And if you say she is forbidden, then who permitted the daughter of Jethro [a Midianite] to you? The law was hidden from [Moses, who did not know how to respond]." Rashi commented on the question, "[w]ho permitted you to wed the daughter of Jethro? Moses had married her before the Torah was given, and once it was, then the Hebrews, who were still the sons of Noah (and therefore not subjected to the Torah's rules concerning illicit unions) came under the yoke of the Commandments, and so did she, as well as a crowd of idol worshipers (who had come out of Egypt with Moses)" (Talmud, Sanhedrin 82a. Midrash Tanchuma parshas Balak 20–21. Bamidbar Raba, chapter 20, 24–25. Targum Yonasan and Rashi to *Numbers* 25:6). It follows from this teaching by one of the sages of Judaism that although Moses is considered as a model, his marriage with Zipporah could not be seen as an example to follow but rather an exception to the rule, because marrying out became illicit from the moment the Torah was given to the Hebrew people. Phinehas, the zealot who, contrary to Moses, remembered the law banning intercourse with foreign women and eventually killed both Zimri and Kozbi with his spear, receives justification and praise from Talmudic scholars rather than condemnation for this extra-legal murder.

A reference to unions with Black women may also be inferred in the Song of Songs, which is attributed to King Solomon. Indeed, the text contains allusions to race, with the famous verses, "I am black yet comely, O ye daughters of Jerusalem! Look not upon me, that I am swarthy, that the sun hath tanned me." Conversely, when the "daughters of Jerusalem" enquire, "What is thy beloved more than another beloved, O thou fairest among women? What is thy beloved more than another beloved, that thou dost so adjure us?" the female narrative voice answers, "My beloved is white and ruddy, pre-eminent above ten thousand" (*Song of Songs,* 1:5–6, 5:10).[1] It is difficult not to infer a prevailing anti-Black sentiment, against which the female voice behind the poem seems embattled; otherwise, why would she feel the need to defuse the possible hostility of the other women, called "daughters of Jerusalem," toward the differentness of her skin color? And why would her lover's

Whiteness be so distinctive as to make him outstanding among ten thousand, unless unmixed Whites were a rarity in a predominantly mixed-race environment?

Additionally, the dismay of Ezra and his prayer upon seeing the increasing frequency of marriages between Israelites and Canaanites provide a valuable insight into the separation of races. "Now when these things were done, the princes drew near unto me, saying: 'The people of Israel, and the priests and the Levites, have not separated themselves from the peoples of the lands, doing according to their abominations, even of the Canaanites, the Hittites, the Perizzites, the Jebusites, the Ammonites, the Moabites, the Egyptians, and the Amorites. For they have taken of their daughters for themselves and for their sons; so that the holy seed have mingled themselves with the peoples of the lands; yea, the hand of the princes and rulers hath been first in this faithlessness.' And when I heard this thing, I rent my garment and my mantle, and plucked off the hair of my head and of my beard, and sat down appalled" (*Ezra,* 9:1–3 and 10–13). Ezra is recognized, along with the prophet Nehemiah, as a major reorganizer of the Jewish state after the captivity in Babylon. Edmond Fleg asserts that "Ezra was adamant to the point of demanding that the Hebrews who had remained in Palestine repudiate their Canaanite wives and deny the children they had had by them."[2] Likewise, it is difficult to know what led the Israelite prophets to reject race mixing while interracial unions were very common in their new home, Canaan. Why could Ezra not consider converting the Canaanite wives and their children born to Jewish fathers, instead of casting them out? The historian Salo Wittmayer Baron offers the following explanation: "Since Ezra and Nehemiah and, particularly, since the enactment of the 'eighteen' separatist prohibitions, intermarriage with Gentile women encountered a serious obstacle in the talmudic [sic] insistence upon conversion to Judaism as an indispensable prerequisite."[3] Even then, Rabbi Simon Qayyara, who authored the legal treatise *Halakkot gedolot* in the eighth century CE, "declared intercourse with a slave girl (even after she had undergone the partial conversion via ablutions and observance of Jewish law required of all slaves) to be a cumulative violation of fourteen different prohibitions."[4] Likewise, in a decree from the ninth century C.E., the Babylonian Rabbi Gaon Natronai stated, "if a son of Israel is caught with his slave . . . she is to be removed from him, sold, and the purchase price distributed among Israel's poor. We also flog him, shave his hair, and excommunicate him for thirty days."[5]

These examples show how interracial unions became relegated beyond the pale of purity in Jewish law and assimilated to hypogamy. The US anthropologist Kimberly Arkin notes,

In a certain kind of context, this project [Ezra's] is not about racial separation but about ritual purity; . . . it is about managing structural dangers, not the physical or biological created by non-Jews. In fact, Jewish historians have argued that the threat of social and cultural proximity between Jews and non-Jews fueled ever more rigorous attempts to establish boundaries in certain places (intimacy and marriage) while necessarily leaving others (commerce, daily interactions) rather open . . . This is very different than either presuming stable ontological difference (race) or attempting to create the presumption of that difference through absolute hierarchical segregation.[6]

Still, the US historian Salo Wittmayer Baron stressed how this led to a form of obsession with genealogy:

Emphatic observance of family purity was, indeed, another eminently eugenic means of national preservation. While retaining its theocratic-democratic character, in this respect Judaism developed aristocratic features. Priestly families were obliged to keep detailed family records, and the lay aristocracy, too, prided itself on its descent. "Well-born, very well-born" (*eugenes, eugenestatoi*) were Greek terms frequently used by distinguished Jewish citizens.[7]

With respect to racialization, Rabbi Ishmael Ben Elisha, an influential figure who taught Talmudic literature in the second century C.E., and "who generally evinced great interest in physical beauty, was also extremely proud that Jews were neither as fair as Germans, nor as dark as Negroes, but of an intermediate color, 'like an ebony tree.' Although not racially conscious, the ancients at times indulged in such verbal displays of national superiority."[8]

The conflation between lineage and the virtue of purity ultimately suggests the notion of a holiness of a "Jewish race," entailing fears of seeing such purity tainted by intermarriage. The warning against actually introducing "enemies of God" into the Chosen People was expressed in unambiguous terms by Rabbi Ishmael: "he who marries an Aramaean [Gentile] woman and raises children with her will ultimately raise enemies of the Lord."[9] Regarding marriage, Rabbi Simon Ben Laqish recommended to "not only choose the spouse in general, but also pay special attention to physical traits such as size and complexion," which Salo Wittmayer Baron explains in historical context as follows: "The sages believed that a union between two very tall or very small, very fair or very dark-skinned, persons might lead to undesirable further accentuation of these characteristics in the offspring."[10]

These remarks amply demonstrate how intermarriages, whether in ancient or medieval Judaism, appeared as a form of transgression that seemed to call for specific bans. These may also be due to their persistence, as Salo Wittmayer Baron emphasizes: "Prohibitions did not always prove effective, however, as is evident from their very reiteration century after century."[11] In other words, despite the fears tied to intermarriage, race mixing remained frequent in the history of what is designated today as "the Jewish people," with enslaved Ethiopian women often appearing as dangerous rivals for Jewish women.[12] This leads us to ask what remains of this legacy of intermarriages in the contemporary Jewry and particularly in France, and how is Jewishness defined with regard to interracialism?

ATTITUDES TO INTERRACIAL MARRIAGE IN CONTEMPORARY JUDAISM

Rabbinical recommendations about interracialism still remain in force, as they shape the attitudes of Jews in France and the Diaspora to outmarriages. The French sociologist Sébastien Tank-Storper explains,

> The contemporary Jewish world, in Israel or in the diaspora, is thus faced with a paradox: the great majority of Jews depart from the normative dimensions of Judaism and create for themselves an identity that is partly ethnic, partly religious, partly cultural, and partly national. However, the official modalities for entering into Jewish identity are a monopoly in the hands of religious institutions that are often extremely intransigent. In this way, there develops that which we have called, taking inspiration from a formula by Judith Butler, real Jewish "trouble."[13]

Hence, in spite of the distaste of French Jewish institutions for mixing and the gatekeeping observed in contemporary Jewry, race mixing is still happening and triggering fears of a loss of identity, whether racial or cultural. As the sociologist Jocelyne Streiff-Fenart points out, the concept of mixed couple, which is prevalent in French social sciences, "suggests, rather than defines, a type of union characterized by a difference in nationalities, ethnicities, races or religions between the two partners."[14]

In the present case, the term designates partners of different faiths but also partners sharing the same religion but with different ethnic backgrounds, typically Sephardic and Ashkenazi. This confirms the French geneticist Albert Jacquard's statement that "what makes a marriage interracial depends on where you build the fence. And the line along which you decide to build that fence is entirely arbitrary."[15] Yet, in spite of the arbitrariness of their definition and the inherited ideologies banning their existence, interracial and interethnic couples are numerous enough to be objects of study, even in France where racial and ethnic statistics are forbidden by law. The sociologist Séverine Mathieu,[16] building on a survey published in the Jewish journal *L'Arche* in 2002, observed an upward trend in interfaith unions, with

40 percent of married respondents under thirty having a non-Jewish spouse, and an even higher proportion in unmarried couples. According to Guershon Nduwa, one of the spokespersons for Jews of African descent in France and himself in an interracial couple, out of the 250 families who he says reached out to his organization, fifty or so are made up of Blacks living with either an Ashkenazi or a Sephardic partner. I myself have obtained interviews with twelve interracial couples, seven of which had been married officially and at a synagogue and five were living together. I have also considered the aspirations of young men and women who are single and actively seeking to marry a Jewish partner. My point is indeed to interrogate the ways in which intermarriage between Blacks (whether Jewish or other) and Jews is addressed in the French Jewry today.

People today meet outside of Jewish milieus as well as inside: in school or in the workplace, in leisure centers, or on religious holidays. Sometimes conversions occur after marriage, as in the case of Ruben, a man of Spanish descent, and Michelle, his Martiniquan wife, who were high school sweethearts and decided to tie the knot while they were respectively Catholic and Protestant. This is what he had to say about Jewishness and intermarriage: "When we met, each of us knew where they were coming from, but it wasn't an obstacle, because even if we had different faiths, it was the same thing at the end of the day. The forms of worship may have been different but in the end, we had the same faith. Before I met her she was already seeking her spiritual path in the same way as I did, more or less, so when I found my way [in Judaism], when I found my answers, my wife had also done her spiritual homework on her end at the same time, and she got the same type of confirmation I did" (Ruben, June 2020). The couple's decision to go through conversion was influenced by their friendship with a Sephardic couple, who directed to the Reform movement, known in France as the liberal Jewish movement: "this was when we met this Tunisian Jewish family, we became friends because we did lots of things together, and they spoke a lot about traditions and their families and all that. This is how we came to our faith eventually" (Ruben, June 2020).

Interracial couples elicit two types of reactions in Jewish milieus in France. On the one hand, the White Jewish in-laws welcome the Black addition to the family if the couple's marriage is anchored in religious practice. This is illustrated by the case of Marah, a former Evangelical preacher from Congo who converted to Judaism. In conformity with the prescriptions of the (Orthodox) Consistory, he married a Jewish-born Sephardic woman of North African descent. Guershon Nduwa, whose wife is Ashkenazi of German descent, says he was accepted without any qualms by his in-laws and Ashkenazi milieus in general: "It never posed any problem to the Ashkenazim, they had a very positive attitude. Things happened naturally. Everybody likes me. Outsiders looking from afar may think that there's a problem, but Germany today is not Germany from the past, really. There was absolutely no reluctance. I can say that very often, people give Ashkenazim a bad name, but when you really know them, you realize that they don't deserve this, honestly" (Guershon, July 2020). Additionally, when the Black spouse is Jewish, the marriage can also entail a return to the practice of Jewish religious norms, thus fulfilling the White Jewish in-laws' hopes. This is the case for Dov, an Ethiopian Jew, whose union with a Sephardic woman of Marrano ancestry was very well received by her family, for she had thus returned to the faith of her origins after first marrying a Muslim man. Likewise, when the Jewish-born partner has become estranged from their birth religion, the conversion of the Black partner often brings them back into the fold. This is how Florence, a woman from Guadeloupe who was born in a Catholic family, led her fiancé Oscar (of mixed Ashkenazi and Sephardic descent) to rediscover Judaism as he followed her conversion process. This is how he describes it: "I was less involved in spiritual life than Florence, in the religious sense of the term, until she decided to convert, and that's when I rediscovered the religion, actually. I attended with her all of the courses taught by Rabbi Berkowitz [then the head of the Reform Judaism movement in France], and I rediscovered the spiritual dimension of Judaism with Florence" (Oscar, November 2011).

But on the other hand, when one of the two partners is a non-Jew, the couple sometimes has to face rejection. Danielle, a Martiniquan woman raised as a Catholic, married an Ashkenazi, and they each decided to keep their birth religion, although neither of them was a practicing believer. Her version was telling: "the family's reaction was more complicated on my husband's side, because he was the only son in the family, and one of the last to bear the name of that branch of the lineage. His father was frustrated with his choice [of a non-Jewish woman]. Later, he came around and accepted his son's choice, but it was a bit more complicated because he had pictured something different for him. In his mind, his son would marry a Jewish woman, of Jewish descent; his concern was with the children. He [her father-in-law] was in a mixed couple, with a Catholic wife. . . . I'm not sure, but maybe in his mind, my father-in-law wanted to spare his son the complications he had known after the war [World War II]. I think that from his standpoint, maybe he wanted his son to follow the path of a woman, reasoning as a seventy-year-old man, from that generation" (Danielle, July 2020). The reasoning she alludes to defines women as the transmitters and gatekeepers of Jewishness. Although the father-in-law's three sons had eventually converted to Judaism (including Danielle's husband) as well as their mother, he hoped for them to choose Jewish wives to return to the rule of endogamy.

In effect, when Black women are confronted with the rejection of their Jewish in-laws, the cause is not so much racism as the concern with preserving the transmission of Jewishness and religious practice. Danielle is even more eloquent when asked if she has been faced with racism from her in-laws: "not at all, I have never experienced racism, to be perfectly honest I've been privileged to never have experienced it. At any rate, with my in-laws I've never felt any racism, never ever. It was on a different plane, it was rather a question of breaking the transmission of Jewish traditions which might pose problems, you see. If I had been a Falasha [Ethiopian] Jew or a Black descendant of a Jewish family, it would have been less complicated for them to handle, you see. It was not a question of skin color" (Danielle, July 2020). However, the rejection of her in-laws went so far as to boycott the wedding ceremony. The reason, she explains, is that her father-in-law is a Holocaust survivor whose parents died in concentration camps. He broke the taboo of exogamy at the end of the war by marrying a Catholic woman, who later converted—a rare outcome at the time—but he clearly did not want his sons to emulate him.

Danielle assumes that things would have been simpler had she been a Beta Israel Ethiopian Jew, for her in-laws would have been assured their son would remain in the Jewish faith; but retention is not always guaranteed in this configuration. Indeed, an Ethiopian Jew whom I also interviewed told me that her Ashkenazi husband, who was formerly very religious, had become an atheist and had shaved off his long beard out of disgust with the racism he had encountered in Jewish milieus. In her case, then, race-based prejudice had undeniably prevailed over the need to preserve a Jewish lineage through the women, since the Jewishness of Beta Israel Ethiopians has been certified and approved by Israeli authorities.

When it comes to the reactions of Black in-laws, respondents all seem to confirm that the White partner is not faced with any cold shoulders. Marah, a Congolese-born convert, explains it as follows: "well, of course, as you know, Black folks—I'm not generalizing here, but we've never had a hard time accepting others, we've always been welcoming, we've always found it natural to share because there's always enough for everybody. Really, my parents were anything but feeling superior, telling me, 'Don't forget she's a White woman, always be extra careful with another family's child'" (Marah, November 2020). As for Danielle, she dismissed the very idea that Caribbean families might reject an addition on the basis of race, possibly generalizing her own family's open-mindedness:

> in Martinique racism is not even a subject, I mean, a racist person in Martinique would have to be crazy, really, because they'd be denying their own roots! Because things are complicated back home. On my family's side, well, we're very different [from the metropolitan French] in the West Indies because our traditional family circles, in the West Indies, are very multiracial in the first place. So the main concern for my father and mother was not the person's

origins, but rather the person himself—who is he, what does he do for a living, what's his life plan, is he capable of being a good father and husband, someone trustworthy, and what are his parents like? These were my parents' concerns, they genuinely cared about the person's character. So they had no business with anything like race, identity, and belonging to this or that community. They cared about very tangible matters, not metaphysical or philosophical or religious matters. To begin with, my father's agnostic and my mother is a very practicing Catholic, and yet it never posed a problem that my future husband was Jewish. (Danielle, July 2020)

Past the first reactions from the families to the choice made by their child, the non-Jewish partner may sometimes opt for conversion with the explicit goal of transmitting Judaism to the couple's offspring. Danielle ascribes her multicultural outlook to her Caribbean origins, but in certain areas around Paris, people befriend others from all walks of life, ethnicities, and religions, as Florence explained: "Sarcelles is very multicultural, so I decided to see what was positive in the various religious faiths surrounding me. At no point in time did I tell myself, 'Oh, okay, he's Jewish so I'm going to join the Jews'—at no point in time did I tell myself that. But I kept seeking. When I met Oscar, without even talking about religion, we got to know each other without even mentioning religion, and I really liked his mindset and his way of life so I told myself, 'why not convert, so we'll have a common basis and we'll know in what direction we're going to raise our children.' Which I think is more difficult when you're in between two faiths" (Florence, 2011). The importance of having an officially Jewish offspring is so predominant that if the woman is not Jewish, she is often compelled to convert. For instance, Elie's Martiniquan mother was made to convert by her Ethiopian Jewish husband before they had any children together.

As endogamy is strongly recommended, exogamy becomes undesirable, if not shunned. The transmission of Judaism to the next generation is the prerequisite of a well-balanced marriage and family. However, a conversion prompted by the intention to marry a Jewish person is not acceptable from the Consistory's Orthodox perspective. As the sociologist Sébastien Tank-Storper explains, "[i]t has become customary to read the Orthodox milieus' suspicion of conversions as overemphasizing the principle of direct line of descent (in short, the ethnic principle) in defining Jewishness. Conversely, more inclusive policies—which are generally attributed to 'modern' Judaism, such as Reform Judaism or the Masorti movement—are generally seen as an assertion of a Jewish identity which is not so much defined in terms of descent, but more as an ethics which it becomes possible to embrace."[17] Danielle is a good example of the latter understanding of Jewishness: like others, she attends worship services at the Reform Judaism movement "Judaïsme En Mouvement" (JEM) because her spouse is Jewish and considers herself to be a Jew neither by descent nor by conversion, but out of a sentiment of belonging.

Whether they identify as Jewish or not, these significant others are confronted with reactions of either acceptance or rejection. The first type of reaction is often found among interviewees who joined Reform Judaism or Masorti communities. These respondents were almost unanimous in saying that they had never experienced prejudice in these milieus. Laure, a fifty-five-year-old woman born to an Ashkenazi Jewish father and a mother from French Guiana and Guadeloupe, gave a representative example in her life story: "I am what you may call an image of race mixing, since my father is an Ashkenazi Jew; he was born in France to immigrant parents . . . and my mother was also born in metropolitan France, to Caribbean parents—my grandfather who was from Guadeloupe and my grandmother, from French Guyana. I am a product of mixing and I have always embraced mixing as my philosophy. Mixing means openness to the Other, without being judgmental. . . . I personally joined the Reform Judaism movement, where I feel very comfortable: people are open-minded, not judgmental, many of them are mixed themselves so I really like that there's no staring at anyone and judging their differentness and their racial mix, you are who you are. That's what I like about it. People who join the Reform Judaism movement do so because they have chosen to, as opposed to synagogues [of the Consistory], where you go because you've had a Jewish upbringing, because you are a Jew who just follows tradition, period" (Laure, October 2020). The sociologist Jocelyne Streiff-Fénard explains that in France, interracial marriages, being "considered as the strongest proof of integration, are generally praised by public opinion, apart from the voters of the National Front. . . . They are seen as a sign of open-mindedness, modernity, and making decisions for oneself."[18] However, among Jewish milieus, this attitude is more prevalent in Reform Judaism and Masorti communities, who tend to interpret interracialism as evidence of a will to assimilate, while in the Consistorial Orthodox branch, it is perceived as a source of crisis. Only very few respondents have said they had felt welcome in Consistorial milieus, the vast majority complaining instead of rejection. Danielle, the non-Jewish spouse of an Ashkenazi man, made the following remarks on the Consistory: "when you go there as a partner in an interracial marriage, you are not recognized by the Consistory. At any rate they [rabbis] try to discourage you and ask you why you chose to marry a non-Jew and start lecturing you right off the bat. It is very difficult for an interracial couple to go through conversion at the Consistory. You need to have the right connections, and then insist a lot—we've got an example of someone who did that in the family. It is a real ordeal" (Danielle, July 2020). Still, interracial couples may be found in all branches of Judaism in France, which prompts us to ask whether these are evidence of a successful integration of Black members in the French Jewry.

At first sight, the very presence of these couples is a testament to the transformation of the racial and ethnic makeup of the French Jewry, for it sheds light on the commingling of Jews from diverse backgrounds in spite of resistance to interracialism, further highlighting the heterogeneity of the French Jewry. Yet the Reform Judaism movement is clearly the most open to diversity, as opposed to the Consistory. This modern dimension of the Reform and Masorti branches of Judaism has been analyzed by the French sociologist Joëlle Allouche, who emphasized that in addition to religious pluralism, "both also insist on the extremely modern premise that there exists more than one way of identifying at Jewish. While they prioritize the religious identity, they also accept that other expressions of Jewishness are possible, such as the historical, cultural, secular, or atheistic one. They consider that in a post-Holocaust world, it is no longer possible to lump all Jews into a single box. This is why more than one branch of Judaism aspires to be open to all forms of expression of Judaism, whether they be religious (of all hues), secular, cultural, or artistic."[19]

These observations help fathom the depth of the ideological gap between communities from the Reform Judaism and Masorti movements and those from the Consistorial Orthodoxy, which tends to disqualify any other Jewish identity than the religious one. This situation entails a strong imbalance when it comes to the marriageability of Black Jews, who face unusually high difficulties finding partners among predominantly White communities, regardless of where they worship. All unmarried respondents have expressed deep suffering in this respect. Young members of the Orthodox movement in particular find themselves in a deadlock as a result of the uncompromising stance of the Consistory, which adamantly rules out conversion for matrimonial purposes. Sébastien Tank-Storper analyzed this position as follows:

> The requirement of a pure intention was a problem because the great majority of requests for conversion were made by people who desired to marry. Logically, the rabbis should have refused such requests without any further discussion. This decision should have been all the more certain, to the extent that the question of conversions within marriage raised the question of an institutional response to religious transgression. The mixed marriage was in effect the sign that one of the most important prohibitions in Judaism had been violated: the rule of endogamy. The conversion of the non-Jewish spouse in a mixed marriage might therefore signify the a posteriori validation of this violation or transgression. Even more, the religious practice of candidates for conversion, in the great majority of cases, did not satisfy the requirements of the rabbis. When the latter demanded that candidates rigorously observe the commandments, and that they

become "practicing Jews," the candidates responded most often with a conception of religious practice based on feeling and subjectivity.[20]

The connection is clear with the ideologies of preservation of Jewish bloodlines and the rule of endogamy discussed above. Conversely, as is emphasized by the French ethnologist Ida Simon-Barouh, "marrying out puts under the limelight the questions that Jews ask themselves in general, for it coalesces all the issues pertaining to Judaism (the religion), Jewishness (the ethnicity), and the ways of performing and transmitting both."[21]

This situation, resulting from the prerequisite of endogamy and the taboo of exogamy, necessarily causes suffering among Black Jewish men and women seeking to marry a Jewish partner. This is exemplified by Ruth, an African woman who converted via the Consistory; she answered my question about getting married as follows: "it's a bit complicated. In fact, God willing—if Hashem wants me to meet a Jewish person, [I will] but it's not so easy for us converts, because I don't have that many Jewish friends, let alone single ones, and the people I hang out with are families with children, so people who don't necessarily have singles in their entourages. And let's face it, being a Black woman and a convert is an actual handicap for me" (Ruth, 2010). Single Black converts who are members of the Consistorial branch logically seek to marry a Jewish partner, including fellow converts, who may be mamzerim, that is, people born to non-Jewish mothers and Jewish fathers. Ruth's frustration is perceptible in her description of the options offered to her by the Consistory:

> So I was planning to either resort to Shidduch—Shidduchim are more or less arranged marriages, where you are introduced to people—or to matchmaking websites and singles clubs. At the end of the day, these are the few options I have; otherwise, I'll have to make babies on my own, by this I mean with a non-Jew, and then I would have children that I could raise as Jews. One last possibility—of course this would be the very last resort, but for me it would be the most negative one—is that I could build a family with someone who would not be Jewish but would not object to my raising the children [in the Jewish faith]. But this would cause problems anyway, because it would be a devious thing to do to go through conversion, only to say you are going to live with someone who doesn't share your faith. I confess that this is a real issue, I confess that it's a question I intended to ask the rabbi, is there any after-sales customer service, once you have converted and you are thirty years old? A woman has got to find a suitable party, if she is to raise a Jewish family. So this is a job for the Consistory and, why not, the organization [Federation of Black Jews] also. Maybe it's easier to live with someone who looks like you and is a Jew, even if he was born a Christian. I think it's important enough for the organization [FJN] and the Consistory to address the problem. (Ruth, 2010)

Evyatar Marienberg, as he addressed the principle of non-admission of an individual into the Jewish community, discussed the condition of the mamzer, a person defined as the "offspring of an incestuous, adulterous, or 'irregular' intercourse, which bars them from marrying a Jewish man or woman until the tenth generation, unless they marry a fellow mamzer, or else a convert."[22] On paper, then, marrying a fellow convert of whatever race should not be a problem. But in fact, matrimonial options prove to be even more restrictive, for two reasons: first, because there are few Black Jews in France, and then, because French Jews are scattered among a variety of branches, which precludes Orthodox Jews marrying Jews from the Masorti or Reform Judaism movements, regardless of race. Indeed, such unions would not be validated by the Consistory, which is the self-proclaimed gatekeeper of Jewish purity. Rabbi Rivon Krygier, who is the leader of the Masorti movement in France, had this to say when I asked him about the Consistory's position in this respect:

> It puts us in a difficult situation, exactly like a person holding a passport from a pariah state, if you will. Well, that person will not be able to visit other countries; which means that a person who has converted into a community like ours [the Masorti] won't be able to have a wedding in a Consistorial community. . . . I can't say we are happy with this situation; it's a very unpleasant situation which weighs people down, for it has a psychological cost. Whenever people are frowned upon as heretics by other people, it's not a desirable self-image to have. Thankfully, most people are able to ignore this and embrace their Judaism in every aspect of life, and they have their place in a large Jewish community. (Rabbi Rivon Krygier, August 2012)

Additionally, the ethnic rivalry between Ashkenazi and Sephardic Jews further complicates Black Jews' matrimonial quests, to the point that those interviewees who are single and hoping to get married seem to have next to no chances to reach their goal. Indeed, they often worship at Ashkenazi or Sephardic synagogues whose members are overwhelmingly if not allWhite, which makes it improbable to meet anyone but White singles. Ismaël, a respondent of Danite Jewish descent, described his predicament as follows: "it's really tough, and I hope things will change and evolve at least a little bit, but it's tough because these are preferences that prevail. Sephardic or Ashkenazi Jews are not necessarily racist, they just hope their daughter will date a Moroccan [Jew] because they're Moroccan or a Tunisian [Jew] because they're Tunisian. . . . They want their daughter to date fellow Ashkenazim or fellow Sephardim, that's all" (Ismaël, 2020).

Ashkenazim and Sephardim being themselves in a love-hate relationship with one another, filled with condescension, they rarely consider as an option a Black Jewish addition, who will generally be seen as not Jewish, or not Jewish enough. A majority of respondents described Sephardim as less open-minded than Ashkenazim when it came to accepting a Black Jew into the family. Guershon, in particular, insisted on this distinction when speaking of rejection:

> Among Ashkenazim, no, as I said, there was no suspicion. It's rather, I'm sorry to say, among the Sephardim that it's a catastrophe, I won't mince my words, they're so racist. Anti-Ashkenazi propaganda causes the feeling that *they* are racist, but that's not true. Of course, you can find a few racists in the bunch. But in general, Ashkenazim are less problematic than Sephardim, because Ashkenazim have more experiences with rejection, as they suffered more rejection in Europe. Sephardim had some issues with the Arabs, but they were better treated. I personally never felt anything racist about Ashkenazi Jews, really. Now I must confess that Sephardim really aren't my cup of tea, I dislike their behavior. (Guershon, July 2020)

Birds of a feather flock together, as the saying goes, and here it must be said that in choosing a partner, Black spouses tend to resemble their White spouses to the point of internalizing their Ashkenazi or Sephardic ethnic markers. Consequently, those who have married Ashkenazim, like Guershon, tend to praise this group at the expense of Sephardim, and vice versa, with casual remarks like "for us Ashkenazim," "now I love and think as a Sephardi," for example. Marah, a Congolese-born convert whose wife is Sephardic, says: "since the mother is the one who makes you a Jew, my children are Jewish. But the father is the one who chooses the color of their Judaism between Ashkenazi and Sephardic, even if he is a convert. I opted for the Sephardic tradition" (Marah, November 2020).

Beyond the Ashkenazi/Sephardic divide, White Jewish families also consider social prestige when assessing a potential addition. Yann, another Congolese convert who joined the Masorti movement, makes this point unambiguously:

> I think it's not so much a matter of religion as a matter of social status. People hide behind [categories], "You're a Muslim, you're a Christian, you're a Jew." But behind these categories, Africanness means poverty and under-development. If I were American, I'd be married already [laughs]. If the guy's a Black American, problem solved—they won't ask if he's Black, he'll be welcomed immediately into the family. (Yann, 2010)

This observation on the preferential treatment of African Americans over Africans and French Caribbean people in French society is frequently heard and dates back to the two world wars, which fostered a sense of gratefulness and fascination with Americanness in the French population. This was studied by the sociologist Emmanuel Todd in his work *Le destin des immigrés, Assimilation et ségrégation dans les démocraties occidentales*.

Other young respondents have expressed deep suffering over the interference of anti-Black sentiment in their matrimonial projects. Enoch, a twenty-four-year-old man from Cameroon who converted to Judaism in the Orthodox Consistorial movement, told me that he had dated a Sephardic woman until her father put an end to the relationship with these words, "My daughter will never marry a descendant of Ham!" (Enoch, November 2017). The Biblical myth of the curse of Ham thus finds a new lease on life when families want to reject a Black suitor or girlfriend with a definitive argument. This also appears in the 2005 film *Live and Become* by Radu Mihaileanu, where the young Ethiopian-born protagonist, Shlomo, sees his father's White Israeli girlfriend tell her, "I want you to stop hanging out with this boy, he's Satan's minion." Later in the film, Shlomo's fiancée asks him if an Ethiopian can marry a White woman, and he answers, "wait, I'll go inquire." That he should need to inquire about this matter shows that interracial marriage is not treated lightly by either White or Black Jews, even in Israel, which recognized the Jewishness of Ethiopian Jews. The answer given to the protagonist by an elderly rabbi from Ethiopia, acting as a father figure to him, is equally telling: "Yes, an Ethiopian man can marry a White woman, but from the day she marries an Ethiopian, the White woman becomes Black."[23] Although this is a work of fiction, the film still reflects the challenges to the social integration of Black Jews and the issues pertaining to Black/White interracial marriages, even in Israel, where, presumably, the question of the Law of Return's application to a couple's offspring is a non-issue. A specialist of Ethiopian Jews' integration issues in Israel, the anthropologist Lisa Anteby-Yemini writes that "in the religious sphere, they are also perceived as a separate group within the realm of marriage proceedings, in which the Jewishness of the partners is only examined by one single rabbi, chosen by the community."[24]

In the French context, it is remarkable that those Black respondents who are members of the Reform Judaism and Masorti movements are the most open-minded in imagining their matrimonial prospects. For example, Yann, a thirty-year-old member of the Masorti movement, described his future as follows:

> My obligation is in transmission, in our community we are all about transmission. I know that this duty, this obligation to transmit my heritage comes from African culture, Western culture, Israeli culture, and as such I can only be open-minded. I don't absolutely *have to* marry a Jewish woman, I just have to marry someone to start a family—well, not just anybody, the person must be capable of accepting my Jewish identity for the marriage to work, because I

have to pass it on to the kids, because of course I'll have kids, and I have to pass it on to my children. If this is not okay, if she won't play that game, well I guess I'll remain single for many, many years [laughs]. (Yann, 2010)

Another interviewee told me that Yann had since then married a White Jew and had children; unfortunately, I was not able to contact him for another interview. Still, the response he gave me ten years ago is a good reflection of the mindset of the Masorti and Reform Judaism movements, which do not necessarily exclude non-Jews, but insist on the transmission of Judaism. This also appears in the response given by Rébecca, a member of the Reform Judaism movement, whose choices are clearly unfettered by religious constraints:

I live with someone I met six years ago, I'm not married yet, and I have no kids. My partner is not Jewish, he's from Guadeloupe. I never obsessed over finding a Jewish significant other, because I'm mixed-race myself, and to me, race mixing is the future of mankind. I hadn't set my mind on finding a Jew and no one else, because if I don't, I'm not going to miss a love story just because the person I met is not Jewish. So, things happened naturally, he's from Guadeloupe and I didn't choose it, it happened just like that. (Rébecca, June 2020)

The case of Danite Jews from the Ivory Coast is slightly different, as they identify as Jews but are not (yet) recognized as such by the Consistory of France. The ensuing lack of exposure and legitimacy in the French Jewry puts them in a difficult situation, making it impossible for them to build families whose Jewishness would be guaranteed. A young member of that community expressed his frustration in the following terms:

My girlfriend's folks have a very negative attitude, especially her sister, and her father is even worse. In the end I told myself, it's not worth the trouble. I'm not going to spend the rest of my life fighting people who reject another person just because he's different, Black, and named Kohen. . . . They never had the nerve to say it to my face, but it's always been at the back of their minds, and sometimes I felt it in their gestures. I visited them often, and I could feel the negative atmosphere, and a smatter of hypocrisy. I was told things indirectly, and even sometimes when she was on the phone with her father, I was standing close by and I could hear her father tell her incredible stuff, like, "he's not a Jew, he's a piece of shit, he's not worth sacrificing everything for." Her father considers me as a subhuman being, in fact. My girlfriend did try to defend me, I'm not denying it, but she is herself a sort of outcast in her own family because she's always dated Black guys, so she was always less than. Because she dated Blacks, she was told they're not Jewish, and now that she's found one who is a Jew, it only made matters worse, because I wasn't Jewish enough! Her father and her sister in particular insisted that I go through conversion. I have no business applying for conversion; if today, as things stand, I am not accepted as I am and I'm not invited, I certainly won't be better accepted after conversion. (Gilad, 2020)

Here, rejection is due both to race-based prejudice and a lack of legitimacy of the community he comes from. Indeed, even though the Danites have sparked genuine interest in Israel, a Sephardic family like his girlfriend's can feel entitled to demand conversion of a man whose family name has been Kohen for generations, and in spite of the Consistory's position against conversions motivated by love. Had he acceded to their demand and converted to the religion he had been practicing since he was born, would he have been welcomed as an addition to their family? I have shown earlier how even Black converts admitted by the Consistory still remain Othered by their fellow Jews; therefore, it seems clear that the family's conversion demand is simply a pretext to camouflage their racial animus.

I have also met Black Jews who were born to Jewish mothers, but could not show their parents' ketubah, or marriage certificate; they too were confronted with the uncompromising stance of the Consistory of France. Indeed, according to the Talmudic treaty "Kiddushin," "anyone born to a Jewish mother is a Jew. In the eyes of the Halakha, children whose father is Jewish but whose mother is not, will not be considered as Jews under this definition. But Jewishness may also be acquired by conversion. Therefore, Judaism is equally transmitted by lineage and by adhesion."[25] The stakes are described as follows by Gabrielle Atlan: "we can say that two positions stand side by side. The first, which is traditional, orthodox Judaism, only recognizes a child's identity on the basis of matrilineal descent, which means that the mother alone determines her child's identity. In other words, a child is not Jewish unless the mother is. The second position, held by Reform Judaism, is that the principle of the child's patrilineal descent should also be taken into account. If he is a Jew, the father should also be considered to have birthed Jewish children even if their mother is not Jewish."[26] Because the Consistory is less flexible when confronted with mixed marriages, some children of Jewish fathers decide to circumscribe it. For example, Rébecca, an interviewee quoted earlier, is the biracial daughter of an Ashkenazi father and an unconverted Martiniquan mother. She chose to ignore the Consistory's demand of conversion and joined the Reform Judaism movement to live her life as a Jewish person recognized by a Jewish community. This is how she describes her decision: "Jewishness is important without necessarily focusing on the religious aspect, the list of taboos. You find out, when you go to Israel, that ninety percent of the population there is Jewish. Yet a good many people in Israel are very liberal and not very religious, and still, they feel deeply Jewish" (Rébecca, June 2020). The freedom to transmit a Jewish identity is increasingly being reclaimed over the obligatory arbitration of religious authorities which often appear as a sort of "religious police" in the recognition of Jewishness. This is illustrated by the case of Liana, another biracial interviewee, whose mother is a Sephardic Jew while her father is a non-Jewish Guadeloupean. Identifying as a Jew by virtue of matrilineal descent, she is fluent in Hebrew after spending seventeen years in Israel, from the age of thirteen until that of thirty, when she returned to France. There, she was faced with the Consistory's demand that she convert, due to her inability to show her parents' ketubah; yet, the same religious instance had precisely refused to deliver a ketubah to her parents thirty years before, considering that her father's petition for conversion was not sincerely motivated. She explained to me that the Consistorial authorities back then had not only refused to perform a religious marriage ceremony, but also urged her mother to split. The divorce ultimately occurred, and her father moved to New York City and is now a Buddhist, while her mother lives in Israel, but no longer practices Judaism because of her disappointment in rabbinical authorities, Liana says. Liana herself has decided to comply with the Consistory's demands of conversion, for the following reasons: "instead of converting my father, they put massive pressure on my mother until they got her to file for divorce. . . . I'm only accepting conversion because I want to be able to marry, I would hate for my future children to have to go through the same issues I'm facing" (Liana, 2012). While she could have joined the Masorti or Reform Judaism movements to obtain recognition of her Jewishness from them, she did not really have a choice, because she wants to spend the rest of her life in Israel and the Consistory in Paris is the only instance in France that can deliver a certificate of Jewish identity, a necessary document for a religious marriage, duly sanctioned by the ketubah that her mother was denied.

The ketubah is defined in these terms by Gabrielle Atlan: "[d]esignated as Ketubbah in Aramaic, the marriage certificate is a legal document with rabbinical origins, likely attributed to Simon Ben Shetah, the brother of Queen Salome Alexandra, a century before the Common Era. It is a legal document that is handed over to the bride during the wedding ceremony—which itself was instituted by the rabbis to officialize the union of the betrothed—and it contains a list of all the duties the husband vows to fulfill towards his wife, and also a list of the duties he or his heirs will have to fulfill in the event the marriage becomes dissolved either by divorce or by his own death."[27] In this case, the ketubah works like a sieve that helps sort out those Jews born to couples married in Orthodox synagogues by Consistorial rabbis. Black men and women who identify as Jews but cannot show a ketubah, along with those who have converted outside of the Consistory, are mechanically rejected as non-Jews, which further complicates any plans for a religious union.

Three types of reactions to this institutional normativity may be observed. First, some respondents, like Rébecca, choose to do without the Consistory's approval in pursuing their matrimonial project, but they still put a premium on the transmission of Jewish identity by passing on Jewish values: "it was important for me to find someone who was open-minded enough, because I was determined to be able to raise my children in Jewish culture—not necessarily religion, but Jewish culture, with traditions, like the ones I was raised in. So whatever my partner believes in doesn't really matter, but what does matter is that he should accept my passing on certain values to my children. . . . I wasn't specifically looking for a Jewish person, but at least someone accepting" (Rébecca, June 2020). The second type of reaction comes from Black Jews like the Danites, who have actually practiced Judaism from childhood in spite of the lack of recognition by the Consistory of France. Transmitting Judaism is even more complicated for them as they take their Jewishness very seriously and therefore insist on marrying Orthodox Jewish partners. Ismaël explains, "we have often been asked for our parents' ketubah. We can't show a ketubah, because it wasn't necessarily part of our traditions, because this is something which was introduced later to sort out Jews from non-Jews, so no, we don't have any" (Ismaël, 2020).

Handling the issue collectively, by means of community organizing, is another option for these involuntary celibates. This would be facilitated by the existence of Shidduch, a Jewish matchmaking tradition mentioned above, which consists in organizing encounters between marriageable men and women seeking to get married. This practice, which presumably dates back to Biblical times, is encouraged by rabbis and families in Orthodox milieus. Single Black Jews are also willing to resort to Shidduch, as Marah successfully did. This is how he described it: "the system of Shidduch aims to respect the tradition which expects the parents or a capable member of the community to handle these matters for their children. This person has to collect information about the person seeking a partner, i.e, their age and background, their level of religious practice, how they want to evolve and in what domain. In the end, this person asks loads of questions and tries to see if there's a match for your criteria. Then he sees if there's actually a good fit, and he sets up a first encounter. This allows the two people, who already know that they have things in common, to begin exchanging to see if the chemistry works between them. That's the system I used to meet my wife" (Marah, 2020).

While resorting to the Shidduch was the best option for Marah, other respondents have complained about the way the system was applied to them. At a meeting of AM-I-FA in 2017, the younger members of the community organization said that their rabbi never introduced them to anyone. Enoch sneered, "whenever a girl has a disability, then I become a suitable party!" (Enoch, 2017) while Ismaël noted that he is often introduced to women who are so much older than himself that they are past their childbearing years. The year before, the group chat Shidduch FJN had been created by Guershon Nduwa, who explained his initiative as follows: "young Black Jews are given a hard time here. I'm not surprised, because the Sephardic milieus have difficulties opening up to different people. This led me to create a Shidduchim group via WhatsApp, which works very well, it's brand new" (Guershon, July 2020).

But while both AM-I-FA and the FJN are led and made up of Black Jews from various branches, those in need of a ketubah still have to comply with Consistorial rules. Marah criticizes the latter in eloquent terms:

> this is real, and it doesn't necessarily mean that there's no need or desire on the part of White Jewish men or women to marry Black Jews. The thing is that the system connecting the two is not really adequate. Let me put it this way: what I mean is that Blacks who convert [to Judaism] have a positive image in France, but that system will never label them "excellent" or rather, call it "an honor for any family to give their daughter in marriage to such men." I know how the Consistory works, and I recognize they work seriously, because just spending two or three years studying doesn't make you a champ of the Torah. And that's why the families that are observant and entrust this Shidduch system with their children's future feel reluctant; because they have doubts on the actual level of practice of the African converts, and they know that there's only one place they can really trust. If you haven't jumped through those particular hoops, then you're done for because they'll reject your application. That's because they know the level is not up to par, and you can see a lot of that in the Black Jewish community in Paris, it's a really mixed bag, from those who converted with the Orthodox, to the "wannabe" Jews who aren't recognized, to those who converted with the Reform movement, so families don't feel safe handing over their daughter, who's kept her virginity and done everything the Torah prescribes, to some person who maybe is going to challenge overnight everything she's always believed in for the twenty years she's spent on earth. I *know* that the reason why the Shidduch system doesn't work well for Blacks is the disparity in the levels of conversion. What that means is that we have to overperform, we don't have a choice; otherwise a guy will always be labeled as the solution of last resort, or as the African who takes nothing seriously. So I would say that the system as it's built doesn't favor us, it doesn't give us an advantage. But from the moment there is a possibility to confirm that the person converted in the most serious manner, and has demonstrated the most uncommon evolution, so that everyone can sign with both hands a certification saying his conversion is an honest one, there is no problem anymore. Or if there *is* a problem, then it's because of racism. (Marah, November 2020)

This criticism, as expressed by a convert who has since then become a rabbi in Israel, is quite revealing of the institutional community framework of the French Jewry: even as it welcomes and converts Black candidates to conversion, it does not actually dispel all shadows of doubts around the authenticity of their Judaism. This leads to the next question Marah is raising, namely, are sincerity and competence enough to durably validate these converts' claims to Jewish authenticity? One of the first female members of a French President's cabinet, Françoise Giroud, famously said that the gender problem will be solved from the moment everyone can see a not-so-bright woman in a high-responsibility position, and not make a fuss about it—as is routinely done with similarly gifted and situated men, she implied. The same could be said of the racial issue in Jewish milieus, especially as many Jews spontaneously acknowledge that converts are held to much higher expectations than those born to Jewish mothers within wedlock.

Yet another reason why Shidduch does not work for Black Jews is that outmarriage, as Jocelyne Streiff-Fénard says, "is the polar opposite of the socially arranged marriage, since by definition, it is never in compliance with a marriage rule, but in opposition with the social norm that presides over normal or licit marriages, which are always between insiders."[28] Indeed, normativity and the strict control of the Consistory contribute to creating, rather than blurring, boundaries between minority groups and the mainstream, White group; and this leaves little to no choice to Black Jews seeking a Jewish partner. This is clearly expressed by Ismaël, a Danite Jewish interviewee:

> The perfect scenario would be to marry a Jewish girl with the same convictions that I have, the same vision; but you know, sometimes things can be complicated with the girl's family. I've seen it happen to my younger brother: he was rejected by his girlfriend's family, who are White. He made all the efforts required of him, but the outcome was negative. In the end, he had to quit. Because of that, I am not entirely excluding the idea of marrying a, quote unquote, goy. . . . Because it's hard to find a Jewish partner. I hope things will change and evolve at least a little bit. (Ismaël, 34 years old, 2020)

Those respondents who identify as Jewish on the basis of ethnicity—not unlike Ashkenazi and Sephardic Jews—and a self-attributed legitimacy, but do not strictly comply with Jewish religious practice, are not averse to the prospect of marrying a non-Jew. Such is the case of Aurélie, who considers herself to be Jewish on the grounds of her Peul (Fulani) origins. She attends a Reform Judaism synagogue in Rouen, Normandy, but refuses the offers of conversion extended to her there, replying she is already a Jew. Yet in spite of this claim, she is willing to consider marrying a non-Jew, because she assumes that her children would automatically be Jewish, notwithstanding her lack of recognition by the rabbinical system. This is what she had to say:

> I am not looking for a Jewish man, I don't care. My priority today, at forty, is to find a partner that is on the same page as me, understands my values and respects me, that's all I'm asking for. I'm not looking for someone who has the same religion as me, not at all. Anyway, from the moment a woman is

Jewish—Jewishness is not given by the men. It's more difficult for a Jewish man to marry a non-Jew, because he's not the one passing on Jewishness, but the woman is. (Aurélie, 2020)

Consequently, even though she seeks neither conversion nor recognition of her Jewishness and is not bent on finding a Jewish spouse, Aurélie still places the transmission of Jewish identity front and center of her matrimonial aspirations. Similarly, at the garden party hosted by White members of the Bnai Brith for the second anniversary of AM-I-FA, on June 28, 2016, I met an African man named Christian, who played the balafon (an African xylophone) for the occasion. He told me he was from Cameroon, and when I asked him if he was Jewish, he retorted that he was, adding, "you too are a Jew, since you're from Congo Brazzaville, because all the Bantus are Jews." Then he quickly began telling me about his life: having read Afrocentric books (see chapter 2), fully convinced of being legitimately a Jew, Christian became romantically involved with a White Jewish woman who became pregnant with his child. But his Sephardic in-laws not only rejected him, but also denied his claims to Jewishness and even to the paternity of their biracial granddaughter. Unwilling to be forcibly estranged from his girlfriend and their child, Christian insisted on going to the synagogue every Saturday to see them, but the Consistorial security service there systematically denied him entry. I have lost track of this respondent and am unable to say if his story had any further developments, but his distress was clearly genuine.

The Consistory's distrust of interracial marriages is also probably linked to the implications on the children's religious identity, and the fear of a loss of Jewishness among the following generations. Beyond all the criticism leveled at the Israelite Consistory of Paris, analyzing the data from the respondents from the Reform or Masorti branches allows a better contextualization of interracialism and race mixing, by shedding light on the stakes of the redefinitions of Jewishness at work in multiracial families. Whatever their category or branch of Judaism, Black Jews are often focused on transmitting Jewishness to their offspring, whether existing or future. Quoting the verse from *Deuteronomy* (4:9) commanding, "make them known unto thy children and thy children's children," Rabbi Haïm Korsia emphasizes that it is "the model of transmission in Judaism which has value only if beyond teaching something, we also learn how to transmit this thing with a simple principle, which is, learning in order to teach. This verse reiterates above all that the fundamental institution which is absolutely crucial to transmission is the family, the natural place of exchange, discovery of oneself and others, and above all, a loving place."[29] The imperative of transmission is therefore central to Jewish identity. But can African and Caribbean Jews meet this obligation or demand? This appears as a nagging question through the interviews given by Black Jews who sincerely seek to live as Jews and actively participate in Jewish community life.

Still, the institutional insistence on bloodlines works in a quasi-normal manner for some respondents, like Marah, who married a Sephardic woman and has chosen to live in Israel, which also facilitates the transmission of Jewish norms to their children:

> Everything works really well and is quite hassle-free because we're in a country where everything is Jewish, so we don't need to worry about what they will eat for lunch in school, whether it's Kosher or not. Or if they go to school with a cap or a kippah on their heads, you don't need to worry if they're going to be judged because they're mixed-race and Jewish, because all the schools in the neighborhood are Jewish schools. Then again, some parents choose to send their kids to a religious school, and everything is done to facilitate a religious education, even for parents who are not devout Jews. (Marah, 2020)

For others who have remained in France, the necessity of transmission nearly turns into a source of anguish when they want to have children and transmit them Judaism, since it is an uphill battle for them to find a Jewish mother for their offspring.

In conclusion, interracial marriages are often perceived by Jewish authorities and believers—save in the Reform and Masorti movements—as transgressing the rule of endogamy. Such transgression, as Sébastien Tank-Storper notes, may be "internalized as a problematic choice, a betrayal of the bloodline, especially with regard to the children's identities. Jews are fond of the saying that switches the usual order of identity: someone is a Jew if this person has Jewish children, rather than if his or her mother is Jewish. The conversion of the non-Jewish bride or wife therefore appears as a way to mend the transgression and allow the transmission of Jewishness to the children (since the mother's status determines her children's)."[30] Séverine Mathieu questions this aspect in the following terms: "When one of the partners is not Jewish, how do the couples define Judaism, or more precisely Jewishness, i.e., Jewish identity in the broad sense of the term, beyond traditional religious practice? The consciousness of being Jewish, much as in the couples where both partners are Jewish, but in a more acute fashion in this configuration, is mingled with other identities. Among the respondents surveyed, social homogamy prevails over religion. Religion is not front and center in their lives and educational choices; However, any time this thee comes up, they refer to Judaism and craft for themselves a sort of customized Judaism. Interestingly, in so doing they make a distinction between what they say pertains to either culture or religion, and assume they favor a mode of transmission based essentially on the former dimension. Why and how do they choose to claim this Jewishness? How do they define this necessity of transmission that they can't seem to escape? How do they express it? What does it mean to be a Jew when you live with a non-Jewish partner?"[31] All the questions that guided Séverine Mathieu in her sociological study of couples that were mixed, but not interracial, are quite relevant to discuss the multiracial families I have interviewed for the present work.

THE TRANSMISSION OF JEWISH IDENTITY IN INTERRACIAL FAMILIES

Although transmission is one of the major motives of conversion among women in particular, some respondents who either self-identify as Jews without any permission from the Consistory or belong to the Reform branch still insist on raising their (existing or future) children as Jews. Rébecca, a twenty-six-year-old biracial woman whose mother is non-Jewish, stresses that she was the one who transmitted Jewish values and traditions to her and her siblings: "the thing is, my father is Jewish and my mother is not, but although my mother is not a convert, she sort of embraced the Jewish religion in the sense that she has converted in her heart, so to speak. She did not go through the conversion process, but still, she has insisted on raising us in the Jewish religion and teach us the values and traditions. So in fact it's my mother who's the leader in the family when it comes to religious holidays, more than my father actually. That's really special, you see, because while not being Jewish herself, she's the leader, she's the one organizing the family get-togethers and all that. For her, passing traditions on to the next generation really matters. In fact, these are values she identifies with, even if she doesn't necessarily share the same religion" (Rébecca, June 2020). I also interviewed Rébecca's mother Danielle, who explained her position in the following terms:

> this is because my husband comes from a tradition that's very Ashkenazi and very affected by the Holocaust, a very sad history, so that for a very long time they kept under a veil what they really were, in an effort to forget this painful episode, up to the present day. You see, certain scars just don't heal and never will, so you have to live with them. Now my own problem is that—personally I've always transmitted my Creole roots to my children and always insisted on immersing them in the culture every time we went on holidays to see their grandparents in Martinique, I wanted them to really have that DNA. But on the other hand, I couldn't understand why the extraordinary history of what makes a Jew in his Jewishness should not also be put under the limelight and borne by my children. Anyway, it's not as if we had a choice, that's who they are, they have this double imprint, but my husband is just sitting there doing nothing. For starters, he's agnostic, he's against all the festivals and he hates

religion—honestly, he couldn't care less about religion. My in-laws keep Shabbat because of the circumstances, and my husband participates in the transmission because we celebrate the holidays. For him that was enough, you see, he did no more than that. (Danielle, 2020)

Clearly, the importance of family rituals and mothers' special role in the transmission of Judaism and Jewishness has a particular appeal for certain men and women. Even if Danielle was raised a Catholic, she undeniably behaves like a Jewish woman and mother, valuing Jewish culture and traditions more than her Jewish-born husband, to the point of insisting on transmitting them to their children in spite of his lack of motivation. It could be surmised that a feeling of guilt for not being the ideal Jewish daughter-in-law expected by her husband parents is behind her insistence on behaving as a protector of the Jewish bloodline of her children. At any rate, her example makes it abundantly clear that even when one of the partners is not Jewish, there is an actual need to transmit Jewishness, that is, Jewish values, traditions, and history.

For those respondents who are converts living with practicing Jewish partners, the norms dictated by the Jewish law (Halakha) always prevail, whether they have embraced the Orthodox, ultra-Orthodox, Masorti, or Reform branches. Other multiracial families are not really practicing, but still entertain and transmit the sense of their Jewishness and feel the need to transmit it to the next generations. I therefore share Séverine Mathieu's string of questions:

[w]hat, then, do you transmit when you self-identify as Jewish, but are not practicing and live and raise children with a non-Jewish partner? From a sociological perspective, how do mixed couples including a Jewish and a non-Jewish partner, and living in a secularized society, craft practices specific to Jewish tradition, even if the people concerned do not necessarily consider these as religious practices? How does the non-Jewish partner perceive and experience the other partner's Jewishness? Will they opt for circumcision or out of it? What dishes are prepared in the kitchen?

In her study, Séverine Mathieu offers answers to her questions along two major lines of analysis. On the one hand, the Jewish partner may, for themselves and others, "craft" a multilayered identity where references to a tradition and a history may well play no role at all—in which case their Jewishness disappears. On the contrary, these references may remain effective, albeit at a barely perceptible level, and in this case the claim to a certain form of Jewishness remains. Hence the rise of a subgroup, the "New Israelites," as the sociologist Dominique Schnapper had defined them in her 1980 book *Juifs et Israélites,* for whom Judaism is a culture and a destiny—a frame of mind that the non-Jewish partner in the couple may also choose to appropriate.[32]

It follows that the issue of transmitting Jewishness remains an essential one even for those men or women who are not practicing Jews or have non-Jewish partners. It is done by selecting the Jewish identity markers from a familial perspective. Rébecca discussed her own non-Jewish partner in the following terms:

> He is an atheist and has never been baptized. His father used to be a Jehovah's witness and his mother too, but he was never baptized. His parents always let him choose what he wanted to do. I, on the contrary, am deeply involved in Jewish values, which he finds very close to the values his parents gave him. So, besides the religious aspect that he doesn't share, he does find an echo in the values and traditions I have received. Just as my [non-Jewish] mother is moved by certain things, he too is moved by certain aspects of Jewish values. (Rébecca, June 2020)

The Jewish identities elaborated by the multiracial families I interviewed are thus constructed on a variety of elements that help them delineate what Jewishness means to them: religious practice, circumcision, the cooking and consumption of Kosher foods, loyalty to the state of Israel and the preservation of the memory of the Holocaust. Those who are attached to the strict practice of the Halakha transmit Jewishness as a coherent whole, as does Rabbi Marah, a native of Congo who converted in the Orthodox movement, married a Sephardic woman, and now lives in Jerusalem:

> It's difficult to single out any particular element because Jewishness is a bloc: it's the Shabbat and Kosher food and Hebrew and the *tzitzit*—all of this is passed on at the same time. There's no room or any possibility to pick and choose, because everything comes at the same time. [My children] always see me wearing my tzizit and my tefillin, they see me going to the synagogue and say the blessings before and after each meal, they see me going to the museum or studying or teaching and all of this is Judaism, you don't choose this or that, but you live as a Jew. (Marah, 2020)

Florence, the convert from Guadeloupe who married a man of Ashkenazi and Sephardic descent, attends a Reform Judaism synagogue with her husband, and the family they have built live in the practice of Judaism: "Yes, we make Shabbat with my in-laws, and I really like also when we get together just the four of us, we make Shabbat every Friday" (Florence, 2011).

Yet other families cultivate a sense of belonging to the Jewish people without religious practice. Laure's story provides a good illustration of this type of families:

I've always been Jewish, always lived in the Jewish religion, but you have to know that Ashkenazi Jews after the war had few notions of belonging to the religion, they were rather focused on belonging to the people, and also on Zionism and the state of Israel, and this was not done from a religious perspective. And my grandparents escaped from Poland and Romania where they knew poverty and hopelessness, to become religiously emancipated, so they asserted themselves as Jews, but they weren't practicing. Being practicing is, for example when we were growing up, we celebrated Kippur and Pesach and the other important holidays and I went to Jewish summer camps and went into Jewish milieus. (Laure, 2020)

Religious festivals but above all community gatherings and family reunions stand out as crucial elements underpinning Jewishness in the dynamics of ethnic singularity and transmission. Even if certain Jewish partners are not practicing, their feeling of belonging is still strong and meaningful. His analysis of the petitions for conversion sent to Jewish institutions leads Sébastien Tank-Storper to question the definition of what constitutes a legitimate Jewish identity and the nature of the bond uniting Jews with one another. Is it "a common origin (i.e. and ethnic definition of Jewishness)? A common destiny (i.e. a definition of Jewishness in terms of nationhood)? Common beliefs and practices (i.e. a religious definition of Jewishness)? In other words, what does it mean to become a Jew? Does it mean incorporating oneself into a people and embrace its destiny? Does it mean integrating a nation-state, namely Israel, with its laws and political institutions? Does it mean embracing a way of life or a culture? Does it mean adhering to a system of beliefs and a worldview?"[33] All these distinctions imply that whoever feels concerned by Jewish identity may find a form of Jewishness they can relate to. As for non-Jews, they can embrace this feeling of belonging to Jewishness by sharing the life of a Jewish partner in the domestic sphere. Séverine Mathieu notes, "[t]oday in France, the definition of Jewishness is based more on self-identification than on the recognition of matrilineal descent. Jewishness is part of a complex, multilayered identity: today you are at the same time a Jew, a parent, a representative of an organization or charity, and a professional."[34] This is echoed by Danielle, the Martiniquan partner of an Ashkenazi husband, who is not Jewish but feels satisfied with her feeling of belonging to the community and having strong ties with its members:

You can be Jewish without being a practicing Jew! For one, I am not a religious person at all, I am more connected to the festive dimension [of Judaism] because where I'm from in Martinique, we party very often. It's always time for a party, so I thought it was really wonderful because it was a way to stay connected beyond the pretext of maintaining traditions, it's a very strong family bond. I've always found this super important and interesting, so I'm always interested in practicing Jewish tradition under that angle of family ties, and family get-togethers for the big family events, when the bonds are strengthened. So we've always been inspired by that, we celebrated at home and we celebrated at the in-laws. Being a Jew doesn't mean going to the synagogue and praying. Being a Jew is really a state of mind, you were born a Jew, and you can become one of course but it has nothing to do with religiosity. It's a state of mind, a tradition, a history, you see. (Danielle, 2020)

This respondent has embraced Jewish identity to such an extent that she is the current PR person for the French Reform Judaism movement, of which she is a member as well as her husband and children, although she has never converted to Judaism. Whether they practice the Jewish religion or not, the women living with Jewish partners often say they feel responsible for the transmission of Jewishness to their children. The respondents have typically emphasized the importance of passing on the culture and tradition.

In particular, because the space of the kitchen functions as "a special locus of memory and sharing in the transmission of Judaism,"[35] Kashrut rules are also elaborated daily in multiracial families in two ways. When both parents are practicing Jews, they choose to keep Kosher and transmit it to their children. When one of the two partners is not Jewish, Kashrut rules are applied on the basis of an individual selection by the family members. In certain families, both the parents and children keep Kosher; in others, either the parents or the children choose to follow Kashrut rules. Very often, non-practicing parents or their children do not keep Kosher but still are Jewish, or identify as such. The interviews reveal a diversity of situations. For instance, Laure is the daughter of an Ashkenazi Jewish father and does not identify as a religious person; she eats pork, but her children do not. They attended Talmud Torah, yet they do not identify as practicing Jews. Rébecca, who is also the daughter of an Ashkenazi father, does not identify as a religious person; she eats pork but feels strongly Jewish. As for Ismaël, who is a devout Jew seeking a Jewish wife, he told me that he is surrounded only by White Jews who eat pork.

Understandably, the transmission of religious values is also shaped by the ethnic customs of each partner, as is shown by Marah, the Congolese convert who now lives in Israel as a rabbi:

The education they receive at home is a mix of natural Judaism because we live in the Jewish and African cultures we ourselves grew up in, we keep Shabbat and celebrate the holidays in the Jewish and African traditions . . . Because Sephardic Judaism is a way of eating and dressing and reading the Torah, it's a whole set of sounds, a distinct way of pronouncing the letters, a world of fragrances, and all this is automatically part of their mother's daily life; They receive this culture in a daily routine that is colored by North African traditions . . . I pass on the language [Lingala] and Congolese food, and by this I mean I adjust Congolese recipes and incorporate them into the Jewish calendar: for instance, for the festival of Channukah, when every Jew is used to eating sufganiyot, which are deep-fried doughnuts, well, I cook Congolese doughnuts and these are the sufganiyot we have at home, and for Shabbat we eat beans cooked Congolese style. I make sure I introduce Congolese cuisine so [my children] may know that their Congolese half also implies a language and a way of eating certain dishes. They are used to it because they are also Congolese. (Marah, 2020)

Many interracial couples are also concerned with the transgenerational transmission of the trauma of the Holocaust.[36] Among the biracial respondents in particular, this trauma is emphasized as inherited. For instance, Rébecca, whose mother is from Martinique and whose father is Ashkenazi with Polish origins, is well situated to evoke the two legacies, as a descendant of both slaves and survivors of the concentration camps. She was seventeen when she first told me her life story: "I feel closer to the legacy of the Shoah than to that of slavery, to be honest. The legacy of slavery is more distant in time, as opposed to that of the Holocaust, which is more recent, with my grandfather often telling me about it. My grandfather was deported to Auschwitz. On the contrary, my mother never tells me about slavery" (Rébecca, 2011). As a teenager, she had such a deep interest in the history of the Holocaust that she collected newspapers from the 1940s and her favorite films—*Schindler's List* by Steven Spielberg and *Life is Beautiful* by Roberto Benigni—all revolved around that theme. Having been struck by the degree of passion with which Rébecca spoke about the Holocaust as a person directly affected by the trauma, and the contrast with her near indifference to the history of slavery, I decided to ask her mother Danielle about this discrepancy and her own involvement in transmitting the memory of her husband's parents in preference to her own heritage as a native of Martinique and therefore a descendant of enslaved French people. She explained it to me in the following terms:

I think that we in the Caribbean haven't resolved the question of slavery as far as legacy is concerned. By this I mean that there is a deep denial of this foundational scar on which Creole societies were built, in that we are not Africans, we are not Europeans, we are not Amerindians, we are not Spaniards, but we are all of these identities. We are the whole and everything at the same time, you understand? But this is rooted in a painful memory, which was built on tragic and cruel historical facts. This is why the older generations (I'm thinking of my grandparents) did their best to erase that part of their history from their genes . . . and decided that their history began in the Caribbean islands and not before. So they had to create a new society, the Creole society, with its specific Negritude, but starting from a new and multiple history. This means that we bear the marks of slavery on our bodies because we are Black . . . It's clear for all to see that Caribbean society is a mixed-race society, you see a person's head, and their hair, and their eyes and their skin color—there is so much diversity in these features that you can plainly see that there's some Blackness in them, or traces of Blackness. But it's been so tragic that the history we've also learnt in school has led us to deliberately ignore that period, the three centuries revolving around the slave trade and the creation of new societies born from the colonies and colonization. Maybe I've been wrong in not finding any sort of deep reason to remind [the children] where they are from. That's because with us it's visible, it's obvious, so I don't need to remind them. And it's not really something you can forget when you bear the marks on your skin and in your flesh. But I confess there hasn't been an effort on my part to do anything special on the 8th of May, which is for us the date of the end of slavery in our city, I haven't taken part in marches to commemorate this crime against humanity. Then again, it's a history you don't forget. But this is something I didn't do—I must confess, I didn't. But it's not something that we celebrate spontaneously, it's something buried deep down and that we don't talk about, it's a history we know we are the results of, but we don't want to talk about it, it's nothing to be proud of. Mind you, we are proud of who we are and what we've created, and what we've become today. (Danielle, July 2020)

Danielle's perceived need to justify herself is telling. The assumption that race is equated with cultural heritage is recurrent in her response, in contrast with Jewishness, which is implicitly represented as necessitating more showing and telling due to its racial invisibleness. Her emphasizing the children's paternal heritage over her own may be analyzed as evidence of the tendency of women in interracial couples to compensate, and possibly overcompensate, for their partners' lack of involvement with the transmission of their own cultural heritages—a finding present in literature on Black/White interracial couples.[37] But it is also undeniable that slavery, following its abolition, has long remained a taboo in the French Caribbean, so that its cultural legacy is rather repressed than reclaimed in the life stories of West Indian or part-Caribbean Jews. Indeed, this is how the existence of the taboo was confirmed by another respondent, Laure, who was born to an Ashkenazi father and a West Indian mother hailing from Guadeloupe and French Guiana:

There's the Holocaust and on the other side there's slavery, so if you close your eyes, you tell yourself, yikes, that's a big load of suffering to bear; but I have no stories to tell on the side of slavery, since people didn't talk about it, you know slavery was actually a taboo. Slavery was abolished in 1848 and my grandfather was born in 1898 so he was born a free man, that's definitely something, it's part of History and it's my history ... It's my history because when people speak of the French Caribbean they necessarily imply slavery ... But no, my children aren't curious about it, it's a distant thing, probably because I talk less about it, while my father kept talking about the Holocaust and we were soaking it up, it's a heavy load to bear. On the contrary, my mother was like, the West Indies is where life is good, but that was her personality and her family's history too, so that she did not bring everything back to slavery. That's all. The history of the Holocaust was a constant topic of conversation, and we were really soaking it up, to such a point that whenever I hear there's a documentary on the Holocaust I buy [the DVD] and I read a lot [on it], I also visited quite a few concentration camps. They say it's a trauma that got transmitted across generations and it's true, it's a trauma that I have and I did tell the children a lot about it, and made them go to museums with me . . . What did I transmit the children? Well it's not just the religion, it's the culture and the history. That's what I've passed on to them. Our family history. What I also passed on is that my grandfather's mother and my grand aunt survived the Holocaust in Romania and they left for Israel in 1947, you know, the story of Exodus and they got jailed in Cyprus; so the creation of the state of Israel is also part of my history and that's not about religion, that's what being a Jew is all about. (Laure, October 2020)

The silence of Caribbean parents around the slave past contrasts greatly with the transmission of the legacy of the Holocaust and the greater popularity of the research on this theme in France, even though both histories are traumatic for the descendants. Clearly, the stigma of the Holocaust has been successfully inverted so that it no longer entails self-hatred, but rather a collective effort of cultivation of a memory that plays a central part in the current definition of Jewishness and identity claims in French society. The family trauma caused by the Holocaust remains tied to collective memory that is elaborated in a nation grappling with both an antagonism between the legacies of slavery and the Holocaust, and persistent expressions of antisemitism and racism (see chapters 1 and 7).

Due to the social tensions around Jews and Blacks around the world and in France, biracial Jews who have inherited the two legacies feel they have to position themselves vis-à-vis each of them, taking the French and global contexts into account as they do so. Rébecca at seventeen was emotionally involved in cultivating the heritage of the Holocaust and did not contest the silence of her mother's family around slavery. Almost ten years later, in 2020, in an atmosphere transformed by the viral video captures of the murder of George Floyd and the subsequent globalization of the #BlackLivesMatter movement, she gave a new answer to my question, knitting the two legacies more closely in her response:

As far as slavery is concerned, I think that its being more distant in the past, and us no longer having first-hand witnesses, makes it more complicated, so what it is really all about today is our skin color. Sure, the duty to preserve memory is important when you see what's going on today, with for example George Floyd in the United States and other people like him who died simply because they were black, and there are things like that, for example Jews who died simply because they're Jewish like Mireille Knoll in Paris, [an octogenarian] who got murdered by a neighbor who believed she had a lot of money. These are things that don't make any sense, just for a question of money she gets slaughtered. Or a kid [Ahmaud Arbery] who goes out jogging and gets killed—people think he's a criminal because he's Black and he gets killed by police [*sic*], these are things that shouldn't exist anymore so, yes, it's an important duty we have to cultivate memory. So for Black people, beyond slavery there are more recent things such as all the forms of segregation which are even more recent than slavery today, these are things that shouldn't exist anymore. Today all men are equal, that's the universal concept so the duty to preserve memory is important also. (Rébecca, June 2020)

In her understanding of the notion of "duty of memory," which was introduced in French political speech and popularized in public opinion following the rise of negationist scholars and the National Front in the 1980s, Rébecca reflects a hierarchy between the two legacies of slavery and the Holocaust. First, the presence of living survivors is clearly a major factor of identification in her eyes, which tends to relegate slavery to a dimension of the past that she presumes has no implications on the present lives of Black French people, as distinguished from Black Americans. Second, the taboo around slavery that is observed in French society—both in the Caribbean and in continental France—makes her spontaneously dissociate slavery from segregation, as if the two were not inscribed in a historical continuum.

Israel, which appears in the responses as a result of the universal link tying the Jewish state to the Jews of the Diaspora and French Jews in particular, involves multiracial families in a process of strong identification. This is particularly palpable among those who have relatives that they visit in Israel, while others go there as tourists or on pilgrimages. A last group has relocated in Israel thanks to the Law of Return (Aliyah), as exemplified by Marah, who is now a rabbi there, as mentioned earlier.

Conversely, Black Jews' connection with the African continent is more ambivalent, particularly in multiracial families. On the one hand, a natural attachment to Africa is expressed by African-born Jews, who recently migrated from the continent. On the other hand, among Caribbean French respondents, Africa appears more distant, but still elicits emotion because this is where the Middle Passage began for their ancestors. This is how Danielle puts it, speaking both from her own viewpoint and as a spokesperson of all Caribbean French:

For me Africa is a dilemma, because for us it's a very remote land that was hidden from people of my generation. It was something that had to be concealed and it was a faraway place where slaves came from, those who suffered and who must not be mentioned again because it's too heavy a burden to carry. I discovered Africa on a humanitarian trip to Senegal, on which I went twice. It was wonderful to look at the people, Black people from elsewhere, the original Black people. For me it was an epiphany, I was very emotional during that trip, especially when I went to the island of Gorée. But for me it remains a faraway place, the land of my fathers, the land of the ancestors. At any rate in my family, it's complicated because I have a great-grandfather who is a Béké, you know, a former planter. And slavery is also present on my father's side since he is Cuban, he was dark-skinned. I am a fierce defender of my Caribbean history, because we've had a second life after slavery. See, we created that space called the Caribbean and due to this, Africa to me is a faraway place. To begin with, I'm trying to understand where I come from by looking at my environment, my immediate surroundings. I have always been very admirative and very observant of the friends and other people who claim strong ties with Africa, in the way they dress and put Africa front and center. Yet I have always felt as if it were a bus passing me by as I remain on the sidewalk. I never got on that bus, or at least I never managed to get on board. (Danielle, 2020)

Among these respondents, trips to African countries may be frequent, infrequent, or nonexistent. Biracial interviewees often mention the shock and frustration of being considered as Whites by the natives when they travel to Africa. On the contrary, certain African converts remain very engaged by the social and political events taking place on the continent: Marah, for instance, may be living in Israel but he is so attached to his native DRC that he has been among the candidates for presidency in that country regularly since 2011.

At times, interracialism triggers misunderstandings based on religion, as in the case of Dov, an Ethiopian Jew whose spouse, a Jewish woman of Marrano (crypto-Judaic) Portuguese descent, had been previously married to a Muslim man with whom she had had children. Dov explained that he sometimes experiences interreligious conflicts as a stepfather of children who are defined as Jewish by matrilineal descent:

I think that my being Jewish was valued by my in-laws. But my wife had a life before me, and she had two sons by an Arab. Her parents disapproved of that union and kept telling her that it wasn't going to work. Now that they've split, the boys are still here, and growing up they caused me a lot of trouble. One day, one of the boys told me, "I want to become a Muslim." (Dov, 2009)

Even if some non-Jewish spouses accept the Jewish "injunction" to transmit Jewish values, sometimes reluctance arises and persists, as in the case of Rébecca's partner, who refuses to embrace the tradition of circumcision: "there are a few things that pose a bit of a problem, like circumcision and suchlike, and these are a bit complicated, but when it comes to raising children in the culture, in the [Jewish] tradition, that's not an issue. Circumcision is, because he's opposed to it, he's not circumcised himself" (Rébecca, 2020). Indeed, while most Africans are circumcised regardless of their religious tradition, French Caribbean men have been raised in a Catholic environment from which circumcision was banned. This certainly accounts for the resistance of Rébecca's partner, who was born in Guadeloupe. Besides, as was mentioned earlier, Rébecca herself is more attached to Jewish cultural values than to the religious tradition per se. This is the case of many other respondents, such as Laure, who explained, "our children are the product of two cultures mixing with each other, so we can't force them to choose sides. We just give them an upbringing and then they do whatever they want with it. At present, what I'm interested in is not religion in itself, but the culture that goes with the religion" (Laure, October 2020). Sometimes, compromises are brokered with the non-Jewish members of the family. For example, Florence has forced her family to adjust to her Jewish way of life: "my mother knows I don't eat pork, so she tries to avoid cooking pork, but that doesn't stop me from eating blood pudding sausages when I go to Guadeloupe. I try not to, but sometimes it's difficult. Knowing that I'll be coming, she'll refrain from cooking what used to be my favorite pork-based food" (Florence, 2011). Interfaith dialog is also part of the dynamics of multiracial families, as with interracial couples: for instance, Rébecca admitted that when she goes to Martinique, she still accompanies her grandmother to church, and Danielle said she was organizing her son's wedding with a Catholic woman and planning the ceremony with a rabbi and a priest.

In the end, even if it is unproblematic in several families, for Black Jews the moral obligation of transmission is still being negotiated, because their identification attempts are often thwarted by attitudes of avoidance from the religious institutions or their fellow Jews, whether Ashkenazi or Sephardic. Consequently, the impossible transmission of their hard-earned Jewishness looms large for many respondents who either have converted to Judaism or identify as Jews and hope to raise their children as Jews. As Sébastien Tank-Storper puts it, the point is "to be able to birth Jewish children and raise them in a Jewish home, without necessarily defining that home in religious terms."[38] Whether or not they are converts, Black Jews are now a minority within the French Jewry, which is itself a minority in France but behaves toward them as a majority group. Ethnocentrism among Ashkenazi and Sephardic Jews often thwarts or undermines interracial unions, as Jocelyne Streiff-Fénart explained:

> ethnocentrism (simply defined as the tendency to prefer the values and members of one's own group) represents an important factor in restricting interethnic relations in general, and in the fields of dating and marriage in particular.

Individuals' ability to marry out of their group are strongly affected by that group's positive or negative attitudes towards intermarriage, as well as by the means it effectively deploys to prevent outmarriages. Hostile attitudes and strategies of resistance to intermarriages may be characteristics of majority as well as minority groups; but in either case, it represents a way to maintain social distance and delineate the frontiers of the club.[39]

Yet if Black Jews are confronted with the rejection and suspicion of families and institutions within the French Jewry, it now remains to be seen how their dual identity is received within the broader French society, with its claims to secularism and colorblindness.

NOTES

1. Translations from The Hebrew Bible in English according to the 1917 JPS Edition. http://www.mechon-mamre.org/e/et/et0.htm.
2. Edmond Fleg, *Anthologie juive des Origines au Moyen Âge* (Paris: Editions G. Crès et Cie, 1923), 296.
3. Salo Wittmayer Baron, *A Social and Religious History of the Jews, Ancient Times*, Vol. II *Christian Era: The First Five Centuries* (New York and London: Columbia University Press, second edition, 1952), 223.
4. Baron, Vol. IV, 195.
5. Baron, Vol. IV, 195.
6. Arkin, 155–56.
7. Baron, Vol. II, 234.
8. Baron, Vol. II, 238.
9. Baron, Vol. II, 232.
10. Baron, Vol. II, 237.
11. Baron, Vol. II, 232.
12. Baron, Vol. II, 238.
13. Sébastien Tank-Storper, "Jewish Trouble. Mixed Marriages, Conversions and Boundaries of Jewish Identity," *Ethnologie française* 43, no. 4 (October 2013): 592. Translated from the French by Cadenza Academic Translations. https://www.cairn-int.info/article.php?ID_ARTICLE=E_ETHN_134_0591#xd_co_f=OTUwNmEwYmYtY2VlYi00OTg2LWIwMjQtZWI3NWMxODg5NjJj~.
14. Jocelyne Streiff-Fenart, "mariage mixte," *Vocabulaire historique et critique des relations inter-ethniques,* Cahier n°6–7, Pluriel Recherches (Paris: L'Harmattan, 2000), 77.
15. Albert Jacquard quoted by Augustin Barbara, *Les couples mixtes* (Paris: Bayard, 1993), 15.
16. Séverine Mathieu, "Identités plurielles: couples mixtes et transmission du judaïsme," *Diversité urbaine* 10, no. 1, (2010): 4, https://doi.org/10.7202/045044ar.

17. Sébastien Tank-Storper, "Ce que devenir juif veut dire," *La conversion, Théologiques* 21, no. 2 (2013): 159–78. Online publication: February 3, 2015, https://id.erudit.org/iderudit/1028466ar.

18. Jocelyne Streiff-Fenart quoted in Gilbert Charles and Marion Festraëts, "L'intégration par l'amour," *L'Express* on line (lexpress.fr) posted on May 9, 2002, updated on June 1, 2006, https://www.lexpress.fr/societe/l-integration-par-l-amour_499095.html.

19. Joëlle Allouche-Benayoun, "Comment être juif croyant et moderne dans la France d'aujourd'hui?" *Sociétés* 2, no. 92 (2006): 5–22. DOI: 10.3917/soc.092.05. URL: https://www.cairn-int.info/revue-societes-2006-2-page-5.htm.

20. Tank-Storper, "Jewish Trouble," 594.

21. Ida Simon-Barouh, *Juifs de Rennes, Étude ethnosociologique* (Paris: L'Harmattan, 2009), 137.

22. Evyatar Marienberg, *Niddah. Lorsque les Juifs conceptualisent la menstruation* (Paris: Les Belles Lettres, 2003), 164.

23. Radu Mihaileanu, *Live and Become,* Elzévir Films, 2005.

24. Lisa Anteby-Yemini, "Peau noire, masques blancs: Les immigrants éthiopiens en Israël," *Pardès* 1, no. 44 (2008): 112.

25. Talmud, Kiddoushin, 3:12, p.9.

26. Gabrielle Atlan, "Le statut juridique de l'enfant dans la Loi juive. Journée d'études Liberté religieuse de l'enfant: *Égalité ou différence de traitement? La question particulière des discriminations au regard de la liberté religieuse de l'enfant*, Maison Interuniversitaire," *Société, droit et religion* 1, no. 3 (2013): 195–208. DOI: 10.3917/sdr.003.0195. URL: https://www.cairn-int.info/revue-societe-droit-et-religion-2013-1-page-195.htm.

27. Gabrielle Atlan, "Le statut de la femme dans le judaïsme," *Société, droit et religion* 1, no. 4 (2014): 33–46. DOI: 10.3917/sdr.004.0033. URL: https://www-cairn-info.libproxy.york.ac.uk/revue-societe-droit-et-religion-2014-1-page-33.htm.

28. Streiff-Fénard, "L'intégration par l'amour," 85.

29. Haïm Korsia, "La transmission dans le judaïsme," *Inflexions* 1, no. 13 (2010): 33–40.

30. Sébastien Tank-Storper, "Ce que devenir juif veut dire," *La conversion,* Géraldine Mossière ed., *Théologiques* 21, no. 2 (2013): 159–178. Online publication: February 3, 2015, https://id.erudit.org/iderudit/1028466ar.

31. Séverine Mathieu, *La transmission du judaïsme dans les couples mixtes* (Ivry-sur-Seine: Editions de l'Atelier, 2009), 119.

32. Séverine Mathieu, *La transmission,* 27. See Dominique Schnapper, "Les Nouveaux-Israélites: identité sans tradition?" *Commentaire*1, no. 9 (1980): 41–48, accessed February 1, 2021, https://www.cairn.info/revue-commentaire-1980-1-page-41.htm?contenu=resume.

33. Tank-Storper, "Ce que devenir juif veut dire."

34. Séverine Mathieu, "Identités plurielles: couples mixtes et transmission du judaïsme," *Diversité urbaine* 10, no. 1, (2010): 4, https://doi.org/10.7202/045044ar.

35. Séverine Mathieu, *La transmission,* 77.

36. Yoram Mouchenik, "Réflexion sur l'identité chez l'adolescent juif," *Champ psychosomatique* 1, no. 25 (2002): 119–28. DOI: 10.3917/cpsy.025.0119.

37. Cécile Coquet-Mokoko, *Love Under the Skin: Interracial Marriages in the American South and France* (London: Routledge, 2020), 169–75.

38. Tank-Storper, "Ce que devenir juif veut dire."

39. Jocelyne Streiff-Fenart, "mariage mixte," 80–81.

Chapter 7

Being Black and Jewish in France Today

When discussing Judaism in France, people rarely, if ever, think of Black Jews, because the prevalence of Ashkenazi and Sephardic ethnicities is such that they leave little room to Jewish identities from elsewhere.[1] However, from the beginning of the third millennium, the presence of Black believers has been documented in significant ways in the French Jewry. But in spite of this, being Black and Jewish in France often means experiencing one's religion in secret, due to both the French Jewry's indifference and the ignorance of French society. This poses the question of how Black Jews live their lives as Blacks and Jews within the two environments.

BEING BLACK AND JEWISH IN FRENCH SOCIETY

When asked how their friends and/or families had responded to the news of their conversion or Jewishness, the interviewees have emphasized both warm acceptance and rejection. Florence, a convert of Caribbean descent who joined the Reform Judaism movement, says she did not have to face resistance from her family because they are open-minded and her mother only goes to church occasionally. They even went so far as to accompany her in her conversion ritual: "my mother was present when I converted, and so was my sister, and my mother prepared the meal. It was important for me to have a meal after the mikveh (the ritual bath), and have the people I care for be there with me, for us all to share the moment together" (Florence, 31, interview given in 2011).

Significantly, just as circumcision marks a man's conversion to Judaism, for women, the ritual of the mikveh is also linked to notions of purity.[2] Aurélie remembered no negative reaction from her family when she expressed her decision to identify with the Jewish people. She explained it by the fact her family is very diversified in terms of religious affiliations: "We're a very diverse family, with Messianic Jews, Pentecostals, Orthodox Christians, and then also Buddhism, and Islam. We are a family with a lot of religious plurality. We're a large family too, with a lot of race mixing" (Aurélie, 40, interview given in 2020).

While for such respondents, the news of their conversion was met favorably by their loved ones, for others, it was the polar opposite. For example, Micheline (who hails from the Ivory Coast) said that she had been on the brink of a divorce:

> My husband did not like it one bit, no, not one bit! My conversion got this close to breaking my marriage, but I was ready for anything, I knew what I wanted. So I told him, I said, "now that I've finally found God, there's no man who can keep me from praying God." I didn't have a shade of doubt. But my husband was anything but accepting, he didn't want me getting into praying. Because you know, everyday I went to the synagogue to pray, and then on weekends it was Shabbat so I was not at home anymore! But I just couldn't go on as it I hadn't found what I was looking for, I felt so good now. And then I was taking the kids with me, so he was not happy with that either and I told him if he disapproved, he could just get a divorce. If he had asked me to choose between him and my [religious] practice, let me tell you I wouldn't have chosen him. I'm listening to God, not to a man. If I'm still with him, it means that God wants me to stay with him . . . All the time he's outside chilling with his friends, he wants me to stay at home and wait for him, doing nothing with myself but waiting for my husband. Now I've found God, with Whom I feel good, and I'm supposed to let go of God? Well, this is *not* happening! One day he told me he was going to file for divorce but today he's still with me. (Micheline, 52, dentist, interview given in November 2020)

This respondent's words give a valuable insight into the traditional gender roles assigned to African women as wives in heterosexual couples. The latter's daily life displays both a tension and an evolution toward a redefinition of each partner's role. "The instability of values, attitudes and feelings blurs the boundaries of the domestic space and the rules of the game within it" as the Senegalese psychiatrist Omar Sylla and the Belgian psychologist Geneviève Platteau noted.[3] Indeed, with the rising assertion of feminist awareness among African women, more and more of them, while being wives and mothers, challenge the way society assigns them this double role. In her life story, Micheline, like many other African women, clearly expresses her frustration with the normative gender roles shaping African couples' daily lives. It may be surmised that Judaism, and more precisely the communal ties characterizing the practice of the religion, offered her a way out of the loneliness she was facing in her married life. Some tensions are clearly gender-based, as several women converts, especially those respondents who joined the Reform and Masorti branches, found in Judaism a lever to offset male domination and eventually create a more balanced relationship with their life partners. This has been a recurrent observation with women converts belonging to these two branches, who emphasized that they particularly appreciated the gender equality distinguishing them from the Orthodox and ultra-Orthodox branches, where they say women are deprived of an education and assigned the sole mission of childbearing. But even if some respondents have had to face strong resistance like Micheline, as a rule, their relatives' reactions to the news of their conversion to Judaism were overall favorable.

However, they reported less positive reactions from their social and friendship networks. Myriam, who joined the Masorti movement, explained:

> You know, it's weird, because on the one hand my friends and even folks I don't know asked me "why?" and on the other hand, my parents never asked me why I wanted to convert. They just said converting is a good thing, they didn't even try to understand why. As if it was a normal thing to do. That's a really good reflection of our family ties. (Myriam, interview given in 2010)

Similarly to Myriam's experience, other respondents mentioned that their entourage expressed puzzlement on learning of their Jewishness or conversion and that the ensuing tensions had sometimes led to conflicts and the loss of friends. As the French sociologist Loïc Le Pape noted,

> [c]onversion initiates a transformation that is meant to be irreversible, since the convert embraces new beliefs, new rituals, in short, a new culture. This irreversible character affects more than just the individual themselves because the consequences reach so much further than the strict boundaries of the personal: the reactions of the families and friends are anything but anecdotal when considering a conversion process. Hence, from the outset, conversions represent a good example of bifurcation.[4]

The spiritual quest at the root of their intention to convert to Judaism often implies a severance from their family traditions, which are Christian in a majority of cases. As these interviewees live in a society where self-assertiveness is valued, they tend to frame the decision-making behind their conversions as a highly individual and intellectual process. But the strategies they found themselves implementing to face their entourage's reactions are multiple. On an individual scale, what they say of their interactions with friends, neighbors, or colleagues manifests a form of identity crisis resulting from the widespread ignorance of the existence of Black Jews besides the Beta Israel and particularly, of the presence of Black Jews in France. Consequently, several ended up hiding the visible signs of their Jewishness, such as the Magen David, the kippah, and the tzitzit. Others, on the contrary, asserted their faith to make it visible to fellow Jews as well as in their social and professional environments, by asking for leaves of absence for Jewish holidays, particularly Yom Kippur, by having their friends and families adjust to their Kosher diet, or by displaying signs of their Jewishness (including the Israeli flag). Such individual initiatives translate their will to be identified as both Black and Jewish by fitting into the cultural norms of the country, even if the display of religious identities in public spaces is, at best, tolerated rather than encouraged in France. In doing so, their departure from a solely racialized minority status reframes Jewishness as a crucial social issue. This is evidenced in what respondents shared about the unwelcoming reactions from strangers they encountered in Jewish spaces: "the first time I went to a library, it was the one on [name of the street] and not only were they unwelcoming, but the salesperson told me that these books were not for people like me" (Dov, 38, realtor, interview given in 2009); "when I to a Kosher grocery store, the salesperson was with his son and the kid said, 'Look, Dad, there's a Black man wearing a kippah!'" (Moshe, interview given in 2009).

This general ignorance of the existence of Black Jews complicates the integration of Black students in Jewish schools, as they find themselves singled out from the rest. Hortense Bilé described the case of a Canadian Black woman who had enrolled her two children in a Jewish school in France but eventually had to return to Montréal for the sake of their mental health. This is corroborated by the ethnographic study conducted by Kimberly Arkin in three Jewish schools in the greater Paris area, which showed how young French Sephardim's self-perception left no room for the presence of Black classmates in their midst. Arkin quoted "Joshua," a student who, while aware of the existence of Black Jews in France due to the presence of a few Black students in his school, still asserted, "we just do not notice them." As for Salomé, a student Arkin describes as Black, "she remained nonetheless a 'half-Jew,' a term that directly indexed quasi-biological notions of 'half-blood' and illicit intermixture." Relating a discussion between students that she observed, Arkin notes that

> Jason, who had always been in a Jewish school, could not even acknowledge the possibility of black Jewishness. Even after Brith Abraham [the school] sanctioned Salomé and Eric's Halakhic status by accepting them as students, Jason still maintained that he had never seen a black Jew in France. If François Grunwald's name and whiteness exiled him to the category "French" [as opposed to the Sephardic self-designations "Moroccan," "Algerian," or "Tunisian"], Jason suggested that dark skin left Salomé and Eric equally non-Jewish, even "Arab." Jewishness thereby remained the exclusive province of those most like Jason and Joshua.[5]

As a matter of fact, while Black individuals' displaying of their Jewishness elicits expressions of surprise, puzzlement, or hostility in Jewish environments, this is also true in professional, social, or friendly environments. Emmanuel is scared to tell his best friend, a man of Algerian descent, that he is Jewish for fear of losing him. Two respondents admitted they had lost friends since doing so. Dov, the Ethiopian Jew quoted above, said:

> Many of my friends were unaware that I am Jewish. As I told you, I have just begun awakening and becoming spiritual. That is something they see. Some of them have issues with it, I don't want to know what exactly their problem is, but I am ready for anything. I have seen some of them trying to use me as a scapegoat—"I'm a Black Jew, I'm the guy you love to hate" [une tête à claques]. These were Black men doing this to me, another Black man. (Dov, 38, realtor, interview given in 2009)

This is the context in which most of the respondents said they had to cope with antisemitism, coming from Africans, Caribbeans, Arabs, or Whites alike. Hortense Bilé, the community organizer, confirmed this as follows:

> The problem we've had is rather with other Blacks who tell us, "Being a Jew is being ashamed of your race." I think not all Blacks know we are Jewish because sometimes when we attend get-togethers, I say, "Well, I don't do this," and all, especially when I'm at a party, so they're like, "But why?" "Well, we do things this way and that way," and they tell me, "that's being ashamed of your race!" The Arabs are the same, "it's being ashamed of your race." . . . Arabs find it shocking when people opt for Judaism. . . . I don't see what's shocking about it. I'm certainly not sorry I converted, I did it because I wanted to choose my religion. Catholicism didn't allow me to choose. I was baptized six days after I was born and I didn't have a choice. (Hortense, interview given in 2017)

Other interviewees have told me that they had had conflicts with coworkers or employers as a result of their religious identity when they asked for leaves of absence for Jewish holidays. Although France is a secular country, the major Catholic religious holidays are still bank holidays and Jewish or Muslim citizens have a legal right to leaves of absence for the festivals of their respective religions. One respondent said he had lost his job after asking for recognition of his Jewish faith in the workplace.

In public spaces, they are also frequently confronted with expressions of puzzlement or hostility. For instance, on the day of his interview with me, Ismaël Yayir Kohen was wearing his kippah and this was noticed by an Arab sanitation worker, who called him out with these words, "But why? Why, why? A Black man has no business being Jewish, he should be either a Muslim or a Christian!" This incident gives an idea of the micro-aggressions entailed by the public's ignorance of the existence of Black Jews in France. The lack of legitimacy also appears in expressions of antisemitism in Black milieus, which often emphasize a perceived need to safeguard the Christian heritage. While I was doing fieldwork on Black Jews in the Boston area, an African American respondent, Tifferet, recalled being rebuked by an African American bus driver who had felt offended, after asking her to what church she was going for Easter service, by her answer that she was not Christian, but Jewish. He told her, "An African American has no business being a different religion from her Christian ancestors, especially if they were Protestant."[6]

This also partly explains why many of the respondents have experienced an identity crisis that led them to silence or conceal their Jewishness. Yann, who is of Congolese descent, discovered Judaism in Israel, where he used to wear a kippah every day. On arriving in France, where he felt the need to convert officially, he decided to stop wearing it in public: "in France, I no longer wear it on the street, instead I put in on when I'm in the synagogue, because in this country people's stares are enough to make you ill at ease" (Yann, 34, interview given in 2009). On the contrary, others have stopped concealing their Jewish faith and chosen to display it, like Moshe, a convert from Guadeloupe: "I kept hiding my Magen David and my kippah because it was too much trouble having to explain all the time that I was Jewish, but now I am done hiding. You hide when you're at war, not in a free country like France" (Moshe, 45, interview given in 2009).

Ultimately, displaying one's Jewish faith while Black ends up being a double whammy, as it makes the person a target of both the rampant antisemitism and the hostility of French Jewish milieus. Enoch, who is a member of the Consistorial branch, was ironic about his own community when I asked him if he expressed his Jewishness in public spaces:

Being Jewish in your own private space is very challenging, it requires a lot of work on a spiritual and outer plane. It's rather within the community that the problem arises. Because when I'm on the street and I see non-Jews, I'm wearing my kippah, I have it on my head all the time, even when I board the metro at Barbès on line two [a majority Muslim part of town], I'm wearing my kippah. I have no problems with non-Jews as a rule, even if, sadly, you can always run into a madman. But the problem is actually within the community, and it's always the same issue, it's as if we weren't real Jews, and that's a really big problem. I wasn't prepared to face this in the community, I thought it would be the other way around, and that I was going to experience that contradiction with non-Jews like this in town. Sadly, that happens within the community, and it's a shame. . . . I think that on a daily basis, in my private life, being a Jew is not easy, being a Jew is an extremely heavy burden to carry, it really is. Now, within the community, it's an uphill battle to be a Black Jew in France, it's not easy at all, unfortunately we're forced to assert our individualities, there's no other alternative. There's always some drama going on and, sadly, there's ignorant people, so we have to push back against that. (Enoch, 24, chef, interview given in 2017)

Still, the rejection manifested in Jewish circles, especially within the Orthodox branch, is not enough to deter them from feeling a sense of belongingness to the Jewish people. Instead of staying away from such environments, some, like Enoch, have decided to make them acknowledge their existence. This same need to exist and be recognized led some Black Jews to organize in order to combat discriminations and fight for visibility both within the global Jewry and the French Jewish landscape (see chapter 5).

FROM ANONYMITY TO THE DISPLAY OF BLACK JEWISH IDENTITY

It would seem that since Black Jews began organizing, they have experienced fewer instances of rejection within the French Jewry, but it is not the case yet. However, they did manage to obtain positive results in certain domains. For example, the FJN drew the attention of the Chief Rabbi of France, Gilles Bernheim, to the existence of the (aforementioned) siddur to be recited on seeing a Black or disabled person, which was still in circulation in 2003. The successful mobilization in reaction to this racist prayer resulted in the excision of these words in the subsequent editions of the prayer book; on December 28, 2011, the Chief Rabbi of France himself informed the FJN of this change when the new edition of the *Siddur Kol Hanechama* came out.[7]

It could be assumed that the Black Jewish believers have won the fight against exclusion and rejection, but nothing is further from the truth. Indeed, because discrimination is so common in their experience, it also infuses their religious practice within the French Jewry and even in their domestic lives. The question many have to grapple with is whether they should eventually accept the distance created by their White fellow Jews or keep fighting to close the gap. Marah offered an answer to this conundrum at the FJN's general convention in 2010, when he said:

There's a mistake we shouldn't make, which is to say that the moment when Black Jews can finally be part and parcel of the French Jewry, there will be no more discrimination. There's friction between Ashkenazim and Sephardim, and even among the Sephardim, between those from Tunisia and those from Morocco, and even among the Ashkenazim, between those from Poland and those from Russia. Such friction is what makes the strength of a community, you want to know why? Because a person who attacks you is not indifferent; they are someone who had become aware of your existence and what you can bring them. By this I mean that if Black Jews want to do things, they shouldn't expect it to be a bed of roses, or to hear things like, "Well, this year no one's been expelled from a synagogue," or "this year, no one said, 'How come you're Black and Jewish?!'" I would even say that we need that because when we cause this type of attitude, it means that people have definitely become aware of our presence. (Marah, general convention of the FJN, 2010)

Indeed, White Jews are gaining some awareness of the existence of Black Jews other than the Beta Israel, for they often draw a lot of attention in Jewish circles. This is especially because Caribbean and African Jews wear taleths, Magen Davids, kippot, and tefillin during services, whether they are Orthodox, Lubavitch, or members of the Reform Judaism movement. However, due to this they are also framed both in Jewish circles and in the other social environments they inhabit. As discussed earlier, they can be barred access to synagogues (typically Orthodox ones) in spite of their signs of belonging to the Jewish faith. When they are not taken seriously, they may even be derided. Enoch, a young man born in Cameroon who converted at the Consistory, shared the following experience:

> I am a serious, practicing Jew, I respect everything holy, I keep Kosher and I wear the talith and all that. Some of them, when they see me coming, they view me as a walking paradox, it's as if I was playing some game. See, I am a Jew, a practicing one, but I'm Black, so that can't be, there's something wrong about it. They tell themselves, "That can't be, what's the catch? How is it that this guy who just showed up, he's got a Te'udat Hamara [a written certification of conversion to Judaism] and keeps Kosher and everything, it just can't be." Some of them told me, "It's impossible, we can't wrap our heads around it." They must think I'm running around in some costume, because each time they ask me how I ended up becoming a Jew and how that can be! (Enoch, 24, interview given in 2017)

The reason behind the doubts over the actual Jewishness of these converts is that in French society, only Ashkenazim and Sephardim can be Jews, while Black people never can. However, while in Enoch's case the wearing of Jewish ethnic signs does not facilitate acceptance in communities, in other cases it elicits reactions of sympathy from White passers-by who share the same faith. Danielle, a Caribbean-born woman in an interracial marriage, told me that when she was walking the streets with her children, who wear the Magen David (and can pass for Sephardim, by their own account), other Jews came up to them with friendly attitudes to inquire whether they were Jewish. Such manifestations of curiosity may also be linked to the dogma of matrilineal transmission, as outsiders may surmise that Danielle is the children's stepmother rather than their mother—as is often the case with multiracial families. I was the witness of another similar scene while interviewing Moshe in a fast-food restaurant in the tenth arrondissement of Paris: a young Black woman interrupted the exchange and introduced herself as Myriam, saying she was an Ethiopian Jew. She asked Moshe, "I see you are wearing a kippah, are you Jewish?"[8] If visible signs of Jewishness can cause curiosity and sympathy among fellow Jews, they more often trigger hostile reactions of antisemitism and racism.

BLACK JEWS CONFRONTED WITH ANTISEMITISM

In France, bearing or wearing ethnic markers is always risky, as it is commonly considered to be a form of criticism of the Republic's colorblind universalism. This is especially true of Muslim ethnic markers, but also of Jewish ones. Rébecca shared with me the following experience:

> What really struck me was something that happened to me on the [Paris] metro. I was holding my cellphone and the case had an Israeli flag design, it was a souvenir I had bought in Israel. So there was this young boy on the metro who saw my phone case and asked me if I was Jewish. And then he started calling me names. He was an Arab, and just for that reason, he went on with a rant on Israel and Palestine and all that, so at first, I let him speak for a while and then he also got a dressing-gown, yeah. (Laughs) In the end, this was someone who, just because he's an Arab, was taking sides with the Palestinians without knowing about the facts of the conflicts. I certainly went to Israel more often than him, and I believe I know more about the conflict than does a person who doesn't know anything about Israel and has never been there. This stayed with me because it was the first time I had been verbally abused this openly. (Rébecca, 27, interview given in 2020)

Likewise, Josué told me he had been called an ethnic slur by a young Arab on the street, while he was in the company of his fellow Lubavitch and dressed like them. As for Éthan, he was also attacked on a train because he was wearing a Magen David:

> Yes, I was attacked by supporters of [the comedian] Dieudonné on the RER [Paris suburban train]. I think that since Dieudonné started his war on the [Jewish] community, in the outskirts of Paris there are more and more attacks of this kind. I was sitting on one of the benches facing each other and I was wearing my Magen David. They spotted that, and I was sitting on my own and there were three of them sitting right next to me. They noticed my Magen David before I could cover it, so they immediately got up and came to sit down around me. I had my cellphone in hand and one of them began saying, "hey, that's a cool phone, wouldn't it be a good thing to pinch it off this bastard from

the Mossad?" He got up and gave me a headbutt, and then it was all three of them against me. Thankfully, I do combat sports so I was able to defend myself. (Éthan, 22, interview given in 2011)

Undeniably, the brand of antisemitism that is most feared and denounced comes from Muslim circles. When I gave a paper at a conference organized by ISSAJ (The International Society for the Study of African Jewry) at the Paris Museum of Art and history of Judaism in November 2015 (just before the terrorist attacks), I had to answer a question on antisemitism in Black milieus. One of the Black Jews in attendance, who had come from Lille in the north of France, came up to me to say that I had answered incorrectly: "anti-Semitism doesn't really come from Black milieus but Arab ones. In the inner city where I live, I can't even wear my kippah any more. Every time I wore it, I took flak." I also personally witnessed such hostility when going to an appointment with one of my interviewees. While sitting on one of the folding seats on the Paris metro, I took my notes out of my bag to rehearse the script of questions. Two young men of north African descent were standing close to me and looked at it over my shoulder; they burst out laughing and began mocking me loudly. I got off at the next stop and changed cars to avoid escalation, but it gave me a better insight into the type of situations described by my interviewees.

Yet, while my interviewees were confronted with antisemitism from fellows Africans and North Africans, they also had to face anti-Semitic hostility from Whites. Hannah, an Ethiopian Jew who was among those rescued by the state of Israel, now lives in France where she works as a psychologist. She, too, was assaulted at one of the Versailles train stations because of her Magen David:

I used to wear a Magen David, but I no longer do. At the Versailles Chantiers station, I was waiting for a train with my daughter when a man came up to us and said, "Why are you wearing this? You have no right to." I said, "Why can't I wear this?" and he went, "you have no right to wear this, what country are you from?" I answered, "I'm an Ethiopian" and he said, "They finally bought you out." So I asked, "Why are you saying we're on sale?" He tugged at my Magen David and the small chain broke. I picked it up and put it in my bag, and no one even lifted a finger. He did that just because I'm a Black woman, which proves to what extent people still have issues with us being Jewish. He was a White guy, there were lots of people around, but no one stirred. Today, I no longer wear my Magen David, because I'm afraid. It's not because I'm Black, but because I'm Jewish. In Israel I used to wear it, but in Israel I feel safe because I'm at home. If I could, I'd return to Israel, because over there you can go wherever you want, you don't have that problem. There are inner problems of course, as in any other country in the world, but we don't have that religious issue of "you're a Jew, you're a Muslim, you're this and that." We've got other problems. (Hannah, 54, interview given in 2010)

This interviewee raised a key issue, which is the prevailing ignorance of the existence of Black Jews. Had a White Jewish woman been the target of such an assault, the onlookers would quite probably have reacted to protect her. The reason why they failed to do so is not that they are all anti-Semitic, but probably that they themselves were unsure that she was really Jewish, in spite of her Ethiopian origins. This evidences that Black Jewish identity is not yet recognized in the mindsets of social players in France.

Besides, if White antisemitism seems to have receded behind the rise of so-called working-class antisemitism (namely, that harbored by Arabs and Blacks), it is mainly because the media have chosen to propel the latter to the headlines and, following the lead of the provocateur Éric Zemmour, emphasize this brand of antisemitism as part of a broader "anti-White racism." French right-wing rhetoric today pits against each other the White/Jewish pair with the Arab/Black pair, even though antisemitism has no color. In reaction to the antisemitism expressed by all groups, but especially North African ones, Black Jews choose to distance themselves from the latter group, even if this means losing friends they deem too intolerant. They also refrain from making their Jewishness visible in public places, especially if they are isolated. But when antisemitism becomes overt as in the case of Black public figures Dieudonné or Kemi Seba (the founder of the Afrocentric community Tribu Ka), Black Jews express their dissent. In 2006, when a march was organized to protest the murder of Ilan Halimi (a young cellphone salesman who was kidnapped and tortured by a gang led by an Ivorian Muslim), the Black men and women who wanted to join the protest were manhandled by members of the Betar and the Ligue de défense juive (LDJ), who were acting as security officers. In reaction to this race-based violence, around thirty members of Tribu Ka paraded in the Jewish section of Paris, particularly the emblematic rue des rosiers (the site of a terrorist bombing in 1982), to confront the members of the Betar and the LDJ, who they said had dared them to come.[9] Following this act of provocation, Guershon Nduwa and members of the FJN organized a counter-movement on the same street, waving Israeli flags, wearing kippot and Magen Davids, and using a megaphone to send reassuring messages to their fellow Jews while proving that one could be Black and Jewish.

Unsurprisingly, Guershon told me that he had experienced backlash:

Well, I've been called all kinds of names by extremists, particularly Dieudonné and Kemi Seba, who called me an ape and a slave to the Jews. . . . It made me very uncomfortable, I was the first person to denounce Dieudonné's behavior.

> . . . Dieudonné has always been an anti-Semite; those who hadn't understood have now discovered it, but I know the man. . . . No, we won't reach out to him because he's very violent. We are okay with debating—if there is a debate organized—in order to show that there's prejudice behind the accusations levelled against Jews. Jews are not the wealthiest people in the world, many of us are unemployed, and many are poor. People shouldn't hide their anti-Semitism behind this form of accusation. But I have opposed him from the start, as I did with Kemi Seba and the Tribu Ka. (Guershon, interview given in 2009)

I received a similar testimony from Yann, who had just arrived in France from Israel when he met Dieudonné by chance, at the university of Nanterre where the latter had come to promote his show:

> Dieudonné may have a charismatic appeal with the crowd, but I did not know in depth what he was saying. He was comparing the situation of Palestinians in Israel with apartheid; saying that Black people over there are enslaved and people hate them. I've been on a mission in Israel and I had another perspective. I asked for the microphone and I said, "You know, Black people who live in Tel Aviv are much better off than Black people living in France! I've lived over there, I was fed by White Jews, I was in a terrible shape when they picked me up, no better than a mop, I had no parents and I was rescued as a child, at an early age, and when I was sick, they were here for me, when I was hungry, they were here for me, when I went to college, they were here to help." . . . They muted the microphone and silenced me. It took place in a lecture room at Nanterre (university) and I left the place in the midst of heckling. (Yann, 34 years old, chef and philosophy student, interview given in 2009)

Regrettably, it has become impossible now to discuss antisemitism in France without mentioning Dieudonné and the recurrent controversies around his statements.[10] But it is important to mention that the latter trigger pushback not only from the League of Human Rights or SOS Racisme, but also Black Jews who often choose to confront the comedian, including on social media, to demonstrate their loyalty to Israel and fellow Jews, but also disprove the growing tendency among the French to assume that all Black people harbor anti-Semitic biases.

By increasing their presence on social media, the members of FJN and AM-I-FA take positions on ongoing debates and topical issues related to Jewish communities in France, Israel, and the rest of the world, making sure their voices can be heard, especially in the wake of terrorist attacks. For instance, Guershon Nduwa explained to me that his organization had implemented an outreach program against antisemitism, in which they visit schools in the greater Paris area where White Jews would be viewed with more suspicion, wearing their kippot and other signs of Judaism (in spite of the ban on wearing ostentatious religious signs in school premises) to raise awareness and help the younger generations of residents deconstruct anti-Semitic prejudices. This can be viewed as translating a form of guilt on the part of Black Jews when antisemitism reaches such extreme levels as in the murder of Ilan Halimi or the taking and killing of hostages by Amedy Coulibaly at a Kosher supermarket in January 2015. Every year on the anniversary of his death, the members of FJN and AM-I-FA commemorate the passing of Ilan Halimi by posting his picture on their websites and (except during the lockdown periods) going in front of the store where he worked to pay tribute to his memory. However, the multiplication of terrorist threats worldwide has understandably reinforced prejudices and reactions of fear in Jewish milieus. Ismael, a Danite Jew from the Ivory Coast, explained how his entire family were searched and frisked on the day of Yom Kippur by the security officers of the synagogue they wanted to enter in the greater Paris area; even the baby's diaper was removed. Understandably, the situation was considered deeply humiliating and they chose to worship elsewhere. Josué, a convert from Cameroon who worships at a Lubavitch synagogue, shared the following experience:

> On the day when Ilan Halimi died [of his wounds], I told myself I should go to the synagogue to pray. But when I got there, I was shocked to see people glaring at me, as if to say, "Haven't you had enough already with what you did? What business do you have here?" (Josué, 52, interview given in 2009)

These testimonies are revealing of a relatively recent sense of uneasiness in relations between Blacks and Jews in France, with any Black person being increasingly assumed to be an African Muslim and Black Jews feeling both compelled to answer for the anti-Semitic statements or attacks initiated by Blacks, and blamed by their communities of faith who, instead of comforting them, make their burden heavier by making them unwelcome.

I personally experienced this situation on joining, on invitation of the FJN, a protest for the liberation of Israeli private Gilad Shalit, which had been organized by the CRIF on the place du Trocadéro, below the Eiffel Tower in Paris. When I arrived at the meeting place, I first met the cordon of the French national police, which let me in without any questions; but after walking half a yard, I was halted by the second security cordon, made up of members of the Jewish community who asked me why I was there, while the White people who came to join the march at the same time were neither stopped nor questioned. Aware that this discrepancy was due to my skin color, I answered that I had responded the FJN's call and they let me in. After walking another half-yard, I was halted again by another Jewish security cordon; this time, as I happened to be standing beside a White woman, they asked her if I was her husband. When she said no, they let her in but stopped me, asking me why

I was there; I gave the same answer as before and they let me in. I saw that there were only three Black protesters, two of whom were wearing a kippah, a Magen David, and tefillin and were draped in an Israeli flag while the third one was bearing a placard declaring her love for Israel. I inferred that it was their need for legitimacy in Jewish circles that led them to display so insistently their signs of belonging, to the point of out-Heroding Herod, so to speak. This is probably why my coming without even an Israeli flag made me even more conspicuous and suspicious in the eyes of the community's security officers. I barely escaped being assaulted by a group of young extremists from the Ligue de défense juive who began hemming me in as if they were ready to pounce on prey, but who, noticing a (White) photographer taking a picture of their flag, turned away to beat him up right under my eyes. On seeing this, I got closer to Moshe, whom I had already interviewed, to gain some of the legitimacy that radiated from the markers of Jewishness he was wearing. I asked him why there were so few Black people, and he answered, "they wouldn't bother to come here."

I came away from this lived experience with two findings. The first one was that the FJN had indeed earned the consideration of Jewish milieus, even if it was still a work in progress. The second one was that I had just experienced some of the hostility and difficulties my interviewees described when answering my questions on their conditions of access to Jewish spaces.

Granted, the rise in antisemitism in France is largely responsible for the heightened level of vigilance on the part of both law enforcement and Jewish security forces; but paradoxically, this very desire to protect the community makes it harder to integrate for Black Jews. This context led the President of AM-I-FA, Hortense Bilé, to write the open letter discussed earlier when a young Danite Jew was humiliated by yet another bodily search at the entrance of a synagogue in Sarcelles, in the greater Paris area. In this long, eloquent letter, she pleaded,

> all Black people are not Coulibaly, the murderer of a Caribbean woman and of the Jewish customers of the Hyper Cacher, just as all Orthodox [Jews] are not Yigal Amir, the murderer of Itzhak Rabin. We denounce this way of killing our souls, the first victim in Scriptures is called Abel, a name that means "blowing, breathing." No Jew has the right to bar the entrance of a synagogue—the place of worship for all Jews—to another Jew, no matter where they come from. We, Black Jews, assert our right to pray. "When you smile and feel safe, it is because someone has prayed for you," but when you harm a person's soul, how can you expect that same person to say the Nishmat kol'hai, "let every living soul praise YOUR NAME"?[11]

Although the letter cites as recipients all of the Jewish authorities in France as well as the antiracist organization SOS Racisme copied in, Hortense confessed to me that she never actually sent a copy to the latter, because she was wary a non-Jewish organization could take advantage of the case, but that she had copied them in deliberately to scare the Jewish organizations into action.

As a matter of fact, Black Jews often tend to cover up for their White fellow Jews, to such a point that my fieldwork was hampered at first. Indeed, as many of my interviewees were unsure of my loyalty, they were seldom willing to share any experience of race-based discrimination in Jewish circles. Likewise, their attitude toward the rise in rabid antisemitism often goes beyond lamenting the situation and toward acting in prevention of hate crimes, by seeking confrontation with Black anti-Semites while their White fellow Jews tend to prefer leaving durably for Israel. On January 9, 2015, when the tragic hostage crisis at the Hyper Cacher supermarket was taking place, Hortense Bilé felt she could not stay idle and volunteered to talk to the hostage taker Amedy Coulibaly:

> This was very hard, especially for us Blacks. There was the first attack against *Charlie Hebdo* [January 7, 2015] and that was very, very challenging emotionally; then came Amedy Coulibaly who shot a Black woman [municipal police officer Clarissa Jean-Philippe] in the back, and then went to the Hyper Cacher. I usually do my grocery shopping there either on Thursdays or on Fridays. On the day of the attack at the Hyper Cacher store [a Friday] I was back from a trip and I wanted to go buy some cold meats there because I live close to that store. I saw that the road was blocked and I didn't know what was going on. I turned on my TV set and I saw Coulibaly. I bolted out without putting on a coat, just as I was, and ran to the Hyper Cacher. I told myself, I'll go talk to Coulibaly, speak to him as a Black woman, he can't shoot me, I'll speak to him face to face. But police stopped me and pushed me back, telling me it's their job to protect me and I had no business being there. But you can't imagine the hurt, the pain we felt knowing that it was our Black brother, son, grandson, nephew, friend, one of us shooting others who were also our people. I told myself that God did something wonderful for us on that day, which was that he made it possible for another Black man from Africa to save people [twenty-four-year-old Lassana Bathily, one of the employees of the store, who successfully hid in the cold room some of the hostages, including a baby]. People forgot that good deed and forgot to credit a Black man with it, because it was a Black man who put his life at risk to save Jews and protected them by locking them up there because he knew the place. This lifted our hearts. To pay a tribute to what that Black man did, all the Hyper Cacher stores hired Black employees. God made it possible for a Black man from the same country as the terrorist [Mali] and of the same religion [Islam] to save Jews. (Hortense, interview given in 2015)

When he took hostages at the Hyper Cacher store in Paris, just two days after the attack on the satirical paper *Charlie Hebdo* by the Kouachi brothers, who killed twelve people, the terrorist Amedy Coulibaly was wanted by police for shooting a Caribbean police officer in Montrouge, south of Paris. The day after that murder, he entered the Hyper Cacher store of the Porte de Vincennes, on the southeastern border of Paris, with heavy weaponry and killed four people before he took hostage the rest of the consumers present. Claiming to be a member of the Islamic state, he demanded the lifting of the siege of the printing house of Dammartin-en-Goële where the Kouachi brothers were hiding, as well as the French state's support for the Palestinian cause in Israel and for the right for French women to wear the Islamic veil. As for Lassana Bathily, he was instrumental in not only hiding customers out of the sight and earshot of the gunman, but also facilitating the work of the French police by handing them the keys to the store's automatic curtain, which allowed them to shoot Coulibaly. Bathily's heroic actions earned him French citizenship as well as the praise of Israeli Prime Minister Benyamin Netanyahu[12] when the latter gave a speech at the great synagogue in Paris. He received the CRIF's award at the organization's yearly dinner, under the presidency of Roger Cukierman.[13] Undoubtedly, whenever Africans or Caribbeans are recognized for heroic deeds, there is hope for a better integration of Black people in French society at large and Black Jews in the French Jewry; but it is significant that years after the tragedies, it is the names of the perpetrators that stay in people's memories and media accounts, not those of the saviors.

In this context, Black Jews feel a strong need to play an active role in fighting antisemitism, and Hortense Bilé's brave initiative testifies to it. However, the Islamic Fundamentalists casting themselves as Allah's warriors[14] have little consideration for the African values of respect for mothers that Ms. Bilé was hoping to use in her de-escalation attempt. Their worldview is based on religious antagonisms, not racial ones, and their antisemitism is about importing the Israeli-Palestinian conflict in France, as did Mohamed Merah or Amedy Coulibaly (see chapter 1); this has redefined the forms of antisemitism that French Jews face on a daily basis. Consequently, it is unclear whether French people of African descent have any clear role to play in this imported conflict.

An excellent illustration of this feeling of awkwardness shared by many Black French people when asked about their position on the Israeli-Palestinian conflict was given by the standup comedian Thomas Ngijol in a recent one-man show:

> This whole thing, the Israeli-Palestinian conflict, is really sad; but you know what is really sad for us as French people is that we imported this into our country, you know this as well as I do. You don't need me to tell you. You know,

whenever someone says the magic word, some folks get tense all of a sudden. And since I'm back on stage I told myself, "Yeah, but I have to say something on it, all the same." But as it's a thorny issue and I'm not completely stupid, I went to ask my father for advice first. I told him, "Dad, everyone gets tense the moment someone mentions the Israeli-Palestinian conflict, so I need to know your position on the subject."

"You want to know how I feel about the Israeli-Palestinian conflict?"

"Yes, Dad, please, it's important for me."

"OK, why don't you sit down, son. So I was born in Nyort, a small village south of Douala in Cameroon. I grew up with my father who was a farmer, my mother, and my little brother Thomas who unfortunately passed away and this is why your name is Thomas, you didn't know that, well now you do. And when I turned 16 I left for the city to study in Douala. That's where I met your mother—a beautiful woman. We began flirting a little and then we got married. All your brothers were born there. You are the only one who was born in France, the only White boy in the family, as we say back home. So we left for France, I got here in 1976 under President Giscard, a great president, the best one. At first we lived in a tiny, unsanitary apartment in Vincennes, it wasn't really an apartment but a shithouse. So we left that place to go to Valenton and we ended up in Maisons-Alfort. During all these years I had it rough, I was doing odd jobs as a janitor to pay rent and at the same time I had to go to university to get my degrees validated, well because in France they don't recognize degrees earned in Africa and don't ask me why, I don't have a clue. During that period racism was really tough, not like now. Back in the day, as soon as I entered a café I heard all these slurs, I know they were meant for me, from the moment I stepped in they went, "yeah, I'll get you a tar baby[15] cup" and I knew they were talking to me but I never reacted, I always kept my dignity and pride intact. No violence, ever. I'll tell you what, son. I feel proud, I really feel proud because we made it, 'cause when I see you and your brothers and sisters, you are good people, and to me, that's what matters more than anything else in this life. All this is to say that I don't give a f*** about the Israeli-Palestinian conflict, I really don't! Get outta my face with this BS, I've got to wire some money to your grandma.[16]

This long monolog aims to emphasize the bread-and-butter issues of Black families in France, whose priorities are shaped by racism, job insecurity, and discrimination in housing and the workplace, rather than by a distant conflict. The father has no time to spend having an opinion on the Israeli-Palestinian conflict because it bears no relation to the success of his children or the economic welfare of his mother back in Cameroon. This serves as a useful reminder of the priorities of the vast majority of Black and even Arab families living in working-class neighborhoods in France, even if they may individually empathize with the Palestinians.

Donel Jack'smann, another French-born standup comedian of Cameroonian descent raised the same issue, emphasizing the antisemitism he has been faced with while not being Jewish himself:

> I've been a victim of anti-Semitism, I didn't expect to be and I was shocked, 'cause, well, everybody knows I'm not starring in *La vérité si je mens* [a comedy on French Sephardim], you know what I'm sayin'? I went to Israel when some Jewish friends invited me to do my show in Tel Aviv for the French community. I asked my friends and family for advice. My Black friends told me, "Don't go there, you'll ruin your career!" My Arab friends said, "Don't go, or we'll ruin your career!" and my White friends said, "You have no career!" So I accepted. But as soon as the news was out on social media, I got showered with anti-Semitic abuse. . . . One of the most recurrent insults was "sellout, traitor." Now this is something I couldn't wrap my mind around. Here are these folks who don't even know me but have decided to throw me into a conflict I have nothing to do with and decided which side I'm supposed to be on. Well, thanks but no thanks, 'cause I'm not a Jew, I'm not a Muslim, not an Israeli, and not an Arab. It's a conflict between you guys, you all are cousins, you've got the same looks, the same hair, the same noses, and you all get your dicks clipped [circumcised], that's your thing, okay! It's your thing, you've been fighting one another for decades for a land where there's nothing, nothing to gain . . .[17]

These remarks, made half in jest, are a fairly accurate reflection of the interethnic tension fostered in France by the Israeli-Palestinian conflict. When, in the context of a research project organized by colleagues of the universities of Kent and York,[18] I interviewed inhabitants and community organizations of La Courneuve in the greater Paris area on urban social life in their neighborhood, I found that their daily lives were made difficult by residential and job discriminations, and that the Israeli-Palestinian conflict was far from central to their daily concerns. I surveyed the Cité des Quatre Mille, a housing project built in the 1960s to house the people ousted from Algeria following the country's independence. Describing his experience of growing up in a project where former French settlers coexisted with harkis (Algerian soldiers who had fought in the French Army) and Jews with Muslims and Catholics, the spokesperson of a community organization explained,

> We grew up without any hatred, it was heaven here in fact. This is what I can't wrap my mind around, when I see that fifty years later there's a lot of anti-Semitism here. Now we have a lot of identity politics[19] here, whereas they had just been through a war which involved, quote unquote, hatred. We never had any problems with the Jewish community or the settler [pied-noir] community or the harkis, never ever. That's the whole paradox, 'cause now it's the other way around, it works backwards, with communities that have taken root and communities that don't mix, everyone stays in their group. It's almost as

if, how can I put it, you can feel sometimes there's a little bit of racism. That's something we never experienced in the '60s and '70s, quite the opposite. It's just the same as when we're asked about the Israeli-Palestinian conflict. These guys over there can't find a solution to their problem, and people show up and ask us, "What's your opinion on Palestine and Israel?" Well, we don't have an opinion on it! You know, my guitar player is a Tunisian Jew; I grew up with him and I eat at his place, why should I call him a kike? We grew up together, I wouldn't dream of saying such a thing. But the media have a huge influence in sowing division among the communities, that's the problem. That's how they create the identity politics, you can see it at every election, where they'll favor a certain community because that's where people have a French ID automatically, while they'll ignore all the other communities, and then they'll say, "how come there are homegrown terrorists?" That's not the point. There are young people leaving for Syria or Afghanistan but *you* [elected officials] are the ones to blame for it! We grew up with Jews, we never had any issues, and I personally have nothing against Jews. (Khaled, interview given in 2017)

This reaction perfectly dovetails with what Donel Jack'sman expressed in his show:

I grew up in Villiers-le-Bel and you know, it's a town that is right next to Sarcelles. When I was a kid, Sarcelles was home to the largest number of Jews in France. There were so many Jews in Sarcelles that the place wasn't even a town, it was a synagogue, you see what I mean? I grew up with Muslims, Arabs, Christians, Hindus, Buddhists, atheists, and religion wasn't an issue. We helped each other out. We respected and loved one another. That's the environment in which I grew up. Then later on, I began hearing some clichés because we were so poor, so the first time I heard someone say, "Jews have money" I answered, "No way, they're struggling, they're cash-strapped, just like us!" They had one falafel to share among five people—they were down and out! They were so broke they ate at my place and slept at my place, can you imagine how broke you have to be to get help from a Black person? That's when you don't even have two nickels to rub together, let me tell you! So you can imagine how I felt when I heard dude say, "Jews rule the world." I blew a fuse and said, "That's not true. In Sarcelles they don't rule over shit. They sucked at school, sucked at rap, sports, soccer, flirting, you name it. So if Jews rule the world, then believe me, someone forgot to send an invite to the Jews of Sarcelles!"

Arguably, the rhetoric used in the media and by politicians on the ethnic communities living in the outskirts of big French cities has had an influence in shaping public opinion on these communities' ability to integrate the nation, as well as on antisemitism. Ultimately, racism and antisemitism have more to do with politics and economics than with any other factor, since the economic and social needs of Arab and Black minorities in France are much more pressing than any interest they may have in the Israeli-Palestinian conflict. Their anti-Semitic sentiment is more akin to envy, for even though French Jews have also suffered from economic, social, and political discrimination (see chapter 1), the media and politicians stigmatize them less often than Blacks and Arabs. Because neither Islamophobia nor "negrophobia" or anti-Black racism have gained currency in mainstream French culture, contrary to antisemitism, French Jews are often perceived to be a privileged group and the only ethnic community whose existence is accepted by the French Republic. This has led a number of grassroots organizations, including those fighting racism and discrimination, to emphasize coalition politics in opposition with the mainstream media, which are accused of giving differential treatment to anti-Semitic hate crimes versus Islamophobic and/or anti-Black hate crimes, the latter receiving less coverage and eliciting less public outrage.

This what the left-wing member of Parliament Éric Coquerel (La France Insoumise, Seine Saint-Denis) pointed out while marching at a "Stop Islamophobia" protest, which gathered more than 13,000 people:

> No one rushed to comfort the victims after the Bayonne attack [in which a mosque was torched] and we are still waiting for the highest authorities of the state and the political organizations to call for a march as they did in the past following anti-Semitic aggressions. But in this case, there's been no response. So we sent out the text and it got many signatures, it's a good text, in essence. That's why we're here, and you can see everything's going on smoothly, there are thousands of us marching this Sunday afternoon.[20]

The reactions the elected official was alluding to have been recurrent in French political life, which explains why they may have caused a backlash among minorities which have been more often stigmatized by the far-right as invasive and unwilling to assimilate to the secular, colorblind model of the French Republic. In November 2015 for instance, in the wake of the tragic attack on the Bataclan theater in Paris, a Jewish teacher self-mutilated and called police to signal that he had suffered an anti-Semitic assault. But before police had been able to prove that it was a hoax, politicians across the spectrum had rushed to denounce a rise in antisemitism and empathize with the French Jewish community. The first instance of such hoaxes took place in July 2004, when a young White woman called Marie-Léonie Leblanc lodged a complaint at the police station of Aubervilliers, a town in the greater Paris area, claiming that she had been robbed of her purse and assaulted on the RER D train by six young men of North African and sub-Saharan African descent because she was Jewish; her face was cut and her belly was covered with svastikas. (*Libération*, July 12, 2004) The media outrage and shock were so intense that then-President Jacques Chirac immediately made the public statement that "whoever harms a Jew harms France herself." However, the police investigation rapidly confirmed that the woman was psychologically unstable; she was not Jewish and had self-mutilated, torn her clothes and drawn the svastikas herself on her body to get attention. This example was symptomatic of the way politicians, recklessly investing in the rhetoric of protecting French Jews from a repetition of their country's history of persecutions, have effectively utilized Jewish identity to turn it into one of the symbols of the Republic on an equal footing with the flag in the imagination of social players. While the sham was a mythomaniac craving attention, she had nevertheless chosen to impersonate a Jew to reach her goal, and succeeded in eliciting immediate sympathy. As the sociologist Fatiha Kaoues pointed out, "[i]t is particularly significant that this young woman, while psychologically unstable, had perfectly internalized the clichés and fantasies widely conveyed by the media, particularly those framing young Muslim men of Arab or African descent and denigrating them as macho, radicalized, and potentially racist."[21] As for French Jews, not only have they been weaponized, but also exposed to greater levels of hostility on the part of the less politically organized minorities of the country, which in turn may be tempted to attack Jews in order to vent their frustrations vis-à-vis the French political class, thus initiating a vicious circle and a self-fulfilling prophecy.

Indeed, France seems anxious to repress the disgraceful history of its treatment of its Jewish population. As mentioned earlier in chapter 1, during Nazi occupation, French authorities under Maréchal Pétain participated in a nationwide operation of de-naturalization and discrimination against Jews before it contributed in the Holocaust. President Jacques Chirac,[22] in a memorable speech commemorating the Vel' d'Hiv' Roundup, acknowledged the nation's responsibility in the tragedy—a move that his mentor General Charles de Gaulle had always refused to make on the grounds that he distinguished the French state from Pétain's collaborationist régime. As the French sociologist Martine Cohen notes,

> It is the memory of the Vichy régime which, considered in retrospect in the 1980s, may have combined with the first political disagreements over France's middle-eastern policy to facilitate an expression of distrust towards the State, even as cultural convergence with mainstream society was gaining momentum. Yet, since then, the tables seem to have turned. The State eventually acknowledged its "responsibility" during the Vichy period to fully answer for it and complete the "reparations" process, and stands as an unwavering ally of Jews in the fight against anti-Semitism.[23]

Yet, since past injustice cannot be undone, one way of reassuring French Jews that they will never be persecuted again in France is to scapegoat Arab and African(-descended) minorities as the only ones that still have a vested interest in antisemitism. Lately, in response to the state of Israel's war against Hamas, the leaders of both chambers of the French Parliament called for a march against antisemitism across the country and across party lines, while initially banning any marches in support of the Palestinian cause. President Macron also ignited a controversy over the separation between church and state after attending the lighting of a Hanukkah candle by Chief Rabbi Haïm Korsia in the presidential mansion, the Palais de l'Élysée, at the same time as his Minister for Education banned the wearing by schoolgirls of abaya, a traditional but non-religious garment worn in Muslim countries. As Martine Cohen notes, this narrative on the fight against antisemitism entails a risk besides that of encouraging competition for victim status, which is that it turns Jews into the sentinels of the French Republic:

> Granted, this privileged role may be seen as a badge of honor, as a sentinel, guarding the outposts, keeps watch over those they must keep out of harm's way (namely, France and its Republic); but it also has a riskier side, for the sentinel most often gets hit by the first bullets. Does Jews' attachment to France and its Republic necessarily have to be expressed on the mode of hyperbole and exceptionalism, and what's more, in an exclusively defensive identification to France casting Jews as eternal victims—the so-called victimhood of Franco-Judaism?[24]

Combined with the undeniable influence of radical fundamentalism among young Muslims, particularly those with few economic prospects, and the reality of anti-Semitic crimes, this has led significant numbers of French Jews to leave the country for Israel in the first two decades of the twenty-first century.

Politicians did not remain sitting idly by as this exodus was taking place; following the terrorist attack on the Hyper Cacher, then-Prime Minister Manuel Valls as well as then-President François Hollande separately asserted that "France without its Jews would no longer be France" in an explicit effort to stop French Jews' emigration to Israel.[25] This emotional, wholehearted reaction starkly contrasts with the warning sent in 2006 by then-candidate and future President Nicolas Sarkozy to the country's Arab and African minorities, "if there are people who feel uncomfortable being in France, let me tell them with a smile but firmly, let them feel perfectly free to leave a country they don't love,"[26] thus unwittingly or deliberately sending the message that the French Jewish community is more cherished and deserving of protection than other minorities in politicians' eyes.[27] Consequently, French Blacks and Arabs tend to share a common feeling of frustration and a sense of solidarity in their fight against discrimination, racism, and Islamophobia, while French Jews tend to pursue the struggle against antisemitism separately, within a community that shields yet also isolates them. This situation in turn reinforces the widelyshared impression that the two groups are locked in the zero-sum-game of a "victimhood contest," where each side seeks to draw more media attention and public sympathy than the other by insisting on the historical traumas it suffered and minimizing the other's.

When, following the murder of George Floyd by a White policeman in Minneapolis in May 2020, the #BlackLivesMatter movement was appropriated in France (as in other European countries) by protesters who seized the opportunity to denounce police brutality against racialized French citizens and residents, the marches gathered White, Arab, and Black French people, but Jewish organizations or intellectuals were not at the forefront or in the media as they had been in the 1980s. In this context, at an international workshop entitled "Jews and Whiteness in Colonial Spaces" organized at the London School of Oriental and African Studies by Yair Wallach and Moriel Ram,[28] I was asked whether French Jews had joined the #BLM protests in Paris. I had to admit that while individuals had certainly done so, they had not been visible as collectives; but I also pointed out whenever the CRIF calls for demonstrations in Paris or other French cities to denounce the persistence of anti-Semitic hate, Black and Arab allies are rarely seen at these protests. It is paradoxical that, in a country where human rights organizations linked racism and antisemitism throughout the twentieth century, the victims of racism should thus appear unconcerned by antisemitism, and vice-versa. In her essay, the Franco-Israeli sociologist Ilana Weizman addressed the complex matter of the place of the fight against antisemitism within antiracism, to advocate a convergence between the two.[29] The change in French politicians' rhetoric about French identity and the values of the French Republic since the turn of the twenty-first century, which shifted toward opposing groups presented as "model minorities" to those stigmatized as "undesirable migrants," is certainly responsible for the now-entrenched frustration of the racialized groups presumed to be Muslim.

Still, there exist constructive forms of activism in religious communities in France, be they Christian, Jewish, or Muslim. Although they receive little media exposure, being less sensational than protests, they do participate in building citizenship in harmony with a religious worldview—by means of memberships in clubs and religious-oriented organizations. The latter encourage voluntary gatherings between religious communities, outreach, ecumenical dialog, and awareness-raising workshops on antisemitism, racism, and discrimination. For example, Rabbi Michel Serfaty, founder and chair of the Amitié Judéo-Musulmane de France (AJMF), launched in 2005 a friendship bus tour of France with fellow Moroccan Imam Mohamed Azizi to sensitize communities in the Paris metropolitan area and the rest of the country to the necessity of interfaith dialog and togetherness, stressing the commonalities between Sephardim and North African Muslims.[30] While the initiative has continued up to the present and AJMF has expanded its outreach activities to training sessions in middle and high schools in the greater Paris area, the bus tour is not always well received by the inhabitants of either majority-Muslim or majority-Jewish neighborhoods. For example, a North African resident of La Courneuve asked Rabbi Serfaty, "You [Jews] have a good image, but we Muslims, what's our reputation, huh? Let's be honest—we're called terrorists, we're called fundamentalists, and thieves, and thugs."[31] This reaction is illustrative of the keen awareness that French Muslims have of their media image and its repercussions in public opinion, which is emotionally conditioned to perceive them as "scum" (a term used by Sarkozy in 2005) and potential anti-Semites. France's Chief Rabbi Haïm Korsia is also sensitive to this imbalance; in September 2019, speaking as a guest of an interfaith talk organized by the Fondation pour l'islam de France, he corrected the statements of former President Hollande and former Prime Minister Valls by asserting, "France without the Muslims is not France, just as it wouldn't be without the Catholics, the Protestants, or the atheists."[32] In spite or because of this stigmatization in political discourse and in the media, interfaith dialog and interracial collaboration are still a priority for grassroots organizations, such as the Amitié judéo-noire, which was founded after the uproar caused by the comedian Dieudonné.

BLACK JEWS CONFRONTING ANTISEMITISM AND RACISM

In such a tense context, how do Black Jews position themselves vis-à-vis antisemitism and racism? Being confronted with anti-Black and anti-Semitic prejudices, how do they claim recognition of their dual identity as Black Jews in French society? For Guershon NDuwa, "there's no separating one identity from the other. Whenever the Jewish community is hurt by antisemitism, I am hurt; and whenever Black people are hurt by racism and discrimination, I am hurt. So I don't feel torn, since I experience both situations at the same time" (Guershon, interview given 2009). As for Hortense Bilé, this is what she responded:

> A Black person has to deal with racism from birth, it's part of us, whether we are Jewish or not, a Black person has to deal with racism from birth and it's not something we have any control over. We have to live with it. To continue to exist, whatever our faith is, we Black people have to excel in whatever we do. We have to be creative non-stop; we have to create again and again and invent new strategies all the time to gain acceptance. We have to invent and re-invent things, produce and reproduce moves until they have to say yes because they

have run short of excuses. Whereas the other guy, the White dude, he just needs to write once and he gets an Oscar. (Hortense Bilé, interview given in 2015)

Ismaël concurs: "My father always told me to work ten times as hard as the White guy to have a chance to succeed" (Ismaël, interview given in 2015). For Dov, an Ethiopian Jew,

> It's tough being Black—incredibly tough. I feel the need to never lose track of my history. I would hate to become one of the people you can see everywhere, one of these young Black dudes who are completely uprooted, some of them have literally lost their minds; I don't want to become one of those. I can plainly see there's an identity crisis, it's the rejection they get from this country [France] that makes them go crazy. (Dov, interview given in 2009)

As these testimonies suggest, it is the racial identity, rather than the ethnic one, which is the main source of discrimination in the case of Black Jews, since their Jewishness is an impossibility in the eyes of the majority of their fellow French citizens. Things are less clear-cut in the case of biracial respondents, whose lighter skin often leads outsiders to identify them as Sephardim or even Ashkenazim. In the case of those who pass, such as Laure (quoted above), manifestations of antisemitism usually hurt more than anti-Black racism, because they share the experience of anti-Semitic prejudice with an entire community whose history of discrimination and persecution is acknowledged by the broader French society. But when they have more African features and can be claimed by the two groups, they have to grapple with the issue of dual loyalty and face a double penalty, as does Liana, whose mother is Sephardic and whose father is from Guadeloupe: "When I'm with Black people, I hear unpleasant remarks on my Jewishness, and when I'm among Jews, I experience racism. Once I went to a synagogue and I heard the rabbi say, 'What's the damn n—doing here?'" (Liana, interview given in 2012). Rébecca's African roots are perceptible too, but because she passes for Sephardic, she has experienced antisemitism more often (on the metro, see above) than racism: "Because I'm mixed-race, sometimes people take me for a Moroccan, so I can pass for a Sephardi [laughs], well, one who's a bit dark-skinned, but when people see me, they think I'm Sephardic. To be honest, I never experienced rejection from fellow Jews" (Rébecca, interview given in June 2020). Here again, Sephardic ethnicity appears as a liminal identity which may be used to conveniently de-racialize Black Jews and reinsert them into the familiar binary, without needing to consider the possible existence of anti-Black sentiment within Jewish circles.

In effect, the issue of antisemitism is so prevalent in France that any Jew is expected to have experienced antisemitism. When I asked Ruth, a convert in the Orthodox branch, if she had experienced anti-Semitic prejudice, she answered, "No, I've never been a victim of antisemitism, I'm not a bona fide Jew" (Ruth, interview given in 2010). This response, even if tinged with humor, is nevertheless revealing of the internalization of this representation. When I asked the same question to a Kenyan Jew of the Nairobi community at the conference of the International Society for the Study of African Jewry (ISSAJ) entitled "New Judaisms, New Diasporas, New Perspectives on Jewish Identity in the Twenty First Century," which was held at the University of Nairobi in February 2019, he responded with a development on the Israeli-Palestinian conflict in Israel, rather than on the lived experiences of Kenyan Jews in Kenya.

However, just a few hours before, while trying to find my way to the conference venue, I was walking behind a White lady who I noticed was clutching her purse and looking somewhat scared. She, too, was looking for the conference venue and we ended up sitting side by side; we began to chat before the workshops started. She told me that she was from Israel and had arrived in Nairobi three years before. When I asked her how she liked her life in Kenya, she answered she did not, explaining that she would have returned home had she not been constrained by family circumstances. I took the opportunity to ask her if her feeling was due to anti-Semitic hostility and she said there wasn't any, but that anti-White sentiment did exist in the country. Her family's home had been broken into three times, she said, and the same misfortune happened very frequently to all the White people she knew in Kenya. This accounted for her nervousness when she felt I was walking behind her.

Following the conference, I and the other speakers went on an organized visit of the Jewish community of Kasuku, in the small village of Gathundia, 165 kilometers north of Nairobi. Riding the bus with us were Yehuda Kimani, the son of the community leader Rabbi Yossef Ben Avraham Njogu, and his wife. As we were crossing a town on our way to Gathundia, the rabbi's son pointed out that the town was almost entirely Christian and harbored no Muslims, concluding, "This is why they live in peace." I understood this comment as implying that they practiced their Judaism in a peaceful environment, devoid of antisemitism. On arriving in Gathundia, after the Shabbat service, I chatted with the officiant and asked him whether in the village, everyone was Jewish or if other religions were also present. He answered that there were Catholic and Protestant churches. I went on to ask if he perceived any anti-Semitic prejudice, and he responded, "No, we never did. We used to belong to a Christian community, so we have no problem. There are Christians all around, and we live in peace with the communities established here—the Methodists, Catholics, and with the other villagers we've never, ever had any issues."

What may be concluded from the conjunction of these three viewpoints on antisemitism in Kenya is that it is difficult to isolate anti-Semitic sentiment from the targeting of White expatriates by robbers in urban settings; indeed, the Jewish community of Nairobi today is composed essentially of natives from Israel, the United States, and the Republic of South Africa,[33] whereas the Jews of Gathundia occupy the same economic positions as the rest of the rural community in which they live. As for their mention of Muslim presence as a potential threat, it seems to have more to do with the terrorist activities of the Al-Shabaab militia, which was driven out of neighboring Somalia by counter-insurgency operations and did target an Israeli-owned hotel in Mombasa and an Israeli passenger jet in 2002, but also, more recently, a shopping mall (2013), a university (2015), and a luxury hotel in Nairobi (2019) as well as Christian teachers and police officers. It is possible that the response given to me at the conference just one month after the attack on the Nairobi luxury hotel reflected an effort to appease our fears by focusing our attention on the faraway Israeli-Palestinian conflict as a better example of the daily experience of antisemitism and terrorist threat. But it did not emphasize a long-standing tradition of scapegoating and animus against Jews (of whatever color) in the Kenyan population along the same lines as in Europe or the United States.

Another example of the difference between France and an African country in the reception of Black Jews was given by one of my interviewees, Micheline, who spends her time between Paris and Abidjan, the capital of the Ivory Coast (a former French colony). While waiting for the approval of the Israelite Consistory of France, she self-describes as a convert and lives as a Jew within a fifty-strong community that was founded by an Ivorian man who unsuccessfully tried to be admitted by the Paris Consistory for twenty years. When I asked her how her friends and family reacted to her identifying as Jewish, she answered,

> It's not a secret, but they don't have a clue about what it means [laughs] when I tell them I am a practicing Jew! They just stare at me blankly and ask, "Judaism, what's that?" They don't even know what it is. To be fair, I used to be just as clueless. Until I converted, for me Judaism wasn't even in the picture; sure, we heard about Jews, but we didn't even know that there was a religious practice. People are surprised, they don't have a clue. When I explain they say, "Ah, okay, so it's the religion of the Jews!" And the next thing they tell me is, "But what about Jesus, then? So you mean you don't pray Jesus anymore? Oh no, poor girl, she doesn't pray Jesus!" [laughs] (Micheline, interview given in November 2020)

If, then, Judaism is unknown to most Africans, does it imply that there is no antisemitism in Africa? Micheline answered,

> Here in my country [the Ivory Coast] there's no anti-Semitism, people leave us alone, folks walk around with their Kippahs and they're perfectly safe—no, really, honestly, everything's fine. There's no anti-Semitism here. But of course, if you meet a Muslim or a Lebanese, don't tell them you're a Jew because he's not going to like it. See, I'm a dentist and I had put divine names in my office. One day a Lebanese customer came for dental care and saw the Hebrew letters so he went, "What's with the Hebrew letters?" When they find out you're Jewish, then there's hate. Well *that* guy, I didn't tell him I'm Jewish. [Laughs] (Micheline, interview given in November 2020)

This echoed another exchange I had at a conference. In January 2011, the Mouvement Juif Libéral (now called Judaïsme en Movement since September 2019) had organized a one-day symposium entitled "Jewish Americans and African Americans, a Model for France?" under the aegis of Rabbi Stephen Berkowitz. In attendance was a fellow Congolese who had recently returned from Brazzaville; I seized the opportunity to ask him if he had noticed anti-Semitic sentiment in Congo, since I had spent a long time away from the country. He answered, "No, this doesn't exist back home; what *does* exist is anti-Lebanese sentiment. I personally dislike Lebanese people, because of the way they behave in our country!" In Congo as in many other Francophone African countries, there is a strong presence of Lebanese expatriates, particularly in the sector of small and medium-size businesses.

Although these testimonies concur in demonstrating the absence of a tradition of antisemitism in Africa, it is still possible to observe the persistence in the mentalities of old Christian prejudices on Jews as "the deicidal people." Hortense Bilé, who is also a native of the Ivory Coast, shared her experience in these terms:

> Even back home in the Ivory Coast, the way people see it is that in converting, I rejected [the Virgin] Mary, from the Catholic viewpoint, or I rejected Jesus, from the Baptist viewpoint. And then they're like, "the Jews killed Jesus"—you hear that all the time. As if we were supposed to blame them [Jews] although Jesus died as a Jew! But they go, "the Jews killed Jesus and all that, so it means if you're a Jew you don't know Jesus, and that means going backwards." They tell me I've lost my place, I'm a worldly woman now, I'm lost and I need to be saved. (Hortense, interview given in 2017)

The accusation against Jews as a "deicidal people" for allegedly assassinating Jesus with the help of the Romans dates back to the second century C.E., when several Fathers of the Church built this cornerstone of Christian anti-Judaism; for instance, Melito of Sardis (d. c. 180 C.E.) wrote, "God was assassinated by the hand of Israel." As a consequence, even though the Councils of Trento in 1545–1563 and Vatican II in 1962–1965 officially put an end to this accusation, many persecutions against Jews in Europe were rooted in this belief. It was transmitted to Africans during the colonial period, when they were Christianized by Catholic and Protestant missionaries. For example, my mother, who was not schooled, was Christianized during the colonial period, in the 1940s–1950s. When she visited us on her very first trip out of Congo, I introduced her to a close friend of my wife's, specifying that he is Jewish, and she blurted out in vernacular language, "Oh really, the people who killed the Lord Jesus are still around?" While this reaction may be seen as characteristic of anti-Semitic prejudice, we also noted that each time we cooked Congolese food while she was staying at our place, she would tell us to invite our Jewish friend, because, she said, "I can tell he likes our food." In African cultures, people do not share meals with anyone they consider evil, therefore it seems more likely that she had simply repeated uncritically a belief that she had been taught in her teenage years, and believed Jews to be one of the peoples of ancient times which now bear new names.

On a different note, a group of Congolese comedians critiqued this imported tradition in one of their shows. A character named Rev. Mangobo preaches, "can you imagine, a great king like Jesus was killed on the cross, the Jews killed him on the cross, yes they did!" Then, in a call-and-response exchange with the congregation, the preacher asks, "What did the Jews do?" The congregation responds, "They killed him," and all lament Jesus' agony. But one critical mind, a character named Sans Souci Mokili (Couldn't-Care-Less), interrupts the wailing to taunt the preacher: "But are we the ones who killed him? We aren't Jews." Another character chimes in, "Reverend, I have a question too. I wonder how we Zairians have anything to do with that sin?" A third character steps in to save the preacher's reputation: "Reverend, let me answer them. It's because this problem is a general case, they put him on a worldwide scale. So this sin is ours also."[34] In the end, Africans may be at the same time imbued with dominant ideologies from abroad and critical of the scapegoating of Jews as the "deicidal people" if this means being enrolled again in conflicts that mean nothing to them. In spite of transmitted prejudices, many African ethnic groups claim to be Jewish or convert to Judaism.

NOTES

1. See Édith Bruder, ed., *Juifs d'ailleurs: Diasporas oubliées, identités singulières* (Paris: Albin Michel, 2020).

2. This ritual consists in an immersion in a pool, typically dug at ground level and containing at least 500 liters of non-stagnant water, a part of which comes from a natural source (whether rain, spring, river, or sea), that is accessed by a few steps. It is built following very strict norms and must be approved by a religious decisionmaker to be labeled as Kosher. See Sophie Nizard, "Une pratique corporelle 'discrète': le bain rituel," *Ethnologie française* 43, no. 4 (2013): 601–14.

3. Omar Sylla and Geneviève Platteau, "Le couple contemporain en Europe et en Afrique," *Cahiers critiques de thérapie familiale et pratiques de réseaux* 1, no. 42 (2009): 262.

4. Loïc Le Pape, "Tout change, mais rien ne change."

5. Arkin, *Rhinestones,* 173.

6. Aurélien Mokoko Gampiot, "Black Judaism in France: An Example of the Intersection Between Religion and Ethnicity," Joëlle Allouche and Harriet Hartman, eds., *Contemporary Jewry* 36, Special Issue no. 3, "Transformation and Evolution in the Jewish World: Judaisms and Judaicities in Contemporary Societies" (2017): 323, http://rdcu.be/tGYG.

7. Alexandre Feigenbaum, "Siddour Kol Hanechama: Le Grand Rabbin réagit," accessed January 28, 2012. URL: http://www.fjn-123.fr/spip.php?article885.

8. Although she accepted to give me her contact information for an interview, I was never able to reach her.

9. Benoît Hasse, "La Tribu KA revendique la 'descente' de la rue des Rosiers," *Le Parisien,* May 31, 2006, accessed January 18, 2012. https://www.leparisien.fr/paris-75/la-tribu-ka-revendique-la-descente-de-la-rue-des-rosiers-31-05-2006-2007031948.php.

10. In an open letter published on January 10, 2023, in the Franco-Israeli periodical *Israël Magazine,* Dieudonné apologized to those of his fellow countrymen and women whom he had offended, particularly French Jews. https://www.leparisien.fr/faits-divers/dieudonne-demande-pardon-a-la-communaute-juive-dans-un-journal-franco-israelien-10-01-2023-UJMIIVOED5AFLKYI7AI6CB2JPQ.php consulted on March 28, 2024.

11. AM-ISRAËL-FARAFINA, open letter, "Stop au racisme anti juifs-Noirs-Métisses (*sic*)- Basanés," Paris, April 3, 2017.

12. Post by david illouz, koide9enisrael: netanyahu "remercie" l'employé musulman du supermarché casher de paris, accessed January 17, 2017.

13. Le Point Afrique, "Mali-France—Lassana Bathily primé au 30e dîner annuel du CRIF," *Le Point*, February 23, 2015, accessed January 17, 2017, https://www.lepoint.fr/afrique/lassana-bathily-prime-au-30e-diner-annuel-du-crif-23-02-2015-1907175_3826.php.

14. Carole La Pan, *L'Islam, du Coran aux Guerriers Fous d'Allah* (Montréal: Collection Essais, Édition Quebec-Livre, 2002).

15. The phrase in French contains the N-word.

16. Thomas Ngijol 2, One Man Show, by Thomas Ngijol, Karole Rocher, and Clément Chabault, 90 minutes, November 10, 2015, 1h41, broadcast on the cable channel Canal + France, 2016.

17. Donel Jack'sman, "Les juifs de Sarcelles," YouTube, posted on March 8, 2021, accessed August 8, 2021, https://www.youtube.com/watch?v=sgfzbfcd3da.

18. Aurélien Mokoko Gampiot, investigation into urban social life in la Courneuve, in collaboration with David Garbin, University of Kent and Gareth Millington, University of York. The findings were published in "Territorial stigma and the politics of resistance in Parisian banlieue," *Urban Studies* 49 (2012).

19. The term used by the interviewee in French is "communautarisme," which has the same political weight as "identity politics" in English.

20. Éric Coquerel, member of the French Parliament from the party la France insoumise Seine-Saint-Denis BFM TV Sunday, November 10, 2019.

21. Fatiha Kaoues, "RER D: leçon d'une hystérie médiatico-politique," yabiladi.com, July 21, 2004.

22. "16 juillet 1995: Chirac reconnaît la responsabilité de la France dans la rafle du Vel' d'Hiv,'" *L'Opinion*, Paris, July 16, 1995.

23. Martine Cohen, *Fin du franco-judaïsme? Quelle place pour les Juifs dans une France multiculturelle?* (Rennes: Presses Universitaires de Rennes, 2023), 226.

24. Cohen, *Fin du franco-judaïsme?* 227.

25. See "Déclaration de M. le Premier Ministre Manuel Valls sur la lutte contre le terrorisme et l'antisémitisme, à Paris le 9 janvier 2016," https://www.vie-publique.fr/discours/197653-declaration-de-m-manuel-valls-premier-ministre-sur-la-lutte-contre-le accessed July 25, 2023, and "Manuel Valls bientôt en Israël pour promouvoir l'initiative de paix française," i24News, May 19, 2016, https://www.i24news.tv/fr/actu/international/europe/113762-160518-manuel-valls-bientot-en-israel-pour-promouvoir-l-initiative-de-paix-francaise accessed July 25, 2023.

26. Nicolas Sarkozy, excerpt from a welcome speech to the new members of the Union pour la Majorité Présidentielle, archives of the Institut National de l'Audiovisuel, accessed July 25, 2023, https://www.youtube.com/watch?v=VufQmfXCUU4.

27. For example, this contrast was noted by the Union Juive Française pour la Paix in a statement it published online on March 9, 2016, following the Prime Minister's speech at the CRIF's annual dinner, accessed July 25, 2023, https://histoirecoloniale.net/Manuel-Valls-confond-antisionisme.html.

28. Yair Wallach and Moriel Ram, "Jews and Whiteness," Academic Workshop, SOAS Centre for Jewish Studies, July 1, 2020.

29. Ilana Weizman, *Des blancs comme les autres? Les juifs, angle mort de l'antiracisme* (Paris: Éditions Stock, 2002).

30. Sue Fishkoff and JTA, "Riding the French Countryside in the Jewish-Muslim Friendship Bus," *The Jewish Chronicle*, June 27, 2010, accessed July 26, 2023, https://jewishchronicle.timesofisrael.com/riding-the-french-countryside-in-the-jewish-muslim-friendship-bus/. See also Kait Bolongaro, "A Rabbi, Three Young Muslims and a Minibus: A Tour de France for Dialogue," *Middle East Eye,* November 14, 2016, accessed July 26, 2023, https://www.middleeasteye.net/features/rabbi-three-young-muslims-and-minibus-tour-de-france-dialogue.

31. Report by Thomas Dandois and Alexandra Kogan, "Un Rabbin dans la cité. Sur la route avec l'amitié judéo-musulmane de France," ARTE GEIE/Memento, 2015, http://www.arte.tv/sites/story/reportage/france-un-rabbin-dans-les-cites/.

32. Quoted in Martine Cohen, *Fin du Franco-Judaïsme?*, 227.

33. "Kenya," website of the World Jewish Congress, accessed July 28, 2023, https://www.worldjewishcongress.org/en/about/communities/KE.

34. Groupe NZOI and Groupe MANGOBO, "Papa pasteur 1," YouTube, posted by kokodianzombo, accessed October 17, 2018.

Conclusion

This study began with a question: How is Judaism articulated with Blackness in the life experiences and quest for recognition of Black Jews within the French Jewry? As this study draws to a close, we have gained a deeper understanding of how French Jews situate and express themselves by means of ethnic markers, institutions, and Sephardic or Ashkenazi identities. We have also explored how Black believers seeking for a vindication of their Judaism and/or Jewishness perceive and express themselves, identify with the Jewish people, and carve a place for themselves into the French Jewry. On the one hand, the Jewish component of the French nation was not easily woven into the social fabric, but only after a long ordeal of persecutions, subjugation, forced conversions to Christianity, anti-Judaism, and antisemitism, with occasional resurgences of the latter. On the other hand, the Black component of the French nation went through the hardships of slavery, colonization (both entailing forced conversions to Christianity) economic immigration, and persistent racism. While Jews, despite some conversions to Christianity, remained Jewish in spite of the persecutions, people of African descent embraced Christianity of Islam, but seldom Judaism in the course of their long history of interactions with Europeans. Today, though, we see men, women, and children of African, Caribbean, or African American descent claiming their Jewishness and/or converting to the Jewish faith.

Since conversion to Judaism is first and foremost an institutional affair, individuals' relation to the established authorities is often perceived as normative and prone to conflict. Indeed, Jewish authorities, imbued with their minority situation in France, tend to keep to themselves in an ethnically, culturally, and religiously exclusive community; even if they allow processes of assimilation and conversion in their midst through conversion, the presence of people of African descent among would-be converts complicates the integration of Black fellow Jews.

The experience of converting to Judaism implies a form of identity crisis, for self-identifying as a Jew or claiming one's Jewishness means being in a minority situation on two simultaneous planes. When becoming Jewish, these Black social players are not identified as such either by fellow Jews or by the broader French society, insofar as the vast majority of the French population is not cognizant of the existence of Black Jews outside of Israel and Ethiopia. The life experiences of the respondents give an accurate illustration of this permanent tension. As a matter of fact, since Black Jewish identity is constantly confronted with doubts and rejection, their identification and integration as Jews is never a given and must always be renegotiated.

On the one hand, some of them have enjoyed a warm welcome in synagogues, particularly in Masorti and Reform Judaism movements, and even, in the case of adopted children, hospitality in Jewish families. Others have found friendships, host families, and, in the case of interracial marriages, romantic love. Such marriages, which have been discussed in one of the chapters of this study, carry a strong significance in relation to integration, for they provide unique insights into inter-ethnic relations between White Jews and Black Jews and non-Jews alike. To a certain extent, respondents describe interracial marriage with White Jews as evidencing racial integration; yet, for other interviewees who are still seeking a Jewish soulmate, interracialism becomes the sign of a "dis-integration" due to the color line drawn by potential in-laws who either are ignorant of the existence of Black Jews or consider them to be racially unsuitable.

On the other hand, in spite of the acceptance and welcome, and Black Jews' sincere desire to belong to the Jewish people, rejection and racism effectively block their integration into the French Jewry. Undeniably, Judaism in France represents an exception among the country's established religions, because of its promotion of the ideology of matrilineage. Indeed, ethnicity and religion combine in reinforcing the racial barriers used to legitimize Jewishness. The latter being founded both on a certificate of Jewishness delivered by the religious authorities and on the assessment of the community, the believers whose mothers are not Jewish suffer from a lack of legitimacy. Consequently, the importance of Jewish matrilineage, which plays a crucial role as a factor of inclusion and cohesion within the Jewish community, also works as a factor of exclusion, particularly for Black Jews. Additionally, African-descended peoples from Africa and the Caribbean having been peripheral to the social organization of the Western and Eastern Jewries, Black Jews appear as intruders in groups that now identify as White.

In reaction to these situations of rejection, racism, and discrimination encountered in Jewish milieus, Black Jewish organizations have recently emerged, with the goal of making their White fellow Jews aware of the existence and presence of Black Jews. Even if the numbers of Black Jews are often pointed out as too insignificant to be taken into account by the rest of the French Jewry—an estimated 250 families, residing in the greater Paris area and other big French cities—their very organizing has triggered awareness, albeit slow, of Black presence in and attachment to the French Jewry. It is because this attachment is belittled and considered with suspicion in the French context that the quest for visibility has eventually become a necessity. The risk of separatism from the rest of the French Jewry is not so acute as to lead to a cultural enclave without any exchanges with the Ashkenazim and Sephardim, but the latter groups feel a heightened sense of responsibility in improving the representation of the French Jewry as a whole. The organizing movement has been more successful than individual attempts at making Black Jews more visible within the French Jewry, despite the fact that their claims remain problematic in the eyes of the broader French society, which is deeply attached to the ideology of colorblindness.

Analyzing the life stories of Black Jewish interviewees has offered a better grasp of their situation within the French Jewry. Their organizing has led to a greater awareness of the possibility of a Black Jewishness, stemming from their focus on Black Biblical figures and their questioning of the roots of Hebrew ancestors. These African and Caribbean believers have a sincere attachment to the idea of Jewishness and an understanding of the Torah that is expressed through the prism of their African or Africana cultures. Their rootedness in African or Caribbean cultures does not clash with their feeling of belongingness in Judaism and Jewishness, for they feel at home keeping Kosher, practicing circumcision, and cultivating other aspects of Jewish ethnicity.

This leads to the rising visibility, in Jewish milieus, of Black believers who are increasingly conscious of, and willing to challenge, their minority status within the French Jewry. Consequently, the Black Jewish experience no longer implies concealing one's African or Africana culture when entering a synagogue, and instead breaking away from the long-standing model of Black Jewish faith in France, that is, living one's Judaism on the down-low.

In the end, understanding the Black Jewish experience in France requires a conjunction of two levels of analysis. The first one allows us to acknowledge that these believers are deeply conscious of belonging to the Jewish people. But this identification process is complicated both by the rejection of their White fellow Jews, who often doubt their Jewishness, and by the French Jewry's organization, which is structured by an ethnic binary between Ashkenazim and Sephardim which gives them no space. The second level of analysis shows that there is a risk of separatism, even if there is no such thing as an emergence of community centers that could jeopardize their sense of belongingness and identification to the Jewish people. However, because they are no longer willing to choose between their African or Caribbean cultures and Jewish culture, they often have to negotiate and insist to gain some visibility within the French Jewry. The religious and political authorities representing the latter are beginning to feel the obligation to sensitize the Ashkenazi and Sephardic members of the community to the presence of Black Jews, in order to improve their representations of them.

Indeed, whether Black Jews are converts or native-born Jews, they aspire to be more than curiosities and instead be considered as full-fledged members of the French and global Jewry. The relative reluctance of Jewish authorities to acknowledge the presence of Black believers has led Black Jewish organizations to takes matters into their own hands and expand their media visibility. Yet, African and Caribbean Jews still identify with their White fellow Jews by seeking vindication in a quest for Jewish origins. Some do so in isolation, silence, and painful anonymity, while others have chosen to join community organizations such as the Fraternité international des Juifs noirs or Am-Israël-Farafina, which prove to be spaces where Jewishness may be conceptualized while also celebrating African or Africana cultures. Finally, Rabbi Pinchas Eliyahou Shaday,[1] the head of the Yeshiva Botsina Kadisha, has decided to gather the Jewish institutions of several African countries under his authority as the newlyappointed Chief Rabbi of Africa since August 2023. This testifies to the need for autonomy felt by Black Jews, who appreciate being in control of their own affairs without necessarily embracing a separatist attitude vis-à-vis their fellow White Jews.

It is too early to determine the middle- or long-term effects of the organizing of Black Jews in France, and whether it will lead to the founding of a Black synagogue. Undeniably, French Jews are too unaware of the existence of Black Jews (other than the Beta Israel of Ethiopia) for their presence to become rapidly ordinary and banal. Because of the claims of Black Jews, this inevitably poses the question of diversity in Judaism, particularly in France. As the French sociologist Martine Cohen has noted, "Jews are diverse in their ways of being Jewish and French. This is not new; what is, is the high visibility of such diversity."[2] Therefore it is not surprising to see some French Jewish institutions taking interest in these community organizations, as the CRIF did in admitting the FJN. What has been accomplished thanks to organizing is not limited to a quest for status; it is about obtaining the right to identify as Jews without shame, and without feeling forced to leave their Africanness behind.

As minority groups in France, Jews and Blacks alike have to grapple with prejudice in the shape of antisemitism and racism in their present forms. But the evolution of the French Jewry now offers an opportunity to study the link between religion, race, and ethnicity in a configuration where the majority of Jews can identify with the White French mainstream while remaining ethnically Ashkenazi or Sephardic, which assigns all other Jews, particularly Black Jews, to minority status. African and Caribbean Jews being conditioned by their double minority status, both within the French Jewry and in French society as a whole, are both claiming the validity of Black Jewishness and challenging their minority situation in order to gain social recognition in France, against ignorance and denial.

The emergence of Black organizations in the contemporary French Jewry sheds a light on the functioning of Jewish authorities in their handling of Otherness and particularly Black believers whose presence questions the assumptions of their fellow White Jews. The emergence and growth of the two community organizations (FJN and AM-I-FA) show the development of new poles of identification within the French Jewry that contribute to defending specific interests and give Black believers a sense of belongingness. These community organizations facilitate the socialization of their members by reiterating discourses and reflections on Black Jewishness, including Afrocentric ones. Faced with systemic racism and rejection, many Black Jewish believers find comfort by embracing the Afrocentric ideology and turning into a bulwark its insistence on the anteriority of African civilizations, while the organizations help them fight racism, unite them into marches, and offer them a safer environment within Jewish communities by improving their visibility thanks to media exposure.

Ultimately, in spite of its universal message, Judaism today is often considered as a monopoly, owned by the Ashkenazi and Sephardic ethnic groups in France. This poses the question of the role played by its representative institutions in acknowledging the growing diversity of the global Jewry and accepting the visible presence of Black believers. For instance, at a conference held in Paris on the theme "religions and frontiers," after I had presented a paper on African and Caribbean Jews in the greater Paris area, a White Jewish woman walked up to me to express her satisfaction at hearing about the existence of Black Jews in France, adding that she wished that rabbis would sensitize their communities to the subject because it would help unite Jews and Blacks instead of dividing them over accounts of Black antisemitism. Indeed, in national and international contexts shaped by antisemitism, the situation of Black Jews is ambivalent, as on the one hand, they suffer from it just like their White fellow Jews, but on the other hand, they are assumed to be anti-Semitic by virtue of the racial identity, prejudices, and politics assigned to them, which complicates their interactions with other Jews.

Besides, we are witnessing a political moment when Jewishness in France is increasingly conflated with Whiteness, as is demonstrated by the alliance between the Sephardic far-right provocateur Éric Zemmour and Marion Maréchal-Le Pen, the traditional Catholic granddaughter of the founder of the far-right party Front National. Under these circumstances, Black Jews, in spite of their faith and although the vast majority are French citizens, remain on the "wrong" side of the color line, with identity claims that clearly signal their exclusion from the French mainstream. While some aim to become indistinguishable from the White majority in social, economic, and political terms, others are still wondering whether they will ever be integrated in French society.

In conclusion, this in-depth survey of Black Jews in France offers a novel approach of the articulation between religion, race, and ethnicity through the prism of the African and Caribbean experience of Judaism. It represents an original contribution to the sociology of interracial relations, religions, and Biblical studies, by bringing into play the concept of Scripturalization, which helps us view the Torah and the Bible as embedded in social relations and, in the present case, in Black Jews' relation to the global Jewry of which they are a part.

NOTES

1. Discours d'Intronisation du Grand Rabbin d'Afrique / Swearing-in speech of the Chief Rabbi of Africa—YouTube streamed live on August 2, 2023, accessed August 2, 2023. https://www.youtube.com/watch?v=noAkz32hHqg.

2. Martine Cohen, "Les Juifs de France. Modernité et identité," *Vingtième Siècle, revue d'histoire*, no. 66, Religions d'Europe (April–June 2000): 91, DOI: 10.3406/xxs.2000.4565.

Glossary

bar mitsvah: Rite of passage for boys aged thirteen years old, whereby they become adults from a religious standpoint, and therefore may be counted as part of the quorum of ten men (minyan) required to recite the prayers. On the day of his bar mitsvah, a boy wears a talith for the first time and is called to recite benedictions and read aloud some verses of the Torah. The religious service is traditionally followed by a meal offered to the attendees by the family; the celebration nowadays has become a lavish party where the young man is presented with gifts by his family and guests.

Kashrut: A set of prescriptions describing how to make food (particularly animals) ritually authorized for consumption, and listing pure and impure animals. Only fruit and vegetables are all considered Kosher.

kavvanah: A state of deep concentration and spiritual intentionality, considered necessary for reciting prayers.

ketubah: A marriage contract listing the husband's obligations, written before the wedding and handed to the bride during the ceremony. In Biblical times, it was written in Aramaic and included the payment of a bride price to her father. While opinions differ as to whether the ketubah was imposed by Biblical law or by rabbis, the document is essential to the celebration of a Jewish wedding and is required by all rabbinical authorities. In the twentieth century, the Conservative movement created a ketubah in English including a clause whereby the bride and groom both promise to abide by the rabbinical tribunal's decision in case of divorce, in order to avoid husbands refusing to grant their wives permission to remarry. The Reform Judaism movement tends to prefer certificates in the local language and including no legal and financial specifics.

Kippah (plural: kippot): A round-shaped head covering for men, customarily worn to show one's consciousness of the presence of God above one's head and manifest one's Jewishness. In the Reform Judaism movement, women also wear kippot.

Magen David: The phrase means "shield of David" and is one of the designations of God in one of the blessings recited in synagogues after the reading of a prophetic text. In a fourteenth-century manuscript penned by a Kabbalist, the phrase was associated for the first time to one of the popular geometrical motifs, consisting of two superimposed equilateral triangles forming a star-shaped hexagon, which traditionally decorated seals, buildings, manuscripts, and artifacts such as mezuzot or amulets. The spread of the printing industry helped popularize the hexagon as a heraldic sign, and, following the Emancipation of French Jews in the nineteenth century, as a rallying sign equivalent to the cross for Christians. The Zionist movement chose it for the flag of the future state of Israel as early as 1897.

Mezuzah (plural: mezuzot): A small rectangular case containing passages from the Torah and attached to the right doorframe of a Jewish home's main entrance. It is customary to touch it with one's right hand on entering and exiting the place, to manifest one's consciousness of observing a commandment and express confidence in divine protection.

mikveh: Ritual bath, designed for the purification of persons and utensils. Conversion is not considered complete until the convert has immersed themselves in a mikveh.

Parasha: A section of the Pentateuch, read aloud in the synagogue during the Shabbat morning service.

seder: Name of the ritual family dinner of the first night (or first two nights) of the festival of Pessah (Passover, celebrating the exodus from Egypt), in which a number of symbolic foods and cups of wine are consumed in a precise order (the word "seder" means "order") to teach the children the meaning of the celebration. The first dinner of Rosh Hashanah (the Jewish New Year) is called 'Seder' in Sephardic traditions.

Shidduch: The Talmud makes it an obligation for every man to find a wife for his son. Prenuptial arrangements, including resorting to professional male or female matchmakers (respectively designated as shadkhan and shadkhanit), are designated by the Aramaic term "shidduchin," which means "peace of mind." They involve an engagement by both families to gather the sum required for the bride price (see ketubah) and set a date for the wedding ceremony. As the engagement is celebrated around a meal where a written promise to marry is signed, it is considered highly problematic to renege on this promise. This is symbolized by the two mothers breaking a dish or earthenware item, to show that just as the pieces of a broken dish cannot be put back together, the engagement to marry must proceed until the wedding takes place, even if it ends up in a divorce. In this book, respondents use the term to allude to matchmaking sites or associations aiming to help single men and women to find partners with a similar understanding of Jewish life, while making sure that the two families avoid mismatches. Indeed, marriage options tend to be more restricted for Kohenim, whose families abide by strict purity rules, or for converts, who are rejected by many families and often encouraged to marry other converts or persons born out of wedlock or to non-Jewish mothers.

Talith: A rectangular shawl with fringes (tzitzit) and black stripes, worn by men for certain prayers in observance of a Biblical commandment (*Numbers* 15:38). Feminists within US Judaism have claimed the right for women to wear it also.

Tefillin: Two small quadrangular leather cases containing for passages from the Torah, worn by men from the age of thirteen for morning prayers, out of respect for an injunction inspired by *Exodus* 13:1–10, 11–16 and *Deuteronomy* 6:4–9 and 13–21. One of the tefillin is wrapped around the left arm and the other is attached around the head, with the box on the forehead, just below the hairline and between the eyes. The four scrolls enclosed define the foundations of Judaism, that is, the oneness of God, the acceptance of divine commandments, God's Providence, and faith in the Redemption of the world as symbolized by the exodus from Egypt. They serve as reminders of religious duties and as protection against sin.

tzitzit: Undergarment with fringes at the four corners, worn by men in daytime in observance of *Numbers* 15:38.

All entries are based on Geoffrey Wigoder, ed., *Dictionnaire encyclopédique du Judaïsme.* French edition adapted by Sylvie Anne Goldberg (Paris: Éditions du cerf, 1993).

Bibliography

Alexandrowicz, Ra'anan. *James' Journey to Jerusalem*. Feature film, Lama Films, 2004.
Allouche-Benayoun, Joëlle. "Comment être juif croyant et moderne dans la France d'aujourd'hui?" *Sociétés* 2, no. 92 (2006): 5–22. DOI: 10.3917/soc.092.05. https://www.cairn-int.info/revue-societes-2006-2-page-5.htm
Ake, Dieudonné. *La vérité sur les Hébreux noirs d'Afrique et les Khazars de Palestine*. Ouragan du Midi, 2022.
Amselle, Jean-Loup, and Elikia M'Bokolo, eds. *Au cœur de l'ethnie. Ethnies, tribalisme et État en Afrique*. Paris: La Découverte, collection Poche, 1999.
Anteby-Yemini, Lisa. *Les Juifs éthiopiens en Israël: les paradoxes du paradis*. Paris: CNRS Éditions, 2004.
Anteby-Yemini, Lisa. "Peau noire, masques blancs: Les immigrants éthiopiens en Israël." *Pardès* 1, no. 44 (2008): 107–18.
Anteby-Yemini, Lisa. *Les Juifs d'Éthiopie de Gondar à la Terre promise*. Paris: Albin Michel, 2018.
Arkin, Kimberly A. *Rhinestones, Religion, and the Republic: Fashioning Jewishness in France*. Stanford: Stanford University Press, 2014.
Asante, Molefi Kete. *The Afrocentric Idea, revised and expanded edition*. Philadelphia: Temple University Press, 1998.
Asante, Molefi Kete. "Akhenaten to Origen: Characteristics of Philosophical Thought in Ancient Africa." *Journal of Black Studies* 40, no. 2 (November 2009): 296–309. DOI: 10.1177/0021934707312814. http://jbs.sagepub.com hosted at http://online.sagepub.co
Assan, Valérie, and Yolande Cohen. "Circulations et migrations des Juifs du Maghreb en France, de la veille de la Première Guerre mondiale aux années 1960. Introduction." *Archives Juives* 1, no. 53 (2020): 4–15, accessed August 5, 2023. DOI: 10.3917/aj1.531.0004. https://www.cairn.info/revue-archives-juives-2020-1-page-4.htm
Atlan, Gabrielle. "Le statut juridique de l'enfant dans la Loi juive. Journée d'études Liberté religieuse de l'enfant: Égalité ou différence de traitement? La question particulière des discriminations au regard de la liberté religieuse de l'enfant, Maison Interuniversitaire." *Société, droit et religion* 1, no. 3 (2013): 195–208. DOI: 10.3917/

sdr.003.0195. https://www.cairn-int.info/revue-societe-droit-et-religion-2013-1-page-195.htm

Atlan, Gabrielle. "Le statut de la femme dans le judaïsme." *Société, droit et religion* 1, no. 4 (2014): 33–46. DOI: 10.3917/sdr.004.0033. https://www-cairn-int.info/revue-societe-droit-et-religion-2014-1-page-33.htm

Ba, Aïssata. "L'alliance noire d'un imam et d'un rabbin." *Le monde des religions* (January/February 2011): 16–17.

Badouard, Romain. "'Je ne suis pas Charlie.' Pluralité des prises de parole sur le web et les réseaux sociaux." *Le Défi Charlie. Les médias à l'épreuve des attentats*, January 5, 2016, accessed October 7, 2016. hal-01251253.

Bahloul, Joëlle. "Noms et prénoms juifs nord-africains." *Terrain* 4 (March 1985), posted online on July 23, 2007, accessed November 1, 2019. DOI: 10.4000/terrain.2872. http://journals.openedition.org/terrain/2872

Bajeux, Jean-Claude. "Mentalité noire et mentalité biblique." In *Des prêtres noirs s'interrogent: 50 ans après*, edited by Léonard Santedi Kinkupu, Gérard Bissainthe, and Meinrad Hebga, 57–82. Paris: Karthala, 2006.

Balandier, Georges. *Daily Life in the Kingdom of the Kongo: From the Sixteenth to the Eighteenth Century*. Translated from the French by Helen Weaver. Sydney, Melbourne, Auckland, and London: Allen & Unwin, 1968.

Bancel, Nicolas, Pascal Blanchard, and Sandrine Lemaire. "Ces zoos humains de la République coloniale." *Le Monde diplomatique* (August 2000): 16–17. Accessed September 3, 2001. https://www.monde-diplomatique.fr/2000/08/BANCEL/1944#tout-en-haut

Barbara, Augustin. *Les couples mixtes*. Paris: Bayard, 1993.

Baron, Salo Wittmayer. *A Social and Religious History of the Jews, Ancient Times, Vol. II Christian Era: The First Five Centuries*. New York and London: Columbia University Press, second edition, 1952.

Baron, Salo Wittmayer. *A Social and Religious History of the Jews, High Middle Ages, 500–1200: volume IV, Meeting of East and West*. New York: Columbia University Press, first printing 1957, second printing 1960.

Barth, Fredrik. "Les groupes ethniques et leurs frontières." In *Théories de l'ethnicité*, edited by Philippe Poutignat and Jocelyne Streiff-Fénart, 203–49. Paris: PUF, 1995.

Bastide, Roger. *Les Christs noirs*, preface to Martial Sinda, *Le messianisme congolais et ses incidences politiques*. Paris: Payot, 1972.

Bastenier, Albert. *Qu'est-ce qu'une société ethnique? Ethnicité et racisme dans les sociétés européennes d'immigration*. Paris: Presses Universitaires de France, collection "Sociologie d'aujourd'hui," 2004.

Bauer, Pierre-Yves. "Le processus de la conversion au judaïsme." Accessed January 27, 2012, http://www.viejuive.com/2007/12/le-processus-de-la-conversion-au.html

Bavua Ne Longo. "Les douze tribus d'Israël." *Zaïre actualité*, no. 15 (July 15–31, 1991).

Be'chol. Lashon website. Accessed March 18, 2024. https://globaljews.org/

Beloff, J. R. "Rwandan Perceptions of Jews, Judaism, and Israel." *Journal of Religion in Africa* 52, no. 3–4 (2022): 243–68. https://doi.org/10.1163/15700666-12340230

Ben Gad, Raphaël. *Je suis juif, je suis noir et j'en suis fier!* Saint Maur-des-Fossés: Éditions Jets d'Encre, 2022.

Ben Yehuda, Ahmadiel. "Israel's Rabbinate Reflects Country's Racist Streak." August 2013, accessed January 28, 2017. https://972mag.com/israels-rabbinate-the-rot-of-racism-and-a-return-to-african-roots/77476/

Benbassa, Esther. "Être séfarade ou pas." *L'Express* (December 19, 2007), accessed June 27, 2021, http://www.lexpress.fr/actualite/societe/etre-sefarade-ou-pas_474041.html

Benbassa, Esther. "Enquête sur le peuple juif." *L'Histoire*, no. 343 (June 2009)

Benoist, Jean. "Le métissage: biologie d'un fait social, sociologie d'un fait biologique." In *Métissage Tome II. Linguistique et anthropologie. Actes du Colloque International de Saint-Denis de La Réunion, April 2–7, 1990*, edited by Jean-Luc Alber, Claudine Bavoux, and Michel Watin, 13–22. Paris: L'Harmattan, 1992.

Berthelot, Martine. "Approche des grands courants actuels du judaïsme religieux et laïc en Occident." In *Juifs de Catalogne: Et autres contributions à l'étude des judaïsmes contemporains / I altres contribucions a l'estudi dels judaismes contemporanis* [online], edited by Martine Berthelot, 206–23. Perpignan: Presses universitaires de Perpignan, 2011, accessed March 1, 2022. DOI: https://doi.org/10.4000/books.pupvd.1396

Beylot, Robert. *La Gloire des Rois, ou l'Histoire de Salomon et de la reine de Saba*. Turnhout, Belgium: Brepols, 2008.

Bilé, Serge. *Noirs dans les camps nazis*. Paris: Éditions du Rocher / Le Serpent à Plumes, 2005.

Birnbaum, Pierre. "Décrets sur les noms juifs, 20 juillet 1808." Accessed November 25, 2016, http://www.archivesdefrance.culture.gouv.fr/action-culturelle/celebrations-nationales/2008/vie-politique-et-institutions/decret-sur-les-noms-des-juifs

Biyogo, Grégoire. "Aux origines kemites des hébreux (sémites)." September 5, 2016, accessed January 30, 2017. http://afrikhepri.org/aux-origines-kemites-des-hebreux-semites/

Blanchard, Pascal, and Nicolas Bancel. *De l'indigène à l'immigré*. Paris: Gallimard, 1998.

Blech, Benjamin. "Épouser une convertie." Accessed August 22, 2022. https://www.aish.fr/print/?contentID=442723973&section=/israel/monde_juif

Bolongaro, Kait. "A Rabbi, Three Young Muslims and a Minibus: A Tour de France for Dialogue." *Middle East Eye*, November 14, 2016, accessed July 26, 2023. https://www.middleeasteye.net/features/rabbi-three-young-muslims-and-minibus-tour-de-france-dialogue

Bonkanda w'Ecole w'efe. Bongandanga: CBM, 1920.

Bouillet, Marie-Nicolas, and Alexis Chassang. *Dictionnaire universel d'histoire et de géographie*. Paris: Hachette, 1878, 26th edition, accessed September 3, 2023. https://gallica.bnf.fr/ark:/12148/bpt6k4849m/f3.item

Boulègue, Jean Jean-Pierre Chrétien, Agnès Lainé, Patrick Lozès, Pap Ndiaye, Marc-Olivier Padis, and Nicolas Masson. "Les 'Noirs' de France, une invention utile?" *Esprit* 6, no. 335 (June 2007): 86–98. Paris: Éditions Esprit.

Brackman, Harold, and Ephraim Isaac. *From Abraham to Obama: A History of Jews, Africans and African Americans*. Trenton, NJ: Africa World Press, Inc., 2015.

Breakstone, David. "Pride and Prejudice: The State of Israel vs Yosef Kibita." *The Jerusalem Post*, June 9, 2021, accessed March 17, 2024. https://www.jpost.com/israel-news/pride-and-prejudice-the-state-of-israel-vs-yosef-kibita-657105

Brotz, Howard. *The Black Jews of Harlem: Negro Nationalism and the Dilemmas of Negro Leadership*. New York: Free Press of Glencoe, 1964.

Bruder, Édith.. *The Black Jews of Africa: History, Religion, Identity*. London and New York: Oxford University Press, 2008.

Bruder, Édith.. *Black Jews: Les juifs noirs d'Afrique et le mythe des tribus perdues*. Paris: Albin Michel, 2020.

Bruder, Édith, ed. *Juifs d'ailleurs: Diasporas oubliées, identités singulières*. Paris: Albin Michel, 2020.

Bruder, Édith. *Les Relations entre Juifs et Noirs. De la Bible à Black Lives Matter*. Paris: Albin Michel, 2023.

Bruder, Édith. "Judaïsme africain, Tribus Perdues et traditions orales." In *Actes du 32e congrès de Généalogie juive Tome 3 / Volume 3 Mondes séfarade, proche-oriental et africain Volume 3: Sephardic, Middle-East and African areas*, edited by Joëlle Allouche-Benayoun, 441–46. Paris: Cercle de Généalogie Juive, 2012.

Buadi, Laurent. "AfricaNews: La découverte au Kasaï d'un vase des Pharaons signifie-t-elle que les anciens rois d'Egypte auraient vécu en RDC? - Congoforum.be." AfricanNews, July 7, 2022. https://www.congoforum.be/fr/2010/07/220710-africanews-la-dcouverte-au-kasa-dun-vase-des-pharaons-signifie-t-elle-que-les-anciens-rois-degypte-auraient-vcu-en-rdc/

Burrell, Kevin. "Kushites in the Hebrew Bible." Videoconference on the YouTube channel Archaeological Research Facility, UC Berkeley, May 20, 2021. Accessed August 19, 2021, https://www.youtube.com/watch?v=4w21n0QPunE

Carlebach, Elisheva. "La communauté juive et ses institutions à l'époque moderne." In *Aux origines du Judaïsme*, edited by Jean Baumgarten and Julien Darmon, 312–41. Paris: Actes Sud and Éditions des Liens qui libèrent, 2012.

Causit, Charlotte. "'Je n'aime pas qu'on me dise 'black': Pourquoi, en France, le mot 'noir' reste tabou." France info, June 12, 2020 (updated September 1, 2021), accessed October 1, 2023. https://www.francetvinfo.fr/france/je-n-aime-pas-qu-on-me-dise-black-pourquoi-en-france-le-mot-noir-reste-tabou_4003111.html

Charles, Gilbert, and Marion Festraëts. "L'intégration par l'amour." *L'Express*, May 9, 2002, updated on June 1, 2006. https://www.lexpress.fr/societe/l-integration-par-l-amour_499095.html

Chevalier, Yves. *L'Antisémitisme. Le Juif comme bouc émissaire*. Paris: Éditions du Cerf, 1988.

Cohen, Martine. "Les Juifs de France. Affirmations identitaires et évolution du modèle d'intégration." *Le Débat*, no. 75 (May–August 1993): 97–111.

Cohen, Martine. "Les Juifs de France. Modernité et identité." *Vingtième Siècle, revue d'histoire*, no. 66, Religions d'Europe (April–June 2000): 91–106. DOI: 10.3406/xxs.2000.4565

Cohn, Haïm H. *Human Rights in the Bible and Talmud*. Tel Aviv: Galei Zahal Tel Aviv University, English translation, 1989.

Coquery-Vidrovitch, Catherine. *Des victimes oubliées du nazisme. Les Noirs et l'Allemagne dans la première moitié du XXème siècle.* Paris: Le Cherche Midi, 2007.

Coquet-Mokoko, Cécile. *Love Under the Skin: Interracial Marriages in the American South and France.* London: Routledge, 2020.

Crété, Liliane. *La traite des nègres sous l'Ancien régime.* Paris: Perrin, 1989.

Cuche, Denys. *La notion de culture dans les sciences sociales. Grands repères,* 4th edition. Paris: La Découverte, 2010.

de Rudder, Véronique, Christian Poiret, and François Vourc'h. *L'inégalité raciste: l'universalité républicaine à l'épreuve.* Paris: PUF, 2000.

Dandois, Thomas, and Alexandra Kogan, "Un Rabbin dans la cité. Sur la route avec l'amitié judéo-musulmane de France." ARTE GEIE/Memento, 2015, accessed September 3, 2023. http://www.arte.tv/sites/story/reportage/france-un-rabbin-dans-les-cites/

"Déclaration de M. le Premier Ministre Manuel Valls sur la lutte contre le terrorisme et l'antisémitisme, à Paris le 9 janvier 2016." Accessed July 25, 2023. https://www.vie-publique.fr/discours/197653-declaration-de-m-manuel-valls-premier-ministre-sur-la-lutte-contre-le

"Deux mille ans de présence juive en France." *Le Monde juif* 1, no. 144 (1992): 18. Accessed July 31, 2023. https://www.cairn.info/revue-le-monde-juif-1992-1-page-17.htm

Dewitte, Philippe. *Les mouvements nègres en France, 1919–1939.* Paris: L'Harmattan, 1985.

Diamond, Eliezer. "Chapter 1 Halakhah, Theology and Psychology: The Case of Maimonides and Obadiah the Proselyte." In Hakol Kol Yaakov בקעי לוק לוקה, pp. 5–8. Leiden, The Netherlands: Brill, 2021. doi: https://doi.org/10.1163/9789004420465_002

Dieckhoff, Alain. "Le sionisme et l'Etat d'Israël face au judaïsme: la continuité incertaine." In *Aux origines du Judaisme*, edited by Jean Baumgarten and Julien Darmon, 420–41. Paris: Actes Sud/Les Liens qui libèrent, 2012.

Diop, Cheikh Anta. *Antériorité des civilisations nègres: mythe ou vérité historique?* Paris: Présence africaine, 1967.

Diop, Cheikh Anta. *Parenté génétique de l'égyptien pharaonique et des langues négro-africaines.* Dakar, Abidjan, and Lomé: Les Nouvelles Éditions Africaines, 1977.

Discours d'Intronisation du Grand Rabbin d'Afrique / Swearing-in speech of the Chief Rabbi of Africa. YouTube streamed live on August 2, 2023, accessed August 2, 2023.

Djerrahian, Gabriella. "Le discours sur la blackness en Israël. Évolution et chevauchements." *Ethnologie française* 45, no.2 (2015): 333–42. Accessed February 29, 2024. https://doi.org/10.3917/ethn.152.0333

Doane, Sébastien. "Fils de Dieu, Les évangiles appliquent ce titre à Jésus. Mais, savez-vous que d'autres textes de la Bible apposent ce titre à d'autres personnages?" *Chronique du 13 avril 2012*, accessed October 25, 2019. http://www.interbible.org/interBible/ecritures/mots/2012/mots_120413.html

Dorès, Maurice. *La beauté de Cham: Mondes juifs, Mondes noirs*. Paris: Ballard, 1992.
Dorès, Maurice. *Black Israël*. Production / Diffusion, Les Films Esdés, 2003.
Dorès, Maurice. "La Bible et l'Afrique." *FJN Internationale* (feujn.org), accessed November 30, 2016. http://feujn.org/spip.php?article326
Dorès, Maurice. *Négritude et Judéité: Balades en noir et blanc*. Paris: Édition Indes savantes, Collection 5 points, 2021.
Dorigny, Marcel. "Depuis 1685, Trois siècles de présences en France, Introduction." In *La France noire*, edited by Pascal Blanchard, Éric Deroo, and Sylvie Chalaye, 10–37. Paris: La Découverte, 2011.
Editorial board. "Brice Hortefeux définitivement relaxé pour ses propos sur les Arabes." *Le Monde*, November 27, 2012, accessed May 30, 2017. http://www.lemonde.fr/politique/article/2012/11/27/brice-hortefeux-definitivement-relaxe-pour-ses-propos-sur-les-arabes_1796614_823448.html
Eisenstadt, Shmuel, and Bernhard Giessen. "The construction of collective identity." In *European Journal of Sociology / Archives Européennes de Sociologie / Europäisches Archiv Für Soziologie* 36, no. 1 (1995): 78–79. Accessed February 29, 2024. http://www.jstor.org/stable/23999434
"Entretien avec Kemi Seba, Fara de l'ex-Tribu Ka. Ancien du Parti Kémite et de la 'Nation of Islam.'" Accessed October 16, 2016. http://www.voxnr.com/cc/tribune_libre/EEypZyZZyZUmORMJLo.shtml
Fabre, Daniel. "Les minorités nationales en pays industrialisés." In *L'anthropologie en France. Situation actuelle et avenir*, edited by Georges Condominas and Simone Dreyfus-Gamelon, 293–314. Paris: Editions du CNRS, 1979.
Fath, Sébastien. "Afrique subsaharienne et sionisme évangélique." *L'enjeu Mondial*, January 2017, accessed October 25, 2019. https://www.sciencespo.fr/enjeumondial/fr/odr/afrique-subsaharienne-et-sionisme-evangelique
Fath, Sébastien. "Le sionisme évangélique africain. Impact géopolitique d'une identité narrative." Conference Juifs et protestants, 5 siècles de relations en Europe, organized by P. Cabanel at the Musée d'Art et d'Histoire du Judaïsme, 2021. hal-03100482
Fayyad, Salam. "Toulouse: Merah face au RAID, stratégie d'intimidation et d'épuisement." *L'Express*, March 21, 2012 (updated March 22, 2012), accessed October 17, 2016. http://www.lexpress.fr/actualite/societe/tueur-au-scooter-les-hommes-du-raid-en-action-a-toulouse_1095906.html
Feigenbaum, Alexandre. "Siddour Kol Hanechama: Le Grand Rabbin réagit." Accessed January 28, 2012. http://www.fjn-123.fr/spip.php?article885
Fila-Bakabadio, Sarah. *Africa on My Mind: Histoire sociale de l'afrocentrisme aux États-Unis*. Paris: Les Indes savantes, 2016.
Fishkoff, Sue, and JTA. "Riding the French Countryside in the Jewish-Muslim Friendship Bus." *The Jewish Chronicle*, June 27, 2010, accessed July 26, 2023. https://jewishchronicle.timesofisrael.com/riding-the-french-countryside-in-the-jewish-muslim-friendship-bus/
Fleg, Edmond. *Anthologie juive des Origines au Moyen Âge*. Paris: Editions G. Crès et Cie, 1923.

France TV info website. Accessed October 22, 2016. http://www.francetvinfo.fr/faits-divers/en-seine-saint-denis-le-ras-le-bol-de-la-communaute-chinoise-ici-tout-le-monde-a-subi-au-moins-une-agression_1730965.html

François, Stéphane, Damien Guillaume, and Emmanuel Kreis. "La Weltanschauung de la tribu Ka: d'un antisémitisme égyptomaniaque à un islam guénonien." *Politica Hermetica*, no. 22 (2008): 107–25.

Friedmann, Daniel, and Ulysses Santamaria. *Les enfants de la Reine de Saba: les Juifs d'Ethiopie (Falachas), histoire, exode, intégration*. Paris: A.M. Métailié, 1994.

Ghiles-Meilhac, Samuel. "Les juifs français sont-ils (devenus) des Blancs comme les autres?" In *Juifs d'Europe: Identités plurielles et mixité*, edited by Ewa Tartakowsky and Marcelo Dimentstein, 27–40. Tours, France: Presses universitaires François-Rabelais, 2017. Accessed June 27, 2021, http://books.openedition.org/pufr/16086. DOI: https://doi.org/10.4000/books.pufr.16086

Gibel Azoulay, Katya. *Black, Jewish, and Interracial. It's not the color of your skin, but the Race of your kin, and Other Myths of Identity*. Durham and London: Duke University Press, 1997.

Gibel Mevorach, Katya. "Les identités juives au miroir de l'héritage du racisme aux États-Unis." *Pardès* 44, no. 1 (2008): 119–32. Accessed March 3, 2024. https://www.cairn.info/revue-pardes-2008-1-page-119.htm

Gilman, Sander L. *L'Autre et le Moi. Stéréotypes occidentaux de la race, de la sexualité et de la maladie*. Paris: Presses Universitaires de France, 1996.

Goffman, Erving. *Stigma: Notes on the Management of Spoiled Identity*. Englewood Cliffs, NJ: Prentice Hall, 1963.

Goldberg, Sylvie Anne, ed. *Histoire juive de la France*. Paris: Albin Michel, 2023.

Green, Nancy. "Juifs d'Europe orientale et centrale." Musée de l'immigration, accessed November 25, 2016. http://www.histoire-immigration.fr/des-dossiers-thematiques-sur-l-histoire-de-l-immigration/juifs-d-europe-orientale-et-centrale

Grégoire, Henri. *Essai sur la régénération physique, morale et politique des Juifs*. Metz, France: Devilly, 1789.

Groupe NZOI and Groupe MANGOBO. "Papa pasteur 1." YouTube, posted by kokodianzombo, accessed October 17, 2018.

Guedj, Jérémy. "Les Juifs français face aux Juifs étrangers dans la France de l'entre-deux-guerres." *Cahiers de la Méditerranée* 78 (2009), February 15, 2010, accessed November 1, 2016. http://cdlm.revues.org/4637

Haddad, Paula. "L'espoir d'un centre communautaire judéo-noir en France." *Jerusalem Post* French edition, June 30, 2009, accessed June 30, 2009. http://www.fjn-123.fr/spip.php?article181

Halévy, Joseph. "La légende de la reine de Saba." École pratique des hautes études, Section des sciences historiques et philologiques. Annuaire 1905 (1904): 5–24. DOI: https://doi.org/10.3406/ephe.1904.2491

Hasse, Benoît. "La Tribu KA revendique la 'descente' de la rue des Rosiers." *Le Parisien*, May 31, 2006, accessed January 18, 2012. https://www.leparisien.fr/paris-75/la-tribu-ka-revendique-la-descente-de-la-rue-des-rosiers-31-05-2006-2007031948.php

Heimlich, Geoffroy. *Le massif de Lovo, sur les traces du royaume de Kongo*, vol. 1. Oxford: Archaeopress and G. Heimlich, 2017.
Hervieu-Léger, Danièle. *Le pèlerin et le converti. La religion en mouvement*. Paris: Flammarion, 1999.
Hervieu-Léger, Danièle. *La religion en miettes ou la question des sectes*. Paris: Calmann-Lévy, 2001.
Hitler, Adolf. *Mein Kampf (Mon combat)*. Translated by J. Gaudefroy-Demombynes and A. Calmettes. Paris: Nouvelles éditions latines, 1982, t.2, La Bibliothèque électronique du Québec, Collection Polémique et propagande, Volume 3: version 1.2.
Hitler, Adolf. Speech at the Berlin Sportpalast, January 30, 1942. Jewish Virtual Library website, accessed August 28, 2023. https://www.jewishvirtuallibrary.org/hitler-speech-at-the-berlin-sports-palace-january-30-1941
Hovanessian, Martine, and Richard Marienstras. "La modification des Juifs de France." *Journal des anthropologues* 72–73 (1998): 93–106.
i24News website. "Manuel Valls bientôt en Israël pour promouvoir l'initiative de paix française." May 19, 2016, accessed July 25, 2023. https://www.i24news.tv/fr/actu/international/europe/113762-160518-manuel-valls-bientot-en-israel-pour-promouvoir-l-initiative-de-paix-francaise
Iancu, Carol. "Les réactions des milieux chrétiens face à Jules Isaac." *Revue d'Histoire de la Shoah* 1, no. 192 (2010): 157–93. Accessed September 3, 2023. https://www.cairn.info/revue-d-histoire-de-la-shoah-2010-1-page-157.htm
Jack'sman, Donel. "Les juifs de Sarcelles." YouTube, March 8, 2021, accessed August 8, 2021. https://www.youtube.com/watch?v=sgfzbfcd3da
Jackson, John L. Jr. *Thin Description: Ethnography and the African Hebrew Israelites of Jerusalem*. Cambridge, MA: Harvard University Press, 2013.
Jannot, Céline, Sandra Tomc, and Marine Totozani. "Retour sur le débat autour de l'identité nationale en France: quelles places pour quelle(s) langue(s)?" *Revue de Linguistique et de Didactique des Langues* (2011): 44–78. Accessed on May 31, 2017. https://lidil.revues.org/3139
Jewish Multiracial Network. Accessed March 18, 2024. http://www.jewishmultiracialnetwork.org/who-we-are/
"Jour de colère: quenelles et saluts nazis dans les rues de Paris." *Huffington Post France*, January 27, 2014, accessed October 23, 2016. http://www.huffingtonpost.fr/2014/01/27/jour-colere-quenelles-saluts-nazis-rues-paris_n_4671985.html
Juteau, Danielle. "L'ethnicité comme rapport social." *Mots* 49, no. 1 (1996): 97–105.
Kahn, Rachel. *Racée*. Paris: Éditions de l'Observatoire, 2021.
Kaplan, Steven. "Black and White, Blue and White and Beyond the Pale: Ethiopian Jews and the Discourse of Colour in Israel." *Jewish Culture and History* 5, no. 1 (2002): 51–68. DOI: 10.1080/1462169X.2002.10511962
Kepel, Gilles. *Terreur dans l'Hexagone*. Paris: Gallimard, 2015.
Khosrokhavar, Farhad. *L'islam des jeunes*. Paris: Flammarion, 1997.
Khosrokhavar, Farhad. "La sociologie de la radicalisation." Interview by Anne Châteauneuf-Malclés. Ressources en Sciences économiques et sociales website, January 10, 2016, accessed October 23, 2016. http://ses.ens-lyon.fr/articles/la-sociologie-de-la-radicalisation-entretien-avec-farhad-khosrokhavar-291659

Korsia, Haïm. "La transmission dans le judaïsme." *Inflexions* 1 no. 13 (2010): 33–40.
Kra-Oz, Tal. "Israeli Chief Rabbi Calls African Americans 'Monkeys.'" *The Tablet*, March 21, 2018, accessed September 10, 2022. https://www.tabletmag.com/sections/news/articles/israels-chief-rabbi-calls-african-americans-monkeys
La Barbe, Franck. "Les juifs pour Jésus." In *Les minorités religieuses en France. Panorama de la diversité contemporaine*, edited by Anne-Laure Zwilling, Joëlle Allouche-Benayoun, Rita Hermon-Belot, and Lionel Obadia. Paris: Bayard, 2019.
La Pan, Carole. *L'Islam, du Coran aux Guerriers Fous d'Allah*. Montréal: Collection Essais, Édition Quebec-Livre, 2002.
Lange, Dierk. "Origin of the Yoruba and the Lost Tribes of Israel." *ANTHROPOS* 106 (2011): 579–95.
Larané, André. "Les juifs en Europe: L'antijudaïsme médiéval, de 610 à 1492." Hérodote, October 30, 2021, accessed August 17, 2023. https://www.herodote.net/610_a_1492-synthese-24.php
Le Monde website. "Le ministre de l'emploi fait de la polygamie une 'cause possible' des violences urbaines." November 16, 2005, updated November 17, 2005. http://www.lemonde.fr/societe/article/2005/11/16/le-ministre-de-l-emploi-stigmatise-la-polygamie_710615_3224.html#Ot5aRL1BExLeMyxE.99
Le Pape, Loïc. "'Tout change, mais rien ne change.' Les conversions religieuses sont-elles des bifurcations?" In *L'enquête sur les bifurcations. Les sciences sociales face aux ruptures et à l'événement*, edited by Michel Grossetti, Marc Bessin, and Claire Bidart, 212–23. Paris: La Découverte, 2010. DOI: 9782707156006. http://www.editionsladecouverte.fr/catalogue/index-Bifurcations9782707156006.html. hal-01077023
Le Point Afrique. "Mali-France—Lassana Bathily primé au 30e dîner annuel du CRIF." *Le Point*, February 23, 2015, accessed January 17, 2017. https://www.lepoint.fr/afrique/lassana-bathily-prime-au-30e-diner-annuel-du-crif-23-02-2015-1907175_3826.php
Le Roux, Magdel. *The Lemba, a Lost Tribe of Israel in Southern Africa?* 2nd edition. Pretoria: Unisa, University of South Africa, 2015.
Leglaive-Perani, Céline. "De la charité à la philanthropie: Introduction." In *Le "moment" philanthropique des Juifs de France (1800–1940)*, edited by Céline Leglaive-Perani, *Archives juives* 1, no. 44 (2011): 4–16. Paris: Les Belles Lettres. Accessed August 7, 2023. https://www.cairn.info/revue-archives-juives1-2011-1-page-4.htm
Liberman, Jeff. *Remerging: The Jews of Nigeria*. Documentary, 2012.
Lis, Daniel. *Jewish Identity among the Igbo of Nigeria, Israel's "Lost Tribe" and the Question of Belonging in the Jewish State*. Trenton, NJ: Africa World Press, 2015.
Liverani, Mario. *La Bible et l'invention de l'histoire, Histoire ancienne d'Israël*. Paris: Bayard, 2008.
Lorriaux, Aude. "30% des collégiens des quartiers populaires ne sont pas vraiment 'Charlie.'" *Slate French edition* (September 22, 2015), accessed October 23, 2016. http://www.slate.fr/story/107191/collegiens-charlie-etude-afev

Macina, Menahem. *Chrétiens et juifs depuis Vatican II. État des lieux historique et théologique. Prospective eschatologique*. Avignon: Éditions du Docteur angélique, 2009.

Malinovich, Nadia. "What's the Color of a Jew? Les Juifs, la blanchitude et le multiculturalisme aux États-Unis à l'époque contemporaine." In *La place de l'autre*, edited by Michel Prum, 37–52. Paris: L'Harmattan, 2010.

Malki, David. *Les Sages de Yabneh, Le Talmud et ses Maîtres-II*. Translated from Yiddish by Edouard Gourevitch. Paris: Editions Présences du Judaïsme, Albin Michel, 1983.

Maltz, Judy. "This Jew by Choice is Testing Israel's Landmark Ruling on Conversions." *Haaretz*, June 27, 2021, accessed March 17, 2024. https://www.haaretz.com/israel-news/2021-06-27/ty-article/.highlight/this-jew-by-choice-is-testing-israels-landmark-ruling-on-conversions/0000017f-e51c-d9aa-afff-fd5c97ed0000

Maltz, Judy. "Appeal to Grant Israeli Citizenship to Ugandan Convert Rejected." *Haaretz*, January 5, 2022, accessed March 17, 2024. https://www.haaretz.com/israel-news/2022-01-05/ty-article/.premium/appeal-to-grant-israeli-citizenship-to-ugandan-convert-rejected/0000017f-f659-d318-afff-f77b823c0000

Marienberg, Evyatar Niddah. *Lorsque les Juifs conceptualisent la menstruation*. Paris: Les Belles Lettres, 2003.

Marr, Wilhelm. *The Victory of Judaism over Germandom*. Bern: Rudolph Costenoble, 1879, accessed August 17, 2023. https://www.jewishvirtuallibrary.org/wilhelm-marr

Masorti Matters Blog. "Ugandan Jew Threatened with Deportation after Interior Ministry Ruling." December 13, 2021, accessed March 17, 2024. https://masorti.org/ugandan-jew-threatened-with-deportation-after-interior-ministry-ruling/

Masorti website. https://masorti.org.uk/articles/what-is-masorti/ accessed September 28, 2023.

Mathieu, Séverine. *La transmission du judaïsme dans les couples mixtes*. Paris: Éditions de l'Atelier, 2009.

Mathieu, Séverine. "Identités plurielles: couples mixtes et transmission du judaïsme." *Diversité urbaine* 10, no. 1 (2010): 3–59. https://doi.org/10.7202/045044ar

Maurouard, Elvire. *Les Juifs de Saint-Domingue (Haiti)*. Paris: Éditions du Cygne, 2008.

Maurouard, Elvire. *Juifs de Martinique et Juifs portugais sous Louis XIV*. Paris: Editions du Cygne, 2009.

Mbaye, William Ousmane. *Kemitiyu*. Documentary film, 2016, broadcast on TV5 Monde on November 26, 2016.

Meyer, Jean. *Esclaves et Négriers*. Paris: La Découverte / Gallimard, 1986.

Miles, William F. S. *Jews of Nigeria: An Afro-Judaic Odyssey*. Princeton, NJ: Markus Wiener Publishers, 2012.

Milewski, Jacky. *Naissance d'une identité: Conversion au Judaïsme dans l'œuvre de Maïmonide*. Paris: Safed éditions, 2004.

Mokoko Gampiot, Aurélien. *Kimbanguisme et Identité noire*. Paris: L'Harmattan, 2004.

Mokoko Gampiot, Aurélien. *Les Kimbanguistes en France, Expression messianique d'une Eglise afro chrétienne en contexte migratoire*. Paris: L'Harmattan, 2010.

Mokoko Gampiot, Aurélien. "Les Juifs africains et antillais en région parisienne." In *Religions et frontières*, edited by Fatiha Kaouès, Chrystal Vanel, Vincent Vilmain, and Aurélien Fauches, 131–41. Paris: Éditions du CNRS, 2012.

Mokoko Gampiot, Aurélien. "Being a Black Convert to Judaism in France." In *Converts as Commuters: Conversions in the Mediterranean World*, edited by Olivier Roy and Nadia Marzouki, 115–38. London: Palgrave-MacMillan, "Islam and Nationalism" series, 2013.

Mokoko Gampiot, Aurélien. "La quête des origines chez les Juifs noirs en France." In *Mondes Séfarade, Proche-Oriental et Africain*, Vol. 3, edited by Joëlle Allouche-Benayoun. Paris: Cercle de Généalogie Juive, 2014.

Mokoko Gampiot, Aurélien. "The Color of Judaism: Black Jews in France." In *The Shadow of Moses: New Jewish movements in Africa and The Diaspora*, edited by Daniel Lis, William Miles, and Tudor Parfitt, 75–89. Los Angeles: TSEHAI/Loyola Marymount University, 2016.

Mokoko Gampiot, Aurélien. "Black Judaism in France: An Example of the Intersection Between Religion and Ethnicity." *Contemporary Jewry*, Vol 36, Special Issue no. 3, *Transformation and Evolution in the Jewish World: Judaisms and Judaicities in Contemporary Societies*, Joëlle Allouche and Harriet Hartman, eds. (2017): 309–31. https://link.springer.com/article/10.1007/s12397-017-9227-4

Mokoko Gampiot, Aurélien. "Les Juifs noirs: Fédération internationale des Juifs Noirs (FJN) et Am-Israël-Farafina." In *Les minorités religieuses en France. Panorama de la diversité contemporaine*, edited by Anne-Laure Zwilling, Joëlle Allouche-Benayoun, Rita Hermon-Belot, and Lionel Obadia, 847–63. Paris: Bayard 2019.

Mokoko Gampiot, Aurélien. "Les Convertis noirs au Judaïsme en France." *African Diaspora*, no. 15 (2023): 1–27. DOI:10.1163/18725465-bja10030

Mokoko Gampiot, Aurélien, and Cécile Coquet-Mokoko. *Kimbanguism: An African understanding of the Bible*. University Park, PA: Pennsylvania State University Press, 2017. http://www.oapen.org/search?identifier=627658

Mokoko Gampiot, Aurélien, and Cécile Coquet-Mokoko. "The Transnational Dynamics of Black Jews in France." In *Imagining the Religious "Other": The Public Face of African New Religious Movements in Diaspora*, edited by Afe Adogame, 85–104. Farnham, UK: Ashgate/Inform Series on Minority Religions and Spiritual Movements, 2014.

Morin, Edgar. *Le monde moderne et la question juive*. Paris: Seuil, 2006.

Mossière, Géraldine. "La conversion. Retour à l'identité." *Théologiques* 21, no. 2 (2013). https://doi.org/10.7202/1028460ar

Mouchenik, Yoram. "Réflexion sur l'identité chez l'adolescent juif." *Champ psychosomatique* 1, no. 25 (2002): 119–28. DOI: 10.3917/cpsy.025.0119

Mulongo, Freddy. "Nduwa Guershon, premier rabbin noir de la région parisienne?" Radio Réveil FM International, May 22, 2009 at 11:44 AM, audio.

Ndaywel è Nziem, Isidore, Abraham Constant Ndinga Mbo, and Tharcisse Tshibangu Tshishiku. *Hommage à Théophile Obenga—Afrique Centrale et Égypte pharaonique*. Paris: Éditions du Cygne, 2020.

N'Diaye, Tidiane. "Les Bantous: Entre dispersion, unité et résistance." *Pambazuka News*, November 13, 2012, accessed January 10, 2017. https://www.pambazuka.org/fr/governance/les-bantous-entre-dispersion-unité-et-résistance

Nduwa, Guershon. Interview by Elikia M'Bokolo. *Mémoire d'un continent*, Radio France Internationale, August 16, 2009, audio.

Nduwa, Guershon. "Les Noirs sont-ils les descendants de Cham, le maudit?" Accessed October 12, 2010. http://www.fjn-123.fr/spip.php?article160

Nduwa, Guershon. *Manifeste des juifs noirs*. Orthez, France: Publishroom Factory, 2016.

N'Guessan, Annick. *Être juif et noir en France*. Production TV Mondiapress, 2014.

Nillon, Pierre. *Moïse l'Africain. La véritable histoire de Moïse*. Paris: Menaibuc, 2001.

Nillon, Pierre. *La Véritable Bible de Moïse*. Paris: Anibwé, 2009.

Nizard, Sophie. "Une pratique corporelle 'discrète': le bain rituel." *Ethnologie française* 43, no. 4 (2013): 601–14.

Obenga, Théophile. *L'Afrique dans l'Antiquité—Égypte ancienne—Afrique noire*. Paris: Présence Africaine, 1973.

Obenga, Théophile. *Les Bantu, Langues-Peuples-Civilisations*. Paris: Présence Africaine, 1985.

Obenga, Théophile. *Origine commune de l'égyptien ancien, du copte et des langues négro-africaines modernes Introduction à la linguistique historique africaine*. Paris: L'Harmattan, 1993.

Peretz, Pauline. *Le combat pour les Juifs soviétiques, Washington-Moscou-Jérusalem, 1953–1989*. Paris: Armand Colin, 2006.

Pieterse, Jan Nederveen. *White on Black, Images of Africa and Blacks in Western Popular Culture*. New Haven and London: Yale University Press, 1992.

PR. "Pèlerinage: 300 chrétiens protestants évangéliques ivoiriens en Israël pour prendre part à la Fête des Tabernacles." October 11, 2019, accessed October 25, 2019. https://news.abidjan.net/h/664582.html

Rahmani, Moïse. *Juifs du Congo: la confiance et l'espoir*. Saint-Gilles, Belgium: Institut Sépharade européen, 2007.

Renan, Ernest. "Le Judaïsme comme race et comme religion." Conference at the Cercle Saint-Simon on January 27, 1883. Paris: Editions Calmann Lévy, formerly Michel Lévy Frères, 1883.

Rosenbaum, Alexis. *L'antisémitisme*. Paris: Bréal, 2006.

Sabbah, Messod, and Roger. *Les secrets de l'exode, l'origine égyptienne des Hébreux*. Paris: Éditions Jean-Cyrille Godefroy, 2000.

Saday, Marah. *Tu seras juif mon fils*. Paris: Biblieurope, 2013.

Salmona, Mushon. *Une jeunesse israélienne*. Film, 2007.

Sand, Shlomo. *The Invention of the Land of Israel: From Holy Land to Homeland*. Translated from Hebrew by Geremy Forman. New York and London: Verso, 2012.

Schnapper, Dominique. "Les Nouveaux-Israélites: identité sans tradition?" *Commentaire* 1, no. 9 (1980): 41–48. Accessed February 1, 2021. https://www.cairn.info/revue-commentaire-1980-1-page-41.htm?contenu=resume

Schuder, Ben, and Niko Philipides. *The Village of Peace*. Affinity Vision Entertainment, USA, 63 minutes, 2014.

Seeman, Don. *One People, One Blood: Ethiopian-Israelis and the Return to Judaism.* New Brunswick, NJ: Rutgers University Press, 2010.

Seeman, Don. "Pentecostal Judaism and Ethiopian Israelis." In *Religious Conversions in the Mediterranean World*, edited by Nadia Marzouki and Olivier Roy, 60–76. London: Palgrave-MacMillan, "Islam and Nationalism" series, 2013.

Shambuyi, J. O. *Tshimanga Mujangi. Baluba et leurs origines juive et égyptienne antique.* Kinshasa: Éditions CODEKOR, 2019.

Shimoni, Liron. "Les Hébreux noirs du désert." *Jerusalem Post*, French edition (February 26, 2013), accessed January 26, 2017. http://www.jpost.com/Edition-fran%C3%A7aise/Israel/Les-H%C3%A9breux-noirs-du-d%C3%A9sert-304581

Simon, Pierre-Jean. "Ethnisme et racisme, ou l'École de 1492." *Cahiers Internationaux de Sociologie* XLVIII (January–June 1970): 119–52.

Simon, Pierre-Jean. "Aspects de l'identité bretonne." *Pluriel* 19 (1979): 23–43.

Simon, Pierre-Jean. "Propositions d'un schéma pour l'analyse des attitudes et des politiques dans le domaine des relations interethniques." *Bastidiana*, no. 23–24 (1986): 167–81.

Simon, Pierre-Jean. "Ethnicité." *Vocabulaire historique et critique des relations interethniques, cahier n°2, Pluriel Recherche*s (1994): 14–20.

Simon, Pierre-Jean. *Pour une sociologie des relations interethniques et des minorités.* Rennes, France: Presses Universitaires de Rennes, 2006.

Simon, Pierre-Jean. *La Bretonnité, une ethnicité problématique.* Rennes, France: Éditions Terre de Brume presses universitaires de Rennes, 2006.

Simon-Barouh, Ida. *Juifs à Rennes. Étude ethnosociologique.* Paris: L'Harmattan, 2009.

Singh, Robert. *The Farrakhan Phenomenon: Race, Reaction, and the Paranoid Style in American.* Washington, DC: Georgetown University Press, 1997.

Spurdle, A. B., and T. Jenkins. "The Origins of the Lemba 'Black Jews' of Southern Africa: Evidence from p.12 F2 and Other Y-chromosome Markers." *Am J Hum Genet* 59, no. 5(November 1996): 1126–33.

Streiff-Fenart, Jocelyne. "Mariage mixte." *Vocabulaire historique et critique des relations inter-ethniques*, Cahier n°6-7, Pluriel Recherches, 77–86. Paris: L'Harmattan, 2000.

Sylla, Omar, and Geneviève Platteau. "Le couple contemporain en Europe et en Afrique." *Cahiers critiques de thérapie familiale et pratiques de réseaux* 1, no. 42 (2009): 255–66.

Szerman, David. "Les Danites de Côte d'Ivoire." La Source de vie, broadcast on France 2 TV channel, June 16, 2013.

Szerman, David. "Les Danites de Côte d'Ivoire. Qui sont-ils?" Interview by Manton Gouine. Updated November 16, 2013, accessed December 29, 2016. http://mantongouine.free.fr/index.php?option=com_content&view=article&id=139:les-danites-de-cote-divoirequi-sont-ils&catid=1:actualites&Itemid=8.

Taboada-Leonetti, Isabelle. "Stratégies identitaires et minorités." *Migrants-formations*, no. 86 (1991): 54–73.

Taguieff, Pierre-André. *La Judéophobie des modernes, Des lumières au Jihad mondial.* Paris: Odile Jacob, 2008.

Taguieff, Pierre-André. *L'antisémitisme.* Paris: PUF, 2015.

Taguieff, Pierre-André, and Michel Vieworka. *Le Racisme-Le Multiculturalisme, Cahier du CEVIPOF*, no. 20 (1998).
Tank-Storper, Sébastien. *Juifs d'élection. Se convertir au Judaïsme*. Paris: CNRS Editions, 2007.
Tank-Storper, Sébastien. "Jewish Trouble. Mixed Marriages, Conversions and Boundaries of Jewish Identity." *Ethnologie française* 43, no. 4 (October 2013): 591–99. Translated from the French by Cadenza Academic Translations. https://www.cairn-int.info/article.php?ID_ARTICLE=E_ETHN_134_0591#xd_co_f=OTUwN mEwYmYtY2VlYi00OTg2LWIwMjQtZWI3NWMxODg5NjJj~
Tank-Storper, Sébastien. "Ce que devenir juif veut dire." *La conversion, Théologiques* 21, no. 2 (2013): 159–78. Online publication: February 3, 2015, https://id.erudit.org/iderudit/1028466ar
Thomas, Mark G., Tudor Parfitt, Deborah A. Weiss, Karl Skorecki, James F. Wilson, Magdel le Roux, Neil Bradman, and David B. Goldstein. "Y Chromosomes Traveling South: The Cohen Modal Haplotype and the Origins of the Lemba—the 'Black Jews of Southern Africa.'" The American Society of Human Genetics (February 11, 2000).
Thuram, Lilian. *Mes étoiles noires, de Lucy à Barack Obama*. Paris: Éditions Philippe Rey, 2010.
Todd, Emmanuel. *Le destin des immigrés. Assimilation et ségrégation dans les démocraties occidentales*. Paris: Seuil, 1994.
Tomasovitch, Geoffroy. "Dieudonné demande pardon à 'la communauté juive' dans un journal franco-israélien." *Le Parisien*, January 10, 2023, accessed on March 28, 2024. https://www.leparisien.fr/faits-divers/dieudonne-demande-pardon-a-la-communaute-juive-dans-un-journal-franco-israelien-10-01-2023-UJMIIVOED5AFLKYI7AI6CB2JPQ.php
Trigano, Shmuel. "La logique de l'étranger dans le judaïsme. L'étranger biblique, une figure de l'autre?" *Pardès* 2, no. 52 (2012): 95–104.
Van Slageren, Jaap. *Influences juives en Afrique. Repères historiques et discours idéologiques*. Paris: Éditions Karthala, 2009.
Vaudano, Maxime. "À Paris, une manifestation attrape-tout contre François Hollande." *Le Monde*, January 26, 2014, accessed on June 5, 2017. http://www.lemonde.fr/societe/article/2014/01/26/a-paris-une-manifestation-de-colere-attrape-tout-contre-francois-hollande_4354734_3224.html
Verbunt, Gilles. "Culture, identité, intégration, communauté: des concepts à revoir." *Hommes et Migrations*, no.1180 (October 1994): 6–9.
Vignaux, Hélène. *L'Église et les Noirs dans l'audience du Nouveau Royaume de Grenade*. Montpellier, France: Presses Universitaires de la Méditerranée, 2009. Accessed November 11, 2016. https://books.openedition.org/pulm/496
Waintraub, Judith. "Nicolas Sarkozy souligne les 'racines juives' de la France." *Le Figaro*, February 9, 2011, accessed on May 30, 2017. http://www.lefigaro.fr/actualite-france/2011/02/09/01016-20110209ARTFIG00725-nicolas-sarkozy-souligne-les-racines-juives-de-la-france.php
Weizman, Ilana. *Des blancs comme les autres? Les juifs, angle mort de l'antiracisme*. Paris: Éditions Stock, 2002.

Wieviorka, Michel. *L'antisémitisme expliqué aux jeunes*. Paris: Éditions du Seuil, 2014.
Wieviorka, Michel. "Introduction." In *Le racisme, une introduction*, edited by Michel Wieviorka, 7–12. Paris: La Découverte, Poche / Essais, 1998. https://www.cairn.info/le-racisme-une-introduction--9782707128669-page-7.htm
Wigoder, Geoffrey. *Dictionnaire encyclopédique du Judaïsme*. French edition adapted by Sylvie Anne Goldberg. Paris: Éditions du cerf, 1993.
Wimbush, Vincent L. *White Men's Magic: Scripturalization as Slavery*. Oxford and New York: Oxford University Press, 2012.
Wimbush, Vincent, ed. *Scripturalizing the Human: The Written as the Political*. New York and London: Routledge, 2015.
Winock, Michel. *La France et les Juifs, de 1789 à nos jours*. Paris: Editions du Seuil, 2004.
World Jewish Congress website. "Kenya." Accessed July 28, 2023. https://www.worldjewishcongress.org/en/about/communities/KE
Zadi, Jean-Pascal. *Tout simplement noir*. Film, 90 minutes, 2020.

Index

INDEX RERUM

Abayudaya, 58, 109. *See also* African Jews
African Jews, 5, 54, 151, 152, 159, 164, 212. *See* Abayudaya; Baluba; Bantu; Danite; Ethiopian Jews; Ibo; Kongo; Lemba; Lost Tribes of Israel; Tutsi; Yoruba
African diaspora, 4
African Hebrew Israelite, 3. *See also* Black Hebrew Israelite
AJTM. *See* Alliance pour un judaïsme traditionnel et moderne
AJMF. *See* Amitié Judéo-Musulmane de France
Aliyah, 53, 85, 91, 92, 96, 110, 162, 199
Alliance pour un judaïsme traditionnel et moderne (AJTM), 126, 153, 165. *See also* Reform Judaism
Am-Israël-Farafina (AM-I-FA), 7, 148n13, 149–65, 166n6, 234n11, 240
AM-I-FA. *See* Am-Israël-Farafina
Amitié Judéo-Musulmane de France (AJMF), 46, 227
Amitié judéo-noire, 46, 150, 151, 228
anti-Black racism, 7, 26, 29, 43, 140, 169, 182, 224, 228, 229

anti-Judaism, 13, 26, 27, 31, 94, 99, 100, 233, 237. *See also* antisemitism
anti-Muslim prejudice, 43
antisemitism, 7, 26–47, 50n61, 94, 99, 133, 140, 145, 151, 152, 162, 198, 209–10, 213–33, 237, 240, 241
Aryan, 27, 28, 29, 30, 32, 125
Ashkenazim, 2, 20, 125, 132, 133, 152, 153, 154, 158, 160, 164, 173, 174, 180–81, 211–12, 229, 239
assimilation, 3, 4, 14, 15, 20, 28, 36, 38, 121, 124, 126, 182, 237

Baluba, 62, 77n38
Bantu, 60, 77n30, 144, 189
Bataclan, 224
Beta-Israel. *See* Ethiopian Jews
Beth Din, 130, 151
Black Hebrew Israelite, 58, 75, 92
#BlackLivesMatter, 198, 227
Blackness, 4, 5, 23, 26, 27, 39, 47, 73, 79n82, 79n83, 91, 110, 111, 129, 158, 162, 164, 197, 237

Canaanite, 56, 65, 71–73, 74, 168, 170
Charlie Hebdo, 40–41, 219, 220. *See also* terrorism

263

Christianity, 3, 6, 12, 14, 22, 25, 26, 57, 66, 81, 86, 94, 95, 98, 99–100, 101, 105, 124, 129, 138, 141, 237
circumcision, 57, 59, 128, 201, 222
Code noir, 21, 23
Conseil Représentatif des Associations Noires de France (CRAN), 46, 150
Conseil Représentatif des Institutions Juives de France (CRIF), 5, 19, 34, 37, 45, 155, 164–65, 183, 217, 220, 227, 234n13, 235n27, 240
Consistory, 5, 7, 15, 19, 20, 84–85, 87, 89, 93, 96, 100, 110, 123–24, 130, 131, 133, 137, 143, 144, 149, 151, 152, 153, 155, 158, 164–5, 173, 176, 177–80, 183–89, 191, 212, 231
conversion, 3, 5, 12, 14, 81–86, 89–96, 99–101, 103, 105–6, 108–9, 111–14, 116n1, 116n15, 116n34, 121–24, 129, 130, 131, 132, 133, 138, 140, 144, 145, 149, 155, 157, 166n13, 170, 173, 174, 176–79, 183–85, 187–91, 194, 202n13, 203n17, 203n30, 205–7, 212, 237, 244. *See also* Maimonides; Obadiah
Council Vatican 2, 31
CRAN. *See* Conseil Représentatif des Associations Noires de France
CRIF. *See* Conseil Représentatif des Institutions Juives de France
culinary, 2, 62, 128, 151–52
curse of Ham, 27, 43, 68, 69–74, 137–38, 168, 182

Danite, 57, 92, 155, 162, 180, 183, 188, 217, 218
differentiation, 2, 35, 36, 39, 44, 63, 74, 224
discrimination, 12, 14–15, 21, 25, 26, 29, 31, 32, 36–37, 38, 42, 46, 110, 124, 128, 134, 137, 142, 147, 150, 150, 154, 156, 157, 160, 162, 203n26, 211, 219, 221, 222, 224–29, 238

Egypt, 20, 66, 83, 245
emancipation, 14, 15, 16, 18, 21, 22, 23, 25, 122, 124, 244
Ethiopian Jews, 2–3, 5, 53, 54, 58, 80, 91, 95–96, 108, 110, 113, 119n38, 141, 159, 167, 182. *See also* Beta-Israel; Falasha; Falash Mura
ethnicity, ix, 1–2, 3, 6, 42, 93, 103, 111, 114, 116, 119n37, 121, 126, 133, 137, 152, 159, 164, 179, 188, 229, 239n6, 238, 239, 240, 242

Falasha, 53, 63, 91, 141, 175. *See also* Ethiopian Jews
Falash Mura, 95. *See also* Ethiopian Jews
Fédération internationale des Juifs noirs (FJN), ix, 7, 97, 104, 108, 127, 131, 137, 141, 144, 149–65, 165n1, 179, 186–87, 211–12, 215, 216, 217, 218, 240, 241. *See* FJN
FJN. *See* Fédération internationale des Juifs noirs
food. *See* culinary; Kashrut; Kosher; locusts; seder
Franco-Judaism, 17, 18, 226, 235n23, 234n24, 236n32
French Revolution, 14, 16, 17, 124

Halakha, 58, 59, 84, 118n27, 122, 139, 152, 184, 192, 193
Haredi, 84
Hebrew, 3, 8n15, 16, 19, 27, 53–64, 65, 66, 68, 69, 70, 72, 74, 75, 77n24, 79n73, 82, 83, 89, 91, 92, 93, 94, 96, 100, 103–4, 105, 106, 107, 110, 112, 113, 114–15, 121, 128, 129, 130, 134, 148n16, 149, 150, 151, 153, 158, 159, 162, 168, 169, 170, 185, 193, 202n1, 232, 239
hierarchization, 2
Holocaust, 31, 32, 39, 88, 99, 103, 115–16, 145, 146, 156, 175, 178, 191, 193, 196, 197–99, 225

Index

Hyper Cacher, 40, 218, 219–20, 226. *See* terrorism

Kashrut, 11, 15, 58, 128, 151, 152, 195, 243
kavvanah, 92–93, 243
Kemitism, 64, 79n61
ketubah, 130, 184, 185–87, 243, 245
Kongo, 59, 61, 77n27, 77n33, 144
Kosher, 54, 57, 92, 103, 128, 135, 139, 151, 152, 155, 159, 190, 193, 195, 208, 212, 217, 234n2, 239, 243
Kushi (racial slur), 74–75, 110, 141, 148n16, 169

Ibo, 54, 55, 164
immigration, 7n3, 24, 25, 33, 34, 96, 237
Inquisition, 13, 144
inter-ethnic relations, 1, 207, 238
interracial marriages, 7, 23, 25, 43, 92, 128, 145, 167–204, 238
Islamophobia, 41, 224, 226
Israel, state of, 19–20, 31, 39, 40, 43, 55, 58, 62, 72, 84, 96, 97, 107–11, 118n35, 162, 193–94, 198, 214, 226, 244

Jewishness, 2–7, 13, 15, 17, 18, 20, 26, 40, 47, 47n18, 53–80, 82, 91, 92, 96, 103, 104, 109, 111, 114, 121, 123, 125, 129, 135, 136, 139, 144–45, 147, 148n18, 154, 158–59, 162, 167, 172–79, 180–86, 189, 190–98, 201, 205, 207–10, 212–13, 215, 218, 229, 237–41, 244
Judaism, ix, 2–7, 8n8, 8n14, 8n29, 8n36, 13, 15–18, 20, 26, 35, 47n4, 49n42, 53–55, 58, 59, 62–63, 68–69, 73, 75, 76n12, 76n14, 76n20, 78n40, 78n45, 79n76, 80n86, 81–119, 121–24, 126, 128, 130–34, 135–36, 138, 139, 140–41, 143, 144, 147, 147n1, 147n9, 148n14, 149–51, 153, 156–58, 161, 166n3, 166n13, 167, 169–74, 176–90, 192, 193–95, 201, 202n16, 203n27, 203n29, 202n31, 202n34, 205–7, 209–10, 212, 214, 216, 226, 230–32, 234n6, 234n23, 234n24, 236n32, 237–42, 243, 244, 245

Lemba, 3, 5, 8n10, 54, 57, 76nn5–8, 77n26, 78n47, 92, 164
locusts, 152
Lost Tribes of Israel, 55, 56, 76n16, 164. *See* African Jews

Masorti, 9n36, 84–85, 87, 109, 113, 119n36, 122–24, 128, 130–31, 137, 147, 149, 151, 176–78, 180–83, 185, 189, 190, 192, 207, 238
mikveh, 205, 244
MJLF. *See* Mouvement juif libéral de France
monotheism, 66–67, 82, 105, 138
Mouvement ju-if libéral de France (MJLF), 149. *See also* Reform Judaism
Muslims, 22, 34, 40, 46, 98, 99, 142, 163, 167, 222, 223, 226, 228, 230, 235n30

non-Haredi orthodox Judaism, 84. *See also* Haredi

orthodox Judaism, 84, 95, 184
Otherness, 1, 2, 103, 241

Palestine, 31, 40, 78n42, 110, 170, 213, 223
police brutality, 45, 227

racialization, 7, 6, 124, 171
racism, 7, 23, 26, 29, 30, 35–38, 41–42, 44–46, 49nn40–41, 50n61, 51n86, 58, 73, 75, 111, 126, 133, 135, 138, 142, 147, 147n1, 148n11, 148n13, 150, 152, 155–56, 162, 166n6, 174, 175, 187, 198, 213, 215–16, 221,

223–24, 226, 227, 228–33, 234n11, 237, 238, 240, 241
Reform Judaism, 16, 84, 95, 105, 123–24, 126, 130–31, 147, 149, 151, 153, 174, 176–78, 180, 182–85, 188, 193, 195, 205, 212, 238, 243, 244

Scripturalization, 6, 9n35, 63, 242
seder, 123, 126, 244
Sephardim, 2, 20, 125, 129, 132–33, 152, 153, 154, 158–59, 164, 180–81, 208, 211–12, 222, 229, 239
Shabbat, 11, 57, 93, 127, 134–35, 136, 143, 192, 192, 195–96, 206, 230, 244
Shidduch, 179, 186–88, 244
slavery, 9n35, 21, 22–23, 25, 39, 61, 69, 72, 73–74, 115–16, 138, 146, 168, 196–200, 237
stigmatization, 14, 34, 40, 124, 228

Talmud, 61, 69, 71, 72–73, 79nn75–76, 83, 84, 85, 92, 95, 97, 116n4, 138, 151, 153, 158, 167–72, 184, 195, 203n25, 244
Talmud-Torah, 85, 95, 153
terrorism, 29, 44. *See also* Charlie Hebdo; Hyper Cacher
Torah, 2, 6, 59, 67, 68, 75, 85, 92, 93, 95, 98, 104, 105, 112, 133, 138, 151, 153, 158, 164, 168, 169, 187, 195, 239, 242, 243, 244, 245
Triangular Trade, 43, 94
Tribu Ka, 42–43, 51n59, 52n92, 215–16, 234n9, 252n29. *See also* Seba, Kemi
Tutsi, 58, 62

Uganda, 58, 109, 118n35, 119n36. *See* Abayudaya
ultra-orthodox Judaism, 84

Vichy regime, 19, 32, 125, 145, 225

Yoruba, 56, 76nn16–17

INDEX NOMINUM

Abraham (Bible), 8n18, 54, 55, 56, 61, 70, 71, 72, 73, 77n29, 82, 83, 103, 105, 111, 113, 161, 168
Asante, Molefi Kete, 64, 66, 78n50, 78n57

Ben Ammi, Israel, 58, 59
Bilé, Hortense Tsiporah, ix, 75, 80n86, 123, 134, 143, 150, 153, 156, 162, 165, 208, 209, 218, 219, 220, 228, 229, 252

Cukierman, Roger, 5, 220

Dieudonné, 39, 41, 43, 45, 62, 78n42, 142, 213, 215, 216, 228, 234n10
Dreyfus, Alfred, 18, 28, 32, 125
Drumont, Édouard, 28, 49n47

Farhi, Daniel, 149
Floyd, George, 198, 227

Grégoire, Abbé Henri, 14, 22, 47n8

Halimi, Ilan, 42, 217
Ham (Bible), 21, 27, 43, 68–74, 79nn66–67, 79nn69–70, 79n80, 137–40, 168
Hitler, Adolf, 28, 29–30, 49nn48–49, 49nn53–55

Isaac, Jules, 31, 50n58
Isaac (Bible), 73, 168

Jacob (Bible), 54, 73, 107, 168
Jesus (Bible), 22, 26, 27, 71, 85, 94–99, 101, 117n12, 117n18, 117n21, 129, 140, 151, 231–33

Korsia, Haïm, 189, 203n29, 226, 228
Krygier, Rivon, 128, 130, 149, 154, 180
Kush, 27, 60, 68, 69–70, 74, 141, 169

Maimonides, 73, 79n77, 83, 89, 104, 116n5, 118n27, 161
Marr, Wilhelm, 26, 27
Mergui, Joël, 5, 84, 137, 158
Moses (Bible), 16, 53, 54, 61, 65–70, 94, 102, 105, 112, 137, 141, 157–58, 164, 168, 169

Nduwa, Guershon, ix, 3, 5, 8n25, 88–89, 97, 131, 137, 138, 147n9, 148n15, 149, 150–53, 157, 158, 160, 162, 163, 164–65, 166n4, 166n9, 166n19, 186

Obadiah, 104, 105, 118n27. *See also* conversion; Maimonides

Saday, Marah Pinhas Eliyahou, ix, 3, 8n24, 162
Seba, Kemi, 42, 43, 44, 52n92, 215–16. *See also* Tribu Ka

Rashi, 71, 79n74, 82, 169
Ruth (Bible), 82, 106, 107, 112

Serfaty, Michel, 227, 228
Sheba, Queen of, 68, 82

Zemmour, Éric, 37, 215, 241
Zipporah (Bible), 67, 68, 105, 112, 141, 143, 157, 164, 168–69

AUTHORS CITED

Allouche-Benayoun, Joëlle, 117n12, 148n21, 165n1, 203n19
Amselle, Jean-Loup, 1, 7n2
Anteby-Yemini, Lisa, 3, 8n13, 54, 58, 74, 76n4, 79n81, 182, 203n24
Arkin, Kimberly A., 47n18, 138, 148nn18–19, 170, 202n6, 208, 234n5
Atlan, Gabrielle, 184, 185, 203nn26–27

Baron, Salo Wittmayer, 79n77, 170, 171, 202nn3–5, 202nn7–12
Bastenier, Albert, 1, 7n3
Benbassa, Esther, 53, 75n2, 131, 145, 148n10
Birnbaum, Pierre, 15, 47n11
Bordes, Chantal, 85, 116n10
Bruder, Édith, 3, 8n9, 8n20, 9n30, 52n93, 54–55, 63, 76n12, 76n14, 78n45, 233n1

Cohen, Martine, 17, 20, 47n16, 48n25, 54, 225, 226, 235nn23–24, 236n32, 240, 242n2
Cohn, Haim Hermann, 72, 79n75, 83, 116n4
Coquery-Vidrovitch, Catherine, 29, 49n50, 146, 148n23

Dieckhoff, Alain, 19, 48n23
Diop, Cheikh Anta, 60, 64, 65, 66, 69, 70, 78nn51–52, 78nn55–56, 79n68, 79n72
Dorès, Maurice, 2, 3, 7n6, 8n8, 61, 63, 77n36, 78n46, 150

Fath, Sébastien, 106–7, 118nn30–31

Ghiles-Meilhac, Samuel, 32, 33, 37, 50n63, 50n67, 51n77, 124, 125, 147n4, 147n6
Gibel Mevorach, Katya, 132, 148n11
Goldberg, Anne Sylvie, 21, 48n26, 245

Hervieu-Léger, Danièle, 4, 8n27, 86, 93, 117n13

Jackson, John L., Jr., 3, 8n15, 59, 77n24

Kaplan, Steven, 110, 119n38
Kravel-Tovi, Michal, 107

Lapierre, Nicole, 3, 8n17, 39, 51nn79–80
Le Pape, Loïc, 81, 116n1, 207, 234n4

Le Roux, Magdel, 3, 8n10, 54, 76n5, 76n8, 77n26
Lis, Daniel, 3, 8n11, 55, 76n9, 76n13, 76n15

Marienstras, Richard, 84, 116n9
Mathieu, Séverine, 151, 166n3, 172, 190–91, 192, 194, 202, 203nn31–32, 203nn34–35
M'Bokolo, Elikia, 1, 7n2, 116n9, 116n19
Morin, Edgar, 13, 47n3

Nillon, Pierre, 67, 79nn61–62

Obenga, Théophile, 60, 77nn29–30

Parfitt, Tudor, 2, 7nn7–8, 54, 73, 76n7, 79n79

Rosenbaum, Alexis, 11, 16, 44, 47n1, 47n5, 47nn13–14, 49n57, 50n60, 52n94

Sand, Shlomo, 16, 47n12
Schnapper, Dominique, 192, 203n32
Seeman, Don, 3, 8n14, 95, 117n15

Simon, Pierre-Jean, ix, 1, 3, 7n1, 8n26, 114, 119n40, 126, 133, 147n7, 148n12, 159, 164, 166n10, 166n18
Simon-Barouh, Ida, ix, 4, 8n28, 155, 166n5, 179, 203n21
Streiff-Fenart, Jocelyne, 147, 172, 201, 202n14, 203n18, 204n39

Taguieff, Pierre-André, 14, 26, 31, 40, 42, 47n7, 49n41, 50n59, 51n81, 51n88, 147n5
Tank-Storper, Sébastien, 81, 82, 84, 116n8, 118n33, 122, 147nn1–2, 172, 176, 177–79, 190, 194, 201, 202n13, 203n17, 203n20, 203n30, 203n33, 204n38
Trigano, Shmuel, 68, 69, 74, 79nn66–67, 79nn69–70, 79n80, 83, 116n3, 158

Weizman, Ilana, 227, 235n29
Wieviorka, Michel, 26, 42, 49n40, 49n41, 49n47, 51n86
Wimbush, Vincent, ix, 6, 9n35, 63, 78n44
Winock, Michel, 19, 47nn9–10, 47n17, 47n19, 48n22

About the Author

Holding a doctoral degree in sociology *summa cum laude* from the University of Rennes 2, France, **Dr. Aurélien Mokoko Gampiot** is presently a senior research associate on the Archiving the Inner City Project at the Department of Sociology of the University of York (UK), a visiting research fellow at the Centre for Religion and Public Life of the University of Leeds (UK), and an associate researcher at the Groupe Sociétés Religions Laïcité (CNRS, France) hosted by the Sorbonne (École Pratique des Hautes Études).

His research discusses the intersection between religion and race in the African diaspora in France. It contributes to the observation of African prophetic religions by studying them from the perspective of the articulation of religion and ethnicity. His book *Kimbanguism, An African Understanding of the Bible* (Signifying (on) Scriptures series, 2017) explores the various modes of appropriation of the Bible by Kimbanguist believers in a comparative approach including other African Initiated Churches with different readings of the Bible, leading them to distinct theologies of Black liberation.

Since 2009, he has conducted pioneering fieldwork among Black Jews in France, and published several articles on the topic. The present work is the outcome of this research.

www.ingramcontent.com/pod-product-compliance
Lightning Source LLC
Chambersburg PA
CBHW031741030425
24529CB00002B/18